# Historians of Economics and Economic Thought

The history of economic thought has always attracted some of the brightest minds within the discipline as a whole. These chroniclers of the discipline's development have helped form our view of it, and it is no surprise that many among them have been at the forefront of new movements in the history of ideas.

This collection summarizes the work of these key historians of economics and attempts to quantify their impact. Some of these writers such as Friedrich Hayek and Joan Robinson are already assured of their place among the greatest economists of the twentieth century, while the collection also stresses the influence of those still active in shaping our perceptions – the likes of Mark Blaug, Samuel Hollander, and Donald Winch.

The collection is authored by an impressive list of contributors, many of whom are themselves well known in the history of economic thought. These include John Creedy, Roger Backhouse, and Neil De Marchi, as well as the editors of the collection as a whole, Warren J. Samuels and Steven G. Medema.

**Steven G. Medema** is Professor of Economics at the University of Colorado at Denver. **Warren J. Samuels** is Professor Emeritus of Economics at Michigan State University.

# Routledge Studies in the History of Economics

# Historians of Economics and Economic Thought

The construction of disciplinary memory

Steven G. Medema and
Warren J. Samuels

London and New York

First published 2001
by Routledge
11 New Fetter Lane, London EC4P 4EE

Simultaneously published in the USA and Canada
by Routledge
29 West 35th Street, New York, NY 10001

*Routledge is an imprint of the Taylor & Francis Group*

Typeset in Goudy by Taylor and Francis Ltd

Printed and bound in Great Britain by Biddles Ltd, Guilford and King's
Lynn

*British Library Cataloguing in Publication Data*
A catalogue record for this book is available from the British Library

*Library of Congress Cataloging in Publication Data*
Medema, Steven G.
Historians of economics and economic thought: the construction of
disciplinary memory/Steven G. Medema and Warren J. Samuels.
p. cm. Includes bibliographical data and index.
1. Economics - history - 20th century. 2. Economics - history. 3.
Economics - historiography. 4. Economists - history. 5. Economists -
biography. I. Samuels, Warren. J., 1993 - II. Title.

HB87 .M35 2001
330'.09 - dc 21

ISBN 0-415-18581-5

# Contents

# Contributors

**Tony Atley**, Department of Economics, University of Newcastle, Newcastle, Australia

**Roger Backhouse**, Department of Economics, University of Birmingham, Birmingham, UK

**Bradley Bateman**, Department of Economics, Grinnell College, Grinnell, Iowa, USA

**Peter Boettke**, Department of Economics, George Mason University, Fairfax, Virginia, USA

**Kenneth E. Carpenter**, Harvard University, Cambridge, Massachusetts, USA

**Charles Clark**, Department of Economics, St John's University, Jamaica, New York, USA

**John Creedy**, Department of Economics, University of Melbourne, Melbourne, Australia

**John Davis**, Department of Economics, Marquette University, Milwaukee, Wisconsin, USA

**Neil De Marchi**, Department of Economics, Duke University, Durham, North Carolina, USA

**Geoffrey Gilbert**, Department of Economics, Hobart and William Smith Colleges, Geneva, New York, USA

**M. C. Howard**, Department of Economics, University of Waterloo, Waterloo, Ontario, Canada

**John King**, School of Business, La Trobe University, Victoria, Australia

**John Lodewijks**, School of Economics, University of New South Wales, Sydney, Australia

**Bruce McFarlane**, Department of Economics, University of Newcastle, Newcastle, Australia

**Steven G. Medema,** Department of Economics, University of Colorado at Denver, Denver, Colorado, USA

**Laurence S. Moss,** Economics Division, Babson College, Babson Park, Massachusetts, USA

**Spencer Pack,** Department of Economics, Connecticut College, New London, Connecticut, USA

**Ingrid Rima,** Department of Economics, Temple University, Philadelphia, Pennsylvania, USA

**Abu Rizvi,** Department of Economics, University of Vermont, Burlington, Vermont, USA

**Warren J. Samuels,** Department of Economics, Michigan State University, East Lansing, Michigan, USA

**Margaret Schabas,** Department of Philosophy, University of British Columbia, Vancouver, Canada

**Jeffrey T. Young,** Department of Economics, St Lawrence University, Canton, New York, USA

# Introduction

*Steven G. Medema and Warren J. Samuels*

The history of economic thought and of the intellectual discipline of economics does not write itself. That is the work of historians of economic thought, among others. Certain books and articles were published, and certain theories and techniques were advanced. That cannot be gainsaid. But what they meant at the time of their creation and what they have meant over time – such is not so simple. Indeed, just as the economy can be interpreted in myriad ways, so too can the history of economic thought itself. Just as one should know who has produced an interpretation of the economy when considering that definition, one should know something about the historians of economic thought who help produce that history. One must study the historian along with the history.

Such a view engenders the question of the role of biography in the study of science. One position is that a scientist's biography helps understand how that scientist did what he or she did and the meaning of it for him or her. Another position is that biography is irrelevant to the truth or falsity of an idea or theory. There is something to both theories. But the latter position suffers from both a conceit and an illusion. The conceit is that what we know is probably true, because past error has been corrected. Of course, believing so in the future means that some of what we consider true today is false. The illusion is that there exists a coherent, unequivocal, univocal body of ideas, whereas at every point in time multiple points of view have existed, however much some or many have been eclipsed by a dominant school of thought. In any event, the truth and falsity of ideas and theories, so hard to come by, is important. But the meaning – *verstehen* – of an idea or a theory is another matter. That is one reason why every generation interprets its own history on its own terms – with multiple stories because of multiple perspectives.

Consider the histories written by John (Lord) Acton, Edward Gibbon, Thomas Babington Macaulay, and Lewis Namier. Consider the intellectual histories written by Harry Elmer Barnes, Henry Steele Commager, Merle Curti, and Vernon Louis Parrington. They approached their subjects from personally more or less unique perspectives. When they wrote the history of the same topic, the difference in perspective made for different histories; sometimes so much so that the topic itself changed.

The same is true of the history of economic thought. The history of the interpretation of mercantilism is as kaleidoscopic and interesting as "the original subject" itself. We use quotation marks to indicate that the meaning of that original subject has varied from interpretation to interpretation and thus from interpreter to interpreter. So too the histories which interpret what Adam Smith, David Ricardo, Karl Marx, Alfred Marshall, John Maynard Keynes, and numerous less well-known economists said and/or meant. So too the meaning of Ricardo's and Marx's theories of value, Keynes's macroeconomic theory, and many other economic theories.

An earlier collection, entitled *The Craft of the Historian of Economic Thought*, published in 1983 as the first volume in the series *Research in the History of Economic Thought and Methodology*, examined the work of a baker's dozen leading historians of economic thought. In the Introduction, Warren Samuels wrote that "doing intellectual history involves complex feats of imagination and self-discipline. Among other things, it reflects the tension between the ostensible raw data of history and the mind of the historian and the forces which operate upon those minds." The same is true with regard to the work of the dozen and a half historians of economic thought examined in this collection.

Too fine a point should not be drawn between the two groups, but one arguable difference between many of the historians included in the two volumes is that those included in this volume are more sensitive to the problems of doing Whig history and of presentism. Whig history tends strongly to celebrate a certain interpretation, a certain school, or the present state of the discipline. Presentist history tends strongly to view and interpret the past not on its own terms – however difficult they may be to decipher – but on the terms formed by the present interests and theories of economists.

Another difference is that most of the historians in this collection have been exposed to and indeed in some cases have helped promulgate new approaches to intellectual history. These include: new approaches to philosophy of science and epistemology (e.g., the meaning of "science"), the social study of science, social linguistics, rhetoric, deconstruction, structuralism, hermeneutics, literary criticism, ideology theory, extensive archival analysis, and so on, as well as older heterodox approaches, such as the sociology of knowledge. These new approaches, and the interpretive insights generated from them, have not been without controversy, but they have added to the richness and depth of insight of our understanding of the evolution of economics and economic thought.

Still another difference seems to be the greater willingness not only to hold the history of ideas at arm's length but to criticize it. The criticisms rendered have varied, of course, with the perspective taken.

Another difference – and again not too fine a point should be put on it – is that many of the historians included in this collection study not only the history of *economic thought/ideas* but also the history of *economics* as a professional, academic, scientific discipline.

One implication of the foregoing is that the work of historians of economic thought has become more variegated, more complex, and, perhaps, more subtle and more highly nuanced than earlier. While the giants of the past could readily walk among those of the present, the giants of the past likely would be quite surprised at the scenery of the present.

# 1 The skills of freedom
## The liberal education of William J. Barber

*Bradley W. Bateman**

### Freedom, Greek and Roman style

In his famous letter "On Liberal Education," Seneca condemns the corrupted and useless tradition of liberal education in the Roman Empire in the first century AD. When he surveyed the contemporary (c. AD 60) practice of liberal education, he was repulsed by the degraded and effete instruction offered to the free (*liberalis*) men of Rome. But while he carefully catalogues the "useless" facts imparted to young, free Romans and attacks liberal education as he finds it, he also carefully constructs an argument for the importance of "true" liberal education.

The conception of liberal education about which Seneca wrote had been first articulated about 400 years earlier in Athens as a means of educating free men for life in a democracy. Many slaves in Athens were educated and used their educations to manage a business, run a bank, or cut a deal for their masters. Some slaves even became wealthy. But the slaves' education was in a skill, or trade. Free men, on the other hand, were believed to need a different kind of education. The *liberalibis studiis*, for the free men, was certainly a "gentleman's education," or one designed for a small male elite, but it was not originally understood as an effete, or impractical, education. Quite to the contrary, if they were to be active citizens and leaders, it was crucial that these men be able to analyze a problem, formulate a response, and understand audience psychology. In short, they needed instruction in rhetoric.

Although the term liberal education does not appear in Plato's dialogue *Protagoras*, the dialogue dates from the same period in Athens and treats the same themes. What is the role of "political–rhetorical skill" in a free Athens? Is it possible to teach these skills? The questions are not idle ones, or for the consideration of idle gentlemen. Athens was surrounded by piranha states, and effective political leadership was the city-state's only hope. Thus, the Greek *eleutherioi technai*, from which the Latin *liberalibis studiis* derived, can be translated not only as "liberal arts" but also as "the skills of freedom." Without the right kind of education in constructing and making good arguments, freedom could not be maintained or defended in the Athens of the fourth century BC or the Rome of the first century AD.

## Freedom, American style

Whatever connotations freedom might have had 2,000 years ago in the Roman Empire, where slavery was still an accepted social institution, it is no less problematic today in the United States. Like all terms of approbation, both the left and the right have appropriated it as a normative criterion. Thus, in the literature of the right, "freedom" is a central concept used to denote the liberty of the individual to act unfettered by the state. In the literature of the left, "freedom" is a central concept used to denote the liberation from poverty, ill health, and homelessness. Partisans of the right demand "individual freedom," while partisans of the left demand "freedom from want."

Americans hear both of these ideological usages of freedom with some regularity, but the older sense of the word that derives from the Latin *liberalis* has little currency today. The small liberal arts college is very much alive and well, and plays an important part in American undergraduate education, but the original meaning of the "liberal" in the liberal education has disappeared from popular usage in the postwar years.

There is some irony in this, for until the great boom created by the "New Economy" during the late 1990s, most students in these small, residential colleges spent a good part of their time worrying about whether they would be employable. Their concern about their future employment was largely a result of the peculiar curriculum of the American liberal arts college. The traditional American liberal arts curriculum differs significantly from the university curriculum in most other industrialized nations in its sacrifice of depth for breadth. Whereas in Britain, for instance, an undergraduate studies in only one area for three years, an American undergraduate studying at a liberal arts college would study for four years, but devote only about one-third of his or her course work to the major area of study. Thus, in the United States, an economics major would normally take only about nine or ten courses in the "major" field, out of a total of thirty-two courses over four years. This limited immersion in the major field of study, when combined with the traditional absence of departments in "professional" fields (such as engineering or nursing) from the liberal arts curriculum, means that students at American liberal arts colleges do not have the kind of special training that makes them immediately valuable to employers upon their graduation.

While the students of these liberal arts colleges in the postwar years did not typically understand themselves as pursuing direct training for a career, this was not because they saw themselves as "free" men or women, for whom employment was unimportant. In some cases, they enrolled because they were following family traditions that had begun when their ancestors had enrolled at one of the many small liberal arts colleges that were the most common institutions of higher education in the nineteenth-century United States. In some cases, they enrolled because of church affiliation, since almost all of the American liberal arts colleges were founded as religious institutions and roughly 90 percent of the American population still reports that they have religious faith. In some cases, they enrolled because they wanted to have small classes and work closely with their professors. This latter would have been especially true after the explosion of large state universities in the 1960s, when classes at those universities began to have enrollments of 500 or more. In the end, however, the students in the small colleges planned to find careers that did not differ significantly from those of students attending the large universities. Thus, for the students at a liberal arts college in the postwar years, freedom would have had roughly the same connotations that it had in the larger culture, and these connotations would not have included any special consciousness that the term related to their own educations.

If the students at these schools were unaware of the particular etymology of the liberal education that they pursued, they were, nonetheless, still very much caught up in the older Greek and Roman ideal of pursuing an education that would allow them the perspective from which to consider the fundamental questions of democratic citizenship. The students at these colleges would have to work for a living like any other citizens; but in a world defined by different kinds of democratic institutions, they understood themselves as political agents with a wide range of opportunities for democratic participation, from voting to public advocacy. "Undergraduate concerns are usually very much linked to their perception of issues in the 'real world'."[1] And during the postwar years, there was "considerable turbulence in American society that in turn ... stimulated noteworthy challenges to the manner in which the academy had become accustomed to going about its business."[2] The most familiar of these changes came during the Vietnam War, but those changes were not the only ones.

While students in the postwar years were often effective in pushing for a more "relevant" education, the changes in the liberal arts economic curriculum in the postwar period were driven from both the supply (the professorate) and demand (student) sides. From the professional side, there was a growing concern first with teaching more quantitative courses, and then with introducing more advanced mathematical theory.[3] From the student side, there was first pressure to teach more courses in what came to be called development economics, and then later there was pressure for courses in comparative systems and environmental economics.[4] These changes from the demand side were very much driven by the set of concerns that the liberal arts students brought in their capacities as democratic citizens.

No one has explained these changes in American liberal education better than William J. Barber, in his retrospective essay published in 1997 in *Daedalus*, the magazine of the American Academy of Arts and Sciences. Published together with an essay by the Nobel Laureate Robert Solow entitled "How Did Economics Get That Way and What Way Did It Get?" Barber's essay helps to lay out a very clear picture of the difference between the economics education at American liberal arts colleges and at American research universities.[5] One of Barber's most important distinctions in this regard is between the faculties at these two types of institutions. He characterizes the faculty at large research institutions as "specialists," while he refers to the faculty at the liberal arts colleges as "general practitioners." The specialists are those who develop (and train the subsequent generations of those who further develop) mathematical and quantitative "sophistication" in the discipline, while general practitioners are those who teach undergraduates, almost none of whom will ever pursue a Ph.D. in economics. The latter group teaches the students who are not yet sure of their career paths, but who have a concern with questions of critical citizenship. These students are not yet sure whether they will work in business, government, or philanthropy, but they want to be educated about the economic dimensions of the contemporary world.

The desire of these liberal arts students for an education in how to think critically about the economy was quite different from the motivations of the typical students in a graduate program in the postwar era. In the article by Solow accompanying Barber's article, Solow describes economics during the postwar period as a modeling science. The normal work of a theoretical economist in a graduate program during these years would consist of building models based on a very small set of initial assumptions. The skills necessary to build such models were more likely to derive from topology (e.g., fixed point theorems) or engineering (e.g., Kalman filters) than they were from history or a knowledge of political institutions. This world of the specialist economists became so focused on the internal aesthetics of modeling by the late twentieth century that a survey of graduate students at the leading graduate schools published in 1987 revealed that 68 percent of the respondents believed that "having a thorough knowledge of the economy" was "unimportant" to success in pursuing the Ph.D.[6] David Colander and Arjo Klamer, the authors of the report containing these findings, concluded:

> graduates are well-trained in problem-solving, but it is technical problem-solving which has more to do with formal modeling techniques than with real world problems. To do the problems, little real world knowledge of institutions is needed, and in many cases such knowledge would actually be a hindrance since the simplifying assumptions would be harder to accept.[7]

Thus, the world of the liberal arts students during the second half of the twentieth century could not have been more different from that of the graduate students in American Ph.D. programs. The liberal arts students were interested in studying the economy and the graduate students were interested in studying the intricacies of the models developed by their mentors, with little concern for how those models might connect to the events in the real world.[8]

## The free scholar

The perceptive reader will have inferred by this point that many of the Ph.D. economists who taught in liberal arts colleges during the late twentieth century lived between a rock and a hard place. On the one hand, their students pulled them to provide an education in the art of thinking critically about the economy. On the other hand, the specialists in the graduate programs pushed them to keep abreast of theoretical developments that were less and less relevant to thinking critically about the way that economies actually work. Now, it would be difficult to find an economist at a liberal arts college during this period that did not think that the means to teaching students how to think critically about the economy did not consist of teaching them the art of applying economic models to real-world problems; but the models being produced at the research universities were increasingly designed with no idea that they would be relevant to an issue like famine or poverty eradication. Thus, the general practitioner was put in the awkward position of choosing between a decision to develop the kind of institutional knowledge that is necessary to successfully apply models to the world, and the decision to master the latest topological and engineering techniques necessary to stay abreast of the newest cutting-edge theory.

It is typical in the world of the small liberal arts colleges that decision making is decentralized and that the tenured faculty have autonomy over their own careers. This career freedom did not provide the answer to the question of how the general practitioners should focus their professional development, but it did mean that every one of them was forced to make conscious decisions about how to shape their careers. No matter whether they chose to concentrate their teaching efforts in mastering the knowledge of the evolving and emerging institutions, or whether they chose to try to master the ever changing statistical and mathematical techniques developed in the graduate schools, they had to make choices about how best to develop their own skills so that they could teach their students how to think critically about the economy.[9]

Another way to characterize this place between the rock and the hard place is, of course, as a position of freedom. The decisions being made were not without considerable consequence. Would one pay heed to the expressed needs of one's students and so maintain the vitality of the connection between student and teacher that is central to liberal education as it is practiced in the United States, or would one try to maintain one's status and prestige in the larger discipline where publication and power are determined almost solely by technical prowess? The further question of whether one could be a good teacher without also being able to work at the cutting edge of theory was also never far from the minds of these general practitioners. But because they had tenure, they were "free" to make the decisions as they pleased. And because they saw themselves very much in the light of their students' self-perception as critical agents in a democratic society, the economists in this position were not unlike the "free" citizens of Athens or Rome. The liberal arts college professor functions very much as a person who must always consider the question of how best to maintain the rhetoric of a successful democracy.

Although thousands of men and women made the decisions that shaped economic education in the American liberal arts colleges after World War II, it is doubtful that any did it with more grace or brilliance than William J. "Bill" Barber. Barber achieved distinction as a scholar in at least two fields, development economics and the history of economic thought, but it would be impossible to understand his distinction in either field without understanding the milieu in which he worked: the American liberal arts college. The particular set of choices open to Barber were defined in large part by his position at Wesleyan University in Middletown, Connecticut; and the way that he made his choices reflects the kind of freedom that is afforded those who devote themselves to liberal education.[10]

## The accidental economist

It is fair to say that William J. Barber became an economist accidentally, although it is also fair to say, without slighting Barber's considerable abilities, that the accident occurred, in part, through the fortunes that arose for him from having received a good undergraduate liberal education. Barber left his native Kansas, in the American Midwest, in 1942 to enter Harvard College, the undergraduate college of Harvard University. He embarked upon a history major, studying with some of the most eminent American historians of the mid-century, including Perry Miller, Arthur Schlesinger, Sr., Arthur Schlesinger, Jr., and John K. Fairbank. After one year, however, he was called to military service, where he served in the U.S. Army in Europe, thus postponing the completion of his history major until December 1948.

Armed with his history major, but having taken two economics courses as part of his broad, liberal education, he returned to Kansas at Christmastime and interviewed for a Rhodes scholarship. Following his successful interview, he was called to the office of the chair of the selection committee, an economist at Kansas State University, and offered employment for the spring semester 1949 teaching introductory economics to Kansas State University students. Now, this offer clearly indicates Barber's intelligence (as well as the selection committee's), but it was only made possible by his broad learning while he was at Harvard.

This opportunity whetted Barber's appetite for more, and when he got to Balliol College, Oxford in the autumn 1949, he enrolled to study in the traditional P.P.E. (Politics, Philosophy, and Economics) track rather than in History, as he had originally intended. This intensely interdisciplinary program would give Barber the chance to pursue economics in greater depth while still affording him some of the breadth to which he had become accustomed in his years at Harvard. At any rate, two years after he entered Oxford, he finished by splitting the top University Prize in economics (awarded on the basis of the university-wide exam). The two years at Oxford had come at a wonderful time for economists, as a large number of the issues in the headline news were tailor made for investigation by economists: postwar reconstruction, the Labour Government's efforts at nationalization of key industries, and the Marshall Plan. Having been educated in this heady environment, Barber returned to the States to take a position as an economic analyst for the federal government in Washington, DC. This experience impressed him more for the limits of bureaucracy, however, than it did for the power of the bureaucrat, and he returned to Oxford in 1955 to pursue a Ph.D. at Nuffield College.

Barber's sense of critical citizenship seems to have remained intact, for he quickly evolved into a student of the emerging field of development economics. A major influence on his thinking at this time was someone whom he met only once, when he was giving a seminar at Nuffield, W. Arthur Lewis. The mainstream in development economics at that time was enamored of Keynesian models that examined developing economies at a highly aggregate level and suggested that development could take place through the creation of sufficient stimulus to increased output. This particular theoretical vantage point "hid" much of the detail "on the ground" and Lewis was developing an alternative model that allowed for the existence of several sectors within the economy, some of which did not meet the traditional assumptions of economic analysis. In particular, Lewis wanted to model the situation when there was a large traditional sector, in which there were vast numbers of people, from which the market sector could freely draw labor. The scale of unemployment in this type of situation was far beyond what might be met by a Keynesian analysis which implicitly assumed that all laborers worked in the market sector and that the capital structure could accommodate all comers when pressed to full usage. This was patently not the case, of course, in most developing economies and Lewis wanted to show the consequences. Barber adapted Lewis's insights into his doctoral research in British Central Africa (which has become the three independent nations of Zimbabwe, Congo, and Malawi). The published result was *The Economy of British Central Africa: A Case Study of Economic Development in a Dualistic Society* (1961).

## An accidental historian of economic thought

If Barber became an economist by accidents of character, education, and fate, he became a historian of economic thought in much the same way. With a career in development economics well on its way, Barber undertook work in the history of economic thought as part of a teaching assignment at his new position as an assistant professor at Wesleyan in 1957. At that time, Wesleyan had a requirement in the economics major that all students take a course in the history of economic thought. The assignment fell to Barber who approached it "as a novice."[11]

Barber did have his intimate knowledge of Lewis's work close to hand, however, and he turned this to his advantage in a brilliant way. Lewis's multi-sector model of the economy was unique for being able to simultaneously demonstrate the insights of Classical, Marxian, Neoclassical, and Keynesian models. Lewis (1954) had, in fact, purposely presented it in this way, and Barber drew from this innovation to build a history of economic thought course around the idea of showing how the crucial concepts in economic models changed through time. Thus, Barber could show how the Classical idea of surplus had been used by Adam Smith to drive a model of economic growth, but had been turned by Marx into a method for demonstrating how capitalists exploited laborers by showing that the surplus had actually been created by the workers in the first place. Likewise, Barber could then narrate the marginal productivity model in neoclassical economics as a theoretical demonstration that in a market driven economy, no surplus would arise to expropriate.

We can only guess at the impact of his first lectures on his students, but ten years later, in 1967, Penguin books published its classic little paperback, *A History of Economic Thought*, the book by which many economists came to know Barber. This book brought to a larger audience Barber's insights about how to compare and contrast the models that define the evolution of economic knowledge. The book went to thirteen printings and was translated into Italian, Spanish, Portuguese (both peninsular and Brazilian versions), Swedish, and Japanese. No book on the history of economic thought published in the postwar years was so readable and so evocative of the power of economic ideas to unlock the secrets of the economic world. Perhaps only Mark Blaug's heavy textbook, *Economic Theory in Retrospect*, was as widely circulated in the second half of the twentieth century.[12]

It was at the same time that Barber achieved his greatest distinction as a development economist, working with the Nobel laureate Gunnar Myrdal on his study of the development prospects of South Asia. Barber was asked to join the team in Stockholm in June 1961 and stayed on until September 1962. During this time, he wrote most of section 5 of *Asian Drama: An Inquiry into the Poverty of Nations* (1968), and six chapters on "problems of labor utilization" that drew heavily from his earlier work on dual-sector labor markets. The book received wide critical acclaim, despite (perhaps because of) its clear-eyed assessment of the situation in Asia.

It would be easy to see Barber as balanced between two different scholarly worlds at this point in his career, having achieved renown in two quite different fields in two consecutive years. But it is just as easy to see him as working to the full potential of a liberal arts college economist, and so not balanced *between* anything. His continuing work in development economics clearly marked out his role as someone working to advance the understanding (and operation) of modern economies. His work in the history of economic thought was a manifestation of his belief that it was "self-evident that students should be expected to make the acquaintance of the discipline's big thinkers through contact with their original works" if the students were to fully understand economics.[13] In this interpretation, there was not so much a conflict between interests in Barber's work as there was a complementarity that arose from continuing to work to develop his own (and his students') "skills of freedom." The evidence seems to point to this second interpretation of Barber's career, for his next major professional work embodied both parts of his professional trajectory.

In 1975, Barber blended the two worlds in which he had achieved distinction with the publication of *British Economic Thought and India: A Study in the History of Development Economics*. Looking back on the classical British economists' treatment of colonial India, Barber offered a perspective on how economic analysis had been intertwined with the practice of colonial administration. This project pointed the way for Barber to his work for the next twenty years.

In the early 1970s, Kermit Gordon took over as director of the Brookings Institution, a major American think-tank in Washington, DC, after a distinguished career in government service (on President John F. Kennedy's Council of Economic Advisers and as director of President Lyndon B. Johnson's Bureau of the Budget). Like the "general practitioners" in the liberal arts colleges, policy analysts in government had a practical interest in economic theory, rather than an aesthetic or engineering interest. Gordon's concern at the time was not esoteric theory, but with the fact that in his experience governmental agencies had short institutional memories and so often had to redo work that had been done elsewhere within the government, at other times, but for the same purposes. Thus, he put together a project headed by Craufurd Goodwin, an economist from Duke University who edited History of Political Economy, to examine how the government produced economic knowledge and how it was used. The particular topic for Goodwin's team was to be the formulation of wage–price policy after World War II, and the primary source was to be the presidential archives from this period. Barber was asked to be a part of this team because of his experience as a part of Myrdal's team dealing with economic policy problems, as well as because he had some expertise in the broad view of economic ideas.

Joining Goodwin's team at Brookings turned out to mark a new direction not just for Barber, but also for the history of economic thought. The work that Goodwin, Barber, and the others were undertaking did not fit into any preexisting subdisciplines of economics as they were then identified. No one working in the history of economic thought in the early 1970s was writing about such recent work in the discipline. The topic Goodwin's team were examining – wage–price policy – could have fit loosely under either macroeconomics or labor economics, but such a historical survey, based in careful archival research, and examining the actual work of policy makers, was very definitely not what "specialist economists" at research universities considered "research." But Goodwin and Barber undertook the work in the spirit of careful historians-cum-program-analysts and produced a report, Exhortation and Controls: The Search for a Wage-Price Policy, 1945–1971 (1975b), that revealed that there had been considerable duplication of effort and lost time during the period in question because of poor communication and bureaucratic amnesia.

The book was so well done that it led to another Brookings study of a pressing contemporary issue, again led by Goodwin, and again with Barber as a member of the team. Energy Policy in Perspective: Today's Problems, Yesterday's Solutions (1981a, 1981b) was prepared in response to the oil embargoes of the 1970s and the various responses that had been mooted within the government. Once again, the members of the team were set to work in the presidential archives to see how the Council of Economic Advisers in various administrations had dealt with energy policy. Once again, they found a situation in which good economists often wasted considerable time because of the problems of bureaucracy and the limits of democratic politics.

Barber's work on these two Brookings projects led him to what many of his contemporaries consider to be his greatest scholarly contribution to the history of economic thought, his work on economic policy making in the administrations of Herbert Hoover and Franklin Delano Roosevelt. In *From New Era to New Deal: Herbert Hoover, the Economists, and American Economic Policy, 1921–1933* (1985), Barber uncovered a lost era in American economics. Until quite recently, historians of economic thought have accepted the Whiggish picture in which American economics arose out of the British tradition in a sequence of great men that began with Adam Smith and David Ricardo, was detoured by Karl Marx (who did his work in the reading room of the British Museum, after all), and then was put back on course by Alfred Marshall, A. C. Pigou, and John Maynard Keynes. In this picture, Paul Samuelson marks the beginning of "real" American economics. Barber's book devastated many of the myths that underpinned this Whiggish picture. He showed the well-developed state of institutional economics in the interwar period, and more especially the extent to which it had driven a whole menu of innovative policy proposals that were championed by Herbert Hoover *before* he became president.[14] This story, in which the institutionalists are not a dissenting band of atheoretical economists, threw open the whole field of study which Mary S. Morgan and Malcolm Rutherford have recently begun to cultivate.[15]

Barber followed his study of the origins of Hoover's policy ideas, with *Designs within Disorder: Franklin D. Roosevelt, the Economists, and the Shaping of American Economic Policy, 1933–1945* (1996). In this book, Barber completed the basic narrative of how economic expertise came to be cemented into American democratic politics in the twentieth century. Roosevelt's four administrations were the ground for the shaping of the institutions that define how economists contribute to policy making in Washington, DC, but the story is tumultuous and unsteady. Roosevelt did not know what he wanted from economists when he came to office, and he regularly employed economists with diametrically opposed views in his administrations, where he set them against each other in battles for his time and attention. Out of this welter arose new theories and new quantitative discoveries that were often more "on the cutting edge" than what was happening in the universities. For instance, Barber shows how the entire argument for using government deficits to "pump prime" the economy was discovered within Roosevelt's second administration and led to policies in 1938 that are "home grown" and not the result of John Maynard Keynes's path breaking *General Theory of Employment, Interest, and Money* (1936).

Barber's term for the environment within Roosevelt's administrations is particularly evocative. He refers to those administrations as a "laboratory for learning," an idea clearly drawing from his own "general practitioner's" background in which economics is "about" developing and teaching the skills of critical inquiry and democratic participation. When Barber looked into the Roosevelt administrations and observed the economists trying to deal with the economic crises created by the Great Depression, he found economist-citizens exercising their "skills of freedom" to develop responses that fit the needs of the larger society.[16] His admiration for those engaged in this work is not partisan; he is as admiring of Hoover and his advisers, people who are often pilloried in the mythology of the Depression, as he is of Roosevelt and his advisers. What impresses Barber is the active life of the democratic citizen and the honest effort to address the problems at hand.

Barber's achievements as a historian of economic thought go beyond his early text and these later two scholarly monographs, however. In the early 1980s he was asked by Piero Barucci to serve as head of the American branch of an international effort to study how economics was institutionalized into university curricula in the nineteenth century. *Breaking the Academic Mould: Economists and Higher Learning in the Nineteenth Century* (1988), which Barber edited, continued his path breaking work into the origins of American economic life, both indigenous and imported. It also continued his intimate concern with the life of economic ideas in the education of American citizens.

Finally, Barber produced the standard edition of the works of Irving Fisher (1997), a project undertaken at the behest of James Tobin, and in which Robert Dimand and Kevin Foster assisted him. This kind of scholarship is essential if serious scholarship is to be done in American economics, for Fisher is one of those giants of American economics who is lost in the Whig iconographies. But, to date, it is the only such standard edition of a major American figure (save the ongoing volumes of Paul Samuelson's *Scientific Papers*).

## The liberal education of William J. Barber

It is still not possible to make the final judgment on Bill Barber's career. Although he retired from active teaching in 1993, he continues to work as if he is on "a permanent sabbatical."[17] He is currently working on "an investigation of the factors shaping the character of American economic discourse" as well as on a project team led by Craufurd Goodwin and Neil De Marchi exploring the nature of art markets.[18] He has clearly worked at full throttle throughout his career, for it would be impossible to produce a scholarly *oeuvre* of this size, while simultaneously carrying the teaching load at an American liberal arts college, without having very well-developed work habits. And he shows no signs of slowing down.

Work habits aside, the most impressive thing about Barber's *oeuvre* is the degree to which it has been shaped by his dedication to liberal education. More than any economist of his generation, his work has been shaped by the desire to be liberally educated and to contribute to the liberal education of others. No one who has read his work would fail to understand the roles and importance of economic analysis in twentieth-century American society. He has shown how the "skills of freedom" have evolved and, in the process, he has shown how they can continue to be cultivated. By his own reckoning, he is a "general practitioner," but we might just as well call him a "liberally educated economist," for he has shown in his work just how an economist can pursue a liberal education.

## Notes

* Fellow, National Humanities Center, and Professor, Grinnell College. I thank Karen Carroll for her careful editing of earlier drafts of this essay. The remaining errors are my responsibility.
1 Barber (1997: 88).
2 Ibid.
3 Cf. Kasper et al. (1991), Bateman (1992), and Barber (1997).
4 To a non-American reader, it may seem odd to say that students had any influence over the curriculum, but when student enrollments shift, so do the allocation of resources to academic departments, and this undoubtedly has an influence on course offerings.
5 There was actually a third essay published with Barber's and Solow's, written by David Kreps. For my comparative purposes, Kreps's piece is not important.
6 Colander and Klamer (1987: 100).
7 Ibid.
8 For those who are incredulous that this description of the difference between the concerns of liberal arts students and graduate students is a close match for reality, it will be instructive to consider the project undertaken by the Social Science Research Council (SSRC) in 1997 to lure top graduate students in economics into summer workshops where they can be introduced to issues in the "real" economy and encouraged to pursue research relevant to policy issues in the "real" world through a system of grants given to students who turn their dissertation work in this direction.
9 The rather large amount of data collected and reported in Kasper et al. would indicate that the vast majority of the general practitioners chose to develop their institutional knowledge of the economy rather than the technical knowledge of the specialists. The Kasper report was a call to give up the profession of the general practitioner at the liberal arts colleges in favor of teaching undergraduates the technical skills necessary to the first-year core courses that are common to all first-year doctoral programs in economics in the United States. Bradley Bateman (1992) is a response to the Kasper report calling for maintenance of the older tradition of the liberal arts economist as a "general practitioner."
10 Barber began teaching at Wesleyan in 1957 and retired from full-time teaching in 1993.
11 Barber (1997: 182).
12 I can also attest that the book had wide circulation in English-speaking Africa in the 1970s. I bought my first copy at the University of Ibadan (Nigeria) bookstore in the autumn of 1978.
13 Barber (1997: 182).
14 Barber's work shattered another myth: that Hoover had been a hapless advocate of laissez-faire economics who was trapped by his ignorance and ideology when the Great Depression hit. The reality is considerably different and considerably more complex than that simple story.
15 See, for instance, the essays in Morgan and Rutherford (1998).
16 Kathryn Jagow Mohrman (1969) studied the undergraduate backgrounds of the top-level administrators in the New Deal and found that two of the three top origins of the administrators were Harvard College and Grinnell College, two traditional American liberal arts colleges.
17 Barber (1997: 188).
18 Ibid.

## Bibliography

Barber, William J. (1961) *The Economy of British Central Africa: A Case Study of Economic Development in a Dualistic Society*, London: Oxford University Press.

—— (1967) *A History of Economic Thought*, London: Penguin.

—— (1975a) *British Economic Thought and India: A Study in the History of Development Economics*, Oxford: Clarendon Press.

—— (1975b) "The Kennedy Years: Purposeful Pedagogy," in Craufurd Goodwin (ed.) *Exhortation and Controls: The Search for a Wage-Price Policy, 1945–1971*, Washington, DC: Brookings Institution.

—— (1981a) "The Eisenhower Energy Policy: Reluctant Intervention," in Craufurd Goodwin (ed.) *Energy Policy in Perspective: Today's Problems, Yesterday's Solutions*, Washington, DC: Brookings Institution.

—— (1981b) "Studied Inaction in the Kennedy Years," in Craufurd Goodwin (ed.) *Energy Policy in Perspective: Today's Problems, Yesterday's Solutions*, Washington, DC: Brookings Institution.

—— (1985) *From New Era to New Deal: Herbert Hoover, the Economists, and American Economic Policy, 1921–1933*, Cambridge: Cambridge University Press.

—— (1988) *Breaking the Academic Mould: Economists and Higher Learning in the Nineteenth Century*, Middletown, CT: Wesleyan University Press.

—— (1990) "Does Scholarship in the History of Economics Have a Useful Future?" *Journal of the History of Economic Thought* 12, 2: 110–23.

—— (1996) *Designs within Disorder: Franklin D. Roosevelt, the Economists, and American Economic Policy, 1933–1945*, Cambridge: Cambridge University Press.

—— (1997) "Reconfigurations in American Academic Economics: A General Practitioners Perspective," *Daedalus* 126, 1: 87–103.

Bateman, Bradley W. (1992) "The Education of Economists: A Different Perspective," *Journal of Economic Literature* 30, 3: 1491–5.

Blaug, Mark (1962) *Economic Theory in Retrospect*, Homewood, IL: Richard D. Irwin.

Colander, David and Klamer, Arjo (1987) "The Making of an Economist," *Journal of Economic Perspectives* 1, 2: 95–111.

Fisher, Irving (1997) *The Works of Irving Fisher*, ed. William J. Barber and James Tobin, London: Pickering Masters Series.

Kasper, Hirschel *et al.* (1991) "The Education of Economists: From Undergraduate to Graduate Study," *Journal of Economic Literature* 29, 3: 1088–1109.

Keynes, John Maynard (1936) *The General Theory of Employment, Interest, and Money*, London: Macmillan.

Lewis, W. Arthur (1954) "Economic Development with Unlimited Supplies of Labour," *Manchester School of Economics and Social Studies* 22, May: 139–91.

Mohrman, Kathryn Jagow (1969) "The Educational Backgrounds of New Deal Administrators," Master's thesis, University of Wisconsin.

Morgan, Mary and Rutherford, Malcolm (eds) (1998) *From Interwar Pluralism to Postwar Neoclassicism*, Durham, NC: Duke University Press.

Myrdal, Gunnar (1968) *The Asian Drama: An Inquiry into the Poverty of Nations*, 3 vols, New York: Twentieth Century Fund.

# 2 Mark Blaug as a historian of economic thought

*Roger E. Backhouse**

## Introduction

Mark Blaug's best-selling and most cited work on the history of economic thought is *Economic Theory in Retrospect*, now in its fifth edition. Its opening pages contain a denunciation of relativist approaches to writing history that will be familiar to generations of students. It is tempting to suggest that Blaug should be judged according to his own standards and that the correct strategy in appraising his work is to ask whether his interpretations of history turned out to be right or wrong. In short, he should be judged by the standards of modern scholarship on the subject. There are, however, at least three reasons for not following such an approach. The first is that if we turn to Blaug's other work, however, we find examples of history that is much more sensitive to historical context than his denunciation of relativism might lead one to expect. Even the first chapter of *Economic Theory in Retrospect* is not completely clear cut: H. D. Dickinson, in reviewing the first British edition[1] justly observed that: "Here the author shows a certain division within himself between head and heart. Intellectually, he is an absolutist; but in many passages his words suggest that, emotionally, he has a strong sympathy with the relativist position" (Dickinson 1965: 170).

The second is that, whatever the merits of an "absolutist" approach when applied to eighteenth- or nineteenth-century writing, it is perilous to follow it when dealing with contemporary work. We are still very close to work published even as long ago as the 1950s.

The third reason is that three characteristics of Blaug's work create potential pitfalls for anyone adopting a purely absolutist approach: (1) he is impatient about minor details; (2) he has opinions on most things and is prepared to exaggerate when this is necessary to make a point effectively; (3) he has changed his mind on some important questions and does not try to conceal this. These points are all important for anyone wanting to "do a Cannan" on him. Thus when Steedman (1995) tried to pick holes in the details of *The Cambridge Revolution*, discussion of careless slips (that were corrected, unannounced, in the reprint) confused the discussion of more substantial issues.

If we are to turn to Blaug's own work for ideas on how it should be interpreted, a better guide is a remark made at the start of his first book, *Ricardian*

*Economics*. In the introduction, in outlining his attitude to Ricardo-criticism, Blaug observes that "the history of ideas is a matter not so much of what was said, but of *why* it was said" (1958: 4; emphasis added).[2] Of course, the question of why something was said cannot be answered without making it clear what was said and it is hard to answer it without forming a view on merits of the case being argued. One advantage of focusing on the "why?" question is that it leaves open the issue of whether one answers it in terms of "the logic of history or the logic of intellectual growth" (1958: 5).

## Life and work

Mark Blaug belongs to the generation whose lives were turned upside down by Hitler and the Second World War.[3] Born in 1927 in the Netherlands, he was sent, at the age of 12, to England and then to the United States. His interest in economics started with Henry George's *Progress and Poverty*, to which he was introduced at the age of 17. In his first year at New York University (1945) he became converted to Marxism, after which he decided to study economics. Disillusion with the Communist Party came in 1952, and he moved away from Marxism gradually over the next eight years. He studied for a Ph.D. at Columbia, supervised by George Stigler, spending two years in the British Museum reading room researching the rise and fall of the Ricardian school, producing the thesis that became *Ricardian Economics* (1958). Starting at Yale in 1954, he soon took over William Fellner's graduate course in the history of economic thought. In his anxiety about the course he over-prepared, collecting the extensive notes that formed the basis for *Economic Theory in Retrospect* (1962). In order to persuade students that his course was relevant to their studies, he emphasized analytical concepts and the modernity of ideas taken from the past. Six years later Blaug moved to England to the University of London Institute of Education where he abandoned the history of economic thought in favour of the economics of education and economic development for a decade, returning to it only in the 1970s. By this time he had become familiar with the work of Popper and Lakatos. He remained at the University of London till his retirement, since when he has held part-time teaching positions at the University of Exeter and the University of Amsterdam. In addition to this he was involved in the foundation of Britain's first private university, at Buckingham, where he also taught the history of economic thought. Politically, he describes himself as having moved progressively to the right, till Margaret Thatcher's government ignored the high costs of unemployment in its attempt to control inflation. Thanks to her, he returned to a "more or less consistent belief" in "capitalism tempered by Keynesian demand management and quasi-socialist welfarism".

Blaug's work can be summarized as falling into five broad categories, each representing a different approach to history:

1   Early writing on classical economics (late 1950s). This includes *Ricardian Economics* and articles on subjects ranging from the Poor Laws and the

Factory Acts to classical attitudes to education (1986a: chapters 1–4, 6, 7, and 9). The characteristic of this work is that it combines incisive analysis with a thorough knowledge of the period's economic history. Blaug was aware not only of what contemporaries knew of developments during this period, but also of the views of modern historians.

2   *Economic Theory in Retrospect*, which went through five editions from 1962 to 1996. Through it, it is possible to chart some of the main changes in Blaug's thinking. Particularly dramatic changes occurred, as will be shown, in his treatments of Ricardian, Walrasian, and Keynesian economics.

3   Methodologically directed analysis of economic writing (mid 1970s onwards). This covers his appraisal of the marginal revolution (1986a: chapter 11), his essay on Kuhn versus Lakatos (1986a: chapter 13), and his second thoughts on the Keynesian revolution (1990a: chapter 4), his appraisals of radical and Marxian economics (1990a: chapters 1–3), the quantity theory (1997: chapter 9) and of Hicks (1990a: chapter 5), and, most important of all, *The Methodology of Economics* (1992).

4   Historical essays written to make specific points relevant to modern economics. These fall into two categories. First are essays that are concerned to make a historical point with a view to changing contemporary attitudes on important economic questions. This includes articles on competition (drawing attention to the Austrian view of competition as a process) (1997: chapter 6), entrepreneurship (1997: chapter 8), marginal cost pricing (1990a: chapter 8). They are concerned to draw attention to serious problems within modern economics – such as the dominance of a deficient view of competition and the absence of any real concept of entrepreneurship. The second category comprises articles that take on historical interpretations that Blaug believes to be erroneous. This covers his article on "Classical economics" in the *New Palgrave* (1990a: chapter 7) and his attack on the Sraffian bias of the *New Palgrave* (1990a: chapter 10).

5   Reference books: *Great Economists Before Keynes* (1986b) and *Great Economists since Keynes* (first edition 1985, second edition 1998) and *Pioneers in Economics* (1991–2).[4] These are books that it would be tempting to neglect on the grounds that they do not claim to be such serious history as his other, admittedly more major, writing. However, the *Great Economists* volumes in particular are important in that, because of the range of economists covered (200 in total) they demonstrate Blaug's breadth of reading in a way that does not always come across in *Economic Theory in Retrospect* where he focused on a smaller number of economists.[5] Though short, the entries provide evaluations of their subjects' work, not simply descriptions of what they did.

The major work that does not fit into any of these categories is *John Maynard Keynes: Life, Legacy, Ideas* (1990b), which grew out of a video he prepared for the Institute of Economic Affairs.

Before turning to the key question of how Blaug has treated some of the major historical issues, something further needs to be said about the three books that arguably stand out as Blaug's main achievements:

1   *Ricardian Economics* arose out of his doctoral dissertation at Columbia. It tried to establish how long the influence of Ricardian economics lasted, and the reasons for both its support and its eventual decline. Blaug thus challenged the interpretations of Ricardian economics offered by authorities as eminent as Schumpeter (1954) and Keynes (1936). The book attracted a small number of reviews but those that did appear were mostly by eminent economists.[6] All the reviewers recognized that the book was scholarly and argued a bold thesis. Stigler, the supervisor of Blaug's dissertation, described the book as "erudite", "comprehensive", "exposition of a high order", and with "clear and proper" exposition of analytical issues. However, he then went on to argue that Blaug's thesis was wrong and that the book would have been better had he paid more attention to the question he set out at the beginning, namely the reasons why Ricardian economics met the fate that it did. Stigler denied Blaug's interpretation of the core of Ricardian economics, arguing that it did not decline until the advent of marginalism.[7] Other historians, on the other hand, have found much evidence to support Blaug's contention that the life of the Ricardian system was very short-lived. O'Brien (1970), for example, came to this conclusion through studying the evolution of McCulloch's thought (James Mill, as early as the mid 1820s, considered McCulloch and himself to be Ricardo's only true disciples).

Hicks echoed Stigler's scepticism about Blaug's overall thesis. He argued that though the theory of the declining rate of profit may have been to Ricardo "the crown of his work", it was anachronistic to think that this could have been "the essence of what Ricardo meant to his contemporaries" (Hicks 1960: 130). *Ricardian Economics* had, Hicks contended, "got its emphasis a bit wrong". In short, Blaug, following Sraffa's lead, gives us the modern Ricardo, capable of sustaining long chains of reasoning, not the Ricardo who made such an impact on his contemporaries. On this point, it can be argued that Blaug, not Hicks, was right. Most of the classical economists took Smith rather than Ricardo as their starting point but even though they rejected virtually all of Ricardo's system, they were unable to ignore it (O'Brien 1975: 43). It could be argued that they were intimidated by Ricardo's powers of reasoning, even where he was clearly wrong (such as on agricultural improvements – see O'Brien 1975: 124–31).

Blaug's own retrospective assessment of the book, written down in the Preface to the Japanese edition in 1980 (1997: chapter 3) was that the book had been over-ambitious, mainly in gliding over the conceptual difficulties involved in evaluating the influence of a school of thought. Such issues are crucial to the question of whether or not the Ricardian system declined soon after Ricardo's death. On the other hand, he provided a list of ten substantial propositions about Ricardian economics that the book got right, and which had survived the enormous literature since then. The footnote listing publications that, in Blaug's view, had significantly increased our knowledge of Ricardo since his book was 22 lines long, whereas the one listing publications that had contributed no more than details was 182 lines long, a characteristically blunt assessment.[8]

2   Economic Theory in Retrospect originated in Blaug's Yale lectures and was intended as a graduate textbook. This explains, at least in part, the absolutist stance that he took. Some students even saw it as a textbook on economic theory rather than one on the history of economic thought. Other important influences were Stigler, his doctoral supervisor, and Schumpeter's History of Economic Analysis. Behind all this, however, lay the period when it was written and the immense confidence many economists had in general equilibrium theory. Blaug had even taken a postdoctoral summer course in mathematical economics with Debreu sponsored by the US SSRC. As later sections will show, this coloured the book's approach to economics. In the second edition he sought to strengthen the argument, replying to critics who had misunderstood the purpose of the first edition. The third, fourth, and fifth editions, however, reveal a progressive movement away from this zeal for general equilibrium theory and greater interest in macroeconomics and Keynesian economics.[9] In youth, Blaug has claimed, he preferred the "hedgehogs" (of whom Walras was one), whereas in later life he preferred "foxes" (amongst whom Smith and Marshall are pre-eminent).

The structure of the book survived intact through all five editions. Aside from chapters on Smith, Ricardo, J. S. Mill, Marx, and "Jevons and the marginal revolution", chapters are organized round specific topics in economic theory and the conceptual problems these raise. In many chapters the focus is on particular individuals (Walras and general equilibrium; Pareto and welfare economics; Marshall and utility; Wicksteed and income distribution; Böhm-Bawerk, Fisher, and Wicksell on capital; Wicksell and money). However, in all cases a thorough discussion of the technical issues is combined with an analysis of what key economists said. The disadvantages of such an approach are that it is sometimes difficult to disentangle what past economists said from modern interpretations and that focusing on key individuals plays down the extent to which ideas emerged from communities rather than from individuals. The advantage is emphasizing the technical questions faced, and often solved, by past economists, and hence their links to contemporary economics. Bearing in mind the depth at which these topics are treated, the breadth of the book's coverage is remarkable.

For a book of such scholarship, Economic Theory in Retrospect received remarkably few reviews. The reason was, presumably, that it was seen by editors as just a textbook. The first edition was reviewed in the Economic Journal, by Hutchison (1963) and H. D. Dickinson (1965), and the second in Economica by Robbins (1969).[10] All three emphasized that it was an impressive, scholarly book, regarding detailed criticisms as minor. Hutchison pointed out that Blaug had "emphatic and clear-cut views on most of the great controversies" presenting his conclusions "so confidently and uncompromisingly" that he hoped the reader would argue back at some points and "take reasonable account of other sides of the questions" (Hutchison 1963: 758–9). In particular, he warned that Blaug was "strongly on the side of Smith, and especially of Ricardo and Marx", and tended to "be rather dismissive of the case for the 'Mercantilists', Malthus and Keynes" (Hutchison 1963: 759). He was also very critical of Blaug's viewing Adam Smith's predecessors in the way that he (Smith) did. Dickinson, also reviewing the first edition, emphasized the book's organization – that it concentrated on eleven key figures (Smith, Ricardo, J. S. Mill, Marx, Jevons, Marshall, Wicksteed, Böhm-Bawerk, Wicksell, Walras, and Keynes), with a further twenty (Malthus to Hansen) getting some consideration, though making "short appearances at very scattered intervals" (Dickinson 1965: 169). He noted that the remainder of the 600 economists mentioned appear merely as commentators and critics. Though admitting that Blaug's absolutist approach emphasized the continuity of economic thought and was valuable for students, Dickinson observed that Blaug did not always make it clear where an economist's contribution ended and more recent interpretations began. Examples included the use of Bortkiewicz and Winternitz to elucidate Marx's transformation problem, and Blaug's "bewildering" use of indifference curves and Hicks's four consumer's surpluses to expound Marshall.

To understand the impact made by the book, it is necessary to consider the alternative texts available in 1962. Roll's *History of Economic Thought* (1973: first edition 1938, revised in 1945 and 1954) was perhaps the main one, though Gray's *The Development of Economic Doctrine* (1931) was also still in use. Robbins described the situation very bluntly: "Most of the relevant introductory textbooks are hopelessly superficial, if not positively misleading; if the student is to acquire his knowledge from them, it were better that he took another subject" (Robbins 1969: 442). Schumpeter's *History of Economic Analysis* was, he wrote, a "masterly history" but "too long and allusive". Given such a situation, Robbins concluded of Blaug's book that "teachers of the subject will regard this edition as an answer to prayer, and wish privately that their own lectures were half so scholarly or half so lively" (Robbins 1969: 443).[11] Its deficiencies were "few and trivial".[12]


3    *The Methodology of Economics* grew out of a survey article of the same title in the *Journal of Economic Literature*. This in turn developed themes from Blaug's earlier article on Kuhn and Lakatos (1986a: chapter 13). In this article, after a summary of Kuhn and Lakatos, Blaug explained the notion of a scientific revolution in economics. This took him into a wide-ranging discussion of Smith, Keynes, the marginal revolution, and Ricardo.[13] After an excursion into the theory of the firm he then turned to the question "Do economists practice what they preach?" Underlying all this, Blaug made clear, was the issue of

whether economists clung too tenaciously to theories. This was also the underlying theme in *The Methodology of Economics*. It explains why, in surveying the philosophy of science, Blaug focused on Popper, Kuhn, and Lakatos. However, rather than taking examples from the history of economic thought, in the book he focused on a series of case studies in postwar economics. These ranged widely: consumption, the firm, general equilibrium, marginal productivity, reswitching, international trade, macroeconomics, human capital, and the family. Compared with the article, the conclusions were stronger – economists *were* playing tennis with the net down.

*The Methodology of Economics* was immensely important in establishing economic methodology as a field within economics. In a sense, therefore, it marks a split between Blaug's work on history of economic thought and methodology that one could see as being confirmed (even if unintentionally) by the removal of the corresponding material from the fourth edition of *Economic Theory in Retrospect*.[14] However, it is worth noting that the case studies are essentially essays in contemporary history of economic thought, albeit focused on a very specific question, namely whether attempts to confront theories with evidence have caused the subject to progress. They share many of the characteristics of Blaug's work on topics that are more traditionally regarded as "historical".

To understand Blaug's approach to the history of economic thought, it is necessary to see how his thinking has developed over the forty years since *Ricardian Economics*. Rather than attempt to summarize everything, three particularly important topics will be selected, in order to show how his perspective on each of them has developed: Ricardo and classical economics; Walras and Walrasian economics; and Keynes and Keynesian economics. The headings are carefully chosen, for in all three cases Blaug has come to make increasingly sharp distinctions between the originators of these traditions and their followers.

## Ricardo and classical economics

Students brought up on *Economic Theory in Retrospect* may be surprised at the historiographic approach on which *Ricardian Economics* is based. The blunt assessment that, outside "the classic commentaries of Wicksteed, Wicksell and Marshall" there were no more than a dozen articles or books on Ricardo that were still worth reading will not be surprising. Perhaps more surprising will be the criticism of Cannan's *Theories of Production and Distribution* (1893). Though Blaug praises the freshness of Cannan's approach, he goes on to criticize him for "rendering classical economics void of sense and logic" (1958: 4). After pointing out that Cannan's rationalization of this through an appeal to historical relativism shows that he "must have realized this", Blaug goes on to present his own view, which merits quoting in full:

Whether we ought to give the "ancients" the benefit of historical insight or look down from present heights at their mistakes, in the belief that truth is concentrated in the last increment of economic knowledge, is largely a matter of taste and purpose. Nevertheless, I cannot suppress the conviction that an appraisal of a historical body of doctrine without reference to the conditions under which it was formulated or the contemporary state of analysis out of which it arose soon becomes an uninteresting display of omniscience.

(1958: 4)

This conviction goes far in explaining his interpretation of Ricardo, which has two main components. The first is that at the heart of the Ricardian system lies not the labour theory of value (Schumpeter) or Say's law (Keynes) but the proposition that "the yield of wheat per acre of land governs the general rate of return on invested capital as well as secular changes in the distributive shares" (1958: 3). The second is that Ricardian economics "emerged directly and spontaneously out of the great corn laws debate of 1814–16" (1958: 6). It is thus natural for Blaug to open his discussion of "Ricardo's system" with a substantial discussion of the period's economic history, in which he discusses what was happening to British agriculture at this time, how contemporaries viewed it, the limited and ambiguous data available at the time, and more recent evidence on the importance of wheat in workers' budgets in the early nineteenth century.

This approach could not be more different from that of *Economic Theory in Retrospect*, published only four years later, with its bold assertion: "Criticism implies standards of judgement and my standards are those of modern economic theory" (1962: 1) and its advocacy of the case for absolutism rather than relativism in the history of economic thought. The concern to understand why Ricardian economics emerged is abandoned in favour of a mathematical formulation of Ricardo's system. The historical context, so important in *Ricardian Economics*, is condensed to the occasional sentence.[15] Instead the reader finds first a graphical exposition of Ricardo's theory of distribution and growth followed, after a more technical discussion of value theory, by an algebraic model that shows Ricardo's fundamental theorem to hold in a model with two commodities (corn and gold) as well as in the simple corn model. Algebraic analysis is used to show that Ricardo's predictions about changes in distributive shares over time depend on his having assumed (implicitly, as a result of his particular numerical examples) very specific functional forms for the production functions.

In both *Ricardian Economics* and *Economic Theory in Retrospect* Blaug argues that Ricardo's influence on his contemporaries was profound. Here, his definition of the heart of Ricardian doctrine is important. If one were to see the labour theory of value as constituting its core, then it would be impossible to avoid the conclusion that Ricardian economics was dead by 1830, if not much earlier. However, by focusing on what he calls the Ricardian doctrine (the relationship between the cost of producing wheat and the rate of profit), relegating value theory to a supporting role, Blaug is able to show the longevity of Ricardian influence. In *Economic Theory in Retrospect*, however, he takes his argument for Ricardo's influence a stage further, seeing Ricardo as having had a profound methodological influence:

> [I]f economics is essentially an engine of analysis, a method of thinking rather than a body of substantive results, Ricardo literally invented the technique. His gift for heroic abstraction produced one of the most impressive models, judged by its scope and practical import, in the entire history of economic theory.
>
> (1962: 127)

Though he goes on to say that "not everyone will consider this praiseworthy", it is clear that Blaug endorsed this view.[16]

In *Ricardian Economics*, Blaug acknowledged the importance of Sraffa's edition of Ricardo's works, going so far as to say that it provided a justification for re-examining the subject. The interpretation of Ricardo that Blaug offered was centred on the "corn model". His response to Sraffa's *The Production of Commodities by Means of Commodities* (1960) was, however, very slow. The first edition of *Economic Theory in Retrospect* did not mention the book,[17] while the second contained simply a single paragraph, tucked away at the end of the "Notes on further reading". This introduces Sraffa's book as "a kind of 'Ricardo in modern dress', containing all the characteristic Ricardian touches" (1968: 143). Blaug observes that, though no writer later than Marx is cited, the argument is related to twentieth-century linear programming models, and that "it is the sort of book Ricardo might have written if only he had gone straight to the point without ifs and buts" (1962: 144). However, though he praises Sraffa's attempt to reinterpret Ricardo, Blaug notes that it is not clear how this could constitute a "Prelude to a Critique of Economic Theory".

In the third edition, this one paragraph was moved from the bibliography into the main text and expanded into a six-page section "Ricardo in modern dress?" He outlines Sraffa's assumptions and the Walrasian nature of his methods (counting equations and unknowns) before explaining the standard commodity and the distinction between "basics" and "non-basics". The "punch of the argument", Blaug suggests, is that relative prices and either the wage or the rate of profit depend only on technical conditions in the production of the standard commodity, and do not depend on those in the production of non-basics. Sraffa has solved Ricardo's problem. However, having conceded this, Blaug then pulls Sraffa's argument to pieces. Joint production undermines the distinction between basics and non-basics; the assumptions about technology undermine any attempt to do comparative statics; increasing returns mean that demand needs to be brought in; the possibility that all commodities in a modern economy are basics. His main criticism, however, is that the argument is hopelessly abstract:

There is hardly a sentence in Sraffa's book which refers to the real world and it is perfectly obvious that the author is only too keen to exchange practical relevance for logical rigor. ... he provides no theory of the behaviour of decision-making units. Profits are equalized between industries but we are not told why. ... [A] final assessment of Sraffa's achievement must involve consideration of the Rip-van-Winkle phenomenon, whereby Sraffa solves a technical problem that Ricardo posed 150 years ago *as if its solution still has substantive significance*!

(1978: 147)

Two years later, Blaug reviewed Hollander's *The Economics of David Ricardo* (1997: chapter 25). Though severely critical of much in the book and in disagreement with the overall picture painted by Hollander, and defending his own youthful interpretation of Ricardian economics, he found much in the book that was well done. In particular he accepted Hollander's demonstration that "Ricardo never held a so-called 'corn-model' whereby the rate of profit is first determined in purely physical terms before the question of pricing has even been raised" (1997: 346). This, Blaug argued, is "Hollander at his best. The idea that such a corn-model can be read into the early Ricardo is part and parcel of the new Marxist mythology that has been created around him" (ibid.). Where he disagreed with Hollander, siding instead with O'Brien (1981) and Peach (1993), was that he saw Hollander as confusing rational and historical recon-structions (1997: 60). Blaug saw it as entirely legitimate to speculate on what Ricardo "ought to have said" or "must have thought" but it was wrong, in the absence of textual support, to suggest that this was what Ricardo actually thought: "Hollander is as guilty of historical reconstructions that are really disguised rational reconstructions as Samuelson is guilty, at least on occasions, of passing off rational reconstructions as if they were for all practical purposes historical reconstructions" (1997: 60). Unlike Hollander, Blaug is open to the possibility that Ricardo (or any other economist) may have made significant analytical mistakes.[18]

Consequently, in the fourth edition of *Economic Theory in Retrospect*, Blaug modified the section on "The theory of wheat profits". Where, in the third edition, he had written, "By this ingenious argument, Ricardo established the central tenet of his system without entering into the question of valuation" (1978: 95), in the fourth he amended this to:

This ingenious argument, which appears to explain the determination of the rate of profit in purely physical terms, without entering into the ques-tion of valuation is known in the literature as the "corn model". It was only in modern times that Piero Sraffa ... detected this line of reasoning as implicit in Ricardo's *Essay*. There is actually no direct evidence that Ricardo had the corn model in the back of his mind, but it is true that the corn-model interpretation neatly rationalizes almost all of Ricardo's argu-ments in his early work. ... Nevertheless, on balance one must conclude that the corn-model interpretation of Ricardo's *Essay* is a modern "rational reconstruction".

(1985: 92)

It is interesting to note that the previous mathematical interpretation, based on the "corn model", was left to stand, subject to this qualification.

A further change in the fourth edition was that, after the section on Sraffa, Blaug included another on "still more modern" interpretations in which the wage rate is variable. At the end of this, he concluded that "it is simply not possible to square *everything* Ricardo said with *one* totally consistent formulation of the Ricardian system" (1985: 144). In the fifth edition he strengthened this by adding the remark that: "The idea that Ricardo never made analytical mistakes, always tied all the ends together in every argument is not just a 'rational reconstruction' of Ricardo's system, it is a super-rational reconstruction" (1996: 140). In conclusion, it can be argued that although Blaug learned much from both Sraffa and Hollander, he ended up defending the position, strongly influenced by Stigler, that he espoused in *Ricardian Economics*.

## Walras and Walrasian economics

In *Economic Theory in Retrospect*, Walras is covered, not in the chapter on the marginal revolution (which is linked primarily to Jevons), but in one entitled "General equilibrium and welfare economics", placed after chapters on Marshall, marginal productivity theories of distribution, and the Austrian theory of capital and interest. The section of this chapter on "Walras and general equilibrium" is important because it is here that Blaug, right from the first edition, discusses formalism in economics.

In the first edition, Blaug admits that Walrasian economics "is thin in substance, stressing form at the expense of content" (1962: 534). He illustrates this with Walras's rule that entrepreneurs make neither profit nor loss. Whereas this might have been the implication of a theory of the firm or the industry, for Walras it was simply the postulate that entrepreneurship is a free service. Outside the theory of consumer behaviour, Walras made hardly any contribution to "substantive economics" (1962: 535). On the other hand, though Blaug is critical of Walras, he praises him for his one big idea (citing Isaiah Berlin's fox–hedgehog metaphor): "the interdependence of all prices and quantities". He describes this as "the first genuine novel idea to emerge in economics since the days of the *Wealth of Nations*" (1962: 535). Note that this implies that interdependence of all prices and quantities is virtually synonymous with general equilibrium. The questions of existence, uniqueness, and stability were "searching" questions, and it was Walras's "genius" to show that they could be solved, at least in principle (1962: 522–3). He concludes the subsection on "the concept of general equilibrium" with the following appraisal:

Yet there is an architectonic quality to the whole performance that has led some commentators to credit Walras with the supreme achievement of theoretical economics. According to Schumpeter, Walras's *Eléments* is nothing less than the "Magna Carta of exact economics".

(1962: 523)

Interestingly, despite the chapter being on general equilibrium, not simply Walrasian general equilibrium, apart from a very brief reference to Hicks,[19] modern economists are not discussed. Edgeworth, Marshall, Wicksell, and Barone are the only others who enter the story.

The second edition reinforces this appraisal of Walrasian economics as the foundation of modern economics, implicitly defending it against critics who argue it is mere formalism. The most notable change is perhaps changing a section "Evaluation of Walras's capital theory" into a more wide-ranging "Evaluation of Walras's contribution". In this section he provides a forceful defence of Walrasian economics against the charge of formalism. First, he argues that "When we complain about Walras's formalism, we must also remember that nearly all economics nowadays *is* Walrasian economics" (1968: 587), citing as examples the theories of money, trade, employment, and growth, together with the "new" welfare economics. He then goes on to cite Hicks's claim that the reason for the "sterility of the Walrasian system" is that Walras did not go on to work out laws of change – "what would happen if tastes or resources changed" (Blaug 1968: 588, quoting Hicks). Blaug amplifies this by claiming that "comparative static analysis, as we know it, is almost wholly the result of the effort of three generations of economists to derive operational theorems about economic behaviour within the general equilibrium framework". His examples include Marshallian partial analysis (where some variables are treated as data), Keynesian income theory (where variables are eliminated by aggregation), and Leontief input–output analysis (where interrelationships between variables are simplified). From this he concludes: "Every day it is becoming more apparent that Schumpeter was right: Walras' *Eléments* was the prolegomenon or Magna Carta of modern economics" (1968: 588). Blaug's support for Schumpeter's view is here made explicit.

In the third and fourth editions nothing was changed, apart from the insertion, in the fourth, of a reference to Jaffé's view that Walras was concerned not to describe the world but to outline a realistic utopia. This might, Blaug suggests, explain why, over successive editions of the *Eléments*, Walras made the world fit his model rather than vice versa (1985: 584).

The dramatic change in Blaug's treatment of Walras comes in the fifth edition. For the first time he suggests that Walrasian and contemporary general equilibrium theory are substantially different. In introducing the concept of general equilibrium, where in previous editions Blaug had moved directly into an analogy between existence of equilibrium and the consistency of a set of simultaneous equations (1962: 522), he now discusses the history of Walrasian economics. Walras, Blaug argues, had a number of followers (Barone, Pareto,

Antonelli, Bortkiewicz, Launhardt, Wicksell, Moore, and Fisher), but "in the great centres of academic economics in England, Germany and Austria his work was dismissed as abstract and remote from life" (1996: 550). Cassel propagated a simplified version of the Walrasian system in the 1920s, and Schultz and Hicks drew attention to his work in the early 1930s. It was only Hicks's *Value and Capital* (1939), however, that "put Walras on the map as one of the great economists of all times" (1996: 550).

After several pages of material on general equilibrium from earlier editions (into which explicit references to Wald, Arrow, and Debreu were inserted), Blaug continues with this story of general equilibrium theory since Walras. Here, however, he gives pride of place to Oskar Lange who used Walrasian general equilibrium theory to attempt to answer the criticisms of socialism offered by von Mises and Hayek. Blaug observes that the significance of this episode, the socialist calculation debate, is that "it was the last time that general equilibrium theory figured in a public debate in more or less the same sense that it had figured in Walras's own time" (1996: 557).

One of the striking features of Lange's article "On the Economic Theory of Socialism" (1936–37) is that it discussed general equilibrium theory exactly as Walras had done, namely as a realistic, although rarefied, abstract description of price setting in a market economy, whether capitalist or socialist. This is striking because by the time we get to Debreu's *Theory of Value* (1959) or Arrow and Hahn's *General Competitive Analysis* (1971), general equilibrium theory is defended as a purely formal representation of the determination of economic equilibrium in a decentralized competitive economy, having no practical value whatsoever. All this is a simply remarkable gestalt-switch in the interpretation of general equilibrium theory over a period lasting but twenty-five years (1996: 557).

Now that Walrasian economics is so clearly distinguished from contemporary general equilibrium theory, Blaug replaces his exposition of general equilibrium theory using Walras's own symbols (1962: 522–6) with a full-blown "reader's guide" to the *Eléments*.

In evaluating Walras's economics, Blaug now abandons his support for Schumpeter's judgement, replacing it with a paragraph in which he juxtaposes Schumpeter's "boundless admiration" for Walras with Milton Friedman's more negative assessment of him as emphasizing problems of form rather than content, and providing an idealized picture of the economic system rather than an engine for analysing concrete problems. In presenting Schumpeter, rather than using the highly memorable "Magna Carta" quotation, Blaug quotes his claim that Walras's general equilibrium system "is the only work of an economist that will stand comparison with the achievements of theoretical physics" (1996: 569), a claim so extreme as to be a priori implausible. He then proceeds to sum up the failure of Walras's "offspring", general equilibrium theory, reaching the conclusion:

> In short, after a century or more of endless refinements of the central core of general equilibrium theory, an exercise which has absorbed some of the

best brains in twentieth century economics, the theory is unable to shed any light on how market equilibrium is actually attained, not just in real-world decentralised market economies but even in the blackboard economies beloved of modern general equilibrium theorists. ... We must perforce conclude that general equilibrium theory as such is a *cul-de-sac*; it has no empirical content and will never have empirical content. ... The real paradox is that the existence, uniqueness and stability of general equilibrium should ever have been considered an interesting question for economists to answer.

(1996: 569–70)[20]

## Keynes and macroeconomics

The first edition of *Economic Theory in Retrospect* provides no evidence of any particular interest in macroeconomics or even that Blaug had read the *General Theory*. The chapter on Keynesian economics describes the "modern neo-Keynesian theory of income determination" (1962: 578). It is the standard textbook IS–LM model of the neoclassical synthesis. A historical element comes in only with the section entitled "The traditional case for public works" and this contains significant mistakes.[21] Keynesian economics was viewed as having been completely assimilated into orthodox economics. Blaug's appraisal was that Keynesian economics was about what happened in disequilibrium and that Keynes's contribution had been to show that loose reasoning about unemployment could be converted into a testable, manipulable model (1962: 601–2). These two points were strengthened in the second edition. Sections were added on "Keynesian dynamics" and "Keynes's contribution to economics". In the latter, the point about testability was linked explicitly to econometrics and the formation of the econometric society in the 1930s.

Changes in this interpretation began to appear in the third edition, but the modifications were only slight. The Clower–Leijonhufvud interpretation of Keynes was introduced, and yet in the new section "Rereading Keynes", Blaug reached the conclusion that lots of the *General Theory* was vulgar Keynesianism. The fourth edition saw the chapter title change from "Keynesian economics" to "Macroeconomics", an inevitable change given that the chapter was now expanded to discuss the Phillips curve, the Natural Rate Hypothesis, rational expectations, and monetarism. The IS–LM model was described explicitly as "one interpretation" of Keynesian economics.

In 1987 Blaug wrote and directed a video, *John Maynard Keynes: Life, Ideas, Legacy*, in which he outlined not only Keynesian ideas but also the historical context in which they arose. Versailles, Bloomsbury, and the economic history of the interwar period were all brought in. He also presented the contrasting evaluations of Keynes offered by Samuelson, Friedman, Hayek, Buchanan and Moggridge and Skidelsky. The approach underlying this was entirely consistent with that of his earlier work. Keynes was presented firmly in historical context, with extensive discussion of the Versailles peace conference, unemployment in the interwar period, and so on. And yet Keynesian ideas were presented as in modern textbooks (though given that the video was aimed at a non-technical audience, this was perhaps inevitable). The text was then published as a book of the same title (1990b).

At the same time, Blaug also changed his interpretation of the Keynesian revolution. In 1972, he had offered a Lakatosian interpretation in which the Keynesian revolution involved a shift from a degenerating research programme to a progressive one. Most of the predictions he listed, however, such as that competitive market economies suffered from a chronic tendency to unemployment, were already well known. In 1990 he defended his interpretation of the Keynesian revolution in Lakatosian terms by arguing that it produced genuinely novel facts such as the low interest elasticity of investment, the high interest elasticity of demand for money, and, above all, that the value of the multiplier was greater than unity.

The picture of Keynesian economics offered in *Economic Theory in Retrospect* was dramatically changed in the fifth edition. Keynes was credited with having transformed our vision of macroeconomics, and the references to the *General Theory* being a confusing book (added in the fourth edition) were removed, as were the references to econometrics. Perhaps most significant, Blaug included a substantial discussion of the novel predictions that underlay the Keynesian revolution. The Keynesian revolution succeeded because it was empirically successful. This is contrasted with real business cycle theory (which replaced monetarism at the end of the chapter) where Blaug argues that the hurdles that such models are expected to jump are not very high. Having accepted that Keynes's *General Theory* is now distinct from contemporary macroeconomics, a reader's guide is provided for the first time. The end result is that, in contrast to early editions, macroeconomics is portrayed as a field that raises important historical and methodological issues.

## Methodology and the history of economic thought

Blaug has, for a long time, been an advocate of what he has described as "unrepentent" Popperianism (1997: chapter 11), regarding Lakatos's methodology of scientific research programmes as essentially Popperian: "Lakatos is 80 per cent Popper and 20 per cent Kuhn, and virtually everything Lakatos ever said is found in Popper in some form or other" (1997: 158). His first systematic application of Lakatos's MSRP to the history of economic thought came in his contribution to the Napflion conference that resulted in Latsis's *Method and Appraisal in Economics* (1976).

In this article, Blaug argues that the central tradition in economics, at least since Adam Smith, is best regarded as a Lakatosian scientific research programme. Its hard core comprised "weak versions" of "what is otherwise known as the 'assumptions' of competitive theory: (1) rational economic calculation, (2) constant tastes, (3) independence of decision-making, (4) perfect knowledge, perfect certainty, (5) perfect mobility of factors, etcetera" (1986a: 243). The positive heuristic comprises statements *such as*:[22] (1) divide agents into buyers and sellers, producers and consumers; (2) specify market structure; (3) create "ideal type" definitions of the behavioural assumptions to get sharp results; (4) define *ceteris paribus* conditions; (5) set up an optimization problem and solve for first- and second-order conditions.[23] The way was then open for Blaug to interpret the emergence of Ricardian economics, the marginal, and Keynesian revolutions in Lakatosian terms.

1   Blaug argues that "the notion that Ricardo is at one and the same time the heir of Adam Smith and his principal critic can be conveyed succinctly *in the language of* MSRP" (1986a: 247). Smith established a research programme, with the Ricardian research programme constituting a problem shift within this programme. However, despite using Lakatosian language, he does not spell out in detail the heuristics of either the Smithian programme or its Ricardian variant. Blaug then proceeds to outline, in clear Lakatosian terms, the degeneration of Ricardian economics after 1848. On the other hand, when he proceeds to the relationship between Ricardian and Continental economics, though he talks of competing research programmes, the Lakatosian framework is used much more loosely. Statements about Continental economics being conceived on the lines of Smith rather than Ricardo do not depend in any way on a Lakatosian perspective.

2   The marginal revolution emerges as involving (a) the abandoning of the Ricardian research programme and (b) a problem shift within the Continental, utility-theory, one.[24] He leaves open the question of whether or not this problem shift was progressive.

3   The Keynesian revolution involved modifications not only to the heuristics of the prevailing scientific research programme, but to its hard core. Pervasive uncertainty and the possibility of destabilizing expectations were introduced into the hard core, and Keynesian economics "bristled with" new auxiliary hypotheses, predictions of new facts, and new interpretations of old facts. In interpreting the Keynesian revolutions, Blaug applies the Lakatosian framework much more rigorously than in the other cases.

This article also contained a discussion of whether economists practise the falsificationism that they preach, concluding that for the most part they do not. Clearly, this was the starting point for *The Methodology of Economics* (1992) where he was strongly critical of "innocuous falsificationism".[25] That same radical critique of economics can be found in the article but rather than endorse it unambiguously, he edges away from it. After a discussion of welfare economics, he writes:

> Nevertheless, every economist feels in his bones that the Invisible Hand theorem is almost as relevant to socialism as to capitalism, coming close indeed to a universal justification for the role of market mechanisms in any economy. It is hardly surprising, therefore, that economists fight tooth and

nail when faced with an empirical refutation of a positive theory involving the assumption of perfect competition. For what is threatened is not just that particular theory but the entire conception of "efficiency" which gives raison d'être to the subject of economics. No wonder then that the "principle of tenacity" – the fear of an intellectual vacuum – looms so large in the history of economics.

(1986a: 256)

He concludes that further research on why economists cling so strongly to their theories may tell us something about the difference between social and natural science.[26]

Blaug introduced a discussion of Lakatos, Kuhn, and scientific revolutions into the final chapter of the third edition of *Economic Theory in Retrospect*, but removed it from the fourth edition, on the grounds that he had covered the material in more detail in *The Methodology of Economics*. Interestingly, however, the rest of the "Methodological postscript" remained. The result was that this chapter returned to the structure established in the second edition: falsifiability in classical economics, falsifiability in neoclassical economics, the limitations of falsifiability, value judgements, and sections on American institutionalism and "Why bother with the history of economic thought?" This falsificationism derived not from Popper or Lakatos, but from his reading Friedman's essay (1953) while working at Yale with Tjalling Koopmans, then writing his *Three Essays on the State of Economic Science* (1957).

## Conclusions

As citations of *Economic Theory in Retrospect* show, Mark Blaug has had a major impact on the history of economic thought. The impact of his work can be attributed to four major characteristics:

1  He is an avid reader and has acquired an encyclopaedic knowledge of economics and the history of economic thought. Where necessary, as in the case of classical economics, this extends also to the relevant history.
2  He forms an opinion on most of the controversial issues in the history of economic thought and given his wide reading is able to defend it vigorously.
3  He always approaches his work with a clear idea of the questions that need to be asked.
4  Underlying all his work, from *Ricardian Economics* to his recent protests against general equilibrium theory, has been a concern with the all-important question of the basis on which theories are accepted or rejected. This is both a methodological and a historical question.

It is also worth noting that, like Keynes, Blaug has been prepared openly to change his mind when confronted with convincing arguments.[27]

One respect in which he has changed his mind is the emphasis he has placed on different ways of approaching the history of economic thought. Espousing "absolutism" in opposition to "relativism" caught the mood of the 1960s superbly, placing him clearly in the tradition of Schumpeter and Stigler. This no doubt played a major role in the success of *Economic Theory in Retrospect* as a textbook. Over the years, however, he shifted his emphasis, moving to the terminology of "rational" and "historical" reconstructions. Whilst still defending rational reconstructions, the mere use of such terminology shifted the balance, for who could be opposed, in history of economic thought, to any reconstruction that was "historical"? In his most recent paper on classical economics (1999), he has reiterated his support for "historical" reconstructions. Though this may look like a reversal of his opinion, it is in fact only a change in emphasis. The belief that ideas can be understood only in historical context was there from the start, which is, perhaps, one reason why his work has been so much better received than that of others who have adopted a purely absolutist approach. This change in emphasis can be explained by the very different state of scholarship in the history of economic thought now compared with the early 1950s and by the need to combat the extreme anti-historical attitude of many contemporary economists.

However, whilst Blaug's strategy has resulted in his making a major impact, it has limitations. Perhaps the main one is that his emphasis on absolutism and rational reconstructions has sometimes led to the playing down of the historical reconstructions to which, as *Ricardian Economics* and many of his other writings show, he attached such importance and at which he also excelled. Historical analysis is present throughout *Economic Theory in Retrospect*, but its extent and importance can sometimes be missed amidst the rational reconstructions. Some important points are even made in the bibliographies rather than in the main text. Furthermore, the historiographic statements in the book are appropriately qualified, but the qualifications are easy to overlook.

The history of economic thought is a field where the knowledge accumulated over many years can place someone in a much better position to write a major, broad interpretation of the subject as a whole than is possible for someone early in their career. Blaug conceded this in saying that *Ricardian Economics* was a book he should have written at the end of his career, not at the beginning. Given the extent of his reading and his understanding of what he has read, which most of those who know him will testify to be exceptional, he is ideally placed to write an interpretation of the history of economic thought on the scale conceived by Schumpeter. But he has not attempted this. Instead, he has produced a series of works that, in comparison with the three books discussed in the second section above, are minor. The two volumes in which he writes about the lives and works of 200 economists, even though they contain an impressive range of information and analysis, are no substitute for a more comprehensive history, though they show clearly how well qualified Blaug is to write such a history.

Blaug's *magnum opus* remains *Economic Theory in Retrospect*. In important respects this rivals Schumpeter's history, avoiding some of its weaknesses.

However, its origins as a textbook in which he worked under the constraint of presenting history in such a way as to make it relevant to learning economics have left their mark. The chapters on classical economics, for example, do not have the breadth of *Ricardian Economics* and the historical background necessary to understand the period's economics is cut down to the absolute minimum, if not beyond it. This is even more true of twentieth-century material where Blaug's advantage *vis-à-vis* many other historians of economic thought must be very marked. To put it starkly, Part III of *The Methodology of Economics*, valuable though it is, is no substitute for the comprehensive history of postwar economic thought that he could have written.

Why is this? One possible answer is that he recognized the near impossibility of such a project. Another is that he simply had not the inclination for it. A more substantial explanation is that Blaug's big project, and his main contribution from the 1970s onwards, was not history but methodology. Though we may see him as having contributed primarily to the history of economic thought, he remained at heart an economist, seeking to make a contribution to economics. With *Economic Theory in Retrospect* he sought to influence the way economists were trained – to wean them away from a narrow non-historical curriculum. He then turned to applied economics and when he returned to the history of economic thought in the 1970s his work was infused, to an even greater extent than in the 1960s, with methodological questions relevant to understanding modern economics. Much of his recent writing has been directed towards making points that he believes practising economists ought to take note of.

In his autobiography, Blaug writes that he has retained much of his youthful radicalism and that he has not become an extreme anti-communist in the way that many ex-communists do.[28] However, the influence of Marxism remained. It is hard, especially for someone who has never been attracted to Marxism, not to see in Blaug's fascination with the labour theory of value and his concern to rebut Sraffian economics the passion of an ex-believer. He emerged from Marxism just at the time when general equilibrium theory was at its zenith and described this era in the following terms:

> We *knew* that general equilibrium theory was the last word in theoretical elegance, that input-output analysis and linear programming would soon make it not just elegant but operational, and that "the neo-classical synthesis" had successfully joined Keynesian macroeconomics to Walrasian microeconomics; in short that true economics was one church and that the full truth was at any moment to be revealed to us.
>
> (Blaug, 1997: 11)

By 1991, however, he had come to realize that general equilibrium theory was a cul-de-sac and he could write what he described as "a diatribe against the 'noxious influence' of Walras on modern economics" (1997: 191). In parallel with this was a change in his attitude towards Keynes and towards macroeconomics in general.

Blaug's passion for both history and analytically rigorous economics and his commitment to bringing the two together have been both strengths and weaknesses in his work. It is surely a blind spot that for as long as he remained under the spell of general equilibrium theory he could not achieve a proper perspective on either Walras or Keynes for the first three editions of *Economic Theory in Retrospect*. Against this, on the other hand, has to be set the enormous achievements of his reinterpretation of Ricardo and classical economics, his raising the methodological awareness of a whole generation of economists, and his demonstration, by his own example, that the history of economic thought should be analytically as well as historically rigorous.

## Notes

* I am grateful to Bob Coats, John Creedy, Craufurd Goodwin, Terence Hutchison, and Denis O'Brien for invaluable comments and advice. Responsibility for any remaining errors or indiscretions is, however, mine alone. This paper was written during my tenure of a British Academy Research Readership. I am grateful to the British Academy for its support.

1 Unusually, the *Economic Journal* carried reviews of both the American and British editions.

2 All unattributed citations are to works by Blaug.

3 The contents of this paragraph are taken from Blaug's autobiographical essay (Blaug 1997: chapter 1).

4 The introductions to the *Pioneers* volumes draw heavily on the *Great Economists* volumes.

5 I refer to the "text" of the book here. The bibliographies, containing many incisive comments, make the breadth and depth of reading that always lies behind the text very clear.

6 I am aware of reviews by Stigler (1959), Meek (1958), Grampp (1959), Dobb (1960), Hicks (1960), Hilton (1958), and Knight (1959). Neither *Economica* nor the *Economic Journal* carried reviews, though as the latter announced the book as "to be reviewed" presumably the explanation in that case is that the reviewer failed to deliver.

7 The book's thesis is considered in more detail in the next section.

8 It is also worth noting that the latter list contains many items whose authors would not have seen themselves as concerned primarily, if at all, with Ricardian economics.

9 It is tempting to see this as a gradual liberation from the influence of Stigler, his Ph.D. supervisor. However, Blaug's own account in terms of the general intellectual climate of the 1960s is highly convincing.

10 Denis O'Brien has pointed out that:

> in the sixties there was still around that archetypal Oxbridge suspicion of people who publish too much. There was some wariness about this brash young American academic who kept producing things, and did not even consider economic history to be forbidden territory. By the second edition it had become clear that this was no flash in the pan phenomenon, and people realised Blaug had to be taken seriously.

11 Though this refers to the second edition, Denis O'Brien has pointed out that Robbins was recommending the book to his graduate students as early as 1962.

12 Having said this he went on to criticize the chapter on scholasticism and mercantilism as "not on the same plane as the rest" and to suggest that Blaug was "too contemptuous" of Malthus.

13  This part of the article is discussed in more detail below.

14  I use the word "unintentionally" because Blaug gives the reason for this as the avoid-ance of duplication. Given the length of *Economic Theory in Retrospect*, the pressure to remove such material must have been great.

15  In the bibliography to the chapter on Adam Smith, Blaug observes that reading Smith, Ricardo, and Mill is more interesting if one knows the contemporary institu-tions that are being criticized, referring readers to a textbook on British economic history.

16  It is consistent with Blaug's judgement that, despite Keynes's favouring Malthus over Ricardo on the question of gluts, "It is fortunate for the history of economics that good logic triumphed over bad" (1962: 159). It is also worth noting that the remark about Ricardo quoted in the text illustrates Blaug's attitude to pre-Smithian writers, dismissed in a few pages in *Economic Theory in Retrospect*. If Ricardo invented the technique of economic analysis, what do we make, for example, of Cantillon?

17  Perhaps this was because, though published in 1962, the book went to press signifi-cantly before this.

18  Blaug's (1986c) reaction to Hollander's book on Mill was even more critical.

19  He cites Hicks as having tried to show that the absence of income effects was suffi-cient to ensure stability of multi-market equilibrium, and observes that criticisms of Hicks for failing to make explicit dynamic assumptions "may be said to have led to the emergence of economic dynamics as a new branch of economic theory" (1962: 530).

20  In the middle of this passage Blaug concedes that general equilibrium formulations of economic problems may be interesting, but this is a different issue from the value of general equilibrium theory as understood in the literature he is discussing.

21  He has Churchill attacking the Treasury view in 1929; Hawtrey as the sole opponent of public works policy; and argues that people failed to realize the extent of unem-ployment in Britain in the 1920s before the revision of Beveridge's book in 1931 (1962: 596–601). However, it should be noted that in his review, Hutchison picked out these as amongst the very few errors in the book. Overall his conclusion was that the book contained "commendably few mis-statements" (Hutchison 1963: 759).

22  The words "such as" are important because Blaug does not suggest that any of these heuristics applied throughout the programme's history.

23  When one first gets to this passage it sounds as though these heuristics are intended to apply from Smith onwards, but within a couple of sentences it becomes clear that they apply only to the period after the marginal revolution.

24  It might be argued that this is a "rational reconstruction" of Blaug's argument, for he speaks of the moves from Smithian to Ricardian economics and from Ricardian to marginalist economics as a problem shift within a broader research programme. But the interpretation of the latter transition as a move between research programmes is necessary to make sense of the clear distinction that Blaug draws between England and Continental Europe.

25  In this paper I am giving this book less attention than it arguably deserves on the grounds that it is as much a contribution to methodology as to the history of economic thought. Though methodological case studies of the type Blaug provides in the book are, in a sense, historical exercises, that was not their main purpose. It should be noted that Part II, on the history of economic methodology, is clearly a historical essay.

26  This was answered in *The Methodology of Economics* (1992) with the case studies in Part III.

27  This applies to his applied economics as much as to his historical work.

28  His experience of McCarthyism served as a warning. He was forced to resign from his first teaching post, at Queens College of CCNY, after he endorsed a student peti-tion in support of a colleague who was unjustly dismissed after refusing to testify before the McCarthy committee.

# Bibliography

Arrow, K. J. and Hahn, F. (1971) *General Competitive Analysis*, San Francisco: Holden-Day.

Blaug, Mark (1958) *Ricardian Economics: A Historical Study*, New Haven, CT: Yale University Press.

—— (1962) *Economic Theory in Retrospect*, Homewood, IL: Richard D. Irwin (London: Heinemann, 1964).

—— (1968) *Economic Theory in Retrospect*, second edition, Homewood, IL: Richard D. Irwin.

—— (1974) *The Cambridge Revolution: Success or Failure*, London: Institute of Economic Affairs (reprinted with revisions, 1978).

—— (1978) *Economic Theory in Retrospect*, third edition, Cambridge and New York: Cambridge University Press.

—— (1985) *Economic Theory in Retrospect*, fourth edition, Cambridge and New York: Cambridge University Press.

—— (1986a) *Economic History and the History of Economics*, Brighton: Wheatsheaf.

—— (1986b) *Great Economists before Keynes: An Introduction to the Lives and Work of One Hundred Great Economists of the Past*, Brighton: Wheatsheaf.

—— (1986c) "Review of Samuel Hollander, The Economics of John Stuart Mill", *History of Economic Thought Newsletter* 36, Spring: 23–4.

—— (1990a) *Economic Theories: True or False: Essays in the History and Methodology of Economics*, Aldershot and Brookfield, VT: Edward Elgar.

—— (1990b) *John Maynard Keynes: Life, Ideas, Legacy*, London: Macmillan, in association with the Institute of Economic Affairs (video of the same title, 1987).

—— (1991–2) (ed.) *Pioneers in Economics*, 46 vols, Aldershot and Brookfield, VT: Edward Elgar.

—— (1992) *The Methodology of Economics: How Economists Explain*, Cambridge and New York: Cambridge University Press.

—— (1995) "Reply", in Fred Moseley (ed.) *Heterodox Economics: True or False?*, Aldershot and Brookfield, VT: Edward Elgar.

—— (1996) *Economic Theory in Retrospect*, fifth edition, Cambridge and New York: Cambridge University Press.

—— (1997) *Not Only an Economist: Recent Essays by Mark Blaug*, Cheltenham and Brookfield, VT: Edward Elgar.

—— (1998) *Great Economists Since Keynes: An Introduction to the Lives and Works of One Hundred Modern Economists*, second edition, Cheltenham and Northampton, MA: Edward Elgar.

—— (1999) "Misunderstanding Classical Economics: The Sraffian Interpretation of the Surplus Approach", *History of Political Economy* 31, 2: 213–36.

Cannan, Edwin (1893 [1953]) *Theories of Production and Distribution*, London: Staples.

Debreu, Gerard (1959) *The Theory of Value*, New York: Wiley.

Dickinson, H. D. (1965a) "Review of *Economic Theory in Retrospect*", *Economic Journal* 75: 169–70.

—— (1965b) "Review of Blaug Economic Theory in Retrospect", *Economic Journal* 75: 168–9.

Dobb, Maurice (1960) "Review of *Ricardian Economics*", *Science and Society*, Winter: 263–4.

Friedman, Milton (1953) "The methodology of positive economics", in M. Friedman (ed.) *Essays on Positive Economics*, Chicago: Chicago University Press.

Grampp, W. D. (1959) "Review of Blaug (1958)", *American Economic Review* 49, 3: 419–20.

Gray, Alexander (1931) *The Development of Economic Doctrine*, New York: Wiley.

Hicks, John R. (1939) *Value and Capital*, Oxford: Clarendon Press.

—— (1960) "Review of Blaug (1958)", *Economic History Review* 13, 1: 129–30.

Hilton, George W. (1958) "Review of Blaug (1958)", *Victorian Studies* 2: 70–2.

Hutchison, T. W. (1963) "Review of Blaug (1962)", *Economic Journal* 73: 758–9.

Keynes, J. M. (1936) *The General Theory of Employment, Interest and Money*, London: Macmillan.

Knight, Frank H. (1959) "Review of *Blaug (1958)*", *Southern Journal of Economics* 25, 3: 363–5.

Koopmans, Tjalling (1957) *Three Essays on the State of Economic Science*, New York and London: McGraw-Hill.

Lange, Oscar (1936–37) "On the Economic Theory of Socialism", *Review of Economic Studies* 4: 53–71.

Latsis, Spiro J. (ed.) (1976) *Method and Appraisal in Economics*, Cambridge and New York: Cambridge University Press.

Meek, Ronald L. (1958) "Review of Blaug (1958)", *Kyklos* 11: 557–9.

O'Brien, D. P. (1970) *J. R. McCulloch: A Study in Classical Economics*, London: George Allen & Unwin.

—— (1975) *The Classical Economists*, Oxford: Oxford University Press.

—— (1981) "Ricardian economics and the economics of David Ricardo", *Oxford Economic Papers* 33: 352–86.

Peach, Terry (1993) *Interpreting Ricardo*, Cambridge and New York: Cambridge University Press.

Robbins, L. C. (1969) "Review of Blaug (1968)", *Economica* 36: 442–3.

Roll, Eric (1973) *The History of Economic Thought*, London: Faber.

Schumpeter, J. A. (1954) *A History of Economic Analysis*, New York: Oxford University Press.

Sraffa, Piero (1960) *The Production of Commodities by Means of Commodities*, Cambridge: Cambridge University Press.

Steedman, Ian (1995) "Sraffian economics and the capital controversy", in Fred Moseley (ed.) *Heterodox Economics: True or False?*, Aldershot and Brookfield, VT: Edward Elgar.

Stigler, George J. (1959) "Review of Blaug (1958)", *Journal of Political Economy* 67, 6: 641.

# 3 Bob Coats and the historicizing of economic policy

*Neil De Marchi*

## Why employ economists?

It would not occur to most historians of political economy to ask this question, much less to have it always in mind, but it is one posed almost from the outset of his career and persistently across the decades by A. W. (Bob) Coats, and pursuing its implications is what differentiates him from just about every other living member of the subdiscipline.

What *does* the question imply? In modern terms, if economists are useful in distinguishable ways, then they must have something that other sorts of professionals do not. With the necessary allowances, however, distinguishing expertise on policy questions has been a mark of economic thinkers for centuries, certainly long before there were professional economists. Policy, not professionalization, is the key word here. For as long as public affairs have involved money, prices, interest rates, and inflation; questions of employment, industry, growth, and decay; trade, exchange rates, and terms of trade; the revenue of the "prince;" a monopolizing spirit, enterprise, risk, and return; for so long has there been a need for policy advice by those with an "economic" understanding.

Economic concepts and insights have varied over time, of course, as well as from place to place. And what counts as expertise has everywhere become a great deal more technical, in both statistical and mathematical senses, than in, say, 1620. More intricate and complex too have become the processes by which policy proposals are filtered, shaped, rendered into statutes or executive orders, and implemented. But it is precisely the changing administrative and institutional forms and structures through which economic ideas are transmuted into policy actions – the policy "process" – that fascinates Bob Coats. This preoccupation has not at all excluded study of the ways economic ideas themselves are formed. Nonetheless, Coats has always insisted that ideas as disembodied entities are of little value, and to the extent that he has bothered with economic theory at all, it is with what he calls the empirical basis of economic concepts and ideas, rather than with economic analysis as such.

## Ideas, policy, and events

How ought one to proceed in writing the history of policy as it involves economics? Here Coats has given us strong hints over the years, summarized in 1987 in the form of a schema which indicates the sort of links that he thinks should be attended to. This framework is presented on page 54 of volume 1 of his collected essays (Coats 1992), to which volume all page references hereafter will be made. The framework is offered as a guide to investigating "how, when and in what manner" ideas have exerted influence over policy (1992: 52).

As suggested already, this is only one half of what interests Coats, it is the complement to first establishing how ideas are influenced by "events" or conditions. But the two parts do not receive equal attention. Events as contingencies are not sharply distinguished from tendencies and changes in the underlying "structure" of the economic "system" – all words and phrases quoted from Heckscher without involving Coats in commitment. Coats is wary of ideology, fights shy of crude social or physical conditioning accounts of how ideas are formed, and is alert to the problem of perceptions versus economic facts (e.g., 1992: 32, 50).[1] But all this caution and awareness of complexities makes him unwilling to say much about ideas other than what I have noted above, that they are abstractions from an empirical basis. He adds that broad parallels do exist between conditions and ideas, whether or not these are causal connections, but claims that establishing causality between ideas and policy actions is much more difficult. In matters of policy, one must not only "descend to the study of the particular applications of general ideas," but be aware that attempts to isolate the "economic" element in policy may involve "an unwarrantable degree of abstraction" (1992: 30).

These extra demands notwithstanding, Coats is more comfortable discussing the elements that must be taken into account in the ideas–policy link than in its conditions–ideas counterpart. In the schema in Coats's volume 1, page 54, ideas are dealt with summarily. He starts with events. These are said to pose problems; in that sense I take them to represent crises, points at which choice is thrust upon thinkers and decision makers. Perceptions of these events shape ideas (and vice versa). But that is all. Supposing ideas in hand, however, those bits of them believed to be of policy relevance are first made known and perhaps responded to by political, religious, social, and legal thinkers and interest groups. (It is here that any economic aspect is likely to become disguised, to the point of being unrecognizable.) The repackaged ideas then pass into the hands of administrative and bureaucratic entities and, again reshaped, may go on to decision-making bodies: courts, parliaments, councils, committees, and so forth. All the preceding links may be bypassed if there are powerful individuals who take up the original ideas and introduce them directly to the relevant decision-making bodies. Either way, there may follow specific rulings, statutes, regulations, and, lastly, implementation and enforcement. Rulings etc., and implementation/enforcement, in turn modify ideas.[2] In an earlier summary of the process (1992: 30), Coats insisted that "the key to the history of policy" lies in "the cut and thrust of the legislative and administrative process" and in "conflicts of personalities and interest groups." His 1987 schema maintains this perspective, but elaborates the various steps in the process.

## Descending to the study of particulars

To assess properly the Coats approach we need to go beyond schemas and look at what happens when he investigates specific instances of policy making. To this end I have selected three essays from the immense array of work that he presents. All are republished in volume 1 of his essays; they cover three decades of his work and different historical eras. Each, however, has to do with trade policy in one way or another. The essays involved are: (1) "In defence of Heckscher and the idea of mercantilism", with an updated perspective, "Mercantilism: economic ideas, history, policy" (1987); (2) "Adam Smith and the mercantile system" (1975); and (3) "Political economy and the tariff reform campaign of 1903" (1968), an episode set in larger historical context in the more recent "The challenge to free trade: fair trade and tariff reform 1880–1914" (1985). I shall choose portions of these essays for comment, but direct my remarks to just two issues which they broach. First, the idea of mercantilism, as illustrating the problems of connecting conceptual generalizations with their empirical base; then, the role of economic expertise in the policy process.

### Case study I: Mercantilism: quasi-system, or policy acts and ideas with an empirical base?

Coats has been much exercised by the problem of whether the idea of mercantilism, which we owe to Adam Smith, is a legitimate doctrinal abstraction to describe what would otherwise appear only as "a vast collection of seemingly unconnected writings of no conceivable relevance to any but the issues with which they [were] immediately concerned" (1992: 31). Legitimacy here requires that there be some underlying coherence. We must be able to show that, although "mercantilist" writers might have presented their ideas in relation to specific problems, they "knew how to relate one problem to another and reduce them to unifying principles—*analytic* principles, not merely principles of policy." Schumpeter, whose words these are (quoted approvingly by Coats 1992: 36), thought that mercantilists passed the test, that their ideas comprised a quasi-system.

But where do the unifying principles come from? Coats has felt a need to go beyond Schumpeter in two ways: first, he wants to be able to point to the specific circumstances generating particular mercantilist "policy acts" or stances but, second, also to display such acts as "particular manifestations of general trends of thought and events" (1992: 38). This suggests a commitment to inductive inquiry that Schumpeter probably would have been uncomfortable with. It may reflect Coats's early graduate training under Bela Gold at the University of Pittsburgh. He remembers Gold for, among other qualities, his "profound respect for empirical data" (1992: 5). Coats adds that this held natural appeal for him because of his own historian's instincts. In any event, and by way of illustrating where Coats's instincts diverge from Schumpeter's, an interest in seeking out the empirical basis of doctrinal positions drives Coats's understanding of Smith in his essay on "Adam Smith and the mercantile system." There Smith's impact is attributed less to his analytical ability than to "his exceptional skill in combining analysis with empirical data, with historical examples, and with direct and incisive comments on the conditions and tendencies of his own times" (1992: 141).

A difficulty here is that Schumpeter's analytical stance is stronger and therefore more open to refutation than Coats's. If it were found that mercantilist writings contain only the espousal of views on specific problems, that the maxims offered only rarely interconnect, then they would fail the S-test: mercantilism would not qualify as even a quasi-system. But what would constitute a comparable criterion of compellingness in a narrative designed to manifest the particular within "general trends of thought and events" (1992: 38)? One measure, of a piece with the basically positivist cast of at least Coats's early writings, is the simple rule that a compelling historical narrative must account for as many as possible of the agreed-upon facts. Nonetheless, this remains a completeness and degree-of-intricacy test. To go farther, to ascribe causes to observed events (outcomes) in any single instance, especially where economic and multiple other influences are present or suspected of being present, as in Coats's typical policy situation, is all but impossible. Mill long ago made this quite clear, and Coats knows it only too well. One way out of the difficulty is to opt for multiple narratives; another is to accept that a good narrative can have entertainment value, that unequivocal enlightenment is not everything. A third, which I like for the clarity it brings, is to write deliberately analytical narratives, with relatively strong positions, based on economic theory, and used to probe the facts. Carried to excess this last alternative can seem slightly, or more than slightly, ridiculous, as Coats has pointed out with regard to a 1980s attempt to reduce mercantilist activism to rent-seeking behavior (see Appendix to "Mercantilism. Economic ideas, history, policy").

Coats has not engaged much in open discussion of how to write non-analytical history, being content for the most part simply to steer a course away from what he knows is faulty. Thus he urges that we avoid the one-sidedness of economists' typically casual and superficial accounts of policy – too frequently they "ignore the influence of political interests and conditions, and administrative structures and procedures" (1992: 44); those of economic historians, which "focus … on conditions rather than ideas" (ibid.); and those of historians of economics, which too often stress only theoretical developments or, when ideas and policy are addressed, tend to neglect "the processes whereby proposals are or are not adopted and enforced" (1992: 45). In thus avoiding extremes Coats has more or less adopted complexity as his watchword, though without telling us how we should evaluate his handling of it. In a sense we are invited simply to enjoy – not difficult to do in his case since he writes so engagingly – though without troubling ourselves overly with Millian concerns.

My own (acknowledged) penchant being for the analytical approach, however, I will try and see what added value, if any, it can squeeze out of Coats's work. We are still dealing with mercantilism, and I turn at this point to his chosen illustration – the clearest available, in his judgment. Coats's chosen illustrative case is the controversy over the East India trade which occurred in late seventeenth-century England; he believes it illustrates well both the inter-relationships between mercantilist maxims – Schumpeter's concern – and the links between ideas and their empirical base – his own particular interest (1992: 36). Since what I deem significant in this episode differs in important respects from Coats's emphases, I will tell the story my way, but with pointers to what he elected to stress.

In the 1690s the East India Company found itself at the center of controversies one of which Coats dubs, following one of his sources, "The 'protection' versus 'free trade' issue" (1992: 37). This is misleading because, whereas modern economists associate protection with tariff and non-tariff barriers to commerce erected by governments, without inquiring what form of governance is involved, an important aspect of the debates of the 1690s, however, was precisely who held the power of protecting. The East India Company had long enjoyed exclusive privileges in its sphere of interest, as a matter of royal prerogative. But royal prerogative had been under challenge in various ways since the 1640s, and in the 1690s the circumstances were right for a fresh, strong move to be made in favor of statutory powers, exercised by parliament. Ignoring this aspect of the debates not only narrows to its economic element what was a much larger conflict, an unaccustomed stance for Coats to take, but it risks missing one of the tendencies of the sort that in general he believes should be emphasized, a real sea change in attitudes towards regulation.[3]

In 1689 this change had resulted in the loss of monopoly privileges to the Merchant Adventurers, and in 1698 it would result in parliamentary approval for the establishment of a rival to the East India Company, the New East India Company. Such chipping away at royal prerogative was abetted by a growing perception that limiting exports to the end of securing higher-than-market profits to a single company was no longer what the nation most needed. Growing colonial and reexport trades meant that competitiveness with rival *nations*, and the nationality of producers rather than of merchants (middlemen), increasingly came to seem more important than the needs of private adventurers.[4]

This perception coincided with the replacement of an hereditary (and Catholic) monarch (James II) with one agreed upon by parliament, a body increasingly willing to assert its sway in matters affecting the national interest. The replacement king, William III of Orange, renewed hostilities against the French, in the context of which import replacement, and protection of domestic against (selected) foreign producers, could be viewed as a way to help meet the expenses of war as well as fitting the new international circumstances of England's trade. But the broad shift to *national* interest in trade policy is first apparent in the Navigation Acts of 1651 and 1660. It was given focus by the then-intense Anglo-Dutch trade rivalry, and expressed in a series of officially sanctioned periods of open trade in the 1660s and 1670s. The 1680s involved something of a return to royal prerogative, but this was just a pause in a progressive movement away from the old system.

As far as the (Old) East India Company is concerned, there were several causes of discontent among other merchants. One, of long standing, was the company's continued exports of bullion to cover its purchases. This, as Coats notes, invited a reconsideration of bullion as medium of exchange rather than as wealth. Another was a sense that the Old Company excluded investors, a charge difficult to sustain given open trading in the company's shares, but relevant because it was so strongly linked in the minds of dissenting merchants with the repeated renewal of privileges to the company, the latest in the 1680s, sought by the Old Company and granted by the Crown under urging by its Tory supporters. Even if shares in the Old Company were freely traded it seemed to many inappropriate that the premium they carried reflected privileges not available to all. Finally, as Coats also notes, the company had been importing textiles, and was thus placed in the awkward position of wanting to defend its own freedom to import when the momentum of opinion was shifting toward the view that domestic producers should be protected. The textiles imported by the company were chiefly painted calicoes which, for reasons of their cost, colorfastness, novelty, and lightness and flexibility in use, had attracted consumers across all social strata. They thus began to be identified as a threat by domestic woollens producers.

The Old East India Company, in several respects, was thus out of step with broader developments of a commercial and political character. Indeed, policy acts increasingly display the character of what Adam Smith called the "two great engines [of the Mercantile System] for enriching a country," a policy of restraining imports for home consumption and one of increasing as much as possible exports from domestic production (*Wealth of Nations* 1976: IV.i.35). But this combination of policies owed nothing to the Old East India Company, and little to debates concerning its particular trades and privileges. Instead, it was one of the "changes in the structure of the system" that Heckscher referred to (Coates 1992: 34).

Strangely Smith, like Coats, makes little of the details reflecting these shifts in power and in the national interest, as sketched above. Smith preferred to press the analytical argument against the "monopolizing spirit" of individual companies, and stressed in a distinctly ahistorical manner the mercantilists' supposed obsession with the precious metals. Coats focuses on novel twists to arguments defending the Old Company's trade.

The story I have told differs from both in emphasizing the change in England's trade situation and in governance structures, emphases stemming from my preference for analytical narrative, in this instance focusing on the consequences of a changing regulatory environment. My emphases relative to those Coats chooses may also reflect differences in sources. He relied mostly on older, synthetic histories, in which the East India Company figured prominently, while since 1958 a lot of detailed and nuanced primary research concerning regulation, taxation, and war finance, and the mini-explosion of patents, IPOs, and startups among joint-stock companies in the early 1690s, has become available. Coats's decision to play up new *ideas* in defence of the Company's trade might also stem from his desire to illustrate Schumpeter's notion of mercantilism as a quasi-system of analytic principles. I opted to neglect altogether possible Schumpeterian analytic principles.

Because of their differing emphases our two accounts serve as an example of the multiple narrative option mentioned earlier. Which one is more satisfactory is not a question that can be decided in the absence of clear criteria. It would be interesting to see how Coats would choose to tell his story now, with modern sources to hand, but it is not obvious that even then the two would match closely. Perhaps the greatest value in having more than one account is that it brings into question the notion that an episode can be selected that is "the clearest illustration" of anything; episodes as such illustrate nothing, what is made of them is all important.

## Case study II: Economic expertise and the policy process

This becomes even more obvious in the relatively modern instance of tariff reform in Britain in the first years of the twentieth century. Joseph Chamberlain's tariff reform campaign of 1903 is identified by Coats as a case where "economists had an unusually favourable opportunity to apply their expertise to a problem of outstanding public importance" (1992: 284). There was both "an urgent need for expert 'scientific' advice" (1992: 287) and "a golden opportunity [for economists] to demonstrate the importance of their special knowledge" (1992: 307).

To make this a compelling case study in the role of the economic expert in the policy process would require at a minimum showing that there is a clear economic aspect to the issue under discussion, even if in practice this element became submerged under the weight of demagoguery, while non-economic aspects came to be accorded greater weight in serious attempts to sort out what was at stake. In fact Coats takes a different route into his material, privileging the views of the principal players, and implying that there was no *single* economic issue. He also places great weight on perceptions, or mis-perceptions. His theme is that, whatever economic question was at stake, personalities and propaganda quickly took over. Politicians prevaricated; inquiries were set in motion that served merely as window dressing; public positions were staked out on the basis of outworn slogans and convenient appeals to class interests, fear, or imperial fervor, as well as straightforward desires to acquire, or stay in, power; senior civil servants, past Chancellors of the Exchequer, and other public figures weighed in on the basis of authority alone; academic economists were divided and expressed themselves in ways and through media that did not allow the basis of a conclusion to be grasped; and so on. In his telling, we are back with the "cut and thrust" of the legislative and political process, and in the midst of personality conflicts and jarring interests, from which rational discourse was all but excluded. The result is a tale of frustrated potential, of wasted opportunities – in particular, of the opportunity to engage economic experts in the policy process.

Here, as before, I would like to propose an alternative reading, one which I think might bring us closer to Coats's own goal. As long as one focuses on perceptions, and personal agendas, it must remain unclear just what economic expertise might have contributed, if anything. Even if perceptions occluded, or were for many the only, reality; even if the economic aspect was to become obscured by other elements in the actual political cut and thrust; still, if one is to get anywhere with inquiring into the role of the economic expert, one must try to identify the economic question at issue. Here I share Coats's frustration with the prevailing lack of unity and even of clarity on just what was at issue in the documentary and other materials he found. But there may be value in positing what the issue(s) *might* have been, if only to rule some possibilities out and others in when the evidence is checked.

From the information Coats gives, I extract as the potentially dominant issue the fact that Britain was faced with growing protectionism in Continental Europe, not least in Imperial Germany, and that this was perceived as a threat to the country's manufactured exports. What response was appropriate in these circumstances? Balfour, the Prime Minister, formulated the matter in a helpful way: "*whether a fiscal system suited to a free trade nation in a world of free traders, remains suited in every detail to a free trade nation in a world of protectionists*" (quoted in 1992: 294; emphasis in the original). Importantly, from the economic point of view, this formulation did not at all challenge the benefits of specializing according to comparative advantage, despite a great deal of fulminating about free trade versus protection. Balfour represented the issue rather as one of how best to position oneself to negotiate with other nations so as to secure a better division of the gains from specialization. This, however, was not something on which economists *could* have much to say. The Ricardian principle – specialize (and trade) according to comparative advantage – being satisfied, dividing the gains had been shown by Mill to be a matter of bargaining, and on bargaining processes economic theory at the time of the tariff reform campaign was silent. What possible role was there, then, for the economic expert?

Balfour, again usefully, spelled out three principles that should guide any reform: no protection to any particular industry against reasonable competition; no mimicking of "the continental method," or a stiff increase in tariffs against the world as a whole, followed by selective concessions for those willing to reciprocate; and, no changes that would result in an increase in "the average cost of living to the working man" (1992: 294). The second principle meant that tariffs should be used as retaliation on a case-by-case basis only. This was consistent with Balfour's declared desire to treat the Empire on a preferential basis from the outset. On this matter, however, he appears to have feared that getting the "colonies" to agree to lower their own tariffs on British manufactures would require more than that their agricultural exports not be subject to a British tariff; it would probably necessitate a modest discriminatory tariff on non-British (non-Empire) imported foodstuffs, hence "*some taxation on food in this country.*" But that would violate his third principle.

So far as the economists were concerned, their expertise could come into play only on this last issue: whether a differential tariff regime could be constructed such that the average cost of living to the worker would not rise. This puts it too strongly. Coats rightly points out that expertise was needed also to interpret the Board of Trade figures, and (implicitly) to analyze whether a purported stagnation in British exports was temporary or more permanent, and to what it might be ascribed. Nevertheless, on what I am calling the central policy issue the required economic expertise was strictly limited in the way indicated.

Advice of the required sort and conforming to the constraint set by Balfour's third principle was in fact offered. Three advisers at the Customs House drew up a package which suggested that British exports could be promoted, and preferential rates offered British possessions on a reciprocal basis, without raising the cost of food (1992: 292–3). Percy Ashley, of the London School of Economics, advising Balfour, added that even if the price of food did increase it would not necessarily increase overall poverty, a potentially important empirical point (1992: 292). Treasury officials, on the other hand, objected as a matter of principle to deliberately altering the fiscal code to influence trade flows, and they challenged Ashley's assessment (1992: 293). Coats makes a great deal of these and other divisions, but my reading is rather that we have here considerable evidence that expert attention was given to precisely the matters at issue, and that differences of approach and on empirical details, both of which are always to be expected, were articulated in such a way that they could have been made the subject of reasoned debate. Making this clear would only have added strength to Coats's point that the economic quickly got lost.

There was also one concentrated form of additional expert input, a letter to *The Times* signed by fourteen university economists. This document made two sorts of points, both economic in nature, though the first has to be restated to bring out its essential economic content. This argument was that it would probably be a mis-step to reintroduce protectionist kinds of fiscal changes, since such moves create opportunity and incentives to self-seeking individuals, and invariably result in corruption and unjust redistributions of wealth (1992: 335). Generalized, this later became a central proposition in Hayek's *The Road to Serfdom*, but participants in the tariff reform debate of 1903 would have known that it could be found in Adam Smith or Bentham. It may even have been an element in the Treasury's opposition to tariff reform.

The second sort of economic argument was contained in a set of detailed propositions which invoked, though not openly, particular tools of partial equilibrium analysis which students of Marshall and readers of the text of his

*Principles* (not necessarily the mathematical appendixes) might have been expected to know or at least to have acquired a feel for. The propositions rested on specific assumptions about various demand and supply elasticities and the measurement of areas under curves. Thus, for example, the letter suggested (point 2) that a tax on imported food would raise wages, but by less, causing a lowering of the real wage (true, if we suppose a pool of the unemployed and a labor supply curve fairly elastic in the nominal wage); (point 3) that the burden of a tax on imported wheat would fall mostly on the domestic consumer, not the foreign producer (true, supposing home demand much less elastic than world supply); and (point 6) that the public would not be recompensed for any impost on food since resources would be diverted from their most efficient uses (i.e., producers' surplus would increase), besides which consumers would pay the tax on all the food consumed, whereas tariff revenue would be collected only on imported foreign foodstuffs (tariff revenue would inevitably be much less than the loss of consumers' surplus) (1992: 335–6).

It might be said that these results involve some theoretical nicety, and an understanding of technique that at the time possibly was quite rare. My point, however, is that the analysis to make such arguments plausible was available, and that they therefore represent a potential contribution by economic experts to what I am supposing was the central economic issue. Coats poses certain economic questions (1992: 330, n.107), but these focus, inappropriately in my view, on free trade doctrine and the "facts" of Britain's trade position. He does ask: "What would be the effects on domestic conditions of various types and levels of import taxes?", a question of exactly the sort that I am calling pertinent; but instead of attempting to answer this by reference to contemporary economic theory he at once reverts to the complications introduced "by the uncertainty of Balfour's intentions and the contending forces within the ranks of the tariff reformers." In short, his inclination seems to be to home in on the complexities made for economic experts by the other elements in the situation, and he concludes in this instance that "economic reasoning inevitably tended to be swamped by propaganda" (1992: 297). It is his ready acceptance of this inevitability that I find regrettable, since it deters him from laying out the economic aspect for the ideal circumstance where none of these interferences existed. Only by going through that exercise, I suggest, can one be in a position to know what is lost in the swirl, what the economic expert was in a position to say, and to judge whether it was said at all, said well, said clearly but ignored, was shouted down, or was simply deemed less weighty in the circumstances than some other aspect – political, social, or whatever. It is very clear in the present instance, for example, that the university economists who signed what became known as the "manifesto" to *The Times* failed badly in injecting their expert knowledge in the form of a series of propositions, the rationale for which could not also be given in a brief letter. Whether this was a failure born of academic pomposity or political ineptitude doesn't really matter; it matters that there was economic expertise available, and it matters that we as historians understand what its form and substance was.

### In addition to historicizing economic policy

This has not been a biographical essay, nor has my coverage been at all complete. Bob Coats himself has supplied us with some details of his academic and personal history (see the introduction to volume 1 of his essays), while the eventual three volumes of his essays will convey the scope of his activity – with the exception of his book reviewing, which has been prodigious. I have focused on his approach to writing the history of economic policy making, and have done so critically, since that is what he would want and because it might advance our ability to pursue his enterprise. But this does not begin to capture Bob Coats as scholar and as historian of economic thought. I will therefore conclude with a brief mention of his many lines of thought and work and his personal style, as a sort of acknowledgement of the paths he has charted, and the standards and personal example he has set.

Bob Coats has single-handedly pioneered thinking on the history of economic policy. As an offshoot of this interest he has also pioneered studies of professionalization in economics. While his own expertise is Anglo-American, he has made it his business to put together teams to examine the role of the economist in policy making in comparative fashion, and, in particular, where international organizations are involved. He would not consider himself a methodologist, or a student of administration, yet he has kept abreast of developments in both fields over many years, and in methodology at any rate has contributed significantly to our understanding of the implications of the work of Kuhn and Lakatos for the study of the history of economics. As historian of economic thought Bob has enormously enriched the field, with insights and scholarly work ranging from pre-Smithian through Keynesian and modern subjectivist economics in Britain, and, in the United States, from colonial to institutionalist concerns, to the breakdown of theoretical synthesis in the 1970s. His vision has been broad, with the integration of methodological, ideational, and economic–historical subject matter always his goal. Bob's writing is a delight, his references wide ranging; indeed, each must come close to setting new standards among historians of economics. As mentor he has been extraordinarily welcoming to newcomers, and generous both with time and with his amazing knowledge of several literatures. Always eager to learn, reading incessantly, keen to know the latest, open to criticism, ready to debate ways in which subdisciplines of concern to him are being shaped, encouraging of youth and renewal, Bob Coats is a model scholar and colleague, his work the very measure of openness and freshness.

### Notes

1 I am attributing convictions to Coats on some of these matters where about the only direct evidence is that he cites Heckscher and others in a sympathetic way (see Coats 1992: 40, n.23 – though see also p. 38, where he urges a need "to strike a balance between the ideological and the environmental determinists"). What almost seems like an excess of fairness is a problem in interpreting Coats's work. He shows

himself to be aware of all points of view but like a canny war correspondent does not unnecessarily stick his head above the parapet.

2 There is an element in the framework that leaves me dissatisfied. Perhaps to indicate that there is no single best starting point Coats renders the sequence of processes a complete circle, suggesting that policy implementation affects (and in lesser degree is affected by) "events." If this is taken seriously it turns events into a consequence of the policy process itself, narrowing their character and robbing them of any real exogeneity. Events lose any possible connections with larger "chance" world occurrences, physical or political; and they are set free from general tendencies within the economic system – they become essentially short term. Instead, they take on the character of responses by some participants in the policy process to undesired or unexpected consequences of prior policy interventions.

3 I am indebted to David Ormrod for letting me see a draft of his paper on "The demise of regulated trading in England: the case of the Merchant Adventurers, 1650–1730." I draw heavily on him for details and for the general lines of an argument concerning a shift towards deregulation in the last years of the seventeenth century. For references to some of the other recent literature on the 1690s, see De Marchi and Van Miegrot (2000).

4 Coats is aware of the national versus private interests element in the discussions (1992: 37), but he does not make it an occasion to inquire into the associated change in the underlying system (here the governance structure). More puzzling is that he states that there were neither political nor religious aspects to complicate the discussions of the East India trade (1992: 42, n.50), an assertion belied by the party biases in the affiliations of supporters of the Old versus the New East India Company and one which unduly diminishes the role of the religious convictions that informed the debates leading up to the events of the Glorious Revolution, between divine rightists such as Filmer, on the one hand, and nominally or strongly Protestant "enthusiasts" and Whigs of the Good Old Cause, such as Locke and Shaftesbury, on the other. It is true that the East India trade was not like the French trade; nor are the religious components in the 1690s' discussions as directly injected as in the immediately preceding opposition to and defence of James II; nevertheless, they cannot just be dismissed as Coats dismisses them here. For useful discussion of the Good Old Cause, albeit in an altogether different context, see Cunningham (1989).

# Bibliography

Coats, A. W. (1992) *On the History of Economic Thought: British and American Essays, Volume I*, London and New York: Routledge.

Cunningham, Andrew (1989) "Thomas Sydenham: Epidemics, Experiment and the 'Good Old Cause'," in Roger French and Andrew Wear (eds) *The Medical Revolution of the Seventeenth Century*, Cambridge: Cambridge University Press, 164–90.

De Marchi, Neil and Van Miegroet, H. (2000) "Rules versus Play in Early Modern Art Markets," *Recherches Economiques de Louvain/Louvain Economic Review* 66, Special Issue on the Economics of Art Markets: 145–65.

Hayek, F. A. (1976 [1944]) *The Road to Serfdom*, London: Routledge & Kegan Paul.

Ormrod, David (2000) "The Demise of Regulated Trading in England: The Case of the Merchant Adventurers, 1650–1730," Mimeo, University of Kent at Canterbury.

Smith, Adam (1976 [1776]), *An Inquiry into the Nature and Causes of the Wealth of Nations*, Glasgow edition of the *Works and Correspondence of Adam Smith, volume 2*, General Eds R. H. Campbell and A. S. Skinner, Textual Ed. W. B. Todd, Oxford: Oxford University Press.

# 4 Verve and versatility
## Neil De Marchi and the culture of economics

*Margaret Schabas**

Australia has produced a disproportionately high number of internationally renowned tennis players, opera singers, and historians of economics. Climate might explain the first phenomenon, the large Italian immigrant population the second, but the third is somewhat more mysterious. One possible explanation is that Australian schoolchildren study British history and geography. This gives them (and Canadians) a comparative advantage over Americans, who are less likely to know the difference between a Whig and a Tory, or whether Liverpool or Leicester is by the sea.

Neil De Marchi may not be known for his operatic prowess, but he once played tennis well and, as his name attests, has Italian roots. He also had good reason to pay attention to his lessons in British history, for his grandfather had left Italy to fight for the British in the Crimean War of 1853. This personal link to the distant past was due to the unusual fact that Neil's father was the youngest of nine, and had not married until his forties. He had voluntarily fought in World War I while in his teens and sustained injuries that were to contribute to his untimely death when Neil was a young child. Neil entered the world on Christmas Day, 1939, just as Europe embarked on yet another blood-bath. He was fortunate, however, to be in the remote town of Katanning in Western Australia. Raised in the company of women – his mother, sister, and aunts – this might explain his love for conversation and decorative arts. His martial and agrarian heritage notwithstanding, it would be difficult to picture Neil hunting rabbits or shearing sheep.

For his first degree (1960) at the University of Western Australia in Perth, Neil concentrated on economics and history. A Rhodes Scholarship took him to Oxford where he sat at the feet of Sir John Hicks. Both at Western Australia and at Oxford, many of Neil's courses in economics took an historical approach – an undergraduate seminar on Alfred Marshall, another ranging back to Adam Smith, another an intensive reading of Keynes. While Neil had intended to specialize in economic development, the cumulative effect of so many courses which concentrated on primary sources was to steer him toward the history of economics.

He returned to the Antipodes with a lectureship at Monash University in Melbourne, and then decided to proceed with a doctorate. His mentor at the Australian National University in Canberra was Graham Tucker, and his thesis topic was "John Stuart Mill and the Development of Ricardian Economics." To his good fortune, Terence Hutchison visited ANU during the course of Neil's research and subsequently served as an external examiner of his thesis, along with A. W. (Bob) Coats.[1] Neil completed his doctorate in 1970 and made his way back to England for research courtesy of the Nuffield Foundation.

A year later, in 1971, he began his long affiliation with Duke University in Durham, North Carolina. In addition to his post as assistant professor of economics, Neil served as acting director of a new interdisciplinary program in the history of the social sciences, a role which helped to broaden his knowledge base beyond that of economics. Upon arriving at Duke, Neil came into contact with several like-minded colleagues, Joseph Spengler, Martin Bronfenbrenner, Vladimir Treml, William Yohe. Best of all, he met a young Canadian scholar, Craufurd Goodwin, who had just founded, in 1969, the journal *History of Political Economy* (HOPE). Neil was enlisted as its assistant editor, a task he subsequently came to share with Roy Weintraub under the more esteemed title of associate editor. Neil's efforts on the journal and his cultivation of doctoral students at Duke have played an important role in making that university the leading center in North America for research in the history of economics.

Before considering the body of Neil's scholarship, it would be remiss not to mention a significant detour in his academic career. Already in the early 1970s he began to work on more practical questions, such as Nixon's wage/price policy, Carter's policy on energy, and international monetary reform. After almost ten years at Duke (1971–80), Neil resigned and moved to Amsterdam to work in the Algemene Bank Nederland as an "Adjunct-directeur" of economic research. He held this post for only three years, finding the rapid change of topics in the banking world not to his liking.[2] Whenever free time presented itself, Neil would disappear to the library to feed his love for scholarship. He returned to Duke in 1983 and was promoted to full professor three years later. His final promotion on the academic ladder coincided with a half-time appointment as Professor of the History and Philosophy of Economics at the University of Amsterdam. He held this latter post for five years, from 1986 to 1991, at which point he decided to concentrate his energies at Duke and soon thereafter became departmental chair.

One of the most salient features of Neil's résumé is his frequent collaboration with other scholars. Neil has co-authored one book (1990) and fifteen articles (the first as early as 1973) and, since 1988, edited seven books and one journal issue (five of these are co-edited). One has only to meet Neil for an hour to realize that research for him is rarely a solitary pursuit. I recall vividly my first brief trip to Duke in 1987 and a lengthy stroll in the adjoining gardens while Neil challenged my research ideas. I was to return again several times, including a four-month sojourn in 1991 courtesy of the National Science Foundation. This gave me the opportunity to audit Neil's undergraduate seminar on Adam Smith and see him employ the Socratic method on a weekly basis.

That visit also included a memorable evening attending a Duke basketball game with Neil, and witnessing his passion for the team in the year they first won the national championship. His manifest pride in his institution's athletic prowess is highly incongruous. For Neil has fiercely resisted an assimilation to American culture, let alone Dixie protocol. Although he still manages with an Australian passport, he seems much more European in his manner of speech and dress. Not by accident did he decide to restore the upper case spelling of his name to De Marchi, or come to have a second home in Rome.

Neil's love for intellectual history is evident in everything he does. Several of his students have written to me at my request, and each one contrasts his passion for learning with his exacting standards for scholarship. They also spoke of his open-mindedness and enthusiastic encouragement to explore alternative approaches. Neil seems to resist getting set in his ways; he is eternally young. Most telling of all is the large number of supervisions. Neil has seen to completion some twenty doctoral dissertations. Indeed, an entire generation of Dutch specialists came under his influence, and not just those whom he supervised officially: Arjo Klamer, Bert Hamminga, Jack Birner, Marcel Boumans, Rudy Van Zyp, Jack Vromen, Albert Jolink, Maarten Janssen, and Esther-Mirjam Sent. Add to this his Duke progeny (again some were not formally his supervisees) – Janet Seiz, Kyun Kim, Jinbang Kim, Michael Lail, Paul Harrison, Jane Rossetti, and Robert Leonard – and the list is truly impressive.[3]

Neil began to publish articles while still finishing his doctorate. The first one, "The Empirical Content and Longevity of Ricardian Economics," appeared in a 1970 issue of *Economica*. Although culled from his dissertation, it reads with the same sophistication as his mature works. It challenged Mark Blaug's claim that Mill purposely avoided the extant empirical refutations of Ricardian theory. Mill defended Ricardian doctrine because he had a different time scale to the one assumed by Blaug. We find here already the seeds of Neil's interest in the question of verification that would later bring him to the work of Milton Friedman and Karl Popper. Neil's second article was part of a conference proceedings commemorating the centenary of the revolutionary proclamations of Jevons, Menger, and Walras. This received wide circulation, first as part of a special issue for *History of Political Economy* (1972) and then as a book on *The Marginal Revolution* (1973). Entitled "Mill and Cairnes and the Emergence of Marginalism in England," it argued that there were sound reasons why Mill and Cairnes did not take the steps later taken by Jevons to establish the principle of diminishing marginal utility. Neil here as in his first article already shows a gift for philosophical analysis.

Four more articles on classical economics appeared in close succession (1973–6) and thus established him as an authority on the subject. The first, "The Noxious Influence of Authority: A Correction of Jevons' Charge" (1973), demonstrated that Millian factions had not imposed themselves on the majority of university appointments in the period before 1871, contrary to Jevons's accusations. Neil here shows an adeptness to investigate almost in a journalistic fashion, digging up records of personal intrigue that would not have made their way into mainstream history of economics. Another 1973 article (co-authored with R. P. Sturges) brought us four hitherto unpublished letters from Malthus to

Whewell, along with an incisive interpretation of their historical import. Despite some obvious similarities, Malthus was not won over to Whewell's campaign to demolish Ricardo. Neil tends to write short, terse articles, but his next piece, "The Success of Mill's *Principles*" (1974), was exceptionally long. It argues that Mill's conciliatory stance proved to be the right strategy for dominating the field right up until the mid 1870s. Finally, an article on a more obscure classical economist, Thorold Rogers (1976b), evinced the same flair for detective work as the one on Jevons.

Several years later Neil was to publish a few more pieces on the same period, on James Mill (1983), Nassau Senior (1987), and John Stuart Mill (1986; 1988a; 1989b). Together with the first group, they might well have been worked up into a book on the scientific standing and propagation of economic ideas in nineteenth-century England. But in many respects, the Rogers article of 1976 brought to an end Neil's exclusively historical focus on classical economics. For, as we will see, 1976 marks an important turning point in Neil's *oeuvre*. He had already flirted with questions of verification from the beginning, but now he marched boldly into the murky land of methodology.

Indeed, the two essays on Mill senior (1983) and junior (1986) are explicitly on methodology, particularly on the trade-off between theory and observation. In the first, Neil attempts to paint James Mill in a more favorable light than the portrait offered by Terence Hutchison. In the second, he emphasizes a more accurate historical interpretation of Mill's views on the scientific status of political economy than the one published by Daniel Hausman. It is worth noting that Neil has an unusual ability to challenge the arguments of others without antagonizing them. Blaug, Hutchison, and Hausman were all to collaborate with Neil at a later point in time, suggesting that Neil's criticisms were fully constructive.[4]

But back to methodology. Neil's article "Anomaly and the Progress of Economics: The Case of the Leontief Paradox" (1976a) ironically made his name more than any one of his studies of the classical economists. It was part of a conference proceedings, edited by Spiro Latsis, that explored the relevance of Imre Lakatos to the history of economics. This was a time when the work of Lakatos was much in vogue, and the book sold well beyond the circle of historians of economics. Neil found an excellent illustration of the Lakatosian program in the case of an anomaly generated by Leontief to the Heckscher–Ohlin theorem of trade. Contrary to what the theorem would predict, American export industries were actually labour intensive. How to salvage the theory? Appeal to auxiliary hypotheses, and establish that the theory has empirical value (remains progressive in Lakatosian terms) in other contexts. Also, true to form, the leading mathematical economist of the age, Paul Samuelson, came to its rescue, showing that the theorem was but a special case of a general theory of market exchange.

Neil's early exposure to Lakatos had a strong influence over him for years to come, though fortunately never to the point of robbing him of his initial historical sensibility. His 1991 volume (co-edited with Mark Blaug) entitled *Appraising Economic Theories: Studies in the Methodology of Research Programs,* attempted to assess the relevance of the Lakatosian program for the history of economics. The findings were primarily negative; most case studies under the microscope did not accord with Lakatos's model. But as Neil noted in his introduction, Lakatos still provided the best self-promoted image of economists *qua* scientists. Even one of the contributors, Vernon Smith, found that Lakatos had captured his own views on scientific inquiry with great precision.

Lakatos had inevitably sparked Neil's interest in Popper and, to a lesser extent, Kuhn and Feyerabend. In 1988, Neil issued an influential study entitled *The Popperian Legacy in Economics*. It was motivated by a conference in honor of J. J. Klant, whom Neil had succeeded at the University of Amsterdam. Neil's own entry to the volume gives a detailed account of how a group of Young Turks at the LSE, led by Richard Lipsey, were inspired in their efforts to rebel by the "manifesto" offered by Popper. Ironically, they made very little specific use of Popper. He was more a shield than a sword. For economists rarely if ever rise to the falsificationist standards demanded by Sir Karl, let alone follow his prescription for bold conjectures. Neil's case study resonated well with the findings of most others at the conference, with the exceptions of Mark Blaug and Terence Hutchison. As Neil notes in his introduction, the conference participants were highly critical of Popperian applications to economics:

> there is no very substantial Popperian legacy in economics. ... Its main lesson was to disabuse economists of the idea that they could establish truth and could rest content with criteria for theory acceptance such as plausibility based on introspection, or logical consistency.
>
> (De Marchi 1988b: 12–13)

Neil's interest in methodology inevitably led him to examine the work of Milton Friedman. From this issued two articles and one book, all in collaboration with Abraham Hirsch. The first article was a brief criticism of an interpretation of Friedman put forward by Larry Boland and William Frazer (1984). Despite some superficial similarities and a brief acquaintance, Friedman is not a Popperian. If anything, Friedman has more in keeping with the instrumentalist ideas of John Dewey. A longer essay (1986) for the new journal *Economics and Philosophy* (on whose editorial board Neil also served) hammers home a similar point about the differences between Popper and Friedman, with specific focus on the latter's monetarist arguments. Friedman (and Anna Schwartz) used extensive evidence from American monetary history, not to test systematically his main argument about increased money supply stimulating output, but rather to pile up evidence the way a lawyer would in a courtroom: "Corroborating bits of evidence are offered to strengthen conviction in this hypothesis. To some extent this is done by weakening trust in the alternatives ... the activity of a criminal prosecutor strikes us as providing a useful analogy" (De Marchi and Hirsch 1986: 19). The implication is that Friedman suppresses the less suitable evidence rather than confront it head on the way a true Popperian ought to do.

Neil and Abe Hirsch's book on Friedman (1990) offers a judicious account of the American economist which points to both the strengths and weaknesses of his research and methodological stance. Friedman is very prolific; simply absorbing his output and sifting through the methodological pronouncements is a feat in itself. The authors have done much more, however, in providing a historical context by which to interpret Friedman's mission, and for that the book will remain essential reading for any student on the subject. They cover the intellectual roots that lead up to his famous 1953 essay on positive economics, including the work of John Dewey, W. C. Mitchell, and Frank Knight, as well as the ideas of some of Friedman's main critics such as James Tobin and James Buchanan. The book lends weight to the view that Friedman practiced somewhat selectively what he preached so boldly.

Neil's interest in the empirical validity of economics also led him toward econometrics, guided by the work of Mary Morgan and David Hendry and his own students Jinbang Kim, Michael Lail, and Maarten Jannsen. The result was a co-edited volume (with Christopher Gilbert) on *The History and Methodology of Econometrics* (1989a), and three co-authored articles, one on *ceteris paribus* conditions for the *Proceedings of the Philosophy of Science Association* (De Marchi and Kim 1989) and two for econometric journals (De Marchi et al.1995). All of these speak to Neil's willingness to learn new technical material and his commitment to ground broader philosophical theories in concrete examples.

A few of Neil's articles on the history and philosophy of economics are outliers that are difficult to subsume under a pattern. A 1983 statistical survey (with John Lodewijks) of the journal literature on the history of economics found, quite surprisingly, that HOPE accounted for only 15 percent of output. The next set of non-groupable papers are three entries for *The New Palgrave Dictionary* (1987) on the topics of "Abstinence," "Non-competing Groups," and "Paradoxes and Anomalies." Actually, the third entry has a heavy emphasis on Popper and in that sense fits with his other work. Another outlier is an article for an Annual Supplement to HOPE (De Marchi and Dohlman 1991) on the subject of national security, edited by Craufurd Goodwin. Entitled "League of Nations Economists and the Ideal of Peaceful Change in the 1930s," it nonetheless draws upon his previous study of Bertil Ohlin and more recent acquaintance with the work of the Dutch economist Tinbergen. Yet another (1994, with Marina Bianchi) is on Douglas North's new institutionalism. It challenges North's tendency to fashion all historical analysis using the idea of transaction costs. Somewhat reminiscent of Popper, they point out that there remains the problem of incomplete knowledge at the time historical actors act. Having the benefit of hindsight prompts historians to impute greater rationality to those actors than is perhaps warranted, and this in turn threatens to distort our historical account.

These apparently unrelated papers once again point to Neil's remarkable breadth. How many historians of economics have managed to write seminal articles on both historical and methodological problems, and seem as much at home in the seventeenth century as in the twentieth? Neil not only is a historian of the highest rank, but his versatility insures that virtually every other scholar in the field must at some point in time confront his work. Neil has also matured far beyond his youthful enthusiasm for Popper and Lakatos. Having helped steer his own student Arjo Klamer toward the study of rhetoric and hermeneutics, and under the influence of some of the literary theorists at Duke, Stanley Fish and Barbara Hernnstein Smith, not to mention his close collaboration with Roy Weintraub, it is fair to say that Neil has severed ties with logical empiricism and the growth-of-knowledge legislators – Kuhn, Popper, and Lakatos. He has come to appreciate the work of sociologists of science such as Karin Knorr-Cetina, Harry Collins, and Trevor Pinch, and to assimilate the new experimental realism put forward by Ian Hacking and Nancy Cartwright. Scientific inquiry is much less rule governed than the earlier group had assumed. The constraints imposed by the phenomena themselves, and the social setting of scientific practice, play a much greater role than theoretical consistency would mandate.

Some of this personal evolution is manifest in Neil's introductions to his volumes on Popper and Lakatos, both the ones already mentioned, as well as a 1992 volume, *Post-Popperian Methodology of Economics: Recovering Practice* and a 1994 volume (co-edited with Bert Hamminga), "Idealization in Economics." There one will find essays (though not by Neil) oriented toward hermeneutics and feminism, as well as numerous critiques of Popper and Lakatos. But perhaps the best indicator of Neil's capacity for undertaking new lines of research is his work on the early modern Dutch art markets and the economics of consumption, both of which are in step with the general turn by historians of science toward cultural history. With these microhistorical investigations into the ateliers and auction houses of the Dutch Golden Age, Neil has returned to his first love: contextual history with broader theoretical implications.

Artworks to this day pose something of a headache to the economic theorist. There is some substitutability, some (limited) reproduction, and of course much room for speculation. Aesthetic considerations are relevant, of course, but often the artist's reputation and size of a painting will be a more important determinant of price. A recent brouhaha over a possibly fake and grossly overpriced Vincent van Gogh painting has disclosed just how atypical the art market can be.[5]

Neil is clearly in his element when it comes to making sense of this tension between commerce and art, and in many respects this work is the most pathbreaking of all. He has, for example, explored questions of originality and value in connection to the early modern Dutch guilds and dealers of art, precisely the period during which painting underwent commodification. Neil has identified a sophisticated array of systems of production and distribution in place c. 1600. Art was treated as a capital good, and speculation lent itself to nascent cases of futures markets. Informational asymmetries provided cases of Akerlof's market for lemons, and instances of fraud and false representation made for interesting tales of exploitation and windfall profits. Neil's objectives are to explore the implications of these early market experiments, both legal and illegal, on later market practices. He has also extended this to the period of Adam Smith and Joshua Reynolds, both of whom recognized the value of ingenuity in the production of rare works of art. My only worry is that the more commercial craftiness Neil unearths (even in painters as distinguished as Rembrandt, who put his signature on his students' paintings), the harder it is to appreciate the paintings as objects of beauty. But the work is exciting and innovative, and provides a countervailing current to the ongoing Whiggish stream to which many established historians of economics still belong. There are about ten articles to date, again most in collaboration with other scholars: Paul Harrison, Matt Raiff, and most prominently, with art historian Hans Van Miegroet.

All of this has helped to shed light on both the art market in general and the conditions of early Dutch capitalism, particularly on the subjects of risk and investment. Neil has linked his analysis of the emergent art market to the joint-stock companies of Dutch East India and even to the tulip bulb mania. One article (with Paul Harrison) examines the practice of selling short or "trading in the wind" by Dutch speculators of the early modern period. In so far as it addresses the concerns of many at the time with impropriety, it contributes nicely to a conference volume on the subject of higgling that Neil and Mary Morgan co-edited in 1993. The volume helped to bring out historical concerns with the question of fairness, as opposed to efficiency, in the exchange of goods.

An interest in art markets has also steered Neil, with the help of Marina Bianchi, to reflect upon the theory of consumption, a topic he once noted it had been Mill's misfortune to neglect. This has produced two pieces, "The tasteless theory of choice meets novelty," and "Adam Smith's accommodation of 'altogether endless' desire," and has also guided him toward the work of Bernard Mandeville, who incidentally had things to say – as did Smith – about the pricing of paintings. The most prominent showcase of this research is his 1994 article (co-authored with Hans Van Miegroet) for the *Art Bulletin*, entitled "Art, Value, and Market Practices in the Seventeenth Century Netherlands."

When I tried to think of which economist in the past had a sensibility closest to Neil's, I first thought it was John Stuart Mill, the figure most prominent in his doctoral dissertation. Both are excellent stylists, with a gift for subtle qualification, and both have shown an ability to remain open to new currents as well as deal judiciously with their opponents. Neil also seems to have endorsed Mill's commandment that life should be full of personal experiments, that the conventional life is not worth living. But I have now come to believe that Mandeville is Neil's true doppleganger. There is of course one superficial similarity, that both lived in Holland and England. And while there is no question that Neil is more a fox than a hedgehog, in some sense he is most like a bee, always buzzing about, conversing and exploring new gardens. As Neil once noted, "research lines seem [like] flowers competing for the insects' attention" (De Marchi and Hamminga 1994: 7). As one who always has his hand in more than one project – often in different centuries – Neil seems best characterized by the cross-fertilizing bee. Moreover, the image of the bee captures Mandeville's point that exchange is never just about equalization; there are always externalities. Neil's dialectical techniques would have made Mandeville proud.

More seriously, both Mandeville and Neil have a Shakespearean eye for human frailty and the force of our passions. But they also relish playing the role of *provocateur*, and show a predilection for encoding their messages in metaphor. A memorable incident made this obvious to me. Neil had organized a weekend conference in the spring of 1991 to debate the merits of Philip Mirowski's *More Heat than Light*. After some fifteen presentations, which Neil would subsequently edit into a volume, he stood up to deliver his own paper, only to tell us that the snake had swallowed his tail, full stop. Make of that what one wants, it captures well the enigma that Neil remains. Notwithstanding his brilliant analyses of classical economics, twentieth-century methodological debates, and the Dutch art market, Neil will only be fully understood after the last i is dotted and t is crossed. Let's hope that is still many decades away.

## Notes

*   I wish to thank Neil De Marchi, Craufurd Goodwin, Marina Bianchi, Paul Harrison, Jack Vromen, and Marcel Boumans for their input. With the sole exception of Neil, they are not responsible for the output here.
1   The internal examiner was T. W. Swan.
2   He published about a dozen articles for the ABN *Economic Review*, from 1980 to 1990.
3   The first ten doctoral students (not listed here) worked in areas other than the history of economics.
4   Likewise, when I challenged Neil's article on Mill and Cairnes he was remarkably gracious about conceding the merits of my reading of the record. He recommended that I be the one to write this account here precisely because he knew I had read with care his early papers on the classical economists.
5   See Geraldine Norman (1998).

## Bibliography

De Marchi, N. B. (1970) "The Empirical Content and Longevity of Ricardian Economics," *Economica* NS 37 (August): 257–76.

——— (1972) "Mill and Cairnes and the Emergence of Marginalism in England," *History of Political Economy* 4 (Fall): 344–63. Reprinted in C. D. W. Goodwin, R. D. C. Black, and A. W. Coats (eds) (1973) *The Marginal Revolution*, Durham, NC: Duke University Press.

——— (1973) " 'The Noxious Influence of Authority': A Correction of Jevons' Charge," *Journal of Law and Economics* XVI (April): 179–89.

——— (1974) "The Success of Mill's Principles," *History of Political Economy* 6 (Summer): 120–57.

——— (1975) "[Wage/price policy in] The First Nixon Administration: Prelude to Controls," in Craufurd D. W. Goodwin (ed.) *Exhortation and Controls: The Search for a Wage–Price Policy, 1945–1971*, Washington, DC: Brookings Institution, 295–352.

——— (1976a) "Anomaly and the Progress of Economics: The Case of the Leontief Paradox," in Spiro J. Latsis (ed.) *Method and Appraisal in Economics*, Cambridge: Cambridge University Press, 109–27.

—— (1976b) "On the Early Dangers of Being Too Political an Economist: Thorold Rogers and the 1868 Election to the Drummond Professorship," *Oxford Economic Papers* 28 (November): 364–80.

—— (1981a) "Energy Policy Under Nixon: Mainly Putting Out Fires," *Oxford Economic Papers* 28 (November).

—— (1981b) "The Ford Administration: Energy as a Political Good," in Craufurd D. Goodwin (ed.) *Energy Policy in Perspective*, Brookings Institution, Washington, DC, 395–545.

—— (1983) "The Case for James Mill," in A. W. Coats (ed.) *Methodological Controversy in Economics: Historical Essays in Honor of T.W. Hutchison*, Greenwich, CT: JAI Press, 155–84.

—— (1986) "Mill's Unrevised Philosophy of Economics: A Comment on Hausman," *Philosophy of Science* 53 (March): 89–100.

—— (1987) *The New Palgrave: A Dictionary of Economics*, edited by John Eatwell, Murray Milgate, and Peter Newman, London: Macmillan. Entries on: (a) "Abstinence," Vol. I: 8–9; (b) "Non-competing Groups," Vol. III: 653; (c) "Paradoxes and Anomalies," Vol. III: 796–99; (d) "Nassau Senior," Vol. IV: 303–305.

—— (1988a) "John Stuart Mill: Interpretation Since Schumpeter," in William Thweatt (ed.) *Classical Political Economy*, Boston: Kluwer, 137–62.

—— (1988b) "Introduction" and "Popper and the LSE Economists," in N. B. De Marchi (ed.) *The Popperian Legacy in Economics*, Cambridge: Cambridge University Press.

—— (ed. with C. Gilbert) (1989a) *The History and Methodology of Econometrics*, Special issue of *Oxford Economic Papers*, book edition, Oxford: Oxford University Press.

—— (1989b) "John Stuart Mill," in J. Starbatty (ed.) *Klassiker des Ökonomischen Denkens*, München: Beck, I, 266–90.

—— (1991) "Re-thinking Lakatos," in N. B. De Marchi and Mark Blaug (eds) *Appraising Economic Theories: Studies in the Methodology of Research Programs*, Aldershot: Edward Elgar.

—— (ed.) (1992) *Post-Popperian Methodology of Economics. Recovering Practice*, Boston: Kluwer.

—— (1993) "Introduction" and "History Through the Lens of Social Value Theory," in N. B. De Marchi (ed.) *Non-Natural Social Science: Reflecting on the Enterprise of More Heat Than Light*, Annual Supplement to *History of Political Economy* 25: 1–4; 283–99.

—— (1995a) "Comment on Jurg Niehans' 'Multiple Discoveries'," *European Journal for the History of Economic Thought* 2, Autumn: 275–9.

—— (1995b) "The Role of 'Dutch' Auctions, and Lotteries, in Shaping the Art Market(s) of 17th Century Holland," *Journal of Economic Behavior and Organization* 28 (October): 203–21.

—— (1998a) "Adam Smith's Accommodation of 'Altogether Endless' Desires," in Maxine Berg and Helen Clifford (eds) *Consumer Culture in Europe 1650–1850*, Manchester: Manchester University Press.

—— (1998b) "John Stuart Mill," in John B. Davis, D. Wade Hands, and Uskali Maki (eds) *The Handbook of Economic Methodology*, Cheltenham: Edward Elgar.

—— (1998c) "Putting Evidence in its Place: John Mill's Early Struggles with History," in Uskali Maki (ed.) *Fact or Fiction? Perspectives on Realism and Economics*.

De Marchi, N. B. and Bianchi, M. (1994) "Institutions Rediscovered," in Cosimo Perrotta and Gioia Vitantonio (eds) *Where is Economics Going? Historical Viewpoints*, Lecce: Congedo, 89–110.

—— (1996) "The Taste-less Theory of Choice Meets Novelty," in Andrea Salanti and Ernesto Screpanti (eds) *Pluralism in Economics*, Aldershot: Edward Elgar, 177–90.

De Marchi, N. B. and Dohlman, Peter (1991) "League of Nations Economists and the Ideal of Peaceful Change in the 1930s," in Craufurd D. Goodwin (ed.) *Economics and National Security*, Annual Supplement to *History of Political Economy* 23: 143–78.

De Marchi, N. B. and Hamminga, B. (eds) (1994) "Idealization in Economics," *Poznan Studies* 38, with introduction, *Idealization and the Defence of Economics: Notes Toward a History*, Amsterdam: Rodolpi, 11–40.

De Marchi, N. B. and Harrison, P. (1994) "Introduction" and "Trading 'in the wind,' and with Guile: The Troublesome Matter of the Short Selling of Shares in 17th Century Amsterdam," in N. B. De Marchi and M. S. Morgan (eds) *Higgling: Transactors and Their Markets in the History of Economic Thought*, Annual Supplement to *History of Political Economy* 26: 1–21; 47–65.

De Marchi, N. B. and Hirsch, A. (1984) "Methodology: A Comment on Frazer and Boland, I," *American Economic Review* 74 (September): 782–8.

—— (1986) "Making a Case When Theory is Unfalsifiable: Friedman's Monetary History," *Economics and Philosophy* 2 (April): 1–21.

—— (1990) *Milton Friedman: Economics in Theory and Practice*, Hemel Hempstead: Wheatsheaf, and Ann Arbor: University of Michigan Press.

De Marchi, N. B. and Kim, J. (1989) "Ceteris Paribus as Prior Knowledge," *Proceedings of the Philosophy of Science Association* II: 17–325.

De Marchi, N. B. and Lail, G. M. (1995) "Comment on Neuberg's Review of Mary S. Morgan, *History of Econometric Ideas*," *Econometric Theory* 11: 386–8.

De Marchi, N. B. and Lodewijks, J. (1983) "HOPE and the Journal Literature in the History of Economic Thought," *History of Political Economy* 15, Fall: 321–43.

De Marchi, N. B. and Sturges, R. P. (1973) "Malthus and Ricardo's Inductivist Critics: Four Letters to William Whewell," *Economica* NS 40 (November): 379–93.

De Marchi, N. B. and Van Miegroet, H. (1994) "Art, Value, and Market Practices in the Seventeenth Century Netherlands," *Art Bulletin* lxxvi: 451–64.

—— (1996) "Pricing Invention: 'Originals,' 'Copies,' and their Relative Value in Seventeenth Century Netherlandish Art Markets," in V. Ginsburgh and P. M. Menger (eds) *Recent Contributions to the Economics of the Arts*, Amsterdam: North-Holland, 27–70.

—— (1998) "Novelty and Fashion Circuits in the Mid-seventeenth Century Antwerp-Paris Art Trade," *Journal of Medieval and Early Modern Studies* 28, special issue on Novelty and Markets, co-edited with Van Miegroet: 200–46.

—— (2000a) "Ingenuity preferences, and the pricing of paintings. The Smith-Reynolds connection," in Neil De Marchi and Craufurd D. W. Goodwin (eds) *Economic Engagements with Art*, Annual Supplement to *History of Political Economy* 31: 379–412.

—— (2000b) "Rules Versus Play in Early Modern Art Markets," *Louvain Economic Review* 66: 145–65.

De Marchi, N. B., Kim, J., and Morgan, M. S. (1995) "Empirical Model Particularities and Belief in the Natural Rate Hypothesis," *Journal of Econometrics* 67 (Spring): 81–102; part of *Annals of Econometrics: The Significance of Testing in Econometrics*, ed. Hugo A. Keuzenkamp and Jan R. Magnus.

De Marchi, N. B., Raiff, M. E., and Van Miegroet, H. J. (1998) "Dealer-Dealer Pricing in the 17th Century Antwerp-Paris Art Trade," in Michael North and David Ormrod (eds) *Art Markets in Early Modern Europe*, London: Ashgate, chapter 9.

Norman, Geraldine (1998) "Fakes?" *New York Review of Books* February 5.

# 5   Maurice Dobb, historical materialism, and economic thought

*Tony Atley and Bruce McFarlane*

## Introduction

Maurice Herbert Dobb, arguably the most outstanding British Marxian political economist of his generation, brought to the study of the history of economic thought a penetrating intellect capable of the most lucid articulation of the highest realms of theory. Born on July 24, 1900, educated at Charterhouse School and Pembroke College, Cambridge, his death in 1976 left an impressive body of work stretching across more than half a century which in content traversed the broad spectrum of political economy. Surveying this body of work for the present essay has led to the search for unifying threads to integrate its impressive distribution across the subject matter of political economy. The concentration upon his history of economic thought and his economic history does not do justice to Dobb's ability to understand, comprehensively, the entire breadth of our discipline. Maurice Dobb had that increasingly rare talent to render complex theoretical problems comprehensible to the non-specialized reader. A part of that skill was the casting of principal problems of political economy in an *historical* perspective. For Maurice Dobb historical analysis became a penetrating instrument to expose latent ideologies inside seemingly robust theoretical structures. Dobb's economic history is a masterful articulation of the dynamic process of *social* reproduction within distinctively *classical* categories of political economy. In an age when *technical* virtuosity is blindly celebrated the work of Maurice Dobb stands as a trenchant reminder of the limitations of an excessively formal approach to understanding a complex social reality.

Of critical importance in understanding the evolution of Maurice Dobb's scholarship is the intellectual relationship which he developed with the sparkling genius of Piero Sraffa. In particular, it was the editorial collaboration between Sraffa and Dobb in producing the *Works and Correspondence of David Ricardo* that challenged many of the accepted interpretations of Ricardian doctrine in the history of economic thought. By far the most profound (in terms of its cascading impact upon the development of economic thought) is the rehabilitation of Ricardo and with it the classical framework of a decidedly *political* economy. With such a resuscitation must come the reassessment of Karl Marx, and a revision of that view propagated by Jevons that Ricardo had "shunted the car of economic science onto the wrong line" with Marx's *Das Kapital* its *reductio ad absurdum*. Dobb, himself, puts the matter concisely when he remarked:

> I think we conclusively establish ... that there was no "weakening" of Ricardo's enunciation of the labour theory as time went on: that in fact he reached at the end of his life a position rather close to that of Marx, so that the true line of descent is certainly from Ricardo to Marx, and *not* from Ricardo to cost-of-production theory au Mill to Marshall as the bourgeois tradition has it.[1]

The importance of this discovery cannot be underestimated and its implications are yet to be fully explored. The ramifications of this resuscitation of Ricardo and the labour theory of value were finally to challenge the consistency itself of the whole edifice of bourgeois economics with the appearance of Sraffa's much neglected *Production of Commodities by Means of Commodities* in 1960. The impact of this theoretical contribution is reflected in the intent and purpose of Dobb's final body of work – that is, his two Marshall Lectures, delivered in 1973, and his opus, *Theories of Value and Distribution since Adam Smith*.

## Dobb's economic history

It is important to understand the relationship between economic history and Dobb's view of the history of economic thought. Dobb's first book appeared in 1925 and developed out of his doctoral research on "The Entrepreneur". *Capitalist Enterprise and Social Progress* sought to recast economic theory in a confrontation with a historical critique of the forces which shaped economic development and produced the institutions we have inherited to this day. The historical sections appeared reworked for a broader audience in a book published by the Plebs League entitled *An Outline of European History*.[2] Although later characterized as "an unsuccessful and jejune attempt to combine the notion of surplus-value and exploitation with the Theory of Marshall",[3] *Capitalist Enterprise* contained the kernel of Dobb's economic history which was to find expression over twenty years later in his seminal *Studies in the Development of Capitalism*.

Dobb's *Studies in the Development of Capitalism* (1946) was the first comprehensive study in English of a theme raised by Marx himself and by practitioners of economic history like R. H. Tawney – the nature of the transition from feudalism to capitalism.

The book arose in part out of discussion among historians close to the Communist Party of Great Britain (CPGB) – Dona Torr, Rodney Hilton, Christopher Hill, R. Page Arnot, and others. Dobb was also aware of the research of Soviet economic historians Lavrovsky and Kosminsky. Interestingly Christopher Hill had earlier visited the USSR and knew of the work on feudal manorial systems, some of which soon came out in English in the *Economic History Review* of the British Society for Economic History.

The main message of the book *Studies* in relation to the transition from feudalism to capitalism was that the starting point of analysis should be (1) an account of "exploitation" under feudal "social relations of production"; (2) discussion of the process of petty commodity production; (3) real-world forces operating to determine the precise features of the working out of feudal exploitation – for example, population growth (and hence the labour: land ratio); military conflict requiring higher levels of economic resources in the hands of the ruling elite; the growing influence of exchange relations with the growth of towns.

One of the striking features of *Studies* is that the author sees "feudal relations of production" in a many-sided way. He does not treat them as *purely* a fetter on technical and social change, but as part of their own transformation. Harnessing Marx's analytical tool of the "mode of production" he described the feudal order as dependent primarily on class relations and the "transition" to something non-feudal – hence as the replacement of one mode of production by another.

The perspective Dobb brought to the issue of how to analyse the change in the feudal mode of production brought him into conflict with the view of his predecessor, Henry Pirenne, and a later critic, P. M. Sweezy. Pirenne had maintained that capitalism emerged in Western Europe in the twelfth century when merchant adventurers organized large-scale trading.[4] This new group diverted a large part of the economic surplus previously appropriated by the feudal landowner. One result was that "production for use" was broken up "from outside" by increasing the scope of production specifically for exchange. Sweezy took a similar stance.[5]

By contrast, Dobb argued that merchants were primarily interested in selling dear and buying cheap – they could not *originate* a process of surplus extraction; they could only be, in a sense, parasitical on that process.

Dobb dates capitalism's emergence much later – at around the end of the sixteenth and the beginning of the seventeenth century. A new "social relation" of owners and hired labourers emerged when merchants started to organize craftsmen into a putting-out system and when successful peasants bought up land and farmed by hiring labour. A wage labour versus capital relationship thus emerged.

The implications of the chapters dealing with this process were clear enough: the rise of the merchant-bourgeois was a strong historical force,[6] a necessary but not sufficient condition for a capitalist mode of production to emerge. Here we go back to the idea of two routes to capitalism.[7] This framework, first suggested by Marx,[8] sketches two and not one path for capitalism's emergence. In the first, colonies and their control by mercantilists provide "primary capital accumulation". Elements of the new merchant class became capitalists. This path is non-revolutionary. This merchant class eventually becomes "an obstacle to the real capitalist mode of production and goes under with its development". Thus, said Marx, the independent development of merchant capital is "incapable by itself of promoting and explaining the transition from one mode of production to another".[9] In the second path, emphasized by Dobb, the producer becomes merchant *and* capitalist. This contrasts with the natural agrarian economy and the guild – the constricted handicrafts of medieval urban industries. Here industrial capitalists emerge from the rank of small or medium-sized producers either in the village or in the growing towns. The role of exchange is mainly to make the growth of the towns non-reversible; it is not to specify "social relations".

Such "dissolving" effects that burgeoning twelfth-century commerce might have had on the feudal order, on feudal social relations, were chiefly that some lords of the demesne commuted labour service for a money payment and made their own economic unit more money oriented, less "self-sufficient". Sometimes, argues Dobb, "market opportunities" lead to *intensification* of serfdom's exploitation mechanisms as servile dues were enforced. Growing military and consumption expenditures of the lords likewise acted to intensify exploitation, exacerbating problems because the economic system had a limited capacity to provide an *expansionary* surplus. This fact Dobb refers to as the "inefficiency of Feudalism as a system of production".[10] The intensification of exploitation and the limited economic capacity of the system led to mass defections of serfs, making it even more necessary for the lords to allow commutation of labour services for money.

By the end of the fifteenth century, in Dobb's estimation a new stage had been reached. Serfdom – the key feudal social relation in the extraction of the economic surplus – was disappearing.

Merchants were able to buy up lands, and lords were obliged to mortgage them. The new class of improving peasant farmers could afford now to hire labour power. Accumulation of capital by these elements led to the rise of the "yeoman farmer" who is already far from the social relations of serfdom and feudalism. Here Dobb's confirmed Kosminsky's finding that already in thirteenth-century England, before the final end of serfdom, there existed a "distinct stratum of upper peasantry".[11] Dobb saw the dynamic movement from this stage to the end of serfdom governed by the internal trends in the mode of production. The market expansion and the generalization of exchange relations while present remained secondary. This was the position that Dobb was best known for taking in the transition debate.[12]

*Studies in the Development of Capitalism* not only provoked a new and sophisticated debate within the CPGB and wider Marxist circles,[13] including interest from Japan and North America, it has from time to time been the subject of re-examination and re-evaluation.[14] Some have questioned the consistency of the relative emphasis given by Dobb to the "intensified exploitation" and "disintegrating effects of market expansion".[15] Others have disagreed on his analysis of "growing military needs of feudal lords". His account of the monopoly restrictions used by merchants to exploit craft producers has however, become part of standard economic history. The notion of the merchant turned producer[16] and the crucial role in the labour process of the putting-out system have been developed for Third World systems,[17] although some have questioned whether this is exploitation or merely unequal exchange.[18]

Whatever the final judgement few would deny that in the 1940s Dobb had provided in his *Studies* a major boost both to economic history as a discipline and to Marxist study in providing a comprehensive and insightful application, in concrete terms, of Marxian tools: the mode of production; social relations; method of surplus expropriation. Furthermore, the connection between Dobb's economic history and his approach to the history of economic thought are conditioned by the same methodological commitments. For example, the opening chapter of his *Studies* contains a methodological declaration specifically Marxist in character but with its classical hue clearly evident.[19] Dobb's historical sensitivity precludes any strictly causal–genetic narrative from appearing in his history of economic thought. Excessively quantitative theories of economic development thus for Dobb fail to capture the significance of qualitative influences in shaping the course and influencing the tempo of historical change.[20] The methodological stance assumed in these early pages of his *Studies* reflects the same interpretation of historical materialism which Dobb possessed in his 1937 *Political Economy and Capitalism*, to be discussed below.

## The young Dobb

Dobb's interest in the history of economic thought began in his student days. One can begin by mentioning Dobb's early piece *The Problem of Surplus Value: A Reply to Mr. Withers*. The context of this essay was his youthful association with such socialist propaganda efforts as the journals "Youth" and "Plebs".

At the time of writing *The Problem of Surplus Value*, Dobb was a 20-year-old Cambridge University student. He had not yet made the contacts in London that were to lead him to the CPGB. His was a youthful Marxism reflecting an itch to lock horns with the more rabid defenders of capitalism. It was this theme, evident in this early piece, which with the appearance of the Sraffa critique, Dobb re-evaluates into a tight, compelling argument, explaining the evolution of economic thought.

However, at this time (the 1920s) Dobb had not fully understood the role of the "law of value" and the species of competition employed by Marx to demonstrate his theory of surplus value and profit. Such a youthful exercise may be seen in retrospect to have been refined by his later position that "the crucial problem for Marx was to show how the fact that one class in society drew an income without contributing any productive activity could be consistent with the prevalence of competition and the rule of law".[21]

Dobb notes in this later essay that Sismondi, Thompson, and Bray had all "sought to explain capitalist income by the existence of some form of cheating or *force de majeure*",[22] by which the capitalist underpaid his workers. According to Dobb "such explanations were regarded by Marx as unsatisfactory" and he proceeds to quote with approval Marx's comment that "you must start from the theorem that on average commodities *are sold at their values*" and that "*profits are derived from selling at their real values*. ... If you cannot explain profit upon this supposition, you cannot explain it at all."[23]

The question concerning the distribution of a social product between the classes in the community which produced it remained a central concern. By 1937 Dobb had framed the issues involved in terms of the requirement to explain profit as a category of income accruing to a particular class of people. Was this question "to be interpreted in terms analogous to the theory of rent"[24] – as attempted, for example, in his friend H. D. Dickinson's *Institutional Revenue?* Even in 1973 when considering the question of distribution in the presence of monopoly, that is in imperfect market structures, Dobb maintains the importance of the theory of surplus value while recognizing its close association with the theory of rent in the stage of monopoly capitalism.[25]

Dobb had a deep understanding of the essential preoccupations of classical political economy. Two early pieces by Dobb stand out in the probing exposition of the aims of the classical economists. The first is a lecture "Criticisms of Some Trends in Modern Economic Theory" delivered in Copenhagen in March 1935. The second, of course, is his 1937 book *Political Economy and Capitalism.*

In contrast with orthodox modern theory, the classical economists were concerned with explanations of the laws which guided the *dynamic* evolution of society as a *whole.* This emphasis was conceived specifically in terms of the revenues which accrued to social classes defined in terms of their relation to the factors of production, labour, capital, and land. These class revenues, wages, profit, and rent, were incomes which allowed the *social* reproduction of the labourer, the capitalist, and the landlord. Central to such conceptualization was the dual concept of cost and surplus, and as Dobb points out, it was "on this distinction the division into gross and net revenue turned", and the surplus approach to political economy constructed within the classical tradition.[26]

Dobb highlights and embraces the classical tradition of employing the simplifying device of abstraction as a legitimate attempt to understand complex socio-economic systems.[27] Such was the approach of classical political economy; abstraction was employed as a device to distil the essence of the phenomena given the *deductive* nature of the economic problem. For any given theoretical structure, as generality subsides with the introduction of more realistic assumptions, it is the degree to which the particular abstraction is itself isomorphic with reality which is the only criterion by which individual abstract constructions can ultimately be judged.[28] Dobb points out that Marx inherited the classical framework in which the theory of value was expressed.[29] Likewise in Vol. I of *Capital* Marx employed intrinsically classical assumptions, for example pure competition with an absence of *individual* monopoly power, in which to unfold his critique of capitalism.

The charge levelled by Böhm-Bawerk against Marx's apparent inconsistency between Vol. I and Vol. III of *Capital* was always the subject of scorn by Dobb. In his 1937 book the argument is couched in terms of the validity of the method of abstraction in the context of the settled traditions of political economy.[30] To claim that Marx was unaware of this problem is simply wrong; in a footnote Dobb quotes Marx's chastisement of Proudhon in *Misère de la Philosophie* as a clear statement that the movement from values to prices of production involved modifications in derivative statements when certain assumptions are relaxed (in this case the proportions of constant and variable capital) which did *not* invalidate the approach based upon the labour theory of value.[31]

It is in *Political Economy and Capitalism* that we find the broader features of the methodological approach that Dobb applied to the study of history of economic thought and economic history. In many respects, the theoretical kernel embraced in this 1937 book is very similar to that contained in his seminal *Studies in the Development of Capitalism*.[32] The intellectual influences which shaped this formulation are revealed in a much earlier piece written jointly with J. G. Crowthers and entitled *Marx and Engels*.

With strong "empiricist" philosophical traditions and a certain ideological "isolationism" Marxism did not make any significant impact in England before the First World War. Dobb outlines the penetration of Marxist doctrines into English intellectual and political circles in a piece, written in 1947,[33] which also contextualizes his own early involvement in Marxist organizations, for example the Plebs League.[34] As Brian Pollitt has noted, *Marx and Engels* reveals the influences of European post-Marxist thinkers such as Labriola,[35] Sombart, Croce, and Sorel.[36] The "successive approximation" defence of the labour theory of value is present along with a "monopoly" power explanation of surplus value.[37] These arguments all predate the revival of the classical system by Sraffa and represent an early attempt to interpret Marx within the history of classical economic thought. This theme, of locating Marx within the classical tradition, was to be powerfully reinforced in the implications of Dobb's collaboration with Sraffa in removing the perceived inconsistency in the theories of profit and value enunciated by Ricardo[38] and Marx.

With the publication of *Studies in the Development of Capitalism* in 1946 Dobb completed a revised edition of his *Soviet Economic Development Since 1917* in the following year and published in 1948. These two works along with Dobb's 1937 *Political Economy and Capitalism* marked the end of an intense period of scholarship which established his reputation internationally as a leading figure in Marxist political economy.[39] It was not until 1960 that Dobb published another book, namely *An Essay on Economic Growth and Planning*. This arrest in the prolific output of books by Maurice Dobb in no doubt reflects the absorption which his collaboration with Piero Sraffa entailed in producing the collected works of David Ricardo.

## Dobb on Adam Smith

Adam Smith is regarded by Marx as one of the genuine founders of political economy, a position he maintained in both chapter X of *Anti-Duhring* and throughout the *Theories of Surplus Value*. Dobb basically shares this view, yet his starting point was very different because he had continually to contend with a lifetime of battling against a whole rewrite of Smith by modern neoclassical and laissez-faire writers who chose to ignore what Adam Smith actually wrote.[40]

No wonder, then, that Maurice Dobb accepted an invitation of Signor Damascelli, on behalf of Italian publishing firm ISEDI, in July 1972 to write a thorough introduction to the Italian edition of Adam Smith's *Wealth of Nations*. Dobb also went on the offensive to defend Smith as a classical economist when contributing an article in 1975 entitled "Ricardo and Adam Smith" to Andrew Skinner's celebratory Smith volume, *Essays on Adam Smith*.[41] This opening gave Dobb the opportunity to dispel some of the myths and silly hagiography surrounding Smith and fit him back into the framework of the classical school with its emphasis on economic growth as governed by broad trends and movements in rates of labour force growth, capital accumulation, and technical progress (in the case of Smith "the division of labour is limited by the extent of the market").

Dobb is well known for the advocacy of a *dual development thesis* in the history of economic thought.[42] Such a thesis hinges upon the contention that Adam Smith combined and articulated two clearly identifiable approaches to political economy. Dobb's position regarding the work of Adam Smith is similar in many respects to that of fellow Marxist, Ron L. Meek. Of particular importance in the formulation of this dual development thesis are the differences in theoretical structure between Smith and Ricardo. Both Dobb and Meek emphasize that Smith underlines the revenue category of "profit" as a class income; however, they note the absence in Smith of anything which could be properly constituted as a theory of profit beyond a general reference to its determination by the forces of supply and demand.[43] Dobb acknowledges Smith as the founder of the classical school outside France and characterizes Smithian doctrine as a "parallel and independent generation of ideas"[44] in terms of its relationship to the French school of physiocracy. While Smith accepted the notion of a surplus it was not something which could be equated with the physiocratic notion of the *produit net*.

On the question of price and the determination of natural value Smith employed, through assertion rather than demonstration, the notion of competition as the social process by which an *ad hoc* market price "gravitates" (fluctuates) around its natural price. Hence the classical competitive process was conceived as an inherently *dynamic* social allocation mechanism which possessed sufficient convergence and local stability properties to explain the natural value of things *qua* commodities in an exchange-based production society. It was the sympathetic magic of "pure competition" which served a critical role in closing the imposing intellectual project of what history has identified as classical political economy.

In the context of the analytically more tractable world of Smith's theoretical schema price itself, the "natural value" of any commodity, becomes composed of the "natural rates of wages, profit and rent". These explanatory magnitudes themselves were justified by the apparatus of supply and demand inspired by the pursuit of bourgeois self-interest. Sraffa was appropriately to title such a theory the "adding-up components" theory of price. Indeed as Sraffa points out (in collaboration with Dobb), Smith's theory:

was that "as soon as stock had accumulated in the hands of particular persons" and "as soon as the land of any country has all become private property", the price of commodities is arrived at by a process of *adding up* wages, profit and rent: "in every improved society, all three enter more or less, as component parts, into the price of the far greater part of commodities".[45]

A corollary of such a position, one that would form the basis of Ricardo's criticism of Smith, was that any rise in the price of corn (as the classical wage–good *par excellence*) would be transmitted into increases in the prices of all goods through raising the price of labour.[46]

Since such a theory is specifically associated with an exchange-based capitalist society there is, as Dobb acknowledges, a hint of a "deduction theory of profit" in the work of Adam Smith. In addition to the poorly articulated supply and demand framework employed by Smith to explain natural values and class incomes is the notion of profit as surplus. This aspect of Smith has been considered (e.g. by Marx) an "incipient theory of exploitation".[47]

These two approaches, which were subsequently to evolve into two distinct traditions in political economy, are seen here combined within the eclectic theoretical structure of Smith. On the one hand is the supply and demand framework employed to resolve the problem of the determination of value. On the other is Dobb's treatment of Smith as a surplus theorist, to the extent that Smith committed himself to the view of the "double surplus" in agriculture – agriculture yielding more surplus than did manufacturing even though it was not (said Smith) the exclusive source of "*produit net*". Such a surplus concept was developed by Ricardo and through him transmitted into the theory of surplus value expounded by Marx.

The absence of a theory for the determination of profit beyond a general reference to supply and demand is a major weakness of the Smithian theoretical edifice. As a result, Dobb notes that the fuzzy supply and demand framework in Adam Smith cripples his attempt to construct a logically consistent theory of profit, without which any explanation of class incomes, that is distribution, is necessarily incomplete. On this issue the total discussion of distribution given by Smith is small, in contrast with the central role assigned to it by Ricardo. It is essentially in a small section of the *Wealth of Nations* misleadingly called "conclusion to the chapter", at the end of a long discussion on the history of prices where Smith discusses the relation between the interests of the three classes to the general interests of society. This small appendix considers the idea, rejected by Ricardo, of an identity between the interests of the landlord and that of society.[48] Dobb insists that it was Ricardo and not Smith who formulated what could be considered a complete theory of distribution by developing the physiocratic notion of an *economic surplus* to serve as the basis of a theory of income distribution. Dobb comments on this point in his Firenze piece, *Adam Smith and the Classical School*, that "This is often overlooked by historians of economic thought who tend to speak of the classical economists as a unified whole and Ricardo as merely developing and extending Smithian doctrine in specific aspects."[49]

Dobb complains that the historians of economic thought have misunderstood the great gulf between Smith and Ricardo on questions of value or "natural price". Natural price based upon labour expended was restricted to precapitalist society. His antithetical theory for capitalist society was the "adding-up" theory in which value was composed of the summation of wages, profit, and rent. The only difference between this formulation and Marshall's later cost of production theory was the addition of a subjective notion of real cost to explain the existence of profit as a necessary category of income (thus merging J. S. Mill's Ricardo with the unmeasurable notion of abstinence advocated by the likes of Senior).

## Dobb on Ricardo

Marx considered Ricardo the "last great representative" of classical political economy and was spoken of as being "the economist *par excellence* of production".[50] For Dobb his interpretation of Ricardo became the fulcrum upon which his history of economic thought critically turned. While abstract economic reasoning finds rigorous expression in Ricardo, more so than in Smith or Malthus, it was a political economy consciously designed to illuminate the consequences of practical economic policy.[51] Indeed, Edwin Cannan had noted that "the close connection between the economics and the politics of the Ricardian period … provides a key to many riddles".[52] Such questions as the contextualization of economic theory within a specific social milieu were a distinguishing feature of Dobb's methodological approach to the history of economic thought.

The critical question of the relationship between Smith and Ricardo is given attention in the previously mentioned article *Ricardo and Adam Smith*. It was in this piece that Dobb clearly outlined Ricardo's priority of dealing with the question of distribution and his consequent search for an analytically robust theory of profit. As Dobb had maintained earlier in his career, the explanation of profit as a source of income was a central question in addressing what he liked to term "classical type" problems, for example issues concerning the distribution of income.

Important in understanding the position of the theory of value in the work of Ricardo is its relationship to those "classical type" problems. It is these questions that unified classical political economy, even though the directions in which their answers were sought were to diverge fundamentally. This has no better illustration than in the influence Smith had upon Ricardo in designing and refining his theoretical system.[53]

The "kernel" of Ricardo's theory of profit is to be found in his pamphlet, written in February 1815, designed to influence the parliamentary debate concerning the Corn Laws. The Corn Laws were first introduced into Britain in 1804 to protect the incomes of landowners through a protective duty on imported corn. Ricardo's *Essay on Profit* was heavily influenced by Malthus's

*Inquiry into Rent.* It contained a theory of profit in which profits were determined by the ratio of corn produced to corn consumed, at the agricultural margin of cultivation. Dobb highlights that such a theory can be seen as the "initiator of a type of theory that sees profit as being essentially determined by conditions of production in the wage-good industry; given as a social *datum* the level of real wages".[54]

Ricardo, in passing from a theory of profit expressed in output terms, for example corn, to a more generalized structure, confronted the theoretical imperative of constructing an internally consistent theory of value.[55] It was in the process of writing his 1815 *Essay on Profit* that Ricardo discovered that "curious effect" of a rise of wages upon the products of industry requiring significant amounts of fixed capital. Such a position was reached in contemplation of the Smithian theoretical legacy contained in the *Wealth of Nations*. Specifically it was the consequence of the aforementioned effect of the rise in the price of corn upon the prices of commodities (produced under differing capital intensities) that prompted the supersession and marked the essential features of the Ricardian, as opposed to the Smithian, system. It was this issue that formed the basis of the "second cause" of changes in value which prompted the reformulation of the theory of value undertaken by Ricardo.

As Sraffa was to point out subsequently, classical political economy when confronted with a complex social reality constructed a simplified theoretical apparatus to filter its essential features into a tractable analytical framework. The important features of this abstract construction included an annual cycle of production, capital consisting of wages advanced, and no fixed capital.[56] Such an edifice was not a totally theoretical exercise but one designed to highlight the more concrete aspects of practical economic problems, for example the distributive consequences of the Corn Laws.[57]

Prior to Ricardo political economy did not possess a coherent, consistent, theoretical system.[58] Ricardo's 1815 *Essay* contained the notion of rent as a surplus and likewise this approach formed the basis for his theory of profit. Important in understanding the conceptual unity which Ricardo was able to achieve is the priority of his theory of profit and the subordinated role assigned to the theory of value. In many respects, Ricardo's theory of value was designed to articulate the implications of this theory of profit as an application of what has become known as the surplus approach to political economy. A feature of Ricardo's early theory of profit was its expression in purely product units of measurement. The theoretical advantages of such an approach are manifold: the rate of profit can be unambiguously expressed as a ratio of two *physical* quantities of corn.[59] In such a framework the frustrating paradoxes of value theory remained latent.

Dobb was eventually to interpret Ricardo's corn model from the *Essay on Profit*[60] as an economic surplus model. Rent and profit are considered in Dobb's interpretation of Ricardo as two species of the *produit net*.[61] As a result an essential antagonism between these categories of income exists *systemically*[62] – a part of the institutional framework of capitalism itself.

It is in the context of providing a consistent explanation of exchange value that the classical labour theory of value came to be evaluated and after the 1870s condemned. A modern treatment of derivative theoretical issues, such as the so-called transformation problem, can be found in Pasinetti's *Lectures on the Theory of Production*. Post-Sraffa these problems in the theory of value become transparent and possible to transcend conclusively. It is worth noting that Pasinetti has declared that the correspondence between values and prices in the classical and Marxian system as an issue which "should no longer be open to dispute".[63] Dobb points out that it was the limited historical vision Ricardo possessed – writing at the very beginning of the Industrial Revolution – which prevented him from separating value and price as "distinct categories and to afford a more thorough analysis of their connection and divergence".[64]

It was the mechanism of "pure competition", the appellation to the forces of supply and demand, which was asserted to produce the "natural prices" the economic system required to allow its smooth reproduction. Included amongst these "natural prices", however, were two distributive variables, the wage rate and the rate of profit. In modern parlance, a system of $k$ equations explaining costs in terms of $k + 1$ variables (i.e. $k - 1$ commodity prices plus the profit and wage rate) requires one to be assigned the status of exogeneity and left unexplained by the apparatus supposed to bring about the solution, in this case a set of *relative* prices. Choice of numeraire only solves half the problem; the remaining degree of freedom logically infects the tenability of considering distribution an internal product of the system by requiring either the profit or wage rate to be determined by forces other than "pure competition". The reality of this exclusion implied that, at the very least, the question of distribution must be considered inside some *deeper* socio-economic or institutional framework. To use Marx's term, the determination of class incomes was a product of the *social formation*. As a result the classical theoretical system which Ricardo developed and Marx inherited was effectively *open*.

If anything, the causal necessity of embracing something other than the supply and demand framework in order to close the classical system focused attention upon the processes by which value theory determined prices. A compelling implication was that for the purposes of determining value "pure competition" was seen to be inseparably connected to what was an intrinsically *social* allocation mechanism. Such a question occupied Dobb's attention in locating Marx within the broad stream of classical economic thought. Ricardo, like Smith, never explicitly revealed the anatomy of this process and in his more developed theory it was less transparent, locked inside the riddles of defining value for chiefly theoretical purposes.

It was the inability to recognize the explanatory role of what Marx termed the *social relations of production* outside of a static *natural* social order which arrested the development of classical doctrines of value. On this question Marx himself was acutely aware of the limitations such a position implied and maintained that this was the starting point for further analysis:

Instead of assuming this general rate of profit in advance, Ricardo should rather have investigated how far its existence is in any way consistent with the determination of value by labour time; and he would have found that instead of being consistent with it, *prima facie* it contradicts it, and its existence has therefore to be explained through a number of intermediary stages.[65]

These "intermediary stages" suggest a plurality of possible institutional mechanisms in which a uniform rate of profit is not a necessary feature, in which the presence of monopoly distorted the representation of value by labour time, but did not destroy it. To the modern mind these "intermediary stages" can no longer be used to invalidate the classical theory of value, as they have done in the past, for example as with Böhm-Bawerk's criticism of the Ricardo–Marx value apparatus. Even Marx himself acknowledged this *apparent* contradiction in the case of Ricardo long before Böhm-Bawerk declared it as the fatal flaw in Marx's own theory.[66] In this regard, Dobb points out, classical "competition" was an idealization designed to distil the essential features of the capitalist cycle of reproduction – the beginning of the construction of economic theory and not the end.

## Marx

Many lectures were given by Dobb on Marx, starting in the 1920s with various worker educational groups. Already mentioned is Dobb's 1922 article on surplus value, another is a chapter written with Fleming for a book (never published) which explained the intricacies of the so-called transformation problem.

The most typical and comprehensive piece is probably his *Lecture on Marx*,[67] which is part biographical, part analytical. Thereafter his view of Marx was necessarily coloured by his collaboration with Sraffa.[68] By the time of the centenary of the publication of *Das Kapital* we find Dobb lecturing all over England on the continuing significance of Marxian economics. These 1967–9 lectures reflect the impact of writing *Studies in Development of Capitalism* and the new material and interpretations of Ricardo launched by Sraffa.

Marx is seen here as the logical continuation of that part of the classical tradition constituted by Ricardo. But Marx was much, much more – *Das Kapital* was the economic analysis of the laws of motion of the capitalist mode of production. His opus also contained not only elements of economic history, the role of the state, and political theory, but a critique of the *ideas* that accompanied the evolution, the contradictory evolution, of capitalism.

Dobb never relied upon the "apologetic" accusation as the basis for the dismissal of economic doctrine, although it provided contextual insight into the social function of economic "theory". Moreover he makes the point that Marx's admiration of Ricardo was despite the fact that "no one can have been more essentially an apologist of the new bourgeois order than Ricardo".[69] Dobb's critique of economic theory was essentially two dimensional. First, it employed a historical perspective to locate statements of theory within the social milieu in which they were produced – this was where the apologetic function operated. The second aspect of this critique involved the theoretical confrontation of bourgeois doctrine with its own internal contradictions – this is where his skill in revealing the content of high theory was masterfully employed. To emphasize one aspect of Dobb's analysis of history of economic thought without recognizing the symbiotic role of the other cannot but *mis*-represent the carefully crafted Dobb critique.[70]

What does Dobb underline in his early lectures on Marx? First, the methodology of Marx. Dobb points out that historical materialism provides the focus or vision of Marx. Unlike Schumpeter, he does not think it is possible to divide Marx's writing into neat, separate boxes: political theory, political economy, sociology, etc. Dobb insists, as in his *Political Economy and Capitalism* (1937), that the progression from Vol. I to Vol. III of *Das Kapital* involved the application of the method of successive approximation: that is, moving from generalized structures, for example the model of "pure" competition employed in Vol. I, to specific, more concrete theoretical structures. Marx, Dobb points out, was simply employing doctrines which were a part of "the settled tradition of classical Political Economy" in building his theoretical apparatus to reveal the "laws of motion" of capitalist society.[71]

Second, Dobb highlights the role of the social formation in setting the boundaries for the method of appropriation of the economic surplus. Capitalism idealized in a model of "pure competition" is just that, an idealization. The operation of the "law of value" and competition *must* be studied if the derivative theorems of a logical analysis are to possess any relevance to a constantly evolving, but still essentially capitalist, mode of production.

Third, Dobb places Marx in the history of crisis theory. His views are contrasted with those of Sismondi, Rodbertus, and Malthus who, like Marx, challenged the role of Say's law of markets as obfuscating crisis tendencies in the capitalist system.

However, in the 1960s and 1970s a mature Dobb altered his emphasis somewhat. In fact significant insights into Dobb's attitude towards Marx can be gained from two of these later sources, hitherto neglected. Dobb was fond of writing short pieces for publication in other languages – Italian, German, and East European. Usually these were destined for encyclopaedias or anniversaries, but two most significant ones were introductory essays to accompany republished versions of Marx's *Theorien* (Theories of Surplus Value) and his *Critique of Political Economy*.

The fundamental theoretical premise upon which Marx's economics is constructed is the concept of the mode of production. Dobb's concentration upon such a concept, as the vehicle for a surplus approach to political economy, brought criticism from other Marxists, for example Sweezy. With the resuscitation of the surplus approach to political economy via Ricardo's theory of profit, Sraffa provided the theoretical lever for Dobb to re-evaluate the history of economic thought. Such a research project culminated in his Marshall Lectures and his outstanding *Theories of Value and Distribution since Adam Smith*.

Once armed with the penetrating theoretical conclusions of the Sraffa critique Dobb constructed a forceful argument reinforcing the notion of a dual development in the history of economic thought in which Marx was a significant participant in a *heterodox* tradition. An example of the vulgar criticism directed at Marx's theoretical framework is the charge that it writes the individual out of the historical process. A point worth making is Dobb's persistent denial that Marxism entailed some form of technological determinism. Dobb was at pains to point out that historical materialism was not a dogma in which individuals were reduced to mere puppets on the stage of history: "Within the reciprocal interaction between ideas and economic conditions, the two way influence of each upon the other was not symmetrical."[72] Important in this regard was the concept of the mode of production that for Dobb[73] contained not only the forces of production but also the social relations in which humanity reproduced the social environment in which, as individuals, they existed.[74] The ability to give the mode of production an objective characterization did not, in Dobb's opinion, imply its independence from the individual actions of particular historical actors.

This also applied to the Marxian notion of exploitation. Exploitation was not a metaphysical construct but a description of a factual relationship, which existed between all individuals in classed-based societies. In defending the Marxian theory of exploitation it is important to recognize that Dobb was keen to avoid any moral justification for its employment as a category of analysis in political economy. Dobb frequently highlights the transparent nature of "unpaid labour" in the appropriation of the surplus in feudalism in order to highlight its existence. It was the apparent contradiction which arose in capitalism operating under the law of value which attracted criticism of Marx's theory of surplus value and which Dobb sought to correct.[75]

## The rise of marginalism

The rise of the neoclassical or "marginal" school (so named because of its widespread use of differential calculus) was associated in 1870–4 with the economists Jevons, Menger, and Walras and transmitted in eclectic tradition to Cambridge in the economics of Alfred Marshall (who put his mathematics much less on open display). Maurice Dobb, from his early days, regarded both the focus on the individual economic unit (as for example in his *The Problem of Surplus Value*), and the use of marginal utility to explain value as a reaction amounting to a kind of theoretical revolution *against* the original message of the classical school. Explanations of value, the emergence of an economic surplus, and the distribution of national income should be rooted in the conditions of production rather than exclusively in the sphere of exchange as such questions had been pigeon-holed in the post-1870s emergence of a somewhat inappropriately titled neoclassical school.

Moreover, he considered that Jevons, in attacking Ricardo and portraying his economics as a kind of dead-end of the classical school, was not simply bringing new analytical techniques to the main corpus of economic knowledge but promoting anti-Ricardian writings at the hands of Senior, Say, Bastiat, and Bailey. Dobb also took a much harsher view of the ideological role of Walras than was common then or is taken now (in view of Walras's support for land nationalization and the promotion of the socialistic plan model of E. Barone).[76] These perspectives are comprehensively spelled out in Dobb's last book, *Theories of Value and Distribution since Adam Smith*. It is of great interest to read an earlier version of these ideas in the form of Dobb's two Alfred Marshall Lectures delivered at the University of Cambridge in 1973. As to why these lectures were not published by Dobb it is hard to ascertain. Possibly he wanted to polish and rewrite them to take account of some of the reactions they provoked – enthusiasm and misunderstandings, suggestions as well as criticism – but that he felt that his message was well enough explained in extended form in his book which was shortly to appear.

It was during the last quarter of the nineteenth century that Jevon's *Theory of Political Economy*, Menger's *Grundsätze* (both published in 1871), and Walras's *Élements* (appearing in 1874) introduced a "novel character and direction" to the development of economic thought. Dobb argues that this period should be clearly demarcated from the classical school of thought, which began with Smith, Ricardo, and continued in the work of Marx.

To the extent that this new school of thought of the 1870s sought to introduce distribution as a species of exchange it stood in sharp contrast to the central preoccupations of the classical school. Dobb highlights the feature of the Ricardian system which logically demands that price relations or exchange value be determined *after* the determinants of distribution had divided the social product between the classes attendant to its production.[77] The protagonists of this "Jevonian Revolution" either ignored this consideration or those aware of its role in the determination of price trivialized its impact, for example Weiser.

Dobb points out, and it is a point worth stressing, that this had the consequence of redefining both the scope of political economy and the content of *legitimate* economic analysis. That this has direct *ideological* implications does not we think need stressing. Dobb is rare amongst historians of economic thought in highlighting the socio-political dimensions to any prescriptive social science. In the new orthodoxy to emerge after the 1870s the social was clearly separated from that which was *economic* and since distribution was an incidental element of the pricing process it was a supra-historical question and not a political one.[78] The evil intent of the apologetic had assumed a far bolder stance in developing an all-conquering Ricardian revisionism.

It should not be construed that Dobb regarded supply and demand theories as empty of content but insisted they must rely upon the acceptance of another, and in a more important sense *deeper*, set of factors which *necessarily* preclude such theories from containing a proper theory of distribution. For this reason they are incapable of offering a complete solution to the "classical type of value problem".[79]

## Dobb's methodological perspective

Maurice Dobb was a creative Marxist in his application of dialectics to the study of capitalist socio-economic systems. For him it did not involve embracing Hegel's method of conceptualizing new phenomena in a search for their constituent opposites, or the mysterious "triads" of some Marxists and Hegelians. This had an important impact upon his approach to the history of economic thought. Dobb rejected modern attempts to deny the possibility of an objective search for truth in the social sciences. Historical materialism was not a "mere 'sociology of knowledge'" (in which ideas are explained by the social milieu which gave them expression) to be classified "as yet another doctrine of historical relativism". To the extent that ideology saturates the social sciences, modern orthodox economics possesses a veil of "false consciousness" which once recognized allows progress in the search for the "laws of motion" which govern the reproduction of complex socio-economic systems.

The historical actor like his one-dimensional cousin – the economic agent – was circumscribed by the blunt empirical facts of the conditions of production and the rich fabric of the society in which his ideas and actions found expression. Agency, to use the term frequently used to *explain* actions, was thus seen *not* as the autonomous creation of a Cartesian mind separated from the historical process. In a letter to Mehring frequently quoted by Dobb, Engels was at pains to dispel any such notion that Marxism denies a role for anything other than the impersonal march of material forces.[80] The relationship was organic, expressed in the form of a dialectic, so often misunderstood by the Anglo-Saxon mind.

Dobb's mature statement of the role of ideology in economic analysis is cast in contrast to that presented by Schumpeter in his *History of Economic Analysis*. As a Marxist he recognized the historicity implicit in all social philosophies and as a result produced a sophisticated denial of the Schumpeterian separation of an independent sphere of logical analysis in economic method.[81] An illuminating and lucid exposition of the principles underlying Dobb's intellectual commitment to Marxism is to be found in his *Marxism and the Social Sciences*. This piece consists mainly of a paper contributed to a symposium on dialectical materialism delivered in the Easter Term, 1942.

Facts, for Dobb, were not objective entities to be collected and exposed to the universal rules of logic – "facts never speak for themselves and that even in the process of digging for them presupposes some principle of selection".[82] This phenomenon arises because "the mind is never (and can never be) a passive mirror to events, and there is always an *active* element in knowledge as we acquire it".[83] It was a deep understanding of the historical process that prevented Dobb from embracing logic-driven interpretations of the capitalist growth process. For Dobb, history exists as a continuum – not one with a smooth terrain reflecting harmonious social development but one in which the conjunction of ideas and productive potential, in moments of inevitable contra-diction, give a peculiar uniqueness (but *not* an independence) to each historical event.

It was the criterion by which the content of economic theory is evaluated, both in its internal consistency and its external relevance, that prompted Dobb's criticism of orthodox, for want of a better term, neoclassical economics. A basic criterion evaluating the theoretical scaffolding upon which economic knowledge hangs was, at the very minimum, the *logical* consistency of the structure itself. Dobb highlighted the fact that the post-1870s interpretation of economics did *not* meet this standard. After the capital debates of the 1960s[84] the attempt to restore the marginal productivity theory of distribution as a *logically* consistent explanation of class incomes was a failure, a point admitted by at least some of the neoclassical devotees. To the extent that committed neoclassical economists themselves had to retreat into the metaphysical realm of relying upon an "act of faith" to justify allegiance to a scientific methodology, they are (repeatedly) targeted by Dobb for the criti-cism they deserved for ignoring the distinction between the achievement of, rather than the (quite legitimate) aspiration towards, scientific status for political economy.[85]

Dobb basically regarded Schumpeter's "vision" as the projection of histori-cally relative categories and modes of thought upon economic phenomena. He regarded Schumpeter's contribution of the role of ideology in the social sciences as "the fullest and most serious contribution to the discussion" exceeding the crude "box of tools" interpretation of the nature of economic analysis. For Schumpeter, it was at the level of the "pre-analytical cognitive act" that ideology entered the construction of the theoretical apparatus to explain a complex social reality. Dobb, however, did not ascribe to the emphasis placed on the "emotional commitments" of the economist to explain the penetration of ideological elements into theoretical structures. Rather, he was interested in the ways in which the social formation, to use Marx's concept, impacted upon the theoretical apparatus employed to construct prescriptive economic policy.

The attempt to imbue economic analysis *per se* with a supra-historical char-acter independent of the distortions introduced by the emotional commitments of the individual (in this case the curious and knowledge-hungry social scien-tist) was an unsatisfactory explanation of the means by which ideology penetrated economics. Dobb's position was lucid in replying to Schumpeter's subjective explanation of the source of ideological intrusion into economics *qua* science.[86] If economic analysis was indeed purely formal then it was emptied of economic content, at least so far as economics is concerned with producing causal explanations of socio-economic evolution in the real world.

If, on the other hand, such analysis lays claim to offering explanations about observable economic phenomena then its separation from the answers it gener-ates cannot be maintained. As a result deeply embedded ideological elements, woven into the fabric of theory, will penetrate economic thought *per se* and hence dissolve the supra-historical claims of method as an "independent and objective" form of analysis. Such an argument applies equally well, in Dobb's opinion, to the modern urge to formalize economic propositions in mathematical structures as a device to purge the ideological from within the aspirant science of economics. One recalls Wittgenstein's words on the use of mathematics frequently quoted by Dobb: "In life we use mathematical propositions *only* in order to infer from propositions which do not belong to mathematics to others which equally do not belong to mathematics."[87] Such attempts, in Dobb's opinion, do not resolve this problem but merely attempt to cloud with rigour what is an essential feature of economics as a *veiled* social philosophy. While the tools of economic analysis got sharper with the reception of formalism, they did not cut any deeper.

With regard to the progress, or lack thereof, in economics as an investigative science Dobb casts his explanation in terms which are upon close inspection a dialectical process reflecting his Marxist intellectual framework.[88] Since ideas are derived, in an important sense, from the social *milieu* in which they find expression, the acceptance of this milieu as a constantly evolving organism provides the prima-facie basis for the conflict which litters the history of economic thought. At any point in the historical process it is "inherited ideas and concepts" which provide the "refracting medium" through which social reality is understood. It is the *dynamic* character of the economic system which inevitably creates new ideas and new explanations of contemporaneous economic events. Such new ideas necessarily provide a critique of pre-existing ones and their derivative theoretical structures shaped by historically antecedent (and hence different) social environments.

If ideas are historically conditioned then for Dobb they are similarly influenced by the position of their originator within the complex heterogeneous set of social relationships that in their totality comprise society. Dobb cites this factor as another element in explaining the persistence of competing schools of thought in the history of economic science. The problematic therefore confronting the social scientist is inevitably complicated by the penetration of ideological elements into the theoretical kernel through which meaningful propositions about real-world processes find expression. However, the implications of this should not be construed as a denial of the possibility of constructing a scientific political economy as the following statement reveals:

> Absolute truth is not a Kantian unknowable, even if it could never be reached at any finite point in the historical process: it could be approached asymptotically, and criteria existed by which one could speak about being nearer to it or more remote.[89]

It was exactly the criterion by which economic theories were to be evaluated that occupies so much of Dobb's attention.

## The Marshall Lectures and theories of value and distribution since Adam Smith

When Dobb delivered the Marshall Lecture at Cambridge in 1973 and produced his *Theories of Value and Distribution since Adam Smith* for the Cambridge University Press in the same year, only a relative few knew of his very significant role in both the collected works of Ricardo and the famous introduction to Vol. I written with Piero Sraffa. In the re-evaluation of the history of economic thought made possible by the publication of *Production of Commodities by Means of Commodities* in 1960, Dobb played a critical role. A notable exception to this lack of understanding of Dobb's role was Professor P.D. Groenewegen of the University of Sydney who captured the significance of Dobb's *Theories of Value* when he remarked that the book represented the "first history of economics in the light of the 'Sraffa Revolution', a term which embraces more than the famous re-interpretation of Ricardo, as the note of acknowledgement at the beginning points out".[90]

With the publication of Sraffa's seminal book offering restoration of classical theories of value and distribution Dobb was uniquely positioned to provide an insightful commentary on its implications for accepted interpretations of the evolution of economic thought. However, despite his major role of collaboration in bringing out the Royal Economic Society's edition of Ricardo's *Works and Correspondence*, the major economic journals sought their reviewers elsewhere. It was left to the labour movement in the form of the activist Marxist journal *Labour Monthly* to give Dobb the outlet for introducing Sraffa's "epoch-making book" to a wider audience, this time comprised of self-taught militants as well as a few radical academics.

Dobb in this review highlighted three issues most likely to interest readers with an interest in political economy and the history of economic thought. The first concerned the method used by Sraffa in constructing a standard commodity which measured value independently of the distribution of the social product between wages and profit. Second, the idea of treating means of production entering new rounds of production and circulation as "dated labour". And finally the solution Sraffa offered to the problem left unfinished by Marx of transforming labour values into prices of production. In passing Dobb refers to the successful work of the Russian economist, Dmitriev[91] and the Polish–German von Bortkeiwicz in solving this problem. The implications for the Austrian capital theory of Böhm-Bawerk and the nefarious "period of production" which arose from the Sraffa critique were devastating for the scientific claims of an increasingly recalcitrant orthodoxy.[92]

It seems unlikely that any other person could have written a review of Sraffa's masterly work quite like this, though Ron Meek, another prominent Marxist economist, wrote a thorough and insightful exposition of Sraffa when he reviewed the book.[93] A curio to be added here is that according to G. C. Harcourt, a review that he prepared with V. Massaro and published in the *Economic Record* had every line vetted by Sraffa himself.[94] But consider Dobb's superb qualification to the task at hand: Dobb came to Sraffa's new and seminal book as his long-time collaborator on Ricardian economics; as a friend from whom he had already, in 1928, "gained more by intellectual contact ... than from any single person".[95] There is evidence in Sraffa's papers held in Trinity College Library, Cambridge (file D1/57) that Dobb prepared for Sraffa in the period 1928–30 a background note on values and prices of production, two concepts central to the models of both Ricardo and Marx. He also discussed Bortkiewitz's work on the transformation problem in a document sent to Sraffa (Sraffa Papers, File 1/50). As well Dobb had written on the transformation problem in January 1948 as shown in letters to Dr Rudolph Schlesinger.[96]

This resuscitation of the surplus approach in Ricardo's theory of profit as a basis of a complete theory of distribution is a significant achievement in that it provides a solid theoretical connection between Ricardo and, as Schumpeter noted, his only great follower Karl Marx.[97]

## Conclusion

The Dobb archive, complied by B. H. Pollitt and catalogued by J. Smith for Trinity College Library, runs into hundreds of items of mostly unpublished lectures or drafts. There are fourteen items dealing with Marx as an economist alone. In the field of the history of economic thought there are manuscripts of talks given in Gosplan, Yugoslavia, Hungary, Czechoslovakia, Poland, and Denmark. There is also voluminous correspondence between Dobb and other economists (Meek, Sraffa, Bellamy, Schlesinger, Brus, Osiatynski – to name a few). Clearly, Dobb was always "mucking about" with different lines of research: about a third of it is on history of economic thought. However, the inspiration that prompted his writings on the history of economic thought reveals themes which, although maturing in their form of argument, remain throughout his career. As Tadeusz Kowalik has pointed out in the *Cambridge Journal of Economics*, Maurice Dobb, like Oskar Lange, "regarded social science, and economics in particular, as a tool of the working people in their struggle for social liberation".[98]

As has been discussed above, a major aspect of the "craft" in his Marshall Lectures and his *Theories of Value and Distribution since Adam Smith* consists of his demonstration of two lines of tradition in the history of economic thought and the essential differences between them. In one stream, exchange is treated as a *self-contained territory*, distribution being internal to the pricing process, even if at the expense of some inconsistency, something which Sraffa in 1960 highlighted. The link with Adam Smith arises through the employment of a supply–demand apparatus to tackle classical-type value problems. In the political economy tradition, however, the pricing process is open and linked to both a *social* pattern of distribution and the technical conditions of production and the integument in which the surplus is extracted and redistributed – to what Professor Takahashi called "the social existence form of labour".[99] With the completion of the debates on British economic history within the CPGB and the publication of his *Studies in the Development of Capitalism* Dobb assumed his more mature stance of emphasizing the influence of a particular *social formation*. Such a conclusion, no doubt, reflects Dobb's deep understanding of the historical process and explains his association of classical political economy with a significant degree of historical *relativity*, as opposed to the rather crude assumption of J. B. Clark that marginal economic theory was "supra-historical" – lifted above the existential realities of the social milieu in which economic theorizing finds expression.

In many respects, Dobb's final body of work possesses an unfinished quality, something which he himself acknowledged, especially with regard to this final book *Theories of Value and Distribution*.[100] Such an observation arises because of his reluctance to go beyond that which remains the subject of contemporary discussion. In this regard, he was referring to the unsettled conclusions arising out of the Sraffa critique. "It was for other and younger Marxist economists, I felt, to step into the breach and supply what is missing"[101] he remarked in a letter to Kowalik. However, Dobb remained throughout most upbeat about the value of the study of the history of economic thought, most notably where his Marshall Lectures conclude with the injunction: "History of economic thought, properly interpreted, and not left to bare chronicle, can not only rediscover forgotten questions and *points d'appui*, but also add a new perspective, possibly even a new dimension to current discussion."[102]

## Notes

1 Correspondence, Dobb to Theodor Prager, Port Said, 23 December 1950, Maurice Dobb Archives, quoted in Pollitt (1988: 63).
2 This book, published in 1925, appears to be the only work by Dobb translated into Russian.
3 Dobb (1978: 117).
4 See W. Sombart, "Medieval and Modern Commercial Enterprise" (1940); R. de Roover "The Commercial Revolution of the Thirteenth Century"; F. C. Lane, "Family Partnerships and Joint Ventures in the Venetian Republic" – all items reprinted in Lane and Riemersma (1954).
5 See Sweezy's article in Hilton (1982).
6 See F. C. Lane, in Lane and Riemersma (1954).
7 Resnick (1972: 134–5).
8 Marx (1894: 323–37).
9 Op. cit., 327.
10 Dobb (1946: 42).
11 Op. cit., 61.
12 Hilton (1982).
13 Hilton op. cit., *passim*.
14 Brenner (1978) and Duchesne (1993).
15 Hilton (1982) and Duchesne (1993).
16 Dobb (1946: 120).
17 Resnick (1972).
18 Duchesne (1993).
19 Consider the following statement, for example: "Hence in any given period to speak in terms of a homogeneous system and to ignore the complexities of the situation is more illuminating, at least as a first approximation, than the contrary would be." This is a positive embrace of the intrinsically classical method of abstraction applied

to a historical investigation (Dobb 1947: 11).
20 Once again a textual reference is here enlightening. Consider:

> To avoid misapprehension, it should perhaps be stated forthwith that the
> history of Capitalism, and the stages in its development, do not necessarily have
> the same dating for different parts of the country or for different industries; and
> in a certain sense one would be right in talking, not of a single history of
> Capitalism, all of them having a general similarity of shape, but each of them
> separately dated as regards its main stages.
>
> (Dobb 1947: 21)

21 Dobb (1942) "A Lecture on Marx", reprinted in Dobb (1955: 188).
22 Dobb, op. cit., 188.
23 Ibid. The quotation from Marx is taken from his *Value, Price and Profit* (ed. Eleanor
   Marx Aveling, London, 1899, 53–54) and is repeatedly employed by Dobb to highlight the independence of Marx's theory of surplus value upon any notion of
   imperfect competition; for example, see Dobb (1937: 60) for its early statement and
   Dobb (1973b: 146–7) for its mature presentation.
24 Dobb (1937: 57).
25 Dobb (1973b: 269). For an early recognition of the importance of monopoly as an
   explanatory factor in the accumulation of capital in his economic history see (1925a: 12).
26 Dobb (1935a: 2).
27 This was an early theme in Dobb's work and is a major component of his *Political
   Economy and Capitalism*. See Dobb (1937: chapter I).
28 See for example the discussion in Dobb (1937: 18–19).
29 Op. cit., 70.
30 Dobb employs the argument that abstraction when moving from the general to the
   particular allows one to maintain the conclusions derived from the former if it is well
   constructed. This was precisely the manner in which Marx proceeded from Vol. I to
   Vol. III of *Capital*. He uses the analogy of the abstract representation of the theory of
   rent to highlight this point:

> To use an analogy, let us suppose that one were to enunciate the theory of rent
> on the assumption that all land was of homogeneous quality, stating that rent
> would be equal to the difference between the cost of production and the selling
> price of corn (the latter being determined by the cost of production at the inten-
> sive margin). To introduce the fact of the heterogeneity of land (and hence of
> *different* costs of production on each farm and each acre) as a later approxima-
> tion would then make no special difference to the corollaries based on the
> simpler assumption, provided that the cost of production of corn on the average
> remained the same and bore the same relation to the price of corn. Moreover,
> the corollaries of the earlier approximation would embody certain essential
> truths about the nature and determination of rent (those connected with what
> one may term the scarcity aspect of rent, as distinct from its differential aspect),
> which no formulation of the theory of rent could imply without some reference
> to this relation between the average cost and the average selling price.
>
> Dobb (1937: 74)

Dobb points out subsequently in a footnote that Böhm-Bawerk employs essentially
the same assumption in the construction of his concept of the period of production.
31 See Dobb (1937: 73n.).

32  "Hence in any given period to speak in terms of a homogeneous system and to ignore the complexities of the situation is more illuminating, at least as a first approximation, than the contrary would be" (Dobb 1946: 11). This is a positive articulation of the classical method of abstraction applied to the study of economic history.

33  Dobb (1947).

34  As outlined in Dobb (1978).

35  A *Dictionary of Marxist Thought* contains an entry on Labriola:

> His best known work in English is essays on the Materialist Conception of History (1896), the first two volumes of a four volume study of historical materialism (the last volume posthumously in 1925). Labriola's Marxism was open and pragmatic, and even in his later work he refused to bring all his ideas within one all-embracing scheme of thought. The great value of the Marxist theory of history, in his view, was that it over came the abstractions of a theory of historical "factors".

"The various analytic disciplines which illustrate historical facts have ended by bringing forth the need for a general social science, which will unify the different historical processes. The materialist theory is the culminating point of this unification." But this unifying principle had to be interpreted in a flexible way: "The underlying economic structure, which determines all the rest, is not a simple mechanism, from which institutions, laws, customs, thought, sentiments, ideologies emerge as automatic and mechanical effects."

36  See Pollitt (1988: 57n.). Further references to these Marxist thinkers can be found in Dobb (1947/48).

37  The linking of the theory of surplus value with monopoly is clearly evident in this piece where Dobb echoes Professor Sieber in the contention that the labour theory of value is a "first approximation". As a consequence surplus value is derived "not in proportion to labour performed, but in proportion to power of ownership – monopoly". See Dobb (1947: 12–13).

38  See Sraffa (1951, Vol. I: Introduction).

39  Pollitt (1988: 61).

40  On this point see Harcourt (1994), republished in Harcourt (1995b).

41  Dobb (1975).

42  Dobb, Meek, and Schumpeter are associated with the thesis that there had been a *dual development in the history of economic thought*. The basis of such a thesis revolves around the contention that Adam Smith was the originator of *two* streams of thought, not one as claimed by those who see a single continuous development in the theory of value and distribution. The single line of development thesis arises in no small way out of the emasculation of Ricardo's economics undertaken at the hands of J. S. Mill. The assertion that Ricardo retreated from the advocacy of "embodied labour" as a universal measure of value is often referred to as the *Hollander–Marshall–Canaan* view. See Sraffa (1951, Vol. I: xxxvii–xxxvii) for an outline of this thesis. For its statement see Hollander (1904). A central element in this interpretation is that Smith attributed significant importance to the role of utility and/or demand. Such an assertion forms the basis of Hollander's contention that Smith was an underdeveloped 'general equilibrium' theorist. For a clear outline of the "two distinct and rival traditions in nineteenth century economic thought" which formed the basis of the dual development thesis see Dobb (1973b: 112–15).

43  See Meek (1967: 18–20) and Dobb (1960a: 7).

44  Dobb (1960a: 40).

45  Sraffa (1951, Vol. I: xxxv–xxxvi).

46  See Dobb (1975: 236).

47  See Dobb (1973b: 46).

48  Op. cit., 53–4.

49 Dobb (1960a).
50 Such remarks by Marx occur in Marx (1887: 24) and Marx (1857–8: 97), respectively. Dobb frequently cites them, for example Dobb (1969/70: 3).
51 Bagehot was to call Ricardo "the real founder of abstract Political Economy" cited in Dobb (1972: 1). Ricardo from his first excursion into political economy addressed pressing practical economic problems, such as in his criticism of wartime policy of the Bank of England in the *Morning Chronicle*. His 1815 *Essay on Profit* was likewise an essay directed to consider the consequences of the Corn Laws, indeed its full title was *An Essay on the Influence of a Low Price of Corn on the Profits of Stock; shewing the inexpediency of restrictions on importation*. Edwin Cannan had declared "among all the delusions which prevail in the history of English political economy there is none greater than the belief that the economics of the Ricardian school and period was of an almost wholly abstract and unpractical character", cited in Dobb (1973b: 23).
52 This remark by Canaan is frequently quoted by Dobb, for example Dobb (1972: 2; 1973b: 23).
53 Sraffa's introduction compares the similarities between the *Wealth of Nations* and *The Principles of Political Economy*. Sraffa (1951, Vol. I: Introduction).
54 Dobb (1972: 3).
55 Such a necessity was prompted by the criticism of Malthus which obliged Ricardo to explain how the prices of *other* commodities moved (if at all) when the cost in labour of corn increased. Malthus had answered Ricardo with the assertion that the general level of profits could be influenced by a surge in export demand as much as by the surplus derived at the agricultural margin of cultivation. See Dobb (1973b: 74).
56 See Sraffa (1951–73, Vol. I: Introduction).
57 See Dobb (1972) and Dobb (1969/70: 2).
58 Dobb (1973b: 66).
59 See Dmitriev (1904).
60 Sraffa (1951–73, Vol. IV: 4–91).
61 This view is expressed in *Ricardo and Economic Policy* where Dobb states:

> Regarding the relation between profit and rent he [Ricardo] came very close to saying, but did not say, that they were two (and rival) species of surplus value: "Rent then, [he writes] is in all cases a portion of the profits previously obtained on the land. It is never a new creation of revenue, but always apart of revenue already created."
>
> Dobb (1972: 5)

62 The Ricardian maxim found in the *Principles* spells this out clearly: "It follows ... that the interest of the landlord is always opposed to the interest of every other class in the community" (Dobb1972: 5–6).
63 Pasinetti (1977: 149).
64 Dobb (1969/70: 10).
65 Cited in Dobb (1953: 8n.) as "*Theorien* English edition. Selections, p.212".
66 Op. cit.
67 Republished in Dobb (1955).
68 See Pollitt (1988).
69 Dobb (1935).
70 Refutation by indulging in quotation duelling is never a sufficient response to the purposive elaboration of highly articulate criticism of established doctrine and its subsequent reinterpretation of the historical record. The response of T. W. Hutchison might hit the mark with *some* of the more bolder Cambridge proclamations regarding history of economic thought but it is an unsatisfying reply to the

sophisticated and complex writings of Maurice Dobb. See Hutchison (1978: chapter 9), "On recent revolutionary versions of the history of economics".

71  Dobb (1937: 68).
72  "Historical Materialism and the Economic Factor", originally published in *History*, February and June 1951, reprinted in Dobb (1955: 233).
73  See Dobb (1947/48).
74  Worth mentioning, perhaps, are the more analytical interpretations of historical materialism given by such individuals as G. A. Cohen and his advocacy of functional explanations of social dynamics coupled with the idea of the primacy of the forces of production (which do not include the social relations of production). Dobb was always careful of the consequences of constructing such taut logical categories when driven by the seemingly compelling force of logical analysis.
75  "I refer to class-exploitation, not as moral judgement, but as a factual description of a relationship" (Dobb 1947/48: 17). "If we take the terms 'exploitation' and 'unpaid labour' as a socio-economic description of a relationship (and not *per se* a moral epithet) then it is hard to see how its correctness can be disputed" (Dobb 1967a: 133).
76  Barone's celebrated article "The Ministry of Production in a Collectivist State" describes a socialist state which decides on the desired distribution of income required over a particular time frame and thereafter follows the results of applying the equations of a Walrasian model in the allocation of natural resources, factors of production, and savings. Originally published in *Il Giornale degli Economisti*, it appeared in Hayek (1935: 247–90). An excerpt can be found in Nove and Nuti (1972: 75–91).
77  Dobb (1973b: 169).
78  "The extreme form of this was J. B. Clark's interpretation of marginal productivity as meaning that each factor, and by implication those responsible for its supply, received the equivalent of what it 'contributed' to production: 'the law itself', said Clark, 'is universal and hence "natural" '." (Dobb 1973b: 176)
79  Dobb (1973b: 180).
80  Letter to Mehring, 14 July 1893, *Marx-Engels Correspondence*, trans. D. Torr, 1934, 5132, quoted in Dobb (1951).
81  See Dobb (1973a: Lecture I) and Dobb (1973b: chapter 1, entitled "Introductory: on ideology").
82  See Dobb (1947/48: 9). See also Dobb (1946: 35): "Since classification must necessarily preclude and form the groundwork for analysis, it follows that, as soon as one passes from description to analysis, the definitions one has adopted must have a crucial influence on the result."
83  Dobb (1947/48: 10).
84  See Harcourt (1972).
85  C. E. Ferguson whose "point of view is uncompromisingly neoclassical" is forced to admit that "placing reliance upon neoclassical economics is a matter of faith" (quoted by D. M. Nuti (1969) "Some reflections on the Sraffa system and the critique of the so-classed neo-classical theory of value and distribution: notes on Dobb M. H. 'Some Reflections on the Sraffa System and the Critique of the so-called Neo-Classical Theory of Value and Distribution'", paper for the Conference of Socialist Economists, 10 January 1969, Dobb Archives, Trinity College, Cambridge).
86  Dobb (1973b: 6).
87  Dobb quotes a 1922 edition of Wittgenstein's *Tractatus Logico-Philosophicus* at p.169 in his *Theories of Value* (Dobb 1973b: 8n.) and also in his *Marshall Lectures* (Dobb 1973a, Lecture I: 4). The quotation is taken from proposition 6.211 and can be found in the D. F. Pears and B. F. McGuiness translation of the *Tractatus* published by Routledge (1961: 65). The relationship between Dobb, Sraffa, and Wittgenstein, the successor to G. E. Moore's chair in philosophy, is a relatively unexplored area of research. It is well known that Wittgenstein discussed his major ideas with Sraffa and received serious criticism, while Wittgenstein lodged with Dobb upon his arrival in Cambridge. The escape from

the straitjacket of Cartesian dualism undertaken by Wittgenstein in his posthumously published *Philosophical Investigations* has considerable implications for the defensibility of methodological individualism within intrinsically social sciences.
88  See the Introduction to his *Theories of Value* (Dobb 1973b: esp. 17).
89  Dobb (1951).
90  V. K. Dmitriev, *Essai économiques* (1968), translated from the Russian edition of 1904 by Bernard Joly, p. 38. The essay on Ricardo, which forms the first part of the work, was published in 1898 (Dobb M., "Ricardo and Adam Smith", p. 331).
91  See Groenewegen (1974).
92  This is beautifully illustrated with Sraffa's example of wine and the old oak chest (Sraffa 1960: 37–8). See Dobb (1973b: 253–4) for his outline of this question in the context of the so-called capital debates.
93  Meek (1961), reprinted in Meek (1967).
94  Harcourt (1995a), which later appeared in Medema and Samuels (1998: chapter 9).
95  Dobb to Barbara Nixon: letter of August 1928 held in Dobb Archive, Trinity College Library, Cambridge, and cited in Pollitt (1988: 62n.).
96  Correspondence between Rudolph Schlesinger and Maurice Dobb is contained in eight documents (dated between 1948 and 1969) contained in the Dobb Archives (Pollitt and Smith 1983/87).
97  Dobb registers Schumpeter's comment in *History of Economic Analysis* in Dobb (1973b: 142).
98  Kowalik (1978: 141).
99  See Hilton (1982).
100 Letter to Tadeusz Kowalik, 25 July 1973, Dobb Archives, Trinity College, Cambridge.
101 Ibid.
102 Dobb (1973a, Lecture II: 18).

# Bibliography

Brenner, R. (1978) "Dobb on the Transition from Feudalism to Capitalism", *Cambridge Journal of Economics* 2: 121–40.
Croce, B. (1899) *Materialismo storico ed economica marxistica*, trans. as *Historical Materialism and the Economics of Karl Marx*, 1914, English edition, London: Howard Latimer.
Dickinson, H. D. ([1932] 1966) *Institutional Revenue: A Study of the Influence of Social Institutions on the Distribution of Wealth*, New York: Kelly.
Dmitriev, V. K. (1904) *Ekonomicheski ocherki*, Moscow. English edition, *Economic Essays on Value, Competition and Utility*, ed. D. M. Nuti, trans. D. Fry.
Dobb, M. H. (1920) "The Problem of Surplus Value: A reply to Mr. Withers", *Youth*.
—— (1924) "The Entrepreneur Myth", reprinted in Dobb M. H. (1955) *On Economic Theory and Socialism*, London: Routledge & Kegan Paul.
—— ([1925a] 1980) *Capitalist Enterprise and Social Progress*, Hyperion Press.
—— (1925b) *An Outline of European History from the Decay of Feudalism to the Present Day*, Plebs League.
—— ([1927] 1948) *Wages*, Cambridge Economic Handbooks – VI, Cambridge: Cambridge University Press, May.
—— (1931) "The Cambridge School", in *Encyclopaedia of Social Sciences*, Dobb Archive, Trinity College, Cambridge.
—— (1935a) "Criticisms of Some Trends in Modern Economic Theory", Lecture to the Economics Society in Copenhagen, manuscript: Dobb Archive, Trinity College, Cambridge.

## 90 T. Atley and B. McFarlane on Maurice Dobb

—— (1935b) "A Note on Demand, given at Cambridge University, manuscript: Dobb Archive, Trinity College, Cambridge.

—— (1937) Political Economy and Capitalism, London: Routledge & Kegan Paul.

—— (1942) "A Lecture on Marx", Lecture delivered on 4 November 1942, Cambridge University, reprinted in Dobb, M. H. (1955) On Economic Theory and Socialism, London: Routledge & Kegan Paul, 178–204.

—— (1943) Marx as an Economist, Marxism Today Series, ed. B. Farrington, London: Lawrence and Wishart.

—— ([1946] 1963) Studies in the Development of Capitalism, International Publishers.

—— (1947) "The Influence of Marxism on English Thought", delivered in Warsaw and Prague, September, Dobb Archive, Trinity College, Cambridge.

—— (1947/48) "Marxism and the Social Sciences", The Modern Quarterly 3, Winter: 5–21.

—— (1949) "On Some Tendencies in Modern Economic Theory", Philosophy for the Future, reprinted in Dobb, M. H. (1955) On Economic Theory and Socialism, London: Routledge & Kegan Paul, 104–17.

—— (1951) "Historical Materialism and the Role of the Economic Factor", History, February–June.

—— (1953) "Introduction to the Italian Edition of Theorien Uber Den Mehwert", manuscript: Dobb Archive, Trinity College, Cambridge.

—— (1955) On Economic Theory and Socialism, London: Routledge & Kegan Paul.

—— (1957) "Some Economic Re-evaluation", Marxist Quarterly, Dobb Archive, Trinity College, Cambridge.

—— (1960a) "Adam Smith and the Classical School", Institute for Social Sciences, Yearbook, Florence.

—— (1960b) An Essay on Economic Growth and Planning, London: Routledge & Kegan Paul.

—— (1961) "An Epoch Making Book",Labour Monthly.

—— (1967a) "Marx's Capital and its Place in Economic Thought", Science and Society 31: 527–35, partly reprinted in M. Howard and J. King (1976) The Economics of Marx: Selected Reading of Exposition and Criticism, Harmondsworth: Penguin Books, 131–9.

—— (1967b) Papers on Capitalism, Development and Planning, London: Routledge & Kegan Paul.

—— (1969/70) Some Notes on Ricardo and his Thought, published in a Festschrift for J. Kuczynski, Dobb Archive, Trinity College, Cambridge.

—— (1970) "The Sraffa System and the Critique of Neo-classical Theory", Die Ekonomist.

—— (1972) "Ricardo and Economic Policy", delivered at the AGM of the Royal Economic Society, 6 July 1972.

—— (1973a) "Ideology and Economic Theory in the Nineteenth Century", Marshall Lectures, manuscript: Dobb Archive, Trinity College, Cambridge.

—— (1973b) Theories of Value and Distribution since Adam Smith: Ideology and Economic Theory, Cambridge: Cambridge University Press.

—— (1975) "Ricardo and Adam Smith", in A. Skinner and T. Wilson (eds) Essays on Adam Smith, Oxford: Clarendon Press.

—— (1975/76) "The 'Crisis' in Economic Theory: Some Random Comments on the Debate", manuscript: Dobb Archive, Trinity College, Cambridge.

—— (1978) "Random biographical notes", Cambridge Journal of Economics 2, 2: 115–20.

Dobb, M. H. and Crowthers, J. G. (1925) *Marx and Engels*, Dobb Archive, Trinity College, Cambridge.

Duchesne, R. (1993) "Debating the Transition to Capitalism: A Review Article", *Science and Society* 57, 6.

Groenewegen, P. (1974) "Review of *Theories of Value and Distribution since Adam Smith: Ideology and Economic Theory*", *Economic Journal* 84, March: 192–3.

Harcourt, G. C. (1972) *Some Cambridge Controversies in the Theory of Capital*, Cambridge: Cambridge University Press.

—— (1994) "What Adam Smith Really Said", *Economic Review* 12, 2: 24–7, republished in Medema, S. and Samuels, W. J. (eds) (1998) *Foundations of Research in Economics: How do Economists do Economics?*, Cheltenham: Edward Elgar.

—— (1995a) "How I Do Economics", in draft, published in Medema, S. and Samuels, W. J. (eds) (1998) *Foundations of Research in Economics: How do Economists do Economics?* Cheltenham: Edward Elgar, chapter 9.

—— (1995b) *Capitalism, Socialism and Post Keynesianism: Selected Essays of G. C. Harcourt*, Cheltenham: Edward Elgar.

Harcourt, G. C. and Massaro, V. G. (1964) "Mr. Sraffa's Production of Commodities", *Economic Record* 40: 442–54.

Hayek, F. A. (1935) *Collectivist Economic Planning*, London: Routledge.

Hilton, R. (ed.) (1982) *The Transition from Feudalism to Capitalism*, London: Verso.

Hobsbawn, E. J. (1967) "Maurice Dobb", in C. Feinstein (ed.) *Socialism, Capitalism and Economic Growth*, Cambridge: Cambridge University Press.

Hollander, J. (1904) "The Development of Ricardo's Theory of Value", *Quarterly Journal of Economics* XVIII: 455–91.

Howard, M. and King, J. (eds) (1976) *The Economics of Marx: Selected Reading of Exposition and Criticism*, Harmondsworth: Penguin Books.

Hutchison, T. W. (1978) *On Revolutions and Progress in Economic Knowledge*, Cambridge: Cambridge University Press.

Kowalik, T. (1978) "The Institutional Framework of Dobb's Economics", *Cambridge Journal of Economics* 2: 141.

Lane, F. C. and Riemersma, J. (eds) (1954) *Enterprise and Secular Change: Readings in Economic History*, London: Allen and Unwin.

Marx, K. (1857–8) *Grundrisse: Foundations of the Critique of Political Economy (Rough Draft)*, trans. M. Nicolaus, Penguin Books in association with *New Left Review*, 1973, 1993 edition.

—— ([1887] 1954) *Capital: A Critique of Political Economy, Vol. I, Book One, The Process of Production of Capital*, ed. F. Engels, Moscow: Progress Publishers.

—— ([1894] 1959) *Capital: A Critique of Political Economy, Vol. III, Book Three, The Process of Capitalist Production as a Whole*, ed. F. Engels, Moscow: Progress Publishers.

Medema, S. and Samuels, W. J. (eds) (1998) *Foundations of Research in Economics: How do Economists do Economics?* Cheltenham: Edward Elgar.

Meek, R. L. ((1961) "Mr. Sraffa's Rehabilitation of Classical Economics", reprinted in Meek, R. (1967) *Economics and Ideology and Other Essays: Studies in the Development of Economic Thought*, London: Chapman & Hall.

—— 1967) *Economics and Ideology and Other Essays: Studies in the Development of Economic Thought*, London: Chapman & Hall.

Nove, A. and Nuti, D. M. (1972) *Socialist Economics: Selected Readings*, Harmondsworth: Penguin Books.

Pasinetti, L. (1977) *Lectures on the Theory of Production*, New York: Columbia University Press.

Pirenne, H. (1936) *Economic and Social History of Medieval Europe*, London: Kegan & Paul.

—— (1939) *Medieval Cities: Their Origins and the Revival of Trade*, Princeton, NJ: Princeton University Press.

Pollitt, B. H. (1988) "The Collaboration of Maurice Dobb in Sraffa's Edition of Ricardo", *Cambridge Journal of Economics* 12: 55–65.

Pollitt, B. H. and Smith, J. (1983/87) *The Dobb Archive*, Trinity College, Cambridge.

Resnick, S. (1972) "The Second Path to Capitalism: A Model of International Development", *Journal of Contemporary Asia* 3, 2: 133–48.

Samuel, R. (1980) "British Marxist Historian", *New Left Review*, March–April, No. 120.

Sraffa, P. (1960) *The Production of Commodities by Means of Commodities: Prelude to a Critique of Economic Theory*, Cambridge: Cambridge University Press.

—— (1951–73) *The Works and Correspondence of David Ricardo*, ed. Piero Sraffa, with the collaboration of M. H. Dobb, Cambridge: Cambridge University Press for the Royal Economic Society.

# 6　The craft of William D. Grampp

## Historian of economics

*Kenneth E. Carpenter and Laurence S. Moss*

## Introduction

In 1972, Professor William D. Grampp reviewed a book by Lionel Robbins entitled *The Theory of Economic Development in the History of Economic Thought* (Robbins 1968). After describing Lord Robbins as "one of the grand figures of British economics," Grampp went on to focus on the character of the text itself. Grampp explained, "what [Robbins] says is influential and it is said with a clarity and grace that are rare in intellectual history and show [intellectual history] can be, what it seldom is, a pleasure to read" (Grampp 1972: 539).

Now, nearly three decades later, in reviewing the work of that reviewer, the authors of this essay find that the same can be said about him. In part, this is because of his numerous professional activities, notably co-founding the History of Economics Society in 1973–4, and subsequently serving as its president in 1980–1. In part, it is because he has done major work in the history of economic thought, above all on economic liberalism and the circumstances surrounding Britain's turn toward free trade in the nineteenth century. Grampp has also beautifully demonstrated the applicability of economic analysis to a subject that most, non-economists at least, would have thought outside the domain of the practitioners of the "dismal science," namely, the creation, pricing, and consumption of works of art. In addition to tackling subjects of large importance and widespread interest, Grampp, like Lord Robbins, has written with an eloquence, grace, and clarity that make his work a pleasure to read.[1] And both the nature of the topics and Grampp's style insure that his books continue to be read: they will not be sent to the offsite storage libraries being constructed in institutions across the country.

Grampp received his Ph.D. in economics from the University of Chicago in 1944. The chair of his dissertation committee was Frank H. Knight, and Grampp's topic, "Mercantilism and Laissez Faire in American Political Discussion," was one to which he would return many times. Knight was influenced by Jacob Viner who characterized the goals of economic policy among the classical school writers as alternating between the twin goals of opulence and power, and this analysis would be taken over and adopted by Grampp himself.[2]

Grampp initially worked as a journalist (the year 1944 was not a good one in which to gain university employment), and his published economic writings of that time show a desire to communicate with non-economists, as through articles in such journals as the *Sewanee Review* and the *Antioch Review*.

His first paper in a professional journal, *The Journal of Political Economy*, was on a European topic, "The Italian Lira, 1938–45," and it represents what would be a continuing interest in Europe, as demonstrated by numerous papers in European journals and many lectures at European universities and banks. Grampp also sought to bring together European and American historians of thought by means of internationalizing the History of Economics Society conference held during his tenure as president.

The first decades of Grampp's teaching career, from 1947 to 1980, were at the University of Illinois in Chicago. After achieving *emeritus* status in 1980, he received a continuing appointment as Visiting Professor of Social Science at the University of Chicago in 1980 and more recently, in 1994, an appointment as lecturer at the celebrated University of Chicago Law School. Grampp remains a lecturer on the Chicago law faculty today.

Well after his first retirement, Grampp published a book in 1989 on the curious subject of *Pricing the Priceless: Art, Artists, and Economics*. In it Grampp demonstrated an unwavering commitment to the self-interested rational maximizer model of economic behavior. Like George Stigler, Gary Becker, and others, Grampp now reached out to be a part of the "Chicago school." Whether Grampp himself will agree with our characterization of his most recent writing as "Chicago-style" remains to be seen, but we set out our argument below in the very last section of this essay.

In the next section, we recall the context of academic discussion during the 1960s about the unsatisfactory status of economic policy discussion in economics. The American economics profession, never shy to give advice to policy makers, has debated whether economists give disinterested advice. This raises the issue – in the past as well as the present – of whether politicians choose economists who provide the advice they want to hear, or whether the role of economists is to help shape public opinion and aid the subsequent election of the politicians. The framing of this problem helps us appreciate, in the subsequent three sections, the topical relevance of what we consider to be Grampp's most durable historical papers and arguments about England's turn toward free trade during the first part of the nineteenth century. Grampp has made a lasting contribution to the historiography of this problem. By our reckoning, Grampp did answer the broad questions he set out to answer all the way back to his dissertation work at Chicago. The sixth section, as noted, deals with the work that connects his personal love for fine art with his "Chicago-style" appreciation of economic psychology and its expression through the market mechanism. The seventh section covers a potpourri of some of the other themes, subjects, and historical figures discussed by Grampp in his essays over the years. We conclude this essay with a short assessment of the place of Grampp's contributions to the history of economic thought.

## The 1960s and the call for a theory of economic policy

On December 29, 1964, in his presidential address to the American Economic Association, Professor George J. Stigler of the University of Chicago complained that the economic profession had yet to understand "the relation-ship between [economic] policies and [the] results of policies" (Stigler 1965: 39). Without this understanding, economists really do little more than translate the "ruling values of their societies" into "awe-inspiring professional language" (Stigler 1965: 39). A great deal more is expected and required from the profes-sional economist, especially in the United States, where "American economists, perhaps reflecting their Germanic training, were more interested in policy [than their British counterparts]" (Stigler 1965: 49). Stigler called for a concerted effort on the part of the profession to develop a "theory of public policy" so that the comparative merits of different types of economic organization could be assessed and policy recommendations be supported by a scientific platform. Stigler prophesied that a new dawn was awakening in which "our expanding theoretical and empirical studies will inevitably and irresistibly enter into the subject of public policy, and we shall develop a body of knowledge essential to intelligent policy formation" (Stigler 1965: 57).

Stigler's essay contained much more than simple exhortations and forecasts about the future direction research might take. It offered a stylized history of economic thought in which Stigler took a knight's tour through the historical literature, from Adam Smith in Scotland, through Mountifort Longfield in Ireland, and ending up in Great Britain with Alfred Marshall and F. Y. Edgeworth. Stigler concluded that "from the heyday of laissez faire [until today] ... no economist deemed it necessary to document his belief that the state could effectively discharge the new duties he proposed to give to it" (Stigler 1965: 46). Stigler cited a number of contemporary writers on the issue and emphasized the "slow development" of quantitative tools and that the "growing insistence upon quantification" was about to push economics into "its golden age" (Stigler 1965: 56). Although Stigler cited other writers working on the history and character of economic policy, he took absolutely no notice of Grampp's pioneering essays on the same subject.

Indeed, the same volume of the *American Economic Review* that contained Stigler's presidential address also included Grampp's essay "On the History of Thought and Policy" (Grampp 1965b: 128–35). Here, Grampp, apparently quite independent of Stigler, enumerated the questions that would inform what might be called the "history of economic policy." What the investigator needed to find out is what it was that governments were "urged to do and refrain from doing, what they actually did, what the problems were that policy was meant to manage and how well it did" in solving these problems (Grampp 1965b: 128). More than this, students of the subject must discover how these decisions on the part of government were "influenced by positive [i.e., theoretical] economics, by ethical values, vested interests, and how much was done for no good reason at all" (Grampp 1965b: 128). This was precisely the sort of research program that would engage Grampp himself over the next three decades of his career.

Grampp's vision for a new field of investigation was not quite the same as Stigler's. Stigler wanted an empirical or quantitative economics that would advise the policy makers – perhaps with benefit–cost accounting methods – which of several forms of government intervention was most cost effective. Grampp wanted to understand three things: first, how the governmental process worked, second, how the actual decision that government should intervene had been made in the past, and, third, the shape and form this intervention took in various historical episodes. The historical episode that most interested Grampp was Britain's "turn" to free trade. This episode began in 1820 when Thomas Tooke drafted the "Petition of the London Merchants for Free Trade" and after obtaining about 200 other signatures delivered it to Lord Liverpool who raised the issue in both houses of parliament. Many years later the discussion sparked by Tooke's petition culminated in the repeal of the Corn Laws (1846) and the repeal of the Navigation Acts (1849) (Grampp 1987b). Clearly, the economist and economic writings did play a part in this story but only a part. Grampp was after a full-bodied account of the governmental processes involved, especially in terms of who made the decision(s) and for what reasons. Biography, sociology, and economic reasoning would all play their part in the story Grampp needed to tell.

At one place, Stigler had referred to the "heyday of laissez faire" by which he meant that during much of the nineteenth century Great Britain had been guided by the rule set out by economists that government should assume minimal functions and not interfere with trade and commerce. Stigler argued that most of the economists of the day advocated this view because laissez-faire was a doctrine or ideology, which was held by economists on dogmatic rather than scientific grounds. Stigler's allegations owe something to the work of the Irish economist J. E. Cairnes in 1873 (Cairnes 1873: 228–49). In 1873, Cairnes remarked that most economists of the first part of the nineteenth century advocated and campaigned for a non-interventionist economic policy. Cairnes's "age of laissez-faire view" stuck in intellectual circles, and many professional historians continue to characterize in this way the nineteenth-century British economists who committed themselves to non-interventionism. As Grampp and others pointed out, the textual evidence does not support this view.

Grampp had already, by 1965, come to the conclusion that much of what had been said about the economic policy analysis of the British classical economists was historically inaccurate and in need of a thorough overhaul. He and some other economists of the day sought to show how in fact economic policy had been made in Britain during the notorious "heyday of laissez faire."

## Grampp's analysis of economic liberalism

Grampp's interest in the twin subjects of mercantilism and classical economics, which can be dated back to his graduate school days and the influence of his teachers Knight and Viner, culminated in his two-volume work *Economic Liberalism* published in 1965. The first volume of *Economic Liberalism* is subtitled

"The Beginnings." According to Grampp, a "liberal economy" is one in which individuals decide what is to be produced, how these goods shall be produced and distributed, and so on. It follows then that "economic liberalism" is the economic policy that directs a liberal economy. What was in fact the economic policy that directed the liberal economy? Clearly, there are strategic choices to be made by empowered individuals. Individuals can come together in joint ventures and engage in collective action for particular purposes. That is one choice. They can also reject collective action and instead rely on the decentralized processes of the market to make choices for them. Or, they can decide that the coercive powers of the government should be used to force action in one way rather than another. Thus, in a liberal regime, the most basic question is: "What shall be the economic powers of the government?"

Grampp's study of the literature led him to conclude that the British liberal economists – also called "classical economists" – held to no single view about government that can be dubbed "laissez faire." According to Grampp, a careful reading of the classical literature suggests that British classical economists held the following view: the state can engage in any economic activity whatsoever, so long as two conditions are met. First that the people want the government to act this way, and second, that the government can actually do what it has been instructed to do (Grampp 1965a, I: ix).[3] This is emphatically not "laissez faire." The British group were liberal because they believed that individuals should decide what is produced, how it is produced, and to whom it is given. Grampp argued repeatedly that what is most commonly termed "[English] classical liberalism" was never synonymous with the ideology of laissez-faire. The classical economists were "liberal" but not in favor of laissez-faire (Grampp 1965a).[4]

Those writers who alleged that the British classical school launched Britain onto a policy of limited government interference with business are, Grampp suggested, simply uninformed, even though Stigler and most historians had adopted Cairnes's erroneous characterization of the classical school. One major purpose of Grampp's *Economic Liberalism* was to set the historical record straight on this point.

In the first chapter to *Economic Liberalism*, Grampp drew on some of his earlier published essays that appeared in *Ethics* (Grampp 1951a; 1951b). "The Stoic Origins of Liberalism" argued that the Stoic writers, Marcus Aurelius, Epictetus, and Cicero, conceived of men and women in a most positive way. Individual agents were thinking, responsible, and courageous beings. Indeed, Epictetus explained that it was quite natural for men and women to act in their own interests but that this was not a problem for the social order because the natural world is set up in such a way that "[people] can attain nothing good for [themselves] unless [they] contribute some service to the community" (Grampp 1965a, I: 23). In Cicero's writings and elsewhere, the "main duty of the state is to respect the worth of the individual" (Grampp 1965a, I: 47). According to Grampp, this view led directly to Adam Smith's compelling idea of the "invisible hand," albeit with a detour. The Stoic intellectual tradition did not endure.

It was abandoned during the Middle Ages and was revised only during the "age of mercantilism," which Grampp dates as starting in 1500 and ending in the seventeenth century, when classical liberalism again took root.

It is incorrect to hold that mercantilism is the opposite of classical liberalism. Although Grampp mentioned the popular view of the 1960s that mercantilism was superior to classical economics because it anticipated John Maynard Keynes's 1936 criticisms of classicism, he went on to argue that the mercantilists, to their credit, were more familiar with the market mechanism and how it worked than many modern writers who, calling themselves "classical liberals," lay down strictures about the proper role of the state in a free society. Grampp's close reading of the mercantilist literature, first published in 1952 and then republished in this 1965 work, brought him to the conclusion that "there [is] a close relationship between what the writers saw and their ideas about how to change it – between economic problems and economic policies" (Grampp 1965a, I: xii). The mercantilist writers could understand what the medieval moralists could not, namely, that human selfishness could be "a power for good as well as harm." This mercantilist break with medievalism pointed directly to the best and most influential ideas of the classical economists (Grampp 1965a, I: 97) and gave substance and shape to British classical economics.

Next, Grampp turned his attention to the origins of the American brand of liberalism, especially in the early years of the American republic when Thomas Jefferson and Alexander Hamilton expressed competing visions about the economic organization of the fledgling United States. Of special interest is what the founders meant by the term "regulation of commerce," which was understood to mean powers delegated to the federal government by the state governments. By the end of the Constitutional Convention some of the delegates were convinced that a limited mercantilist government had been created in the United States (Grampp 1965a, I: 110). The Federalist Party (the party of Alexander Hamilton) clearly valued economic and national power over individual liberty. The Republican Party (the party of Thomas Jefferson) initially favored agriculture and strict limitations on immigration so that the moral climate of the United States could be steadily improved without the influence of morally compromised immigrants from permissive cultures. It is difficult to say whether one or the other political party was more "pro-market." Like the mercantilists, markets could be utilized to secure a powerful nation, and so markets and national power were not on opposite sides. Indeed, Grampp's review of the evidence led him to conclude that "from at least 1750 onward [those same authors who] would elucidate the principles of economic liberalism [would also] conclude that state interference was necessary" (Grampp 1965a, I: 130). Clearly, economic liberalism is not "remarkable for its logic" but for its flexibility. In the United States, liberal policy provided for continuing economic growth and national economic development (Grampp 1965a, I: 168). Contrary to the view of Cairnes and later Stigler, liberal policy there cannot be characterized as "laissez faire."

In the next chapter of *Economic Liberalism*, "The Classical Psychology of Liberalism," Grampp summarized Adam Smith's ideas about "economic man." According to Grampp, Smith "implied ... that for the greatest part of the population, happiness, truth, beauty, and goodness depend on real income" (Grampp 1965a, II: 27). Smith raised the status of economic man because "in competitive behavior he saw the requisites of cultural progress" (Grampp 1965a, II: 38). This analysis led Grampp quite naturally to the last two chapters entitled "The Political Ideas of the Classical Economists" and "Liberalism in the Great Century."

When Grampp wrote of "the classical school of economics" he had in mind most of the British writers of the later eighteenth and early nineteenth centuries. This group consisted of Adam Smith, David Hume, Thomas Robert Malthus, James Mill, David Ricardo, J. R. McCulloch, Nassau Senior, and John Stuart Mill. But even J. S. Mill was already of another era because of his utilitarianism, which pointed his brand of classical liberalism away from the importance of the individual and the individual's development as a human being. With utilitarianism came the idea of maximizing general happiness, which meant considerably less emphasis on the individual. The inner corps of the classical school favored free trade so long as it was consistent with national power; otherwise interventionism was fine (Grampp 1965a, I: 65).

Legislation was of interest to businessmen, statesmen, writers, and, of course, the classical economists. However, the views of the classical economists were only one small tributary flowing into the surging ocean of economic policy discussion of the time, and the economists were themselves by no means consistent on the role of government.

Consider, for example, the Factory Acts. On some occasions economists favored enactments to protect factory workers, and at other times they opposed their amendment. Economists adhered to no single identifiable party line about regulation.[5] Classical liberalism was a loose economic policy of "limitation," and scientific argument played a most important part in the debate over factory legislation. At the end of the classical liberal period, John Stuart Mill clearly and expertly pointed to the possibility that each person in a group of self-interested adults may wish to adopt a certain rule of behavior but find it "not in the interest of any individual to adopt the rule for guidance of his own conduct, unless he has some assurance that others will do so too" (Blaug 1971: 108). This important principle implies that all voluntary behavior among consenting adults is not always optimal and that as a matter of scientific logic the state can intervene to raise living standards.[6] As a general rule, Mill believed, government should not intervene in the economy, unless such intervention was calculated to do more good than harm. The burden of proof was always with the advocates of intervention. Absent such well-reasoned grounds for intervention, then, laissez-faire should be the rule.

As Grampp and others have noted, Mill's qualified application of the noninterference principle, that is, the laissez-faire principle, allowed many sorts of government intervention to pass the benefit–cost test. On Mill's influence, Grampp seems to have been ahead of the leading historians of this century

(Blaug 1971: 108; Hollander 1985: 677–769; Grampp 1965a, II: 71). In addition, with Mill making such extensive use of earlier utilitarian ideas, Grampp is quite convinced that Mill's writings mark an abrupt end to traditional classical liberalism. With Mill we have the start of a theory of economic policy that aims at maximizing regional output rather than at protecting rights and promoting the dignity of the individual. Grampp's two-volume study on *Economic Liberalism* closed with the assertion that by Mill's time, a new version of liberalism, one far removed from the Stoic-brand discussed in his book, had entered British economics.

What is the lesson Grampp tried to communicate with work on economic liberalism? And he did attempt to communicate a lesson. To be sure, he aimed to contribute to future discussions of the history of thought, but he also sought to help shape public discussion of policy. The work could, after all, have been published in one volume in a cloth binding by a university press. Instead, it was brought out in two volumes in paper, and in a series promoted by the College Department of Random House, a format that would promote reading by college students and the general public.

According to Grampp, the economic liberalism of the classical school was certainly not the same as laissez-faire. In British classical liberalism the "government may do whatever it can do that the people will have it do" (Grampp 1965a, II: 97). In contrast to that traditional liberalism, the utilitarian liberal position was that the government may do whatever it can do that people will have it do *or can be made to believe it should do* (Grampp 1965a, II: 139, italics in original). Those things that the people might be led to believe the government should do could include measures aimed at improving the people intellectually or strengthening their character. In other words, utilitarianism transformed classical liberalism into the liberalism that was at its heyday in the United States in 1965 at the time of publication of *Economic Liberalism*, and Grampp wanted to make clear the distinction between the different brands of liberalism.

He also wanted to show that classical liberalism was not libertarianism. The classical economists like the mercantilists that preceded them were practical men of affairs. They were willing to use government intervention if the government intervention was expected to achieve a particular desired result, and if the people desired the intervention (see also Grampp 1988).

Why then did Cairnes, an educated and veteran observer, set historians and economists such as Stigler on the wrong trail by branding the classical school as advocates of laissez-faire when they so strenuously did not adopt this position? According to Grampp, "Cairnes' mistake was not unusual. Economists often [make] poor historians, just as historians have been poor economists" (Grampp 1965a, II: 86). Having diagnosed a serious problem with the existing historiography of economic thought, Grampp set off on a research program that would not only help correct the error but open new doors of historical understanding about the exact role of economists in the making of economic policy during the first part of the nineteenth century.

## Setting the record straight about the Manchester school

Grampp was not alone in his efforts to clarify our understanding of the theory of economic policy among classical economists. Valuable work documenting the fact that the classical economists did use a variety of theoretical ideas to assess policy and were not doctrinaire advocates of laissez-faire was appearing in the years before Grampp published his *Economic Liberalism* in 1965. Blaug's study on the debates among the economists surrounding the several Factory Acts had appeared in the *Quarterly Journal of Economics* seven years before *Economic Liberalism* was published, and E. G. West's paper on "Private versus Public Education, A Classical Economic Dispute" had appeared in the *Journal of Political Economy* in 1964. These works benefited from Robbins's *The Theory of Economic Policy* that presented the policy views of the English classical economists as public spirited and intelligent (Robbins 1952: 206–7). And many other papers dealing with the important problem of the classical approach to economic policy (for citations, see Samuels 1966; Coats 1971; 1992) followed the publication of Grampp's *Economic Liberalism* and may have been stimulated by it. A. W. Coats summed up what is now the commonly accepted view of the economic policy of the (British) classical writers, and it is a consensus that Grampp helped to build:

> Contrary to the view expressed by innumerable commentators, [the classical economists] did not advocate laissez-faire, if that expression is taken to mean an essentially negative conception of the economic and social role of government. Unquestionably they were suspicious of governmental activity, believing it ... often partisan, corrupt, or inefficient; but they did not regard the reduction of state intervention as an end in itself. It was a means to a higher end, namely, the attainment of individual freedom in economic, social, political, and religious life. Not only did the classical economists admit many exceptions to the general rule of government non-intervention, they also recognized that the law was supplemented by a variety of "non-legal social controls."
>
> (Coats 1971: 6)

What the classical economists thought about policy was only part of the issue for economists who in the United States were increasingly involved in actually making policy. What about the past? As Stigler put it, economists wanted to understand "the relationship between [economic] policies and [the] results of policies" (Stigler 1965: 39). Did the economists of the classical school who, it was accepted, did much more than translate the ruling values of their times into formalisms and awe-inspiring definitions (Stigler 1965: 39), did these virtuoso performances from the economic pundits of an earlier day have any real impact on British economic policy itself? More to the point, did the writings of the British classical school change anything fundamental about the way ordinary individuals lived and worked?

Grampp made a painstaking effort to answer these questions about the actual influence and effectiveness of economists. A master of what can be termed "historical sociology," he assumed that human beings make history and not forces like "class interest" or "God's will." Grampp first identified the relevant policy makers and then, through their correspondence, diaries, pamphlets, and public speeches, probed their relationship with the economists of the day, all in an effort to determine how and in what ways economic ideas influenced the actual course of political events in Britain. The *Manchester School of Economics* is the excellent monograph in which Grampp investigated in great depth the linkages between economic thought and policy (Grampp 1960). It remains the standard monograph on the subject.

The so-called Manchester school of economics, which suddenly appeared in 1838, was a political movement on behalf of free trade in grain, which, it was expected, would benefit manufacturing interests. According to Grampp, "it was financed and conducted mainly by the mill owners of Lancashire of whom the most prominent were [Richard] Cobden and [John] Bright" (Grampp 1987b: 252). Thus, the very existence of the Manchester school was symbolic of the weakening of the old landlord class in England. This same Manchester school ceased to exist in 1846, after the infamous Corn Laws were repealed. Political movements can die quickly; economic schools do not. And the Manchester school was, in fact, entirely different from the classical school of economists. It consisted of a "group of agitators who meant the government to act in certain ways, and its members spent less time in reasoning and writing about their purposes than in winning the country over to them" (Grampp 1960: vii). According to Grampp, economic ideas, and theoretical distinctions, were "clearly subordinated to political purposes" (Grampp 1960: 2, 15). Furthermore, "none of the well-known economists appear in the register of the Manchester School. Neither the economists nor their doctrines had any lasting connection with the real campaign" (Grampp 1960: 16). And what a campaign it was!

The Manchester school had to contend first and foremost with the classical economists themselves. According to Grampp, most British classical economists were opposed to an immediate, unqualified move toward free trade in grain. Ricardo favored allocative efficiency over free trade and therefore supported a modest tariff on those imports that competed with domestically taxed goods. The idea was to create a "level playing field" by subjecting foreign manufacturers to a similar tax so that resources would not be shifted out of the domestically taxed industry as domestic consumers switched their purchases to cheaper imports. Malthus was a staunch defender of a tariff on imported grain through most of his professional career.[7] Most of the classical economists would have nothing to do with this political movement emanating from Manchester. The movement was contemptuously dubbed a "school" by Prime Minister Disraeli after the Manchester agitators formed the National Anti-Corn League in 1839. The League brought together businessmen who wanted free trade because they believed it would expand exports of their textiles, while at the same time lowering wage costs and expanding job opportunities in Britain. To be sure, not all the businessmen couched their arguments in terms of exports and lower wages. Grampp noted that some business leaders, genuinely caring about alleviating poverty among the working poor, agitated for reform on this most humanitarian basis (Grampp 1960: 7). The major leaders of the move- ment, Cobden and Bright, also favored free trade because they believed that it would promote an international division of labor that would create interdepen- dency and, consequently, foster world peace (Grampp 1986).

This idea was consistent with British classical economics, but little else of the economists' engine of analysis seems to have made its way to Manchester. The Philosophical Radicals – the followers of James Mill – that supported Repeal were utilitarians and not economic liberals. This list included Charles Villiers, John Bowring, William Molesworth, George Grote, J. A. Roebuck, Joseph Hume, Perronet Thompson, and Francis Place. The Radicals wanted to extend the franchise to a broader group of citizens and saw Repeal as another blow against the privilege of the great landowners. Other middle-class radicals included many famous Manchester business leaders such as J. B. Smith, Archibald Prentice, Edward Miall, Joseph Dyer, George Wilson, Joseph Savage, and textile factory owner John Bright. The movement provoked James Wilson to start The Economist in 1843 – a publication whose commitment to free trade has never faltered in a remarkable 150 years of continuous publication (Edwards 1993). Historians Samuel Smiles and George Richardson Porter joined in with their support as well. The movement demanded the repeal of all laws limiting the international export and import of food.

Grampp reported that "the names of none of the well known economists appear in the register of the Manchester School," and he added that "neither the economists ... nor their doctrines had any lasting connection with the real campaign" (Grampp 1960: 16). The reason was quite simple. Grampp insisted that the British classical school writers never supported unilateral free trade. Indeed, Malthus himself had argued that high corn prices caused the worker to receive high nominal wages and that this was in the worker's interest. Protectionism was good for the worker because by choosing not to spend all of his larger nominal budget on corn he could thereby command a greater quantity of (relatively cheaper) manufactured goods and thereby enjoy a higher living standard. In a nutshell, Malthus argued that high corn prices are a blessing to the working man and not a curse, because his real wages were fixed in corn and corn traded off for a greater number of manufactured goods under the Corn Laws. Grampp's rational reconstruction of the constrained maximization model implicit in Malthus's argument quickly became an often-cited article in the history of economic thought (Grampp 1956).

The Manchester school claimed that the working man was harmed by protectionism. The school insisted that the

corn laws ... were bad because they raised the price of food and lowered real wages; they created unemployment by restricting the export of manu- factured goods and their sale on the domestic market; they encouraged manufacturing abroad, and they protected inefficiency in agriculture at home.

(Grampp 1960: 84–5)

In short, the Manchester school found the British classical economists to be enemies of Repeal and not its natural ally (Grampp 1960: 17, 35, 107).

The Irish potato harvest failed in 1845. This tragedy finally led Sir Robert Peel to support Repeal in 1845, even though he initially resigned rather than initiate it. Then, after again assuming power, he brought about Repeal by executive order. Repeal was a crucial decision that brought England to a free trade commercial policy that lasted well into the twentieth century.

What of the more subtle linkages between classical economics and British economic policy? According to Grampp, the Manchester school was an expression of "middle class radicalism [rather] than classical economics" (Grampp 1960: 114). Free trade symbolized the abandonment of the old order in which landlords ruled and were dominant, and it was the old order that Repeal promised to end. Not subtle economic argument, but the dramatic vision of a new social order motivated the agitators. But what motivated Sir Robert Peel?

Was Peel promised a job by the Manchester school business leaders? Was Peel promised funding for his next political campaign? Questions such as these were no longer considered inappropriate and irrelevant for economists. In fact, three years before Grampp published his *Manchester School of Economics*, Anthony Downs's *An Economic Theory of Democracy* appeared. Its startling thesis was that politicians do not seek office to introduce new programs but instead offer programs in order to get into office (Downs 1957; cf. Musgrave 1992). Downs's book was an important milestone in what we now know as "public choice economics." According to historian Dennis Mueller, "public choice has developed as a separate field [in economics] largely since 1948" after the appearance of Duncan Black's seminal papers on group decision making (Mueller 1989; Black 1948a; 1948b). This literature was greatly enhanced with Downs's work, which may have owed something to the work of Joseph A. Schumpeter (1942). Still, the idea that political man and economic man are one and the same was a blasphemy that only radical social critics, progressives, and muckrakers once dared to utter. Now such utterances are commonplace in the public choice literature (Mueller 1989). The field of public choice holds as its fundamental premise that economic behavior is as applicable to non-market decision making as it is to market decision making.

It was George Stigler who set the profession on the road to a new theory of economic policy analysis and who gave direction to the next generation of public choice economists when, in 1971, he proposed that the legislative process be considered a vast mechanism of exchange. According to Fred S. McChesney, the question Stigler posed may be stated as follows: "if some economic agents wanted (demanded) regulation and government provided (supplied) it, was something akin to [voluntary] exchange going on?" (McChesney 1997: 8). Indeed, Stigler's seminal paper of 1971, "The Theory of

Economic Regulation," has established a veritable subfield of economics based around the idea that politicians are like business leaders, self-interested maximizers who are bought off by the bidding of special interest groups (Stigler 1971; Peltzman 1989). The modern theory of regulation shifts the role of economists. Instead of offering advice to politicians based on some normative framework only loosely linked to their analysis, economists have the role of recognizing and quantifying the ways in which government regulation creates benefits for some that were either unavailable except through politics or else more cheaply obtainable through politics than through trade (McChesney 1997: 9–10; and see Peltzman 1989).

In Stigler's view, the roles of both the individual economist and politician are limited and without much historical significance. Indeed, in 1975, Stigler explained that the repeal of the Corn Laws had nothing to do with intellectual argument but instead with the fact that the manufacturing and commercial classes had grown in size and political influence relative to the agricultural classes. Repeal was inevitable because the interest groups had changed in relative power and influence. The individual economists and politicians were unimportant to the repeal of the Corn Laws. Stigler's personal challenge to Grampp could not have been more clearly expressed than it was in the following passage:

> So returning to the Corn Laws. I believe that if Cobden had spoke only Yiddish and with a stammer, and Peel had been a narrow, stupid man, England would have moved toward free trade in grain as its agricultural classes declined and its manufacturing and commercial classes grew. Perhaps a few years later, but not many. In 1846 the agricultural classes of England had fallen to about one-fourth of the labor force. Truly effective import prohibitions would have driven grain to intolerable price levels, and intolerable things are not tolerated.
>
> (Stigler 1975: 319)

Stigler may not have answered the question Grampp posed in 1965, but he showed that he considered to be unimportant the sort of answers that Grampp was providing.[8] Grampp stated that:

> we would like to know about the history of economic policy ... what was said, done, and why – what it was that governments were urged to do and refrain from doing, what they actually did, what the problems were that policy was meant to manage and how well it did, how much the decisions were influenced by positive economics, by ethical values, vested interests, and how much was done for no good reason at all (Grampp 1965b: 128).

The Stiglerian response, especially the one that emerged during the 1970s, was that politicians were simply the brokers of those with a financial stake in the enactment of any policy or regulation. Politicians were the horse traders who either served their constituencies or else suffered certain defeat at the polls.

Could this not-so-flattering description of politicians as brokers of interest groups really apply to those who set Britain on the road to free trade during the nineteenth century, as Stigler insisted?

## The role of the individual in steering Britain's "turn" toward free trade

In 1982, Grampp launched his counter-offensive in the form of a series of important scholarly articles. He offered a detailed examination of economic opinion in Britain at the time when parliament debated the famous Thomas Tooke petition of 1820 (Grampp 1982a; 1987b). Grampp was determined to show that economists, economic policy ideas, and the heroism of politicians really mattered. By his words and deeds, Grampp must be considered an anti-Stiglerian. Individuals are as important if not more so than interest groups.

The episode began when Tooke, a businessman with extensive practical experience in the English–Russian grain trade, drew up the "Petition of the London Merchants for Free Trade" (Grampp 1982a: 498; Blaug 1986: 251). That petition called for free trade, and its signatories were especially those merchants whose trade was constrained by the existing high duties. The Petition was published in the newspapers and brought to the House of Commons for debate by Alexander Baring. According to Grampp, the party leaders of both houses wanted "to liberalize commercial policy measure by measure ... until free trade was a reality" (Grampp 1982a: 501; 1987b: 254). Both houses took evidence by listening to the business leaders of the day. It is a mistake, Grampp maintained, to credit the businessmen and lobbyists with the initiation of a free trade commercial policy for Britain. Based on a careful reading of the parliamentary testimony, Grampp concluded that the businessmen were "cowering timorous creatures" not always completely informed about what is was that they wanted. The politicians were not "low and cunning animals devoid of morals" or horse traders for campaign contributions (Grampp 1982a: 519). Rather, they were politicians of great conscience who balanced the benefits of free trade against the concerns of British power and national defense. Only after much principled deliberation and a searching of their private conscience did they heroically and selflessly set Britain on a course in 1820 that would lead inexorably in 1846 to the repeal of the Corn Laws and finally the removal of all other restrictions on international trade by 1850. There is little of Stigler's idea that the politicians were mere brokers of deregulation for personal gain. The frequently read claim of the economic historians that Britain wanted free trade because of its industrial superiority is also erroneous, according to Grampp (Grampp 1982a: 520). It is Grampp's considered view that it was the statesmen and party leaders who heroically took Britain toward free trade during the first part of the nineteenth century. They did this neither out of a quest for personal financial gain nor out of a calculated bid for campaign contributions; they did it because they believed it was the correct policy, from which the nation as a whole would benefit. Grampp is absolutely clear on this point.[9]

The members of the British parliament received extended praise in another piece that Grampp published in 1982 entitled "Economists and Politicians: Some Cautionary History" (Grampp 1982b). Apparently, it is a misconception worth clearing up that politicians proceeded on one level and economists on another. According to Grampp, culling evidence from Hansard's Reports and "citing the authority of an economist was a common practice in Parliament" although in many instances the politicians completely misunderstood the economists (Grampp 1982b: 16–17). Grampp urged that we remember that interventionism is quite consistent with classical economics since the goal of classical economics was the wealth and health of the entire nation and not the absolute liberty of the individual. Wealth and power had to be brought into balance with liberty, and that was a principal activity of the wise political leader. There was also a longstanding tradition of economists working also as politicians, or else directly advising political leaders. That history certainly dates to the mercantilist period when writers such as Dudley North served as the Commissioner of Customs and the Treasurer and Davenant served as both a Member of Parliament and the Inspector General. Indeed the list of British Prime Ministers who knew economics includes the Earl of Shelburne, William Pitt, Sir Robert Peel, William E. Gladstone, and Lord Liverpool. Grampp concluded that "politicians are not always unlettered in economics or indifferent to it" (Grampp 1982b: 23). Economists, on the other hand, when they are not occupying an elected office and even when they are, find that their opinions, no matter how learned, count for merely one vote (Grampp 1982b). Grampp scolded the economists. He reminded his colleagues that it is the politicians and elected legislators who hold the legitimate authority to make national economic policies. When economists advocate policies in a manner "so confident and authoritative that it suggests no one is entitled to disagree with them," they reveal their inability to accept the basic democratic process under which legitimate political decisions are made (Grampp 1982b: 28).

Perhaps the most famous and well-known instance of economists volleying to have their voices heard by the political leaders took place during the famous Corn Law debate of 1815. Sir Henry Parnell set up a Select Committee of the Commons to decide what was to be done now that the hostilities with France had ended. The spate of pamphlets by David Ricardo, Thomas Malthus, Sir Robert Torrens, and Edward West in 1815 is a milestone in the history of British economic thought and much commented on in the secondary literature (Blaug 1968; Hollander 1979). At once, the various party leaders had to balance the national interest against the economic welfare of the people (Grampp 1983: 148; 1987b: 254). It is not true, Grampp maintained, that the voice of the economist was ignored. Not true at all. According to Grampp, "the ideas of the economists, or what were represented to be their ideas, did figure in the debate" (Grampp 1983: 150). Indeed, the party leaders acknowledged the merits of free trade but did not accept the opinion that free trade alone was the basis for making policy (Grampp 1983: 151). This episode above all else demonstrated that the conventional historical accounts of British trade policy during the first part of the nineteenth century are incorrect. The evidence showed that it was not the ideas of economists, manufacturing inter- ests, class interests, or large impersonal forces that explain what happened in Britain after 1815. What happened after 1815 was the result of the wisdom of a few political leaders who really cared about the welfare of the masses of farmers, manufacturers, and shippers living under their control (Grampp 1983: 152; 1987b: 254).

In a 1987 piece that appeared in the *Business History Review* (Grampp 1987a) Grampp provided the most incisive analysis of the special business inter- ests that lined up around the debate that led to Britain's turn to free trade. The strongest opposition to free trade came from the shipowners and shipbuilders who used the national defense argument in praise of the protectionism that benefited them. The party leaders could have conveniently and profitably succumbed to these interests but they did not. According to Grampp, "the deci- sion for free trade was made because the party leaders wanted it made and arranged matters so that it would be" (Grampp 1987a: 99). Indeed,

> in time what the economists wanted done the politicians undertook to do. One is tempted to take this explanation back a step and make the economists, rather than the politicians, responsible for the [turn to free trade], but that would be mistaken. Economics was influential but the economists were not. ... Smith was influential, and some Ricardian doctrine was. Ricardo was not.
>
> (Grampp 1987a: 100)

Grampp's most important conclusion is that the turn toward free trade was indeed urged by the merchants but that the politicians did not simply supply them with the deregulation the merchants most effectively demanded as Stigler would have stated it (Stigler 1971).

Grampp believed that at least in one historical episode – Britain's turn to free trade – the politicians really did put the public interest ahead of their private financial interests when they supported free trade and that they did so (only) because it would increase living standards for the majority of the population and promote the stature of the nation (Grampp 1987a: 106; 1987b: 254). The policy of the age was not laissez-faire. The long line of historians who have argued that the merchants brought about free trade in 1820, or that the economists supported it without much qualification and out of a blind faith in laissez-faire, are ill informed. Grampp's lasting contribution to the study of the history of free trade in England is to show that with the exception of Tooke (who drafted the famous Petition), it was the politicians who, informed by economic ideas and motivated by public service over personal self-interest or greed, launched Britain onto a course that culminated in the repeal of the Corn Laws and the Navigation Acts, thereby securing higher living standards for all British subjects (Grampp 1987a; 1987b). Based on his extensive reading of the literature, his analysis of the parliamentary reports, and the social biography of the principals involved, Grampp concluded that it was the statesmen, leaders, and committed politicians that made all the difference. There is no evidence that a tiny collection of self-seeking lobbyists enlisted the aid of the crafty and insidious politicians. Grampp's analysis of Britain's turn to free trade must be summarized as fundamentally opposed to the Stiglerian economic theory of regulation and largely at odds with the modern public choice view of economic policy making.

## Grampp and the world of art

The best work in the social sciences comes about when a scholar combines two areas of study that have not been traditionally brought together. Grampp's friends know of his great love of art. Attendance at a conference customarily meant pilgrimages to art museums, and he is one of those individuals who will travel half way across the country to see an exhibition. Despite his love for the art world and his patronage of its leading institutions, Grampp has been mercilessly outspoken about the hubris of the museum officials and art aficionados who claim that art is exempt from the ordinary ebb and flow of market forces. With righteous indignation, the art interests lobby for special subsidies and privileges from the various national governments. We have seen that Grampp was reluctant to apply the Stiglerian model of interest group politics to selected historical episodes in British history out of which the policy of free trade emerged. When it came to analyzing the self-interested behavior of the art museum lobby and the cultural associations, Grampp was a fully fledged member of the Chicago school. Grampp revealed no inhibitions whatsoever about exposing hypocrisy and self-seeking behavior in the land of museum management. His full-length book, *Pricing the Priceless: Art, Artists, and Economics*, is a wise and witty book, one that in some ways is pioneering (Grampp 1989a). His subsequent "A Colloquium about Art Museums: Economics Engages Museology," put forth – and rebutted – the arguments most often used by museum curators to cover up and excuse their outrageous inefficiencies (Grampp 1996).

The book is filled with memorable anecdotes, insightful criticism, and sarcastic humor. According to Grampp, "rent-seeking in the arts differs from that in other areas in being more confident of its legitimacy" (Grampp 1989a: 230; 1989b). Grampp's position is absolutely clear: "art should support itself and do so without government subsidy" (Grampp 1989a: 269). Much of his book is an exercise in the application of the rational choice model to the particular facts and situations of the art market. In Grampp's words,

this [book] is about art and artists, especially about painting and painters, and tries to say something that has not been said before or said in the same way. If it has succeeded, the reason is that it observes them from the point of view of neoclassical economics. That has hardly ever been done and probably never has been done in the way it is done here.

(Grampp 1989a: ix)

We agree.

Grampp insists that "economic and aesthetic values are consistent [in the sense that] if outside the market painting A is said to be superior to painting B then on the market the price of A will be higher than B" (Grampp 1989a: 37). To recent work in the humanities that shows consumer behavior to be the fundamental factor behind the flourishing of the arts in certain periods (see, notably, John Brewer 1997), Grampp would say, "Of course." At one point, Grampp makes the empirical observation that "the price of the work of most artists falls after their death" (Grampp 1989a: 50), and he explains that during an artist's lifetime he is subject to the buyers of his work and their preferences. He can of course paint what he wants and insists that the buyers buy it or go "take a hike," but this business strategy is apt to prove costly to the stubborn artists. In the end it is a give and take, and the division of power between the artist and the customers is evidence of what Grampp calls a "dual sovereignty" model of the market place (Grampp 1989a: 76).

To be sure, there was patronage, but it also involved exchange: Grampp is irreverent enough to remark that "there is scarcely a museum in Italy which does not have a biblical scene that includes a portrait of the donors, usually clerics, depicted in the lower foreground, right and left, in an attitude of devotion" (Grampp 1989a: 47).

In telling the story about the rise of art and the particular circumstances in which it has flourished over the centuries, Grampp draws upon his vast knowledge of history and the history of economic thought. We learn that the Academy of Fine Arts in France that was formed in 1648 did not come into its own until Colbert extended the authority of the French monarchy over the entire economy (Grampp 1989a: 90). This pattern was repeated in other places, and in Spanish South America and elsewhere state building and artist patronage went hand in hand.

The state's involvement with painters extends to the art museums themselves. The fact that they are non-profit organizations should not mislead anyone into imagining that "they are conducted for the benefit of the public at large" (Grampp 1989a: 167). Museums are confused about everything, including their capital assets. There are costs to holding these assets in virtual cold, dark storage. The costs have to do with the fact that the paintings could be sold on the market and the sales proceeds invested in bonds. The interest on the bonds could be used to fund myriad programs for these same museums. But the curators refuse to make such calculations or even assist others when asked to do so.

The National Bureau of Economic Research once made an effort in the 1960s to collect such financial data, but it was greeted instead with the "droll notion" that "art is priceless" and the economists should get lost (Grampp 1989a: 179). Like stubborn Soviet central planners, the museum curators wander in the dark. They have no real understanding of what constitutes the "best use" for their art held in their collections. Indeed, most museum collections are in storage and kept away from the public, with only about 10 percent of the objects on display (Grampp 1996). If the best use were, as the museum officials sometimes say, to make "it visible to the largest number of people," then they would place the art on the "busiest street corners and the most traveled expressways would be lined with the greatest art of the world" (Grampp 1989a: 200). But the museums have other objectives as well, and it is in exploring the "trade-offs" among the various objectives that Grampp's economic analysis of the art world makes the greatest of contributions. Grampp's contributions to the economics of art are the latest evidence of his ability to look beyond commonly accepted formulations.

## Final assessment

Although William Grampp, now in his ninth decade, has not stopped teaching and might very well write more, the general outlines of his scholarly contribution are clear. He has explained, in a widely read work, the transformation of economic liberalism into the liberalism that earlier dominated American policy. He has contributed significantly to the question of how economic policy is actually made and what role, if any, the intellectual plays in its creation. Whether he looked at the course of British commercial policy and the teachings of the classical economists, or the American founders and the great works of economics that most influenced them, or the mercantilists and their attitudes and contributions to statecraft, he concluded that at least in one instance politicians played a decisive role – and that, putting aside their narrow private business or selfish interests, they acted with the goal of bettering social life. Grampp has had little patience for those historical accounts that attribute changes in policy to "the business interests" or to "industrial power." He was also reluctant to apply the "public choice model" and certain simplified versions of the Stiglerian perspective that attribute so much of political behavior to opportunistic wealth maximization of one type or another. Instead, Grampp found, at least in the cases he examined, that individuals matter and that some can rise above petty factional interests and even their personal, narrowly defined self-interest.

Grampp was not the first to argue that individuals can be motivated by principles, by a quest for fame, and a favorable place in the history books. What he has done so well is tie these accounts to the facts, doctrines, and body of analysis of economic thought in the period dating from about 1500 to 1860. Much of his work has endured and receives favorable citations by other historians; here we include his analysis of Malthus's 1815 defense of protectionism as a device to raise the workers' real wages (Grampp 1956); his authoritative account of the Manchester school both in terms of its historical sociology and links to the classical writers (Grampp 1960); and finally, his detailed accounts of the turn that the British parliament took toward free trade starting in 1820 with Tooke's petition and the parliamentary debates inspired by that petition. To these milestones we only mention two papers that raise new conceptual issues in a creative and interesting way. First, we point to Grampp's paper on usury in the seventeenth century in which he brilliantly traces the theory of asset pricing (the pricing of land) as it emerged in the British literature 300 years ago (Grampp 1981). The second paper, "Scots, Jews, and Subversives Among the Dismal Scientists," deals with the variety of arguments deriding the advocates of open markets and free trade because of their ethnic backgrounds and alleged dishonest ethnic practices. Ricardo was repeatedly singled out for his Jewish background. These attacks marginally affected the development of economic policy and constitute some of "the bad, the silly, and the scurrilous" attacks on free trade (Grampp 1976). Grampp's craft as a historian of economics was based on a wide-ranging study of the source material that few have been able to match. That, combined with the economist's keenly analytic mind, his ability to write clearly, his breadth of interests, and his keen sense of the issues that matter have all resulted in work that has been a part of ongoing conversations on various aspects of economics. William Grampp's scholarship has been recognized and valued by his colleagues, as, for example, when he was chosen president of the History of Economics Society in 1980–1; and this master craftsman has left us wiser.

## Notes

1   This is partly the result of his early experiences as a journalist. On his résumé, William Grampp provides a listing of what he calls his "Non-Academic Experience." He lists his association with Akron Times-Press as a reporter and copy reader from 1937 to 1938. From September of 1938 until February of 1939, Grampp served as a correspondent with the Press-Wireless in Paris and the Chicago Tribune in London. Finally, Grampp served as a Vice Consul in the economic section of the American Embassy in Rome from September 1944 until August 1945. His résumé goes on to list his consulting assignments with a score of publishers, both commercial and academic, including Dow Theory Forecasts and the Continental Bank.

2   Professor Jacob Viner joined the faculty of the University of Chicago in 1916 and was promoted to the rank of full professor in 1925. He remained at Chicago until 1946, when he joined the faculty at Princeton University. Viner was an advocate of expansionary fiscal policy during the Great Depression and advised American government agencies during World War II. His brilliance as a scholar and active involvement in public policy debates no doubt influenced Grampp, possibly directing his research interests. Viner is famous for a number of insights but one in particular seems to have guided Grampp throughout his career. We are referring to the idea that especially in the mercantilist literature, the English writers in

> poetry and official documents, [used phrases such as] "power and plenty," "wealth and strength," "profit and power," "profit and security," "peace and plenty," or their equivalents. ... Nor is there any obvious reason, given the economic and political conditions and views of the seventeenth and eighteenth centuries, why power and plenty should not have been the joint objectives of the patriotic citizen of the time, even if he had freed himself from the mercantilist philosophy.

> (Viner 1991: 138–9)

Grampp would argue in his writings that when faced with a choice between opulence and power, most writers and especially the British classical school writers chose power over opulence. Adam Smith himself was quite clear about the need to encumber trade with restrictions, such as the Navigation Acts themselves, so that it could contribute to national power. Grampp like Viner repeatedly emphasized this point (see also Viner 1964).

3   We have had some difficulty determining what types of government intervention Grampp's definition would ever rule out. Rent control might be one example. Suppose the people want abundant low-priced housing and demand, petition, and subsequently lobby so that the government provides it. Surely, the government can raise taxes and put up houses the way it puts up army barracks during war. This the government can do, and so doing is consistent with liberal economic policy. Now suppose, instead of actually building houses, the government simply controls rents by imposing a ceiling price. Low prices are associated with abundance, and so this law makes housing appear to be abundant. Rent control is precisely what the government should not do under economic liberalism because it has not produced an abundance of low-priced housing but rather precisely the opposite; cf. Grampp (1950).

4   There is of course the embarrassing British classical economist, Herbert Spencer, whose basic writings and thoughts seem to be pretty close to what the textbook writers mean when they speak of "laissez faire." Grampp dealt with Spencer under a subhead that fully recognized his contribution as the embodiment of pure laissez-faire. Grampp remarked that a "legislator who went to Spencer for guidance would come away with laissez faire in the purest form in which it ever has been proposed," but Grampp added that "these ideas set Spencer quite apart from the classical economists" (Grampp 1965a, II: 115–18). By excluding Spencer, Grampp disposed of what some might consider to be an exception to his thesis. Grampp did not consider the French liberal tradition which included many writers who promoted strictly laissez-faire ideas. Another possible exception, to the Grampp view that the classical economists did not embrace laissez-faire, is the American John Taylor. Grampp mentioned his contribution as "more thoroughly one of laissez faire than that of anyone else of his age including British liberals" (Grampp 1965a, I: 163). An interesting doctrinal question is whether the logic of the argument of the British classical economists indicated that they should have embraced laissez-faire, not whether they in fact did so. Grampp did not deal with this question.

5   In his notorious *Letters on the Factory Act*, published in 1837, Nassau Senior opposed the ten-hour Bill that in its original form was designed to limit the length of the working day for all workers regardless of gender, age, or willingness to work (in Senior 1966). Senior's calculations revealed that if the work-day were shortened by one hour, factory profits would tumble to 8 percent from 10 percent (Blaug 1971: 110). From this, and perhaps from Karl Marx's critical treatment of Senior (Blaug 1971: 111n.), historians have concluded that Senior was a member of the British classical school and a laissez-faire zealot opposed to all government intervention in the labor market. This is an incorrect interpretation of Senior's considered opinion on the role of government intervention in the labor market. In the same work in which Senior opposed shortening the work-day, he expressed his support for legislation that would limit child labor. Clearly, Senior's opposition to the Factory Acts was confined to the 1833 Act only, and not to the principle of state regulation of the factory system. He did not take a position based on a value judgment that "bargained for" hours of work should be unregulated. Senior was no libertarian. Quite the contrary, Senior carefully explained the economic consequences of "shorter hours on employment and real wages," thus distinguishing his scientific response from that of the ideologue (Blaug 1971: 106). Not a wide-eyed advocate of laissez-faire, Senior was a genuine social scientist (Grampp 1965a, II: 111). In his Oxford lectures given between 1847 and 1852, Senior stated that the duty of government is to intervene if such interventions

will raise the welfare of the governed. Apparently, Senior suspected that the ten-hour Bill would not work to achieve that objective; hence his opposition.

6   This argument lies at the heart of the debate over the proper role of the state in economic life. If the state can promote a series of mutually advantageous trades that otherwise would not have taken place, then the possibility exists that state intervention while restricting individual liberty in some respects may unlock a series of mutually advantageous trades to which all parties might agree (see Baumol 1969). To use a simple example: the state increases an individual's taxes by $10 but then spends the money to create a situation involving collective action wherein the individual gains as much as $100. That individual might feel well compensated for the loss of liberty.

7   The most recent evidence suggests that Malthus may have turned toward free trade in corn after 1826 but that he did not live long enough to edit out fully the old arguments from the second edition of his *Principles of Political Economy* which was published posthumously in 1836 (two years after Malthus's death in 1834). See Hollander (1997).

8   Grampp and Stigler were co-founders of the History of Economics Society. Stigler had served as president of the American Economic Association and urged a new approach to the study of economic policy. From these considerations, it seems likely that Stigler and Grampp had some familiarity with each other's work. We have not found evidence that they disagreed with each other in print.

9   He wrote: "I find it plausible to think the policy was the work of politicians who believed it would increase the total and per capita real income of Britain. ... [Indeed] politicians can act in the general interest" (Grampp 1987b: 254).

# Bibliography

Baumol, William J. (1969) *Welfare Economics and the Theory of the State*, Cambridge, MA: Harvard University Press.

Black, Duncan (1948a) "On the Rationale of Group Decision Making," *Journal of Political Economy* 56, February: 23–34.

—— (1948b) "The Decisions of a Committee Using a Special Majority," *Econometrica* 16, July: 245–61.

Blaug, Mark (1958/1971) "The Classical Economists and the Factory Acts: A Re-examination," *Quarterly Journal of Economics* 26, May, in A. W. Coats (ed.) *The Classical Economists and Economic Policy*, London: Methuen, 104–22.

—— (1968) *Economic Theory in Retrospect*, Homewood, IL: Richard D. Irwin.

—— (1986) *Great Economists Before Keynes*, New York: Cambridge University Press.

Brewer, John (1997) *The Pleasures of the Imagination: English Culture in the Eighteenth Century*, New York: Farrar Strauss Giroux.

Cairnes, John E. (1873) *Political Essays*, London: Macmillan.

Coats, A. W. (ed.) (1971) *The Classical Economists and Economic Policy*, London: Methuen.

—— (1992) *On the History of Economic Thought: British and American Economic Essays*, 2 vols, London: Routledge.

Downs, Anthony (1957) *An Economic Theory of Democracy*, New York: Harper & Row.

Edwards, Ruth Dudley (1993) *The Pursuit of Reason: The Economist 1843–1993*, Boston: Harvard Business School.

Grampp, William D. (1948) "On the Politics of the Classical Economists," *Quarterly Journal of Economics* 62, November: 714–47.

—— (1950) "Some Effects of Rent Control," *Southern Economic Journal* 16, April: 425–47.

—— (1951a) "The Moral Hero and the Economic Man," *Ethics* 61, January: 136–50.

—— (1951b) "Truth and Authority in Economic Organization," *Ethics* 61, July: 314–22.

—— (1952) "The Liberal Elements in English Mercantilism," *Quarterly Journal of Economics* 66, November: 465–501.

—— (1956) "Malthus on Money Wages and Welfare," *American Economic Review* 46, December: 924–36.

—— (1960) *The Manchester School of Economics*, Stanford, CA: Stanford University Press.

—— (1964) "False Fears of Disarmament," *Harvard Business Review* January–February: 28–179.

—— (1965a) *Economic Liberalism*, 2 vols, New York: Random House.

—— (1965b) "On the History of Thought and Policy," *American Economic Review* 55, May: 128–35.

—— (1972) "Robbins on the History of Development Theory," *Economic Development and Cultural Change* 20, April: 539–53.

—— (1973) "Classical Economics and Its Moral Critics," *History of Political Economy* 5, Fall: 359–74.

—— (1976) "Scots, Jews, and Subversives among the Dismal Scientists," *Journal of Economic History* 36, September: 543–71.

—— (1981) "The Controversy over Usury in the Seventeenth Century," *Journal of European Economic History* 10, Fall: 671–95.

—— (1982a) "Economic Opinion When Britain Turned to Free Trade," *History of Political Economy* 14, 4: 496–520.

—— (1982b) "Economists and Politicians: Some Cautionary History," *Review of Social Economy* 40, Spring: 13–29.

—— (1983) "An Episode in the History of Thought and Policy," in A. W. Coats (ed.) *Methodological Controversy in Economics: Historical Essays in Honor of T. W. Hutchison*, Greenwich, CT: JAI Press, 137–53.

—— (1986) "Peace and Trade: The Classical vs. The Marxian View," in H. Visser and E. Schoorl (eds) *Trade in Transit: World Trade and World Economy*, Dordrecht: Kluwer, 17–31.

—— (1987a) "How Britain Turned to Free Trade," *Business History Review* 61, Spring: 86–112.

—— (1987b) "Britain and Free Trade: In Whose Interest?" *Public Choice* 55: 245–56.

—— (1988) "Rights Theory in Classical Liberalism," in Achille Agnati, Davide Cantarelli, and Aldo Montesano (eds) *Essays in Memory of Tullio Bagiotti*, Padova: CEDAM, 621–31.

—— (1989a) *Pricing the Priceless: Art, Artists, and Economics*, New York: Basic Books.

—— (1989b) "Rent Seeking in Arts Policy," *Public Choice* 60, February: 113–21.

—— (1991a) "A Public Choice View of the French Revolution," *Économies et sociétés*, série Oeconomia, Histoire de la pensée économique – P.E. no. 13, July–October: 641–56.

—— (1991b) "The Artist as Entrepreneur: Or the Cuckoo Unhedged," *Bostonia* May/June: 23–39.

—— (1992) "Cantillon Reconsidered," in S. Todd Lowry (ed.) *Perspectives on the Administrative Tradition: From Antiquity to the Twentieth Century*, Aldershot: Edward Elgar, 64–95.

—— (1993) "An Appreciation of Mercantilism," in Lars Magnusson (ed.) *Mercantilist Economics*, Norwell, MA: Kluwer, 59–85.

—— (1996) "A Colloquy about Art Museums: Economics Engages Museology," in V. A. Ginsburgh and Pierre Michel Menger (eds) *Economics of the Arts: Selected Essays*, Amsterdam: Elsevier, 221–54.

Hollander, Samuel (1979) *The Economics of David Ricardo*, Toronto: University of Toronto Press.

—— (1985) *The Economics of John Stuart Mill*, 2 vols, Toronto: University of Toronto Press.

—— (1997) *The Economics of Thomas Robert Malthus*, Toronto: University of Toronto Press.

McChesney, Fred S. (1997) *Money for Nothing: Politicians, Rent Extraction, and Political Extortion*, Cambridge, MA: Harvard University Press.

Mueller, Dennis C. (1989) *Public Choice II: A Revised Edition of Public Choice*, Cambridge: Cambridge University Press.

Musgrave, R. A. (1992) "Schumpeter's Crisis of the Tax State: An Essay in Fiscal Sociology," *Journal of Evolutionary Economics* 2, August: 89–113.

Peltzman, Sam (1989) "The Economic Theory of Regulation After a Decade of Deregulation," *Brookings Papers on Economic Activity: Microeconomics*, Washington, DC: Brookings Institution, 1–41. Reprinted in *idem, Political Participation and Government Regulation*, Washington, DC: Brookings Institution, 286–323.

Robbins, Lionel (1952) *The Theory of Economic Policy*, London: Macmillan.

—— (1968) *The Theory of Economic Development in the History of Economic Thought; being the Chichele lectures for 1966*, New York: St Martin's Press.

Samuels, Warren J. (1966) *The Classical Theory of Economic Policy*, New York: World Publishing.

Schumpeter, Joseph (1942) *Capitalism, Socialism, and Democracy*, New York: Harper Torchbooks.

Senior, Nassau ([1837] 1966) *Two Letters on the Factory Acts*; reprinted in *idem, Selected Writings on Economics*, New York: Augustus M. Kelley.

Stigler, George J. ([1965] 1975) "The Economist and the State," *American Economic Review* 55, March; reprinted in *idem, The Citizen and the State: Essays on Regulation*, Chicago: University of Chicago Press, 38–57.

—— (1971) "The Theory of Economic Regulation," *Bell Journal of Economics and Management Studies* 2, Spring: 3–21.

—— (1975) "The Intellectual and His Society," in R. T. Selden (ed.) *Capitalism and Freedom: Problems and Prospects*, Charlottesville, VA: University of Virginia Press, 311–21.

—— (1982) *The Economist as Preacher and Other Essays*, Chicago: University of Chicago Press.

—— (1988) *Memoirs of an Unregulated Economist*, New York: Basic Books.

Tullock, Gordon (1993) *Rent Seeking*, Aldershot: Edward Elgar.

Viner, Jacob ([1937] 1964) *Studies in the Theory of International Trade*, London: George Allen & Unwin.

—— (1991) *Essays on the Intellectual History of Economics*, ed. D. A. Irwin, Princeton, NJ: Princeton University Press.

West, E. G. ([1964] 1971) "Private versus Public Education, A Classical Economic Dispute," *Journal of Political Economy* 72: October, in A. W. Coats (ed.) *The Classical Economists and Economic Policy*, London: Methuen, 123–43.

# 7 F. A. Hayek as an intellectual historian of economics

*Peter J. Boettke**

## Introduction

F. A. Hayek (1899–1992) is known primarily as an economic theorist and classical liberal political economist. A few scholars have delved deeply into the connection between Hayek's analytical contributions to economics and his visionary political economy of liberalism, but most prefer to divide Hayek's career into two distinct stages: an early stage as an economist primarily concerned with monetary theory and business fluctuations, and a later stage as a social theorist concerned with the critique of socialism and the advocacy of classical liberalism. It is not my purpose to counter this argument in this chapter with an argument for unity in the corpus of Hayek's work.[1] Instead, what I want to emphasize is not so much his analytical unity (which I do believe is largely present), but an *attitudinal* unity with regard to the way one makes an argument in politics, philosophy, and economics. Throughout his career, Hayek possessed a profound respect for the intellectual history of the various disciplines within which he chose to write. He read far into the past of the discipline in order to place contemporary disputes in context and to borrow from older ideas in order to make innovative contributions. For Hayek, saying something old often represented saying something extremely fresh and new. Hayek was part of a generation of economists who believed that knowledge of the history of the discipline was not simply an antiquarian interest, but a vital component of the education and training of any economist.[2]

We do know that Hayek did have a passion for collecting antiquarian books – a passion he shared with Laski and Keynes.[3] But Hayek did not just like old ideas for their own sake. He sought to always put his arguments within a broader and deeper intellectual tradition. History of economic thought was, to Hayek, a tool for contemporary theory construction. He deployed a considerable knowledge of the evolution of economics to place his own, and others, arguments within a context. This situating of argument within the history of the discipline was for Hayek the way in which we could see patterns of thought and get at the underlying issues under review. In social life, the same fundamental disputes emerged again and again. I will argue that Hayek was an *opportunistic* reader of the history of economic thought. Pure *accuracy* of his reading was not his primary concern. Rather, Hayek's main concern was the purpose to which his particular reading could be put in making his own argument. In making this argument I will rely on Hayek's discussion of three central areas to his intellectual enterprise: monetary theory and business fluctuations; equilibrium and the price system; and the critique of rationalist constructivism. Before proceeding to examine Hayek's particular case, however, I want to describe what I mean by an opportunistic reading in the history of ideas.

## Readings in the history of thought

All readings, as the deconstructionists fondly point out, are selective readings. It is in this sense that we can agree with the motto that "All readings are misreadings." Without going into a broad discussion of literary criticism or the epistemological quagmire that is involved, I would object to the implication that this motto implies that all readings are equal. Some readings are better than alternatives and arguments can be intersubjectively tested on this issue. Relativism is not the only alternative to the claim of absolute objectivity.

One way to view the claim that all readings are necessarily selective readings is as a more controversial way of stating the basic methodological critique of historicism that theory-less interpretation of historical phenomena is epistemologically impossible. The writing of history necessarily entails selective reading of the facts. The world is abuzz with data and the interpreter must arrange the facts in some order of importance. That order will depend, to a large extent, on the perspective of the individual doing the arranging and the purpose toward which the tale will be put. That history is always subject to reinterpretation and refinement is an accepted part of the historian's craft. There may be works which are accepted as temporarily definitive treatments, but precisely because there is not a one-to-one correspondence between an event and our rendering of the event there can never be *the* definitive treatment. Works of interpretation are always subject to revision on the basis of the acquisition of new knowledge (either of a theoretical or empirical nature).

The Austrian economists, the tradition of economic scholarship that Hayek was educated in and contributed to, contended that readings of history could be adjudicated on the basis of sound economic theory. Historical interpretations which were guided by ill-conceived or implicit economic theories could be demonstrated to be faulty on the basis of economic theory. The logic of a theoretical argument could be critically assessed by others, independent of the perspective of either its creator or its reader. This was the tactic that the Austrians followed to avoid the trap of relativism that seems to follow from the admission that the facts of the social sciences are what people think and believe them to be (see Hayek 1948: 57–76). How successful that tactic was (is) will not be discussed in this chapter; all I seek to establish is that the Austrian tradition was well aware of the omnipresence of selective reading in history and the social sciences.

What is true of the history of events and physical phenomena is also true for the history of ideas – all readings of an author entail a selective reading. The idea of pure objective accuracy holds sway for particular issues – Marx did write *The Economic and Philosophical Manuscripts of 1844*, Mises did put forth his argument against socialism in 1920, Keynes did argue that aggregate demand failure was responsible for unemployment equilibrium levels of output in 1936, etc. The model of pure objective accuracy in readings, however, does not hold sway once we move from the realm of the trivial to the realm of determining *meaning* and *relevance*. History of economic thought that demands our attention does not just remain at the level of the trivial, but instead seeks to get at the *meaning* of an author and the *relevance* of that author's contribution. Knowing who and when somebody wrote something, what its title and central argument is, are important, but not the most essential elements to our understanding of the worldly philosophy. Accuracy may be a necessary condition, but it is not sufficient for making a contribution to the literature – at least this is the claim that opportunistic readers of texts make.

In the history of economic thought there are various types of readings that can be offered and they can be divided along the following lines – accuracy and opportunistic, Whig and contra-Whig. The matrix of history of economic thought readings Table 1 summarizes the positions.

|  | *Accurate* | *Opportunistic* |
|---|---|---|
| Whig | Doctrinal history *Dogmengeschichtliche* | Rational reconstruction |
| Contra-Whig | Lost problems *hagiography* | Contemporary theory construction |

I define the terms as follows: (1) Whig – history as written by those perceived to have been the intellectual victors of key debates; (2) Contra-Whig – history as written by those perceived to have been the intellectual losers of those key debates; (3) Accurate – primary concern is the intent of the author; and (4) Opportunistic – primary concern is the intent of the reader. Of course, these readings rarely appear in pure form. In order for an opportunistic reading to retain scholarly credibility, for example, it must meet some minimum standard of accuracy whether it is Whig or contra-Whig in spirit. For my purpose, however, all that matters is the claim that all four cells in the matrix represent legitimate contributions to the scholarly literature in the history of economic thought.[4]

Hayek's own readings of the history of economic thought were primarily of the opportunistic variety, but moved between Whig and contra-Whig as the fate of his own Austrian tradition wavered in the context of twentieth-century economic thought.[5] In his early contributions to economics, Hayek wrote from the vantage point of the victorious marginalist revolution in which the Austrian economists were recognized as leading contributors. During the middle of his career, as he lost both the debate with Keynes and the debate with Lange and Lerner, his writings began to take on a more contra-Whig spirit. Wisdom of the past was lost on the current generation, and we had to go back in order to go forward. This becomes most obvious in his later stage when his concern is mainly the intellectual error of two centuries which had manifested itself in the *pretense of knowledge* and *fatal conceit* of the twentieth century. Hayek was not primarily an intellectual historian as that term is understood and practiced by great exemplars, such as Quentin Skinner. Rather, he used intellectual history primarily for his present theoretical purpose. To Hayek, doing intellectual history was one way in which one did contemporary theorizing. When written from the point of view of the victor, it was simply to show that seeds of the argument existed in the earlier great economists and that the current developments were the logical outcome of a grand tradition. When written from the point of view of the vanquished, it was to show that there were serious discontinuities in the development of thought and that knowledge once possessed had been lost. We had traveled down intellectual dead-ends, and that to right the situation required an alternative set of theoretical constructions and methodological precepts. In both cases, Hayek's intent was to engage today by means of yesterday. His reading of Mandeville, Smith, Hume, Wicksell, or Menger was largely a function of what purpose he hoped to deploy them for in his intellectual battles with his contemporaries. He invoked his knowledge of nineteenth-century British monetary economics in battles with Keynes, his knowledge of Continental thought as a critique of British proposals for socialism, and his knowledge of the Scottish Enlightenment, in contrast to the French Enlightenment, to make his case for classical liberalism in the mid to late twentieth century.

Purists in intellectual history will have a problem with my argument for opportunism. It is to Hayek's credit that his exercises in pure intellectual history of economics and political theory were generally well received by his peers. But an accuracy-based intellectual history whose sole purpose is to establish either the intent of the author, or the lost contributions of some ancient intellectual hero, will be subject to the charge that while it may be an interesting hobby, it does not possess a legitimate claim to the education of young economists. Just like it might be nice if aspiring scholars learned Latin, or were knowledgeable of European history, given the technical demands of modern economics training the opportunity cost of learning the history of thought is simply too high. This was precisely the argument offered during the debates at New York University when the history of thought requirement was finally abolished in the Ph.D. program. NYU was one of the last major research departments to cling to a history of thought requirement into the 1990s. The argument certainly did not originate with this debate at NYU, but had been used for at least a generation to eliminate the field from the core of Ph.D. education in economics. The argument has a long history, and probably originated with Frank Knight and his then student George Stigler. Knight argued that all one could learn from the study of the history of thought were the past errors that had been made by earlier thinkers. The discovery of error was not considered a waste of time to Knight, however. In Stigler's hands, though, the argument took on a different edge. He argued that all truly important contributions of the past were incorporated in the present. Whatever was not already incorporated could be rightfully ignored. This argument was consistent with Stigler's basic presumption toward efficiency in "marketplace competition" – in this instance the efficiency of the market for ideas. There simply were no intellectual profits to be had by reading old authors – whatever profit opportunity might have existed had already been exploited. Stigler's argument, like all Whig arguments, in the end reduces intellectual history to an interesting pastime for some, but certainly not a worthy vocation for an aspiring economist.

It seems natural that Stigler would stress the efficiency in the intellectual marketplace and thus invoke the "survivorship principle" in Whig fashion. It is less clear why Paul Samuelson, a major innovator in the theory of market failure, would be so sanguine about the efficient evolution of economic thought. Just like Stigler, Samuelson is a prime defender of the Whig perspective. Anything that was important in the past writers can be found in the current body of mainstream thought. There are no lost gems – no $20 bills lying on the sidewalk of intellectual life. In fact, Samuelson (it could be legitimately interpreted) actually went so far as to postulate that basically anything worth discussing in economics can be found in *his* body of work.

Kenneth Boulding (1971) countered Samuelson brilliantly in his essay "After Samuelson, Who Needs Smith?" Boulding, in classic contra-Whig fashion, argued that we all need Smith because Smith is part of our "extended present." There are arguments and insights in Smith which remain unincorporated in our contemporary theory that once incorporated will improve our understanding of matters. The "market" for ideas is not perfectly efficient – mistakes are made, intellectual resources are wasted, and as a consequence there is indeed intellectual gems laying unexploited waiting for someone to grasp.

This grasping goes on all the time. One way in which contemporary model-building theoreticians work is to read work in other disciplines opportunistically. Paul Krugman (1995), for example, borrows liberally from work in demographics and geography to build models addressing issues in trade and development. When Kenneth Boulding was a young technical wizard of economics, and even later as a grand master of his craft, his models were borrowed from biology and ecology to discuss the evolutionary dynamics of a capital-using economy.[6] The history of economics is filled with examples of theory construction being aided by the opportunistic deployment of metaphors worked out first in other disciplines. Of course, as Philip Mirowski (1989) has pointed out, the central metaphors of modern neoclassical economics were borrowed from physics.

Hayek's use of intellectual history opportunistically followed from both the idea that all that is important in the past is not necessarily contained in the present, and the idea that mining the past might offer concepts which point the way to more productive theory construction today. In his intellectual history work, Hayek is both a rational reconstructivist of older theories to fit in with contemporary needs, and a borrower of older ideas to build new ones. He finds dead-ends in current trends of thought, forces us to reconsider the earlier moment of choice, and then imagines the path that could have been followed instead.[7] That path, to Hayek, is always more promising than the one that was chosen. During his Whig phase, he did this for the future – the path being chosen was identified *ex ante* as bankrupt, for example in his "Trend of Economic Thinking" paper, where he argued that current trends were mistakenly influenced by the vanquished of the German historical school. During his contra-Whig phase, the argument takes on the opposite slant – the path that was chosen has revealed itself *ex post* to have been mistaken, for example the horrors of Soviet communism and German fascism as a consequence of being seduced by the rationalist doctrine of the French Enlightenment rather than the evolutionary rationalism of the Scottish Enlightenment. In the end, salvation lay in choosing the path that Hayek identifies as the intellectually correct one. This is a judgment of great intellectual hubris, the more so as his position deviated farther and farther from the intellectual mainstream. For a man who took as his motto Hume's – to use reason to whittle down the claims of reason – such hubris was uncomfortable. Better to bring along a set of eminent writers to aid your cause.[8] That was Hayek's rhetorical strategy – independent of the merit of any of his particular readings of the history of economic thought (though it does appear that more often than not his reading is accurate enough in order to be effectively opportunistic).

## Hayek's readings of the history of economic thought

Hayek's main contributions to economics and social theory can be found in his analysis of: (1) monetary theory and the trade cycle; (2) the informational role of prices and equilibrium; and (3) the critique of rational constructivism and the defense of the liberal political order. As I have asserted in this chapter, Hayek's career can be divided into these three stages of emphasis. Of course, the lines blur between these stages because, as early as his inaugural address at the London School of Economics (LSE), Hayek was warning of rational constructivism, and as late as the late 1960s he wrote articles about Keynesian economics, unemployment, and the business cycle. But it is probably fairly uncontroversial to assert that these stages are evident in Hayek's work, with the 1920s and 1930s representing his primary work in monetary and business cycle theory, the 1930s and 1940s representing his main contributions to price theory and the market system, and the 1950s and beyond reflecting his preoccupation with the problems of constructivism and social theory. What is most significant for my purpose, however, is not to delineate these periods, but to demonstrate that in each period there is a significant similarity in attitude toward the way one constructs an argument and the manner in which the history of ideas is to be deployed in the task at hand. As stated above, there is an attitudinal unity in Hayek that can be established quite separately from whether or not there is an analytical unity in his work.

The common theme in Hayek is to first situate his own contribution within the broad intellectual context within which this issue has been discussed.[9] In his early monetary theory and the trade cycle period, this is reflected first in his argument that only a monetary explanation can provide an economic theory of economic fluctuations for Say's law that would ensure the automatic adjustment of supply and demand in a natural economy. What follows is a discussion of how various thinkers throughout the history of the discipline – from Cantillon and Hume to more contemporary figures – have sought to analyze the influence of changes in the supply of money upon prices within an economic system. This is followed by a discussion of how production plans of some are coordinated with the consumption demands of others, and how mal-coordination in these plans can emerge from monetary influences (see Hayek 1931; 1933).

Hayek seeks to identify how others have sought to solve the problem and failed, and in the process situates his own contribution to the problem. Discussing the evolution of the way eminent economists have sought to get their hands on an important problem is used as a technique for giving the reader the context for Hayek's contribution. It has been for this reader always a persuasive manner of argumentation, and it can be found in *Prices and Production* (1931), *Monetary Theory and the Trade Cycle* (1933), and *Profits, Interest and Investment* (1939). We are not treated to detailed discussions of other writings, such as those found in Eugen Böhm-Bawerk's *Capital and Interest* (1884), Edwin Cannan's *A History of Theories of Production and Distribution* (1893), or Jacob Viner's *Studies in the Theory of International Trade* (1937). But all of these works share something fundamental with Hayek, the idea that *theorizing in economics proceeded by way of critically examining the evolution of the particular field of study.*[10] It is important to stress, however, that what each of these works saw as important in the history of that evolution depended crucially on the problems their respective author found important in the contemporary situation. In other words, all readings – even the most subtle and well respected – are selective readings, and thus opportunistic in a fundamental sense.

Hayek's notion of plan coordination follows directly from his analysis of a capital-using economy. Production takes place in time and agents must somehow be led to coordinate their activities with others so that resources are invested in projects which satisfy consumer demands. In Hayek's business cycle work, the mal-investment that results from credit expansion manifests itself in a cluster of failed investment projects. This was an example of the negative influence of money on prices within an economy. Crucial to this story, however, is the insight that prices serve as signals which agents within the economy rely on to inform them about how to behave. In retrospect, it seems natural that Hayek would move from his business cycle work to his work on the price system while according the notion of plan coordination a central position.

Hayek defines equilibrium as plan consistency among agents. At the individual level, the notion of equilibrium is non-problematic. Hayek insists, however, that for the interaction of individuals equilibrium can only be reasonably postulated by way of an empirical examination of the way agents *learn* within the economic process. The flip-side of Hayek's argument that the private property market economy provided the institutional backdrop which enabled agents to learn how to coordinate their affairs with others, was that the institutions of socialism would initiate an entirely different process which would not enable agents to coordinate their plans with others through time. In his essays "The Nature and History of the Problem," and "The Present State of the Debate," contained in Hayek's edited volume, *Collectivist Economic Planning* (1935) and reprinted in *Individualism and Economic Order* (1948), the similar pattern of situating his argument within the history of thought in the field can be found again. Each past contribution is presented as it relates to the evolution of an argument which culminates in Mises's critique of socialism.[11] Again, as was asserted above with regard to monetary theory and business cycles, Hayek does not present in detail any argument made by a previous economist for that is not his purpose. Previous contributions are there to aid the story of the logical evolution of the field and to situate Hayek's own contribution – which is filling in the gaps of the existing literature. History of thought is but a tool to be deployed to aid the task of theory construction to address problems that are pressing at the moment.

In the examination of the price system, Hayek argued that previous contributions had tended to assume what in fact was supposed to be demonstrated – namely, how agents obtained the knowledge necessary to coordinate their plans so as to realize the mutual gains from exchange. Hayek's contribution was to switch the analytical focus from looking at market prices as signals about what people have done in the past to viewing market prices as guides for future action. This, he argued, is a consequence of pursuing marginal utility analysis to its logical conclusion. But others had failed to grasp fully the implications of this shift in focus and thus the problem of the *division of knowledge* in society had not been addressed adequately.[12] In perhaps his most well-known essays in price theory, "Economics and Knowledge" and "The Use of Knowledge in Society" (both reprinted in Hayek 1948), the problem of the division of knowledge in society is brought to the forefront of the analysis of the market economy.

This strategy of argumentation is evident even in Hayek's most worked-out critical claim in intellectual history – his attack on the tradition of rational constructivism. In *The Counter-Revolution of Science* (1952), Hayek devotes half of the book to tracing the influence of French rationalism through Comte and on to Hegel and thus Marx. The accuracy of Hayek's reading is not the main point to emphasize for my purpose. All I am suggesting is that this is another case in which Hayek is using the history of ideas for his present purposes of theory construction. The contrast to rational constructivism is Hayek's twin ideas of evolution and spontaneous order.[13] The hubris of scientism is Hayek's great foil, against which his own theory of liberal institutions emerged.

In "Individualism: True and False" (reprinted in Hayek 1948), Hayek lays out the essential argument that would be continually repeated in his critique of scientism. The Cartesian rationalism of the French Enlightenment (e.g., Rousseau) leads inevitably to an argument for collectivism. The more modest claims of English philosophers (e.g., Locke, Hume, and Smith) leads instead to a defense of true individualism. While Tocqueville and Acton developed more successfully the ideas of the Scottish moral philosophers, Burke, and the English Whigs, unfortunately Bentham and the philosophical radicals came under the sway of French rationalism. In an almost ironic twist of intellectual fate, rationalistic individualism is transformed into collectivism.

The reason for the transformation, Hayek attempted to demonstrate, was due to the contrast between design theories of social institutions and spontaneous order theories of social institutions. The social philosophy of the British thinkers of the eighteenth century was the "product of an acute consciousness of the limitations of the individual mind which induces an attitude of humility toward the impersonal and anonymous social processes by which individuals help create things greater than they know" (1948: 8). On the other hand, Cartesian rationalism is born of "an exaggerated belief in the powers of individual reason and of a consequent contempt for anything which has not been consciously designed by it or is not fully intelligible to it" (ibid.).

This theme is reiterated and pursued further in all of Hayek's subsequent work in social philosophy and political economy, such as *The Constitution of Liberty* (1960), *Law, Legislation and Liberty* (1973, 1976, and 1979), and *The Fatal Conceit* (1988). And the style of argument is similar to establish the point – a tour through the history of ideas to show how this false belief in unlimited powers of reason has taken hold of our imaginations to the detriment of the civilization. As I have said, the testing of the veracity of Hayek's claims is not my current purpose, but instead I have sought to demonstrate the use to which Hayek put intellectual history through his scholarly career. Here, as in the other instances, intellectual history is deployed by Hayek as a way of situating his theoretical contribution and a tool of rhetoric in establishing his own argument.

## Conclusion

F. A. Hayek revealed throughout his scholarly career a passion for ideas – where they came from and what were the implications of them when pursued consistently and persistently. He read deeply and widely into the history of ideas. His teaching duties over the years reflect his concern with the history of ideas as well, particularly at the Committee on Social Thought at the University of Chicago, but also at the LSE.

But Hayek rarely did intellectual history for its own sake. Instead, he was part of a generation of scholars in economics and political economy who viewed intellectual history as a way of doing contemporary theory. In this manner, his work often represented a style of theorizing which is only evident in our modern intellectual culture by those doing political theory (e.g., Skinner) and sociological theory (e.g., Giddens). Modern economists do not normally engage in a tour of ancient economic thought (defined as anything beyond ten years old) in order to situate their contribution and trace out the evolution of ideas in the discipline.

In judging Hayek as an intellectual historian, I have decided to focus on the use to which he put the history of ideas in his own work. It is my contention that Hayek is best appreciated as an *opportunistic reader* of the history of political, philosophical, and economic thought, and one who waffles between a Whig and contra-Whig perspective in his readings. The history of ideas represents a live body of thought to Hayek, or as Boulding put it, part of our extended present which possesses intellectual evolutionary potential. We have much to learn from Mandeville, Hume, and Smith, precisely because their work still speaks to us today. When he wanted to, Hayek made significant contributions to pure intellectual history – for example, his work on Thornton's monetary theory, or his work on Mill and Taylor. But of the pieces I have counted from Hayek's bibliography that could be characterized as work in intellectual history, the majority are best described as contributions to contemporary theory which make liberal use of intellectual history to construct the story Hayek wanted to tell about monetary theory and the trade cycle, the nature of the price system and the inability of socialism to replicate its workings, and the principles of the liberal order. My intent, however, was not to criticize Hayek for this, but instead to applaud him. By treating ideas as alive and mining the writings of older thinkers for insights useful for today, Hayek paid the ultimate intellectual respect to his predecessors and demonstrated through his writings that political economy does indeed have a useful past.

## Notes

\*   An earlier version of this essay was presented at the History of Economic Society Meetings. In revising it I have benefited greatly from the comments of Steve Horwitz, Steve Medema, Christine Polek, Andrew Rutten, Warren Samuels, and Edward Weick. The usual caveat applies.
1   Readers interested in the unity interpretation are referred to Boettke (2000).
2   In his bibliography, which includes 19 books, 14 edited volumes, and some 151 articles, Hayek published 4 books which could be classified as works in the history of thought, edited 9 volumes in the field, and published 29 articles. Hayek was particularly fond of the biographical essay: 17 of his 29 articles are biographical in nature. See the bibliography of Hayek's writings contained in Boettke (2000). Hayek's interest in the history of thought is evident from the beginning of his career: for example, Hayek (1927) is an introduction to Gossen's work which Hayek contends anticipated the marginal utility revolution. Hayek (1933–36) introduced and edited The Collected Works of Carl Menger. He had also planned to write an intellectual biography on his cousin Wittgenstein, but this endeavor was ceased because of difficulties in getting access to Wittgenstein's papers at that time. In addition, Hayek's teaching career included a lengthy period where he taught a course on the intellectual history of the liberal tradition at the University of Chicago, and a look at his syllabi from his theory courses at the LSE in the 1930s demonstrates how he attempted to integrate the evolution of concepts into an examination of contemporary theory. On Hayek's teaching at the LSE see McCormick (1992: 44ff.).
3   Hayek informs us that during the war years, Keynes regularly sent Hayek his copy of the Journal of the History of Ideas when he discovered their mutual interest in the history of ideas (Hayek 1994: 91).
4   In recent years there has been a very significant movement among historians of economic thought to treat their subject as a subset of the discipline of the history of science. However impressive I find this work, it is my position that history of

economic thought as a field should not exclusively follow this path. As historians of thought are intellectual historians this does seem to be the most productive direction, but knowledge of the history of one's discipline can also be used in contemporary theory construction. The subfield within economics should encourage both intellectual movements, which entails retaining a foothold in the departments of economics.

5  Hayek's essays in economic biography were focused more on accurate reading. His work on Henry Thornton (Hayek 1939) and Mill's relationship with Harriet Taylor (Hayek 1951), for example, is often considered definitive. But his work on the British versus French Enlightenment and rational constructivism and the defense of liberalism are viewed by some with suspicion as pure contributions to intellectual history.

6  See, for example, Boulding (1981). For an overview of Boulding's contributions to economic thought see Boettke and Prychitko (1996).

7  For an application of this style of contemporary history of thought to the case of Hayek himself, see Boettke (1997, 1998a).

8  McCloskey (1985), in discussing the rhetorical techniques deployed in even the most technical of economic writings, points out how argument for authority is often invoked to advance the author's cause (see e.g. 70–2).

9  McCormick (1992: 45–8) reprints Hayek's syllabi from his "Theory of Value," "Principles of Currency," and "Industrial Fluctuations" classes at the LSE from 1931, 1934, and 1937. Hayek's syllabus for the "Theory of Value" lists Menger, Böhm-Bawerk, Pareto, Wieser, Wicksteed, Davenport, and Knight as required in addition to more contemporary readings. Hayek's syllabus for "Principles of Currency" is even more peppered with history of thought references, including Hume and Ricardo. The syllabus for "Industrial Fluctuations" begins with Tougan-Baranowski's work.

10  I will not develop the argument here, but I believe there are direct parallels between the way Hayek viewed the intellectual development of economic thought and the development of legal thought. The theorist in economics is to be constrained to a considerable extent by precedent and not to be disconnected from previous contributions in the same way that the judge is constrained by the precedent of the common law. Law is not made anew in whole, but instead is the outcome of a slow and cumulative process of discovery through application to particular cases.

11  On the Mises–Hayek critique of socialism see Boettke (1998b).

12  Except perhaps Mises, whose writings, Hayek argued, "contain beyond doubt the most complete and successful exposition of what from then onward became the central problem" which socialist writers had to address in seeking to replace the market process. Hayek argued that Mises had offered a

> detailed demonstration that an economic use of the available resources was only possible if this pricing was applied not only to the final product but also to all intermediate products and factors of production and that no other process was conceivable which would in the same way take account of all the relevant facts as did the pricing process of the competitive market.

> (1948: 143)

13  Hayek informs us that under the influence of Mises, he became a serious student of Bentham's papers at University College. In fact, Hayek became involved with the organization of Bentham's papers before the war, but the project broke down during the war and was not resumed until Hayek had left London. During his study, Hayek claims to have discovered that Bentham was more influenced by the French rationalists as opposed to the Scottish rationalists. See Hayek (1994: 140).

# Bibliography

Boettke, Peter J. (1997) "Where Did Economics Go Wrong? Modern Economics as a Flight from Reality," *Critical Review* 11, 1: 11–64.

—— (1998a) "Formalism and Contemporary Economics: A Reply to Hausman, Heilbroner, and Mayer," *Critical Review* 12, 1–2: 173–86.

—— (1998b) "Economic Calculation: The Austrian Contribution to Political Economy," *Advances in Austrian Economics* 5: 131–58.

—— (ed.) (2000) *The Intellectual Legacy of F. A. Hayek: Politics, Philosophy and Economics*, 3 vols, Aldershot: Edward Elgar.

Boettke, Peter J. and Prychitko, David (1996) "Mr. Boulding and the Austrians: An Essay on Boulding's Contribution to Subjectivist Economics," in L. Moss (ed.) *Joseph Schumpeter: Historian of Economics*, New York: Routledge, 250–9.

Böhm-Bawerk, Eugen (1884) *Capital and Interest*, 3 vols, South Holland, IL: Libertarian Press.

Boulding, Kenneth (1971) "After Samuelson, Who Needs Smith?" *History of Political Economy* 3, 2: 225–37.

—— (1981) *Evolutionary Economics*, New York: Russell Sage.

Cannan, Edwin ([1893] 1967) *A History of the Theories of Production and Distribution*, New York: Augustus M. Kelley.

Hayek, F. A. ([1927] 1937) "Introduction," in Hermann Heinrich Gossen, *Entwicklung der Gesetze des Menschlichen Verkehrs und der daraus fliessenden Regeln für menschliches Handeln* (1854), Berlin: Prager.

—— ([1931] 1967) *Prices and Production*, New York: Augustus M. Kelley.

—— ([1933] 1966) *Monetary Theory and the Trade Cycle*, New York: Augustus M. Kelley.

—— (1933–36) "Introduction," in *Collected Works of Carl Menger*, 4 vols, London: London School of Economics.

—— (ed.) ([1935] 1975) *Collectivist Economic Planning*, New York: Augustus M. Kelley.

—— (1939) "Introduction," in Henry Thornton, *An Enquiry into the Nature and Effects of Paper Credit for Great Britain* (1802), London: Allen and Unwin.

—— ([1939] 1975) *Profits, Interest and Investment*, New York: Augustus M. Kelley.

—— (1948) *Individualism and Economic Order*, Chicago: University of Chicago Press.

—— (1951) *John Stuart Mill and Harriet Taylor: Their Friendship and Subsequent Marriage*, New York: Augustus M. Kelley.

—— ([1952] 1979) *The Counter-Revolution of Science*, Indianapolis: Liberty Fund.

—— (1960) *The Constitution of Liberty*, Chicago: University of Chicago Press.

—— (1973) *Law, Legislation and Liberty*, Vol. 1, Chicago: University of Chicago Press.

—— (1976) *Law, Legislation and Liberty*, Vol. 2, Chicago: University of Chicago Press.

—— (1979) *Law, Legislation and Liberty*, Vol. 3, Chicago: University of Chicago Press.

—— (1988) *The Fatal Conceit*, Chicago: University of Chicago Press.

—— (1994) *Hayek on Hayek*, Chicago: University of Chicago Press.

Krugman, Paul (1995) *Development, Geography and Economic Theory*, Cambridge, MA: MIT Press.

McCloskey, D. N. (1985) *The Rhetoric of Economics*, Madison: University of Wisconsin Press.

McCormick, Brian (1992) *Hayek and the Keynesian Avalanche*, New York: St Martin's Press.

Mirowski, Philip (1989) *More Heat Than Light: Economics as Social Physics, Physics as Nature's Economy*, New York: Cambridge University Press.

Viner, Jacob (1937) *Studies in the Theory of International Trade*, New York: Augustus M. Kelley.

# 8 From Adam Smith to John Stuart Mill

## Samuel Hollander and the classical economists

*Jeffrey T. Young**

No historian of economic thought has raised as much controversy and been the topic of as much debate, even acrimonious debate, as has Samuel Hollander. Reactions to the various installments of his series on the classical economists have ranged from Lionel Robbins's high praise of the Smith and Ricardo books as an "answer to a prayer" to Mark Blaug's condemnation of the book on Mill as "a very bad book indeed" (Robbins 1998: 10; Blaug 1986). Assessing such a body of work is a daunting task indeed.

The purpose of this chapter is to lay out the main lines of Hollander's interpretation of the great classical economists. While recognizing the far-reaching nature of his work, our primary concern will be with the so-called continuity thesis along with some of the key distinctive features of Hollander's interpretation of each of the individuals involved. The continuity thesis, in brief, argues that the core of Ricardian economics, including the other classicals and Marx, is a general equilibrium model which integrates value and distribution theory along the lines of allocative mechanisms in a market economy. Models which assert a fixed subsistence wage and then view distribution as determined prior to pricing at best have grown out of a preoccupation with part of Ricardo, but cannot be said to capture the general framework of analysis (Young 1998). We shall pursue this general line of argumentation through Hollander's books on Smith, Ricardo, Malthus, and Mill. There is still to come a proposed book on Marx, but from what Hollander has already published on him, we can conclude that Marx will also be fitted into this general pattern of working with a general equilibrium model in which the rate of wages, surplus value, and profits are endogenous to the system (Hollander 1981; 1984; 1987). The continuity thesis, then, suggests that the classical economists lie in a direct line of descent to the neoclassicals, particularly Marshall and Walras, in that they share essentially the same underlying paradigm of pricing, distribution, and allocation theory.

The chapter is divided into four parts followed by a brief conclusion. Each part is devoted to one of the four currently published volumes in Hollander's proposed series on the classical economists. In all parts I will focus on particular aspects of each work which contribute to the continuity thesis, for which Hollander is best known. I propose to examine Hollander's position and the nature of at least some of the key pieces of evidence for it in the original texts. I will also consider at least some of the points of controversy in the sometimes bitter debates which followed the publication of the volume on David Ricardo, but my main purpose will be to present Hollander's position objectively. In my review of Hollander's *Classical Economics* (hereinafter CE) I observed that in the debates surrounding his work I thought that Hollander had the better of his critics (Young 1991: 167). I reaffirm this conclusion here. Hollander's work on the classical economists is so thoroughly researched and so internally consistent that it must be taken extremely seriously. With all due respect to other very able, even brilliant, historians of economics, no other body of work on the classical economists is based on the depth and meticulousness of scholarship as that to be reviewed here.

## Adam Smith

With the publication in 1973 of *The Economics of Adam Smith* (hereinafter *EAS*), Hollander announced his intention to produce a series of studies of the great classical economists. This work is the shortest and least controversial of the series to date. While it was generally warmly received at the time, it has since been overshadowed by the sometimes bitter controversies which erupted following the subsequent installments. Even Mark Blaug, one of Hollander's severest future critics, recognized *EAS* as "a major contribution to Smithian scholarship" (1973: 474). Better than a quarter of a century later, *EAS* endures as an outstanding, if not the best ever, book on Smith's pure economics. It convincingly overturns Schumpeter's harsh judgment of Smith's theoretical performance (1954: 184), while laying to rest numerous erroneous positions found in the secondary literature, for example Smith's alleged failure to notice the Industrial Revolution.

There are two central themes which inform *EAS*. First, at the core of the *Wealth of Nations* (*WN*) is a model of competitive resource allocation which shows the operation of the price system in creating the price, wage, rent, and profit structure in the economy. This is a general equilibrium framework which is thoroughly integrated into a dynamic model of economic development which focuses on the growth-enhancing properties of a system which allows capital to freely seek its most profitable investment. Second, Smith's analytical structure cannot be fully determined apart from his applications of it. The brilliance of his achievement as well as the interpretation of some of the "rough edges" of his purely theoretical statements come out most fully in his applications.

Representative of these themes, consider Hollander's treatment of the alleged inconsistency in Smith's Book I and Book II analysis of investment priorities. Some commentators have noticed that Smith's discussion of investment priorities in Book II is "in sharp conflict" with the market allocation processes of Book I (*EAS*: 277). In particular, the latter exposition relies on unimpeded market forces to allocate capital to its highest valued uses via the mechanism of profit rate equalization. As is well known, in Book II Smith then uses the criterion of the quantity of productive labor employed to determine the socially optimal allocation of capital between agriculture, manufacturing, and trade. This would imply a divergence between private and social profitability opening the way for government to redirect market allocations in order to increase the level of employment. Smith, of course, never made this argument, but it does seem to flow as a matter of logic from his Book II hierarchy of investment priorities.

Hollander argues that Smith's true position can be discerned by looking at his applications of the principle. Here we find the hierarchy of investments, which in the natural progress of opulence governs the process of economic development, couched in terms of the principles of resource allocation based on factor price equalization operating in the context of changing relative scarcity. The dynamic model of development is built on the model of static resource allocation and is fully consistent with it. The natural advantage of agriculture, for example, depends on the relative abundance of land compared to labor, thus generating a relatively high profit rate in agriculture (*EAS*: 280ff.). The free play of self-interest is sufficient to direct the first investments of capital into agriculture, and it is only when land becomes scarcer relative to labor that the first investments in manufacturing will come forth. This process generates Smith's "natural balance of industry" which plays a leading role in his critique of mercantilism (*WN* IV. vii. c.43).

This reconciliation between Smith's two positions is only partial, but it is instructive that when the two come into direct conflict, Smith selects against the quantity of productive labor measure of value added:

> Though the same capital never will maintain the same quantity of productive labour in a distant as in a near employment, yet a distant employment may be as necessary for the welfare of the society as a near one. ... It is thus that the private interests and passions of individuals naturally dispose them to turn their stock towards the employments which in ordinary cases are most advantageous to the society. But if from this natural preference they should turn too much of it towards those employments, the fall of profit in them and the rise of it in all others immediately dispose them to alter this faulty distribution. Without any intervention of law, therefore, the private interests and passions of men naturally lead them to divide and distribute the stock of every society, among all the different employments carried on in it, as nearly as possible in the proportion which is most agreeable to the interest of the whole society.
>
> (*WN* IV. vii. c.87–8)

The same principle guides the growth of capital in the dynamic setting. Under conditions of free trade there would be a natural progression whereby a "landed nation" would acquire a fully diversified economy of farmers, manufacturers, and merchants.

The continual increase of the surplus produce of their land, would, in due time, create a greater capital than what could be employed with the ordinary rate of profit in the improvement and cultivation of the land; and the surplus part of it would naturally turn itself to the employment of artificers and manufacturers at home.

[The] continual increase both of the rude and manufactured produce of those landed nations would in due time create a greater capital than could, with the ordinary rate of profit, be employed either in agriculture or in manufactures. The surplus of this capital would naturally turn itself to foreign trade, and be employed in exporting, to foreign countries, such parts of the rude and manufactured produce of its own country, as exceeded the demand of the home market.

(WN IV. ix. 22–3)

The principles of market allocation of resources which operate through the structure of alternative opportunities govern the static and dynamic pattern of capital accumulation and allocation. This structure is in turn governed by the changing patterns of relative scarcity. The hierarchy of investment productivity is accounted for in the context of this changing pattern of relative scarcity with the initial superiority of agriculture rooted in the relative abundance of land in the early stages of economic development. Some inconsistency with the employment criterion remains, particularly with respect to the allocation of capital to trade (EAS: 298–9), but Smith's model is clear and consistent within the context of his applications of it. Hollander concludes:

It is, in brief, not merely the elaboration of the mechanisms of resource allocation which requires attention, but also the particular uses to which the analysis was put, and it is in the course of Smith's treatment of the historical sequence of investment priorities according to the principle of profit-rate equalization, that a fundamental equilibrating mechanism is utilized, namely resource allocation governed by the differential pattern of factor endowments between economies. Despite the overwhelming significance of the mechanism, the reader of the Wealth of Nations will find no hint thereof in the First Book. It is rather in the 'applied' chapters, dealing with contemporary restraints on importation and with the colonial trade, that full and skillful use is made of the mechanism, casting new light upon Smith's contribution to both theoretical and applied economics.

(EAS: 307)

I would suggest that the fundamental problem is that Smith lacks the concept of the marginal product. He instinctively realizes that under conditions of declining marginal productivity in each sector, eventually it will be profitable to invest in those sectors which are lower down in the list of priorities giving a mature, commercial society a full complement of sectors. His explicit model runs in terms of declining profitability in each sector with each increment of investment yielding higher returns in agriculture than in manufacturing and trade. However, within each sector incremental investments yield declining rates of profit causing the lower productivity sectors gradually to become profitable compared to the higher productivity investments at the margin. The lack of the concept of marginal productivity and its associated equimarginal principle of allocation prevents Smith from explicitly stating the model. The result is that his clear understanding of the principle emerges only in the applications of it, and in those applications the Book II criterion of productive labor is explicitly superseded by profit rate equalization analysis.

If we recall that the principle desideratum of productive labor was its ability to add value, then it would be tempting to suggest that Smith's hierarchy of investments based on the employment of productive labor is not all that far removed from the concept of the marginal value product. Agricultural capital's ability to set in motion a larger quantity of productive labor could then be viewed as implying that the marginal product curve of agricultural capital lies above that of manufacturing and trade. The declining profit rate in each sector could then be viewed as declining marginal productivity, and the equalization of profit rates arises from the equalization of the marginal value product in each use. That Smith had officially to replace the criterion of productive labor in his applications, of course, reminds us that he did not have the modern model in mind.

The fact that he understood the basic principle that optimal allocation entailed equality of returns at the margin without having the model itself reinforces the validity of Hollander's conclusion. It is a legitimate interpretive procedure, indeed a necessary one, to seek understanding of a writer's theory in his applications. This, I contend, is particularly true in the early days of analytical economics. Modern concepts of utility and diminishing returns may have been around, but that is not the same as saying either that they were available to a single mind, or that a single mind would understand their importance and be able to integrate them into a logically consistent, complete body of theoretical statements. Moreover, modern standards of rigor in model development and even in definitions of terms were still in the future. It should not be surprising, then, that early theorists, such as Smith, would reveal a deeper theoretical understanding when they are applying economic theory than they are able to do when they attempt explicitly to articulate a theoretical model. In short, the tacit understanding of economics generally runs ahead of economists' ability to articulate the theory rigorously. Looking to these applications in Smith reveals a very modern model of static resource allocation in a general equilibrium framework which is fully integrated with a dynamic model of capital accumulation.

There is much more in *EAS*, such as its very informative and helpful focus on Smith's awareness of the industrial structure of the day and his sensitivity to technical progress. There is also a treatment of utility and demand theory which sets the record straight against a long line of commentators who see in the paradox of value an abandonment of any attempt to relate utility and demand to price determination (Schumpeter 1954: 188; Hutchison 1988: 363). As in the case examined above, Hollander resorts to Smith's applications to show that he did not ignore the role of demand as has been so often deduced from his purely theoretical chapters. However, viewed against the backdrop of Hollander's later work, the central message of EAS is its presentation of Smith as a modern sort of general equilibrium theorist; a theme which when later applied to Ricardo yielded Hollander's highly controversial continuity thesis.

## David Ricardo

Hollander's most enduring legacy as an historian of economics will undoubtedly be his work on David Ricardo, the centerpiece of which is his Economics of David Ricardo (1979; hereinafter EDR). The substance of his interpretation then formed the backbone of his CE text (1987), and his replies to the critics, which reaffirm and extend his position, appeared as Ricardo – The New View (1995a). A perusal of the reviews of EDR quickly reveals a depth and intensity of controversy that is almost unheard of among historians of economic thought.[1] The reason for this is that Ricardo interpretation, though frequently turning on apparently subtle and complex points, has wider ramifications for our understanding of the whole sweep of the development of economic theory in the ensuing century and a half. Indeed, it even relates to contemporary controversies over value, distribution, and growth theory.

Hollander's interpretation is complex and far reaching, and as Blaug, and others, have recognized, it constitutes "a full-scale frontal attack on the entire body of Ricardian scholarship" (1985: 147). Blaug himself has suggested a ten-point breakdown of EDR while O'Brien has produced thirty-two points, and Hollander himself jokingly opts for thirty-nine (Blaug 1985: 147; O'Brien 1981: 354–5; Hollander 1982: 226). At the core of Hollander's position is the belief that the standard textbook interpretation of Ricardo is simply wrong. This interpretation centers on a model that can be found in various degrees of mathematical sophistication in any number of texts and articles. Luigi Pasinetti's mathematical formulation of the Ricardian system represents perhaps one of the best rational reconstructions of the mainstream view of Ricardo (1960). Prominent features are the so-called "corn-model," diminishing returns in agriculture, and the fixed subsistence wage. In the modern era its roots lie in the "corn-model" interpretation of Ricardo's early theory of profits which Sraffa first proposed in his "Introduction" to the Works and Correspondence of David Ricardo (1951).

The salient feature of this model is that it views the agricultural sector of the economy as one giant farm producing one output, corn, using corn, as both seeds and wage good, as the only input. Given the subsistence wage, the rate of profits is determined at the no-rent margin as the physical ratio of the net corn output to the corn capital used as input. Thus, prices in the rest of the economy must adjust to equalize general profits with the agricultural profit rate since no price adjustment of corn can alter the corn rate of profit. With agricultural land being scarce and with the Malthusian population mechanism in place to keep wages at subsistence, as the economy grows via the accumulation of capital diminishing returns in agriculture will cause a falling rate of profit while rents rise. Unless free trade in corn is introduced the economy is on course toward the inevitable stationary state.

This in brief is the textbook Ricardo. Its defining characteristics are the dependency of profits on the conditions of production in one sector, the subsistence wage, the separation of value and distribution, with distribution occurring prior to pricing, and the assumption that long-run adjustments occur instantly in the labor market, but not elsewhere. From this it is concluded that Ricardo has little in common with the neoclassical economics of Marshall and Walras and their twentieth-century offspring. In particular, Ricardo in no way can be viewed as a supply and demand theorist, treating value and distribution as interdependent problems of valuation. It then follows that modern general equilibrium theory and its concomitant concerns about subjective value, optimal resource allocation, and simultaneous determination are completely foreign to Ricardo's conception of the economic process.

This view comes in two distinct variations, the Sraffian and the traditional (Peach 1993). (Bronfenbrenner (1997: 160) further subdivides the traditionalists into Walrasians and marginalists.) The touchstone of the former is Sraffa's famous conjecture from his "Introduction" to the *Works and Correspondence of David Ricardo* that

> The rational foundation of the principle of the determining role of the profits of agriculture, which is never explicitly stated by Ricardo, is that in agriculture the same commodity, namely corn, forms both the capital (conceived as composed of the subsistence necessary for workers) and the product; so that the determination of profit by the difference between total product and capital advanced, and also the determination of the ratio of this profit to the capital, is done directly between quantities of corn without any question of valuation.
>
> (xxxi)

This argument is, of course, correct as a matter of logic. If there is such a production process in which input and output are the same single commodity, then its rate of profit will be set by a physical ratio independently of the pricing process. Indeed, the pricing process will have to be such that other outputs, measured in value terms, must yield the same profit rate when compared to their inputs, also measured in value terms. This logic is sufficiently compelling to lead Sraffa to the conclusion that this, in fact, is Ricardo's position, notwithstanding its absence in the extant papers, published and unpublished.

The transition to the value theory of the *Principles* reflects the need to express essentially the same idea in a world of multiple commodity production where profit appears as a value quantity, not a physical quantity. Sraffa states:

> It was now labour, instead of corn, that appeared on both sides of the account – in modern terms, both as input and output: as a result, the rate of

profits was ... determined ... by the ratio of the total labour of the country to the labour required to produce the necessaries for that labour.

(xxii)

The transition to the labor theory did not vitiate the original hypothesis, so Ricardo's model still determines profits as the value analog of the physical ratio of surplus less rent to capital.

Essentially on the strength of this "corn-model" interpretation, the Sraffians have reconstructed the history of economic thought. The argument is that there is a "surplus" tradition running throughout the history of economics from Petty and the physiocrats to Marx, Sraffa, and even Keynes. While overly simplified, this approach may perhaps be stated as a view of the economic process as one which generates a social surplus which can then be consumed, taxed, or accumulated as new capital. With wages set at subsistence, property income becomes the residual that is available for accumulation and/or taxation. The striking feature of this approach is that traditional supply and demand analysis and resource allocation issues play no role. Distribution is treated as prior to exchange and rooted in certain institutional features of the system, coupled with the exogenously determined wage.

This stands in stark contrast to the allocative, supply and demand economics of the mainstream which views distribution as a pricing phenomenon simultaneously determined with output prices. Supply and demand economics does not deny the concept of surplus as income in excess of that which is needed to maintain a flow of factor services sufficient to reproduce current aggregate output. However, it does not view surplus as the central concept of economic theory, and, since wage income can have a surplus element, it does not make a significant distinction between property and non-property income. In this camp are J. S. Mill, Marshall, Walras, Samuelson, Arrow, etc., while Adam Smith seems to be oddly in both streams.

Ricardo plays a key role in this telling of the history of our discipline. For if he truly belongs with the Sraffian stream that stream itself becomes significantly more important, since without him it is much easier to dismiss it as the irrelevant musings of a few dissidents, who have not progressed analytically beyond Marx. Thus, among Sraffians Ricardo interpretation is an integral part of the program to overthrow neoclassical value, distribution, and growth theory.

Ironically the traditionalists hold a similar interpretation of Ricardo, except that where the Sraffians find strength they find analytical error. Both are agreed, for example, that Ricardo held a subsistence wage theory and that he separated value and distribution, but for the traditionalists this is a weakness, not a strength. This view goes all the way back to the first neoclassicals. Walras, for example, argued that Ricardo's distribution theory is marred by his inability to recognize that he was dealing with an underdetermined system of simultaneous equations. In essence he was trying to solve for two unknowns with one equation, and, therefore, he ended up believing that profit was a residual after rent and wages were determined respectively by the Malthus/West theory of differential rent and the Malthusian population principle (Walras [1926] 1977: 424–5; see also Schumpeter 1954: 568–9; Knight 1935). On this view Ricardo falls short of such contemporaries as J. B. Say for his failure to see distribution as a problem of valuation, and Ricardian economics is, then, judged a "detour" in the history of economics (Schumpeter 1954: 568). Ricardo is further criticized for failure to develop the subjective value theory, apparently believing that utility had nothing to do with pricing. Sraffa's interpretation, which further distances Ricardo from the neoclassical mainstream, was, thus, generally accepted with the result being that the typical textbook presentation of Ricardo today often entails the corn-model approach along with Sraffian stories of the transition to the value theory of the *Principles*. Although there is some variety in the texts, I believe that most contemporary scholars would generally agree with D. P. O'Brien's assessment of both the central place of the corn model in Ricardo's thought and the central focus of his economics:

> The corn-model is quite clearly the fundamental concern of Ricardo's *Principles*. It is a model designed to prove one central proposition: that the existence of the Corn Laws … caused resort to inferior land at home, involving a fall in the average and marginal products of labour and capital and hence bringing about a stationary state in the not very distant future.
>
> (1975: 41)

Terry Peach's recent study constitutes a notable, but partial, exception to this generalization. While he jettisons the corn model he nonetheless maintains in a similar vein to O'Brien that Ricardo's "'primary objective' … was to establish that progressively diminishing returns *must* ('permanently') depress general profitability; and following on from this point, that Ricardo's core analysis of distribution was inextricably linked with his analysis of growth" (1993: 8; emphasis in original).

Now for Hollander this represents a single (very important) application of a general framework of analysis that centers on the inverse wage–profit relation, the fundamental theorem on distribution:

> It will be a main theme of the present work that to single out the theorem relating to a declining rate of return on capital is to exaggerate the import of a particular application of the basic theory. I shall show that Ricardo paid more careful attention to the general principle of the inverse profit-wage relationship than to the particular issue of a falling rate of profit.
>
> (EDR: 12)

The general framework concerns the rigorous analysis of the interaction "between the money price of corn, the money wage, and the money price of manufactures" aimed at demonstrating that a rise in money wages must entail a fall of general profitability (EDR: 11). This would not seem to entail a radical departure from the mainstream except that Hollander further argues that the genesis of Ricardo's framework is found in his journey of escape from the Smithian theory which asserted that a rise of wages leads to an increase in the money price of all goods. This journey predates the "Essay on Profits" and leads Hollander to conclude that the corn model is not the logical core of the "Essay" and that the falling rate of profit is there, as it is in the *Principles*, a value phenomenon (1995a: 35).

Closely associated with this, though logically distinct, is Hollander's "new view" perspective on Ricardo's wage theory. The "new view" first appeared in the secondary literature in the 1970s, and its proponents posit the existence in Ricardo of a more general growth model in which diminishing returns, in the absence of technological change and/or free trade, produces secular decline in both the rate of profits and the real wage (Levy 1976; Hicks and Hollander 1977; Casarosa 1978; Samuelson 1978). In this view the subsistence wage prevails only in the stationary state (it is viewed as similar to the minimum rate of profits at which capital accumulation ceases). Along the path to convergence the wage is set in the market according to the rate which will keep population growing at the rate of capital accumulation, essentially a balanced growth path. However, along this path diminishing returns assure that money wages must rise as the value of corn rises, but the real wage falls. Since the real wage is seen as equilibrating capital and labor growth rates, and since capital growth is slowing (also due to diminishing returns) the real wage must fall to keep labor growth in line. If the real wage did not fall – that is, if the money wage exactly compensated for the rising corn price – an excess supply of labor would develop and the money price of labor would be forced down.

From these basic propositions, much of the rest of Hollander's attack on Ricardian orthodoxy follows. Once we grant that Ricardo's concern was to correct a logical error which he found in Smith's value theory, that the logical foundation of the "Essay" is not found in the corn model, that he developed a general framework centered on the fundamental theorem on distribution as a correction to Smith, and that the subsistence wage prevails only in the stationary state, the bulk of Hollander's interpretation follows as a matter of course. The model is clearly a general equilibrium one in which value and distribution are not only simultaneously determined but also both viewed as value phenomena. Making the wage endogenous and variable undermines the "surplus" interpretation of Ricardo, while focusing on the general nature of the theory makes the Corn Law controversy only one of many practical applications of the model.[2] Moreover, viewing the rate of capital accumulation as gradually slowing to the stationary state would seem to be quite consistent with the idea of a supply function for capital which is positively related to the rate of return. Although it may be stretching the point to place Ricardo squarely in a Walrasian general equilibrium tradition, this view of Ricardo certainly makes him a recognizable precursor of the Walrasian and Marshallian versions of neoclassicism. Regarding demand and choice theory I shall have more to say below.

As I indicated above, this interpretation of Ricardo has proved very controversial. If we abstract from what I would consider side issues, the controversy can be seen as a rivalry between two rational reconstructions, the "corn-model" and the "*new view.*" Each is mathematically sound, and proponents of each can point to passages in Ricardo which suggest the logic of the respective model specifications. In an attempt to evaluate these rival reconstructions I pursue three interrelated arguments. First, I take up Stigler's concept of scientific exegesis as a method for evaluating these rival reconstructions. Second, with any rational reconstruction there is the danger of writing the history of economics backwards, because we are using later developments to explicate and assess earlier writings, specifically in the realm of rational choice theory and the influence of demand on relative prices and distribution in the full-scale Ricardian model. This leads directly into the third area. Much of Ricardo interpretation employs logic, the method of rational reconstruction, as a tool for determining the author's original intent. The presumption is that Ricardo developed an internally consistent analytical apparatus, and, therefore, we can better determine what that apparatus is if we apply logic to textual exegesis. Logic, for example, seems to be the primary basis upon which Sraffa attributed the corn model to Ricardo, and it also looms large in Peach's reaffirmation of the subsistence wage doctrine (1993: 11, 103, 115). The same applies to the "*new view.*" There is a compelling logic to it such that it cannot be dismissed simply because the corn model is a logically tight construction in its own right.

Stigler developed a criterion for scientific exegesis to help determine which interpretation of an author's words is the correct one when the historian is faced with contradictory passages (1965). He concluded that:

> The test of an interpretation is its consistency with the main analytical conclusions of the system of thought under consideration. If the main conclusions of a man's thought do not survive under one interpretation, and do under another, the latter interpretation must be preferred.
>
> (448)

Our immediate problem is somewhat different, but, nonetheless, it comes under the purview of Stigler's criterion. The problem is selecting between two rational reconstructions, both of which claim to be consistent with the main analytical conclusions of the Ricardian system. The issue then becomes how to determine the main conclusions which must be consistent with the given interpretation. One way around this impasse is to invoke Stigler's principle of personal exegesis, which means to determine which best fits "the style of the man's thought" (448), and indeed this is one of Hollander's tactics (1995a: 98 as an example). Alternatively we could adapt the principle of scientific exegesis to the problem at hand. If two interpretations are consistent with the same set of conclusions, but one goes further and incorporates cases that the other does not, then the former interpretation is to be preferred. In this case Hollander claims that the "new view" is consistent with secular wage–profit paths which the traditional "corn-model" cannot handle. In particular, "an initial stage of rising real wages and a subsequent stage of declining real wages, each accompanied by a falling profit rate – simply cannot be accommodated" (1995a: 98).[3]

Much of this would be irrelevant, of course, if one could not find the "new view" cases in Ricardo's extant writings. Space does not permit me to review the textual evidence in depth. However, one key passage, which Hollander cites from the *Principles*, should suffice to indicate the nature of the textual support.

> It appears, then, that the same cause which raises rent, namely, the increasing difficulty of providing an additional quantity of food with the same proportional quantity of labour, will also raise wages; and therefore if money be of an unvarying value, both rent and wages will have a tendency to rise with the progress of wealth and population.
>
> But there is this essential difference between the rise of rent and the rise of wages. The rise in the money value of rent is accompanied by an increased share of the produce. ... *The fate of the labourer will be less happy*; he will receive more money wages, it is true, *but his corn wages will be reduced; and not only his command of corn, but his general condition will be deteriorated*, by his finding it more difficult to maintain the market rate of wages above their natural rate.
>
> (Ricardo 1951: I, 102; emphasis added)

Terry Peach, one of Hollander's severest critics, accepts that there is textual support for the "new view," but he goes on to argue that only the traditional view is "compatible with Ricardo's core doctrine of 'permanent' movements in profitability" (1993: 103). Below, I will show that Peach is wrong; the constant subsistence wage is not a necessary assumption to derive Ricardo's "core doctrine." For now my point is that Hollander is not alone in noticing passages which call into question the subsistence wage interpretation.

There is, however, an obvious and potentially damaging problem with the whole program of attempting to rationally reconstruct past theoretical systems, which is that there is the very real danger of ending up with a backwards history of thought. Since the whole process involves using modern techniques, categories, and models to interpret the past, there is always the possibility of illegitimately reading the present into the past.[4] Despite its widespread acceptance, there is good evidence that this is precisely the origin of the "corn-model" interpretation. Sraffa himself has acknowledged that:

> It should perhaps be stated that it was only when the Standard system and the distinction between basics and non-basics had emerged in the course of the present investigation that the [corn-model] ... interpretation of Ricardo's theory suggested itself as a natural consequence.
>
> (1960: 93)

Add to this the Marxian roots of Sraffa's *Production of Commodities* (namely, in Marx's prices of production and the transformation problem), and what emerges is at least a prima-facie case that attributing a Sraffa-style model to Ricardo is the result of writing history backward.[5]

Should we direct a similar charge to the "new view"? Is Hollander guilty of reading neoclassical categories into Ricardo which are not really there? In fact the critics have made exactly this argument. This, I think, is a much more difficult question to answer as it ranges over a wide spectrum of issues in Hollander's interpretation. In many cases it ultimately seems to depend on what sort of judgment one is willing to make in instances where later ideas may be seen as "consistent" with Ricardian notions, but not necessarily actually there in the text.

The whole of Hollander's interpretation of Ricardian demand theory and the role of demand in his model is a case in point. Received opinion in the history of economic thought has been that Ricardo, and the classical economists generally, lacked a demand theory. Hollander, on the contrary, asserts that Ricardo actually had a "particularly sophisticated" demand analysis (*EDR*: 273). This is a wide-ranging claim which cannot be treated exhaustively here, but consider as a first example Hollander's claim that changes in final demand affect the wage–profit structure, just as they do in neoclassical general equilibrium theory (*EDR*: 299–301; *CE*: 104; 1995a: 195ff.). This is an exercise that Ricardo did not do, and at least one critic suggests that this is good reason to reject Hollander's claim (Hollander 1995a: 195). However, rather than reading something into Ricardo which is not there, Hollander is using Ricardo's own logic, from the famous chapter "On Machinery," in which an exogenous change in the capital structure alters the demand for labor and the real wage. Hollander simply points out that if the capital structure varies across industries then a change in the composition of demand will have a similar effect on wages and profits. Applying the logic of one case, which is in Ricardo, to a comparable case, which is not, does not seem to me to violate appropriate principles of interpretation, particularly when dealing with systems of analytical economics for which the range of possible applications is open ended.

Now consider a more difficult case that really gets to the heart of the matter of reading modern ideas into older texts: Ricardian views on utility. Hollander resurrects Alfred Marshall's view that Ricardo exhibits an understanding of the difference between total and marginal utility when he draws a distinction between value and riches (1995a: 172, 178). In the *Principles* the passage in question reads:

A man is rich or poor, according to the abundance of necessaries and luxuries which he can command; and whether the exchangeable value of these for money, for corn, or for labour, be high or low, they will equally contribute to the enjoyment of their possessor. It is through confounding the ideas of value and wealth, or riches that it has been asserted, that by diminishing the quantity of commodities, that is to say the necessaries, conveniences, and enjoyments of human life, riches may be increased. If value were the measure of riches, this could not be denied, because by scarcity the value of commodities is raised; but if Adam Smith be correct, if riches consist in necessaries and enjoyments, then they cannot be increased by a diminution of quantity.

(1951, I: 275–6)

In seeing diminishing marginal utility Peach argues that Marshall "simply imposed his own meaning on Ricardo's words" (1993: 247). Hollander, however, while agreeing that Marshall is probably right, carefully tries to avoid any such charge of projection of modern meanings onto older texts:

This passage asserts unmistakably (1) that *total* utility is lessened by a reduction in supply, i.e. by increased scarcity, and (2) that "value" per unit is raised by this increased scarcity; it follows immediately that the *increase* in value corresponds to the *reduction* in total utility, i.e. value measures "riches" – *at the margin*. Ricardo did not state this definition in so many words.

(1995a: 178; emphasis in original)

He goes on to conclude that marginal utility did not require a new paradigm, because of Ricardo's "appreciation and widespread application of the scarcity principle" (178). The interpretation does not turn on whether Marshall is right about Ricardo's implicit knowledge of marginal utility *per se*.

I would argue that the concept of a utility function and its first derivative are tools which helped economists later in the century to formalize ideas which were already there in the classical texts, despite some particularly unkind remarks which one must expect when an innovator such as Jevons believes that he is revolutionizing economics. The development of the theory of rational choice is another, related, example. A modern-style theory of choice is clearly implicit in classical population dynamics. For example, Ricardo repeatedly asserted that:

The friends of humanity cannot but wish that in all countries the labouring classes should have a *taste* for comforts and enjoyments, and that they should be stimulated by all legal means in their exertions to procure them. There cannot be a better security against a superabundant population.

(1951, I: 100; emphasis added)

Such statements clearly imply that he saw fertility decisions as rational choices involving the trade-off involving material goods as an alternative to having children.[6] Formalizing this in a model of rational choice using modern techniques and concepts seems to me to be a legitimate exercise in rational reconstruction. The formal model and the Ricardian text seem to me to be saying the same thing about human behavior.

Turning to the issue of the analytical logic of these reconstructions, there is the general presumption that Ricardo's analytical model, whatever it was, would be free of logical error, if properly reconstructed. Hence a rational reconstruction must not only *intersect* with the original text, but also itself be logically sound. Now as a matter of logic the inverse wage–profit relationship is first a relative price phenomenon, second a product of general equilibrium reasoning, and third reflective of the interdependence of value and distribution. Ricardo's fundamental problem here was to explain the determinants of the structure of relative prices in an economy which produces cloth (manufactured good), corn (agricultural good), and, for simplicity, gold (money) using labor and capital (for simplicity in the same proportions). Under conditions of increasing land scarcity the value of corn would rise causing money wages to rise (otherwise the demand for labor would run ahead of the supply). Gold and cloth would not change since the amount of labor and capital required to produce them does not change in the process. With the gold price of labor rising and the gold price of cloth constant gold profits would fall in manufacturing. They would also fall in agriculture, because the gold price increase only compensates for greater labor embodied at the margin, not for the increased money wage. Labor's share of the surplus less rent rises relative to profits. This is the inverse wage–profit result. I do not see how this scenario could be viewed as anything other than a general equilibrium model with value and distribution interdependent and simultaneously determined.

Whether the real wage, labor's command over goods, rises or falls is irrelevant to the fundamental theorem. All that is required is the rise in the gold wage for cloth profits to fall. In agriculture profits will fall if there is any increase in the wage share, no matter how small. This will occur if gold wages rise, no matter how small the rise. This is because Ricardian "money" has the special property of measuring accurately the proportions between wages and profits, causing money wages to rise when the labor embodied in wage goods rises. "New view" dynamics are logically consistent with the fundamental theorem. The secular path of declining real wages and profits is not a contradiction of the fundamental theorem which runs in terms of money, really proportionate, wages. The conclusion of the traditionalist interpretations, Peach's "core doctrine," that diminishing returns entail a permanently falling profit rate, barring technological change and free trade, does not require either the corn model or the subsistence wage. Ricardo's problem was that profits measured in his "money," which stood in lieu of the invariant standard of value, might not accurately predict real-world profits unless the labor theory of value was a close approximation to reality. Hence his tendency to assume that it was.

While the fundamental theorem does not require a specific assumption about the commodity wage, the overall dynamics of the Ricardian system are more logically sound if we assume a commodity wage above the natural wage eventually falling to the natural wage when the economy arrives at the stationary state. The simple reason for this is that population is rising throughout the process, and by definition the natural wage is equivalent to a stationary population. Therefore, the market wage must be above the natural indefinitely, and, since profits are assumed to be falling, the rate of capital accumulation is slowing and so is the growth rate in the demand for labor. Market clearing properties will then insure that the commodity wage falls to keep labor supply growing at the declining rate equal to capital growth. As Samuelson indicates, a "short-circuited" version with the population instantly rising to drive the market wage down to subsistence may have pedagogical value because of its simplicity, but it is not the general model (1978: 1426). Ricardo undoubtedly followed similar pedagogical simplicities, but the "new view" passages serve to warn us that he also had in mind a general model.

The fact that Hollander attributes a general model to Ricardo has also been a source of controversy. O'Brien, for example, in his review of *EDR* is quite indignant that Ricardo should be saddled with a model in which anything can happen, thus changing the status of the falling rate of profit from scientific prediction to only one of several possible outcomes. He suggests that such theorizing is "virtually useless" and, therefore, assumes that Ricardo knew better (385). This, however, will not do. The "new view" cannot be condemned on these grounds. If it could, all of modern economic theory would have to go as well, since supply and demand analyses, both micro and macro, are precisely the sort of theoretical framework Hollander is talking about. Supply and demand analysis makes no prediction of relative price movements without introducing changes in the *ceteris paribus* assumptions, such as an increase in income or a change in the price of a substitute good. "New view" models of the wage path make no predictions without first introducing assumptions about the degree of prudential population control. If Ricardo and the classical economists recognized different possibilities here, it certainly does not render their methods "useless," without predictive capability.

I have attempted to focus on what I consider to be the main lines of Hollander's interpretation of Ricardo, leaving aside numerous points of detail. According to Hollander, there is a general model in Ricardo that is neither a corn model nor a subsistence wage model. It is a model of the relative price structure and its dynamic development with capital accumulation running into land scarcity. As such it is a general equilibrium model in which value and distribution are simultaneously determined. Hollander's main conclusion, that the history of economics exhibits strong continuity within a single paradigm, follows logically from this.

Will Hollander's Ricardo win the day among historians of economic thought? Will the "new view" become standard textbook fare? Will the "soundbite" version of history which most economists know delete the "subsistence wage" concept from its Ricardo? The controversy has been so intense and even bitter that I would be foolish to make a prediction with any degree of confidence. What I believe I have demonstrated is that Hollander's interpretation is logically sound, rooted in the original texts, and defensible against the charge of anachronism, reading new ideas into older texts. Indeed, it is worth noting that some chinks in the traditionalist façade have begun to appear. Textbooks now give some credit to the "new view" (Blaug 1996: 139–40; also Staley 1989: 88–90), and statements such as the following are beginning to appear in unrelated places: "the corn-model of an economy (commonly, but mistakenly, called the Ricardian model)" (Rashid 1998: 25).

The same, however, could be said of the Sraffian interpretation – that it is logically sound, rooted in the text, and defensible against the charge of anachronism. Moreover, one might use Stigler's criterion in its favor on the grounds that it highlights the concept of absolute value, as opposed to relative prices, in Ricardo's writings. Indeed Hollander agrees that there is textual support for the Sraffian reading, particularly in the chapters on value and profits in the *Principles* (Young 1998). He goes on to insist that it cannot be sustained when viewing Ricardo's output as a whole. The issues are complex, and there is no objective standard, Stigler notwithstanding, by which to resolve the controversy. Much depends on the weight to assign various passages. What I hope to have shown is that Hollander's interpretation can stand up to the harsh criticism which has been directed against it. It is at least a reasonable reading of Ricardo, but one over which reasonable people may disagree.

## Robert Malthus

As of this writing, *The Economics of Thomas Robert Malthus* (1997, hereinafter ETRM) is the latest installment of Hollander's series on the classical economists. As in the case of Ricardo and J. S. Mill, it is a massive, complex, and far-reaching volume. It is intended to be a companion piece to EDR, so I will consider it here and treat J. S. Mill in the next section of the chapter. It is undoubtedly destined to become the definitive work on Malthus as an economist.

Despite its size (1,007 pages of closely reasoned text), we can gain a broad appreciation of its importance to the history of economic thought if we concentrate on three interrelated themes. First, and perhaps the most controversial and newsworthy, is Hollander's claim (already announced in the prestigious pages of the *American Economic Review* in 1992) that sometime around 1824 Malthus renounced his stand on agricultural protection and threw his support to the Ricardian vision of Britain's economic future fueled by industrial growth coupled with free trade in both corn and manufactured goods. The upshot is that eventually Malthus joined the classical mainstream with the only substantive point of disagreement being his rejection of Say's law which survived his renunciation of agricultural protection even though effective demand considerations were one of the arguments he had used to support a high-rent, self-sufficient agricultural sector.

Second, Hollander argues that there is a strong physiocratic influence on Malthus, which waned with his reversal on the Corn Laws. The presence of an agricultural bias standing alongside such classical commonplaces as the law of diminishing returns, then, Hollander uses to shed new and interesting light on the difficult interpretive problem of Malthus's consistency. In this way

Hollander significantly elevates Malthus's reputation in the history of economic thought to that of a first-rate economist. He does not raise the issue of the single versus dual paradigms in the history of economic thought that played such a prominent role in *EDR* and its critical reception. However, these points of Malthus interpretation certainly reinforce the continuity claim between Ricardo and the neoclassicals, since at least some of the flash points in the Malthus/Ricardo debates turned on Malthus's use of the physiocratic "surplus" approach in arguing the case for protection.

Third, closely associated with physiocratic themes in Malthus, is Hollander's claim that Malthus adopted the Sraffian corn-model theory of profits along with a Sraffian type of price theory, which we have seen is usually attributed to Ricardo. Since Malthus's explicit discussion of the corn-model theory in the second edition of his *Principles* has been cited as evidence in support of Sraffa's interpretation of Ricardo, Hollander's claim about Malthus is likely to be equally controversial as his interpretation of Ricardo (Prendergast 1986).[7] In this way *ETRM* reinforces the argument of *EDR*. In what follows I will attempt to present the substance of Hollander's case on each of these points.

With regard to the Corn Laws, Hollander's evidence comes from four separate sources dated from 1824 until Malthus's death. They are the nature of certain changes made in the second edition of the *Principles*, an 1824 *Quarterly Review* article on Ricardian political economy, a note added to the chapter on import restrictions for corn in the 1826 edition of the *Essay on Population*, and three letters written between 1829 and 1833.

Space does not permit a thorough review of all the evidence, but we can gain an appreciation of the case by looking at the note added to the *Essay*. The note is long, and it begins with a refutation of one common argument favoring free trade in corn. Among other things the opponents of the Corn Laws claimed that free importation would protect Britain from the distress of a scarcity of corn in the home market. Malthus points out that this may not be the case since the facts point to similar weather conditions in all of the European corn-growing countries causing good and bad harvests to occur simultaneously throughout Europe. Free trade, then, could not be relied upon to stabilize prices and available quantities. At this point, instead of his usual endorsement of the Corn Laws as a necessary exception to the policy of free trade, Malthus states:

> I am very far, however, from meaning to say that the circumstances of different countries having often an abundance or deficiency of corn at the same time, though it must prevent the possibility of steady prices, is a decisive reason against the abolition or alteration of the corn-laws. The most powerful of all the arguments against restrictions is their unsocial tendency, and the acknowledged injury which they must do to the interests of the commercial world in general. The weight of this argument is increased rather than diminished by the numbers which may suffer from scarcity at the same time. And at a period when our ministers are most laudably

setting an example of a more liberal system of commercial policy, it would be greatly desirable that foreign nations should not have so marked an exception as our present corn-laws to cast in our teeth. A duty on importation not too high, and a bounty nearly such as was recommended by Mr. Ricardo, would probably be best suited to our present situation, and best secure steady prices. A duty on foreign corn would resemble the duties laid by other countries on our manufactures as objects of taxation, and would not in the same manner impeach the principles of free trade.

But whatever system we may adopt, it is essential to a sound determination, and highly useful in preventing disappointments, that all the arguments both for and against corn-laws should be thoroughly and impartially considered; and it is because on a calm, and, as far as I can judge, an impartial review of the arguments of this chapter, they still appear to me of weight sufficient to deserve such consideration, and not as a kind of protest against the abolition or change of the corn-laws, that I republish them in another edition.

([1826] 1992: 180)

The allusion to the "present situation" suggests that at least part of what is going on is that Malthus has changed his perception of the balance of costs and benefits associated with free trade, because circumstances had changed. As Hollander points out, by 1826 the liberalization of trade was becoming a reality rendering obsolete Malthus's earlier position which was in part based on the belief that free trade was an unrealizable ideal (*ETRM*: 857; also 1992: 653). Malthus never disputed that free trade was right in principle. He always viewed the Corn Laws as a legitimate exception to a policy of free trade in all other sectors of the economy.

In addition, Hollander argues that the endorsement of Ricardo's plan for export subsidies is actually an endorsement of free trade, not the reverse, as a superficial reading would imply. Ricardo's plan called for a duty on corn imports "to correct for differential taxation imposed on British farmers relative to British manufacturers, and an appropriate drawback on [corn] exports" (*ETRM*: 851). The purpose was to prevent the distortion of resource allocation that resulted when imported corn was not subject to the same taxation as homegrown corn. Despite the ambiguous way Malthus refers to Ricardo's scheme (are both the "duty" and the "bounty" meant to refer to Ricardo or just the "bounty"?), an endorsement of the whole policy package seems to be the most logical interpretation, since Ricardo's proposed drawback does not stand alone as a meaningful policy proposal (*ETRM*: 853).

Also worth noting is that Malthus himself tells us why he did not change the body of the text to reflect his latest thinking on agricultural protection, thus relegating the "announcement" of his new position to a footnote. The importance of the issue made it incumbent upon political economists to give a full airing to all the arguments. In addition, he continued to believe that protectionist arguments were sufficiently meritorious to be listened to and duly considered in the public arena. He specifically did not retain the protectionist passages as a "protest" against the abolition or even change of the Corn Laws.

Hollander's discovery of Malthus's change of mind may prove to be the most controversial point of his work on Malthus. John Pullen, for example, reacted quite negatively to Hollander's initial publication of the discovery, and a debate ensued (Pullen 1995; Hollander 1995b). He argues that the passages Hollander cites are amenable to other interpretations and that some protectionist passages, such as remained in the second edition of the *Principles*, should be given greater weight. In my view, Hollander has successfully rebutted these claims in his reply (1995b). However, Pullen raises an issue, of which Hollander is quite aware, but which is potentially damaging. John Cazenove, the probable editor of the second edition of the *Principles*, and William Empson, a close friend and colleague of Malthus's at the East India College, apparently knew nothing of this recantation (Pullen 1995: 522–3). Both of them thought the second edition substantially complete and in accord with the views Malthus expressed in the first edition. This, of course, would include the continued endorsement of the Corn Laws. Pullen finds it incomprehensible that Malthus could change his views without either Cazenove's or Empson's knowledge. He, therefore, concludes that Malthus must have retained his protectionist position until his death. Hollander admits to being puzzled by the fact that "Malthus's new position has been under wraps for 170 years" (1992: 658), but he has elsewhere provided reasons for downplaying the significance of both Cazenove's and Empson's remarks about the continuity between editions (1998: 251).

I find Pullen's arguments about the textual evidence itself unconvincing in that Hollander's interpretation of the key texts, particularly the 1826 note quoted above, seems to be the most logical, natural reading of them. Until further evidence comes to light I consider Hollander's claim that the problem lies in the unfinished nature of the second edition the best available explanation of the mystery of why no one seems to have known anything about this until Hollander announced its discovery in 1992 (1992: 658).

Important analytical issues are also at stake in the question of Malthus's stand on the Corn Laws. An important attribute of Hollander's reading of Malthus is the presence of a physiocratic bias, more far reaching and ingrained than Smith's, which played a key role in his original stance in favor of the Corn Laws, and which Hollander claims waned with his recantation in the mid 1820s. I will argue that Malthus's physiocracy has far-reaching implications for Hollander's one-paradigm view of the history of economics. Although he does not specifically take up this issue in the book, ETRM significantly strengthens the central thesis of EDR.

That the first two editions of the *Essay on the Principle of Population* contained strong physiocratic influences is well known. Hollander's claim to originality here is that he sees this influence as "more positive, specific, and lasting than usually suggested in the literature" (ETRM: 406). Donald Winch's assessment is perhaps typical in this regard when he labels the physiocratic features of the *First Essay* a "flirtation" and concludes that they were "largely excised three years later" (1987: 61). Particulars include a physiocratic defini-tion of wealth wherein manufacturing income is treated as a transfer payment, agriculture as the sole source of surplus, the view of rent as derived from a Providential gift, the greater productivity of a unit of capital in agriculture compared to either trade or manufacturing, and landlord expenditures as the determinant of aggregate demand. By 1806 Malthus was treating manufacturing and trade as creators of income, but not producers of surplus. Thus, the agricul-tural surplus was still seen as the source of all forms of disposable income – that is, income available for either taxation or accumulation without causing a with-drawal of productive services.

The result was that Malthus continued to look upon agriculture as a special activity. It tended to yield a social rate of return in excess of the private rate (the opposite applied to manufacturing). It also had the special property that, unlike the market for other goods where supply and demand operated as inde-pendent functions, supply created its own demand (*ETRM*: 381). An increase of mouths to feed was sure to follow an increase in food output guaranteeing that the physical corn surplus would always result in a value surplus to be distributed as rent and profits to farmers and manufacturers. Only in the case of corn did Malthus attribute this value surplus to the physical surplus of output above capital consumed (*ETRM*: 379).

Perhaps Malthus's most significant departure from physiocracy was the prin-ciple of diminishing returns that formed the basis of the classical theory of rent, of which Malthus, of course, was a principal founder. At the same time this introduces a scarcity perspective which is at odds with the "surplus" approach. This is reflected, for example, in Malthus's and Ricardo's disagreement over the nature of rent. In Ricardo's view rent arose out of the scarcity of fertile land, and was larger the more severe the scarcity relative to the demand for food (*ETRM*: 380). Rent did not reflect a creation of wealth and a low-rent, high-profit, and high-wages economy was to be preferred over the high-rent economy. Malthus saw rent as a share of the agricultural surplus, a gift of Providence. To him, high rent and high wages went together since a higher money price of corn would increase both real rent and real wages. This economy was to be preferred over a high-profit economy. The high-rent, high-wage economy could support a larger population, and the consumption propensity of landlords would insure macro-economic stability. Malthus recognized land scarcity as a condition for rent to exist, but viewed it as only determining the distribution of the surplus as rent (*ETRM*: 389).

Malthus did seem to be aware that he was trying to reconcile competing doctrines. In addition to the tactic of treating scarcity and surplus as two sepa-rate and necessary causes of rent, he also suggested that the surplus approach should be confined to the special case of necessaries, all other goods governed by relative scarcity via the mechanism of independent supply and demand func-tions (Hollander 1998: 302). However, Malthus does not seem to have been aware that he was dealing with mutually exclusive paradigms of pricing and distribution. The superior productivity of agriculture simply cannot be sustained in the face of diminishing returns in that sector. At the margin, labor must at some point become more productive in manufacturing than in agriculture. Moreover, he could not maintain two principles of price determination, both applicable to agriculture. Corn prices could not simultaneously be determined by the intersection of an upward-sloping long-run supply curve with a downward-sloping demand curve leaving rent as a payment arising out of the scarcity of land (which Malthus upheld) and also be sure that price would always return a value surplus to the farmer since supply created its own demand. In the first instance the supply and demand functions are independent, as they must be, while in the second they are interdependent. Hollander concludes: "He had fallen into a logical trap – insisting upon the physiocratic view of rent as surplus while allowing the differential principle of rent. Malthus's theoretical position was, as Ricardo insisted, untenable" (ETRM: 398).

A further implication of the doctrine of the unique productivity of agriculture is that the unregulated market allocation of resources between agriculture and manufacturing is likely to be non-optimal from the social perspective. Indeed, one wonders if the physiocrats could really have been as committed to free trade in principle as they are generally portrayed (today as well as in Malthus's time).[8] In Malthus's case there is a clear association between physiocratic principles and agricultural protection. The agricultural origin of the surplus renders agriculture more productive per unit of capital invested than manufacturing, and since the surplus does not accrue exclusively to the farmer, the social rate of return in agriculture exceeds the private rate (Hollander 1998: 290, 299). In so far as markets respond to private calculations of gain, the result is that capital will be under-invested in agriculture and over-invested in manufacturing even if the restrictions which favor the latter over the former are removed. Subsidies and import restrictions are called for on utilitarian grounds.

In addition, there are aggregate demand considerations. Malthus claimed, against Ricardo and his school, that capital accumulation was not alone sufficient to sustain growth, and that diminishing returns is not the only inhibiting factor. In particular, he believed that a strong demand for leisure would stunt the growth of effectual demand unless new wants were constantly being created (ETRM: 581). This was one of the functions of trade in his theory. Expansion of aggregate demand was for him a gain from trade separate from and additional to the efficiency gains Ricardo championed. In addition, he feared that investment derived from a reduction in consumption would be unsustainable since there would be an insufficient market for the expanded supply of goods. In short, he feared that if the propensity of landlords to save was too high the capitalists' excess of their investment over their saving was unlikely to be sufficient to bring total investment in line with total saving, thus generating an insufficiency of aggregate demand.

With landlords' marginal propensity to consume being generally higher than that of the capitalists, a high-rent share would tend to alleviate this problem. Hence, agricultural protection was in part advocated to increase aggregate demand and encourage sustainable accumulation (investment financed out of rising profits). This was his version of the model of balanced growth. Over time the agricultural and manufacturing sectors of the British economy would grow together. There would be no secular shift toward manufacturing as the principle of comparative advantage entailed if allocation were to be efficient. Malthus's position on aggregate demand is more complex than this, as we have made no allowance for short-run fluctuations and the analysis of the postwar depression in Britain. However, the connection between agricultural protection, physiocracy, and demand seems to lie in his analysis of the role of demand as a causal factor in generating the secular growth path.

Over time Malthus's physiocratic bias weakened. Although he never completely relinquished it, he did eventually endorse the Ricardian vision of industry-led growth in a free trade regime. The process began with the introduction of prudential control into his population model, which tends to undermine the "surplus" approach, as the wage now becomes an endogenous variable set by the operation of supply and demand (Hollander 1998: 310). This blurs the distinction between surplus and capital. By the 1817 edition of the *Essay* he was beginning to place an emphasis on industry-led growth, and he eventually abandoned the notion that landlord consumption was necessary to maintain aggregate demand (1998: 310–11). This latter derived from his reading of the experience of British growth in the 1820s in which growth in manufacturing exports was clearly the engine of aggregate demand growth. Although he abandoned protection and embraced much of the Ricardian vision, he never relinquished his claim against the Ricardians that aggregate supply growth did not guarantee aggregate demand growth, or that a breach between *ex ante* saving and investment could temporarily interrupt the secular growth process. In this he was clearly ahead of his time.

Malthus has suffered from bad press in the history of economic thought, possibly because of the tendency for the victors to write the history. Keynes famously tried to redress the balance and refurbish Malthus's reputation. However, there has been a tendency to view him as confused, inconsistent, or even worse. Hollander's work along with some other recent contributions shows that there is a coherent analytical structure to Malthus's thought.[9] He also sheds some important light on why Malthus has this reputation. His thought evolved as he grappled with the demands of two conflicting approaches. To make matters worse he was trying to develop a model which was inherently more complex than that of his contemporaries as he attempted to graft an aggregate demand function onto the corpus of canonical classical theory. It is not, therefore, surprising that Malthus should gain such a reputation. *ETRM* goes a long way to set the record straight and give Malthus the historian's long overdue accolade as a first-rate economist.

There remains the issue of Malthus's Sraffian-style value and distribution theory, which is also associated with his physiocratic bias, the surplus approach. Hollander is not the first to suggest that Malthus followed a Sraffian approach, but there is a difficult matter of interpretation here (Costabile 1983). On the one hand, there is a clear Sraffian model in Malthus with value determined by quantities of dated labor, the profit rate determined as the ratio of surplus to capital advanced, and the labor-commanded value measure. This is not in dispute between Hollander and the Sraffians. On the other hand, passages in which Malthus appears to be criticizing the idea of profit as a physical ratio have been used as evidence in support of Sraffa's interpretation of Ricardo (Prendergast 1986). This is where the problem lies. Hollander asserts that it is Malthus, not Ricardo, who spelled out the physical corn profit model with manufacturing profits coming into line via the adjustment of the corn/cloth terms of trade and distribution determined prior to prices (*ETRM*: 435; *EDR*: 722). In the multi-goods case the rate of profit is determined in the wage goods sector. The Sraffians dispute this arguing that Malthus's theory derives the profit rate as a value ratio in the manner of *Production of Commodities*. The interpretive issues are complex, but we can at least gain an appreciation of Hollander's position and its importance to his interpretation of Ricardo.

Malthus always defined the profit rate as a value ratio. However, Hollander points out that

> though the general expression for the profit rate involves value terms, the *agricultural* profit rate is expressed in physical (corn) terms, and the rate thus determined carries over to manufacturing. Second, Malthus spelled out the assumptions required to permit proceeding in physical terms in agriculture; and he cautioned that, in application, the procedure might break down, even should both input and output be composed of the same physical substance. The evidence points: (1) to an *analytical* corn-profit model consciously spelled out ... and (2) to limitations in application reflecting largely seasonal corn-price fluctuations.
>
> (*ETRM*: 436; emphasis in original)

We have here the substance of Hollander's interpretation reduced to two propositions. First, there is a consciously spelled out corn-profit model to be found in both editions of the *Principles*. The evidence is the use of physical measures of input and output in agriculture. Second, there is an explicit rendering of the assumptions necessary for the physical ratio to determine the value ratio. In the scenarios where Malthus uses these assumptions, the lines of causation are from agriculture to manufacturing via the adjustment of the relative price of manufactured goods.

One such example is his exposition of the canonical classical model of growth under conditions of increasing land scarcity in the second edition of the *Principles*. After showing that diminishing returns lower profits and corn wages (note the "new view" flavor of the analysis), Malthus queries:

> In the mean time, it will be asked, what becomes of the profits of capital employed in manufactures and commerce, a species of industry not like that employed upon the land, where the productive powers of labour necessarily

diminish; but where these powers not only do not necessarily diminish, but very often greatly increase?

([1836] 1986: 274–5)

He goes on to answer that:

In the cultivation of land, the cause of the *necessary* diminution of profits is the diminution in the quantity of produce obtained by the same quantity of labour. In manufactures and commerce, it is the fall in the exchangeable value of the same amount of produce.

(275; emphasis in original)

He then explains, using his definition of value as labor commanded, how capital will flow into manufacturing until the value of manufactured goods falls sufficiently to reduce the manufacturing rate of profits to equality with agriculture. From the context it is clear that the agricultural profit rate is ultimately a physical phenomenon involving the relation of corn input (corn wages) to corn output. Consequently the agricultural rate is the governing rate for the system. This is precisely the model that Sraffa attributed to Ricardo (*ETRM*: 447).

Second, Malthus recognized limits to the applicability of the model. As a model of the secular path of wages and profits, it incorporates only the impact of diminishing returns in a world of constant technology. Malthus, of course, was never satisfied that diminishing returns told the whole story. It constituted what he called the "limiting" principle, while the impact of aggregate demand and supply were the "regulating" principle (*ETRM*: 448; Malthus [1836] 1986: 271). If aggregate demand were insufficient, as in a depression or secular stagnation, the rate of profits would fall below that dictated by the marginal product of capital advances in agriculture. Seasonal fluctuations in harvests could also cause the actual rate of profit to deviate from that determined at the margin in agriculture. Short-run supply variation, for example, can cause price fluctuations which affect input and output values differently, even though both are corn. It is considerations such as these which led Malthus to insist that profits are always a value ratio, but this does not rule out a corn model since, as Malthus claims, the value ratio is essentially determined by the interaction of the "limiting" and "regulating" principles, and, as I have shown, the "limiting" principle is a Sraffian model with profits determined in the wage goods sector independently of and prior to prices.

With his recantation of agricultural protectionism, its associated distancing from physiocratic principles, and his ascent to the inverse wage–profit relation, Malthus, as we have seen, moved closer to Ricardianism in the 1820s. However, there remained three essential differences between them; two are substantive and one is erroneous. Malthus erroneously believed that matters of substance depended upon his choice of numeraire, labor commanded, which necessarily rendered the wage basket per unit of labor constant in value. However, as Hollander shows there is no substantive difference here. Diminishing returns generate the same secular trends regardless of whether one uses Malthus's or Ricardo's measuring stick (*ETRM*: 500–1).

The substantive differences are Malthus's use of the corn model to explain the "limiting" principle of profits and his theory of aggregate demand. In the first instance, the key is that while Malthus assumed the money wage was constant (Malthusian "money," unlike Ricardian "money," was produced by a constant amount of unaided labor in one hour of work), money wage variation was the source of profit rate variation in Ricardo's model (*ETRM*: 501). The result is that Ricardo did not use a corn model (although he could have used it as a special case) while Malthus did use it. In the second instance, Malthus once again failed to realize that his doctrine did not depend on his choice of numeraire. One does not need a labor-commanded index to arrive at the conclusion that aggregate supply can exceed aggregate demand. The upshot is that there are indeed differences between the mature Malthus and Ricardo, but they are not as great as Malthus himself believed.

The conclusion must be that Hollander's view of Malthus is largely correct. Indeed *ETRM* is likely to become the benchmark against which all future Malthus scholarship will be measured. That Malthus recanted on the Corn Laws will likely become the received view. On Malthus's physiocracy, the only controversy is its depth and longevity beyond 1803, and on the corn model the evidence is quite compelling. As in the case of Sraffa, Hollander's interpretation of Malthus also has implications for our understanding of Ricardo, and it invites the following set of hypotheses. First, the corn model that Sraffa saw in Ricardo's "Essay on Profits" of 1815 is actually in Malthus, although it does not appear before the first edition of the *Principles* in 1820. Second, the error of attributing it to Ricardo was originally Malthus's error, and Sraffa was simply following Malthus. This is evident from the fact that Sraffa imputed it to Ricardo based on comments Malthus was making. Third, although this is quite speculative because we do not know if Malthus had the corn model in 1815, Malthus could easily have made this mistake if he was himself thinking in terms of the corn model as a theory of the agricultural profit rate since he would have naturally taken Ricardo's assertion in the "Essay" of the leading role of agriculture as an expression of the model. Given the convoluted nature of their correspondence (they could not even come to a mutual understanding over such basic ideas as the "value of labor") and the complexity of Malthus's economics, it is not surprising that it has taken Hollander's monumental effort 170 years later to straighten this out.[10]

## John Stuart Mill

Hollander's *The Economics of John Stuart Mill* (hereinafter *EJSM*) appeared in 1985, more than a decade prior to *ETRM*. As is true of the latter, the two volumes on Mill must be seen as companion pieces to *EDR*. Thus, the Ricardian pedigree of Mill's thought and Marshall's continuity thesis become the central themes of the book: "It has emerged from our investigations that the economics of Ricardo and J.S. Mill in fact comprises in its essentials an exchange system consistent with the neo-classical elaborations" (*EJSM*: 931).

However, the book covers the entire range of Mill's writings including those on methodology, utilitarianism and liberty, theoretical economics, and policy broadly construed to include Mill's concern for basic institutional issues. What emerges is a view of Mill as a consistent thinker embarked on the exceedingly complex task of mounting a multi-faceted attempt to rescue Ricardian economics from the hands of second-rate political economists and various "sentimental enemies" (quoting Mill's *Autobiography, EJSM*: 181). According to Hollander, in the *Principles* Mill adopted a defensive strategy by asserting the provisional, non-universal nature of political economy's main conclusions (*EJSM*: 180–1). In this way he presented political economy as one of several social sciences (the others as yet undeveloped) all taking their place under the umbrella of a hoped-for general social theory: the science of ethology, the formation of national character (*EJSM*: 135). Thus political economy investigated only a slice of human life (that concerned with the production and enjoyment of material wealth) within the institutional structures of a competitive capitalist economy. Moreover, he asserted that this was always the understanding shared by the best of the political economists (meaning Ricardo among others). Mill's intention in the *Principles*, Hollander summarizes as

> the liberation of public opinion from the influence of second-rate economists who gave economic theory a bad name by their apologetic misapplications of theory, and from the false belief that Ricardian doctrine and method itself amounted to social apologetics.
>
> (*EJSM*: 185)

In this way Hollander successfully argues that the characteristic feature of Mill's *Principles*, namely its institutional eclecticism, far from being a departure from Ricardo and a return to Smithian procedures, is actually an integral part of Mill's defense of Ricardian political economy.

In what follows I shall confine myself to a consideration of three interrelated themes in this Ricardian rescue mission: Mill's exposition of the fundamental theorem of distribution, "new view" wage and profit dynamics in the context of Mill's general framework of analysis, and the historically provisional nature of the conclusions of theoretical economics. Admittedly this represents an aggressive elimination of many of the details of the case Hollander has painstakingly constructed through nearly 1,000 pages of text and footnotes. Some of this material, such as Hollander's analysis of the evolution of Mill's relation to Benthamite utilitarianism, is not only brilliant, but also important in its own right.[11] However, in keeping with the spirit of the work as part of Hollander's multi-volume study of classical economics, I will confine myself to only some of the key issues which have emerged in the discussion of the other installments in the series. Thus, for the purpose of assessing Hollander as an historian of economics the continuity thesis and the Ricardian heritage must be our central concerns.

Consider Mill's statement in the *Principles* of the fundamental theorem. Having first assumed money as an invariant standard in the Ricardian sense (691), he presents two cases of a general increase in money wages: a rise in real wages and a rise in the price of provisions in the course of population expansion. In each case the general rate of profits falls, but the argument in the second case is of particular interest:

> Having disposed of the case in which the increase of money wages, and of the Cost of Labour, arises from the labourer's obtaining more ample wages in kind, let us now suppose it to arise from the increased cost of production of the things which he consumes; owing to an increase in population, unaccompanied by an equivalent increase in agricultural skill. The augmented supply required by the population would not be obtained, unless the price of food rose sufficiently to remunerate the farmer for the increased cost of production. The farmer, however, in this case sustains a twofold disadvantage. He has to carry on his cultivation under less favourable conditions of productiveness than before. For this, as it is a disadvantage belonging to him only as a farmer, and not shared by other employers, he will, on the general principles of value, be compensated by a rise of the price of his commodity: indeed, until this rise has taken place, he will not bring to market the required increase of produce. But this very rise of price involves him in another necessity, for which he is not compensated. As the real wages of labour are by supposition unaltered, he must pay higher money wages to his labourers. This necessity, being common to him with all other capitalists, forms no ground for a rise of price. The price will rise, until it has placed him in as good a situation in respect of profits, as other employers of labour: it will rise so as to indemnify him for the increased labour which he must now employ in order to produce a given quantity of food: but the increased wages of that labour are a burthen common to all, and for which no one can be indemnified. It will be paid wholly from profits.
>
> (692–3)

Mill goes on to consider the possibility that the cost of production is not reducible entirely to wages since past accumulations of fixed capital contain profits. Although the case raises complexities which are beyond the scope of the work, he concludes that

> there is nothing in the case in question to affect the integrity of the theory which affirms an exact correspondence, in an inverse direction, between the rate of profit and the Cost of Labour [the money wage expressed in invariant money].
>
> (694)

The proposition had already been stated in Book II in the chapter on profits:

> We thus arrive at the conclusion of Ricardo and others, that the rate of profits depends on wages; rising as wages fall, and falling as wages rise. In adopting, however, this doctrine, I must insist upon making a most necessary alteration in its wording. Instead of saying that profits depend on wages, let us say (what Ricardo really meant) that they depend on the *cost of labour.*
>
> (419; emphasis in original)

Despite having said that profits do not originate in exchange, the chapter ends making the point that the mechanisms by which the result obtains in a market economy entail the operation of the price system:

> The evidence of these propositions can only be stated generally, though, it is hoped conclusively, in this stage of our subject. It will come out in greater fulness and force when, having taken into consideration the theory of Value and Price, we shall be enabled to exhibit the law of profits in concrete – in the complex entanglement of circumstances in which it actually works.
>
> (421)

Taken as a whole, then, it should be clear that when Mill says that "profit arises, not from the incidence of exchange, but from the productive power of labour" (417), he is not asserting the independence of value and distribution. Indeed the contrary is the case. Mill's full statement of the law shows its roots in relative price movements in a general equilibrium framework. The price of wage goods rises relative to other goods in the economy. Value being relative (as is price in the above passage owing to the assumption of invariant money), a general rise of money wages cannot cause a general increase in value; profits have to fall (marginal cost, of course, is assumed to contain no rent). To read this as a general equilibrium model based on the interaction of supply and demand featuring the interdependence of value and distribution does not seem at all far fetched to me. Indeed, it seems to be the most logical reading of the text.

The theorem was not of mere incidental significance to Mill. He believed it was a powerful antidote to the popular misconception that general prices depended upon general wages. We have already seen how Ricardo developed the theorem in response to precisely this misconception which is found in Smith. In fact, the point was of such importance that both Ricardo and Mill believed that its validity did not depend on the device of the invariant standard (*EJSM*: 353). Mill, for example, showed that the popular view collapsed in a *reductio ad absurdum*, since it implied that there could never be an increase in the real wage if money wage increases always resulted in price-level increases to offset them (459–60, 692). Moreover, Mill was greatly vexed at the possibility of ever getting the point across to the general public (*EJSM*: 919), and toward the end of his life he was concerned that a contemporary comparison of British profit rates with American ones appeared to present an empirical refutation of the theorem (*EJSM*: 964).

Neither was the theorem merely an intellectual curiosity. Among other things it had obvious and important implications for international trade since, as Mill points out, "no such advantage is conferred by low wages when common to all branches of industry. General low wages never caused any country to undersell its rivals, nor did general high wages ever hinder it from doing so" (684). This is of the first importance in understanding popular misconceptions of trade which all too readily result in damaging protectionism. The same could be said of Ricardo. Contemporary students of economics, not to mention policy makers, would benefit from a deep and thorough under-standing of Mill's point.

In addition to the general equilibrium nature of the theorem, we may also discern an intention to construct a general framework of analysis rather than to generate specific historical predictions. This is evident in the fact that, first, Mill elaborates the theorem following real wage changes in addition to what is normally viewed as the more characteristically classical concern for population growth under conditions of increasing land scarcity. Second, real wage changes themselves can come about for a variety of reasons, not all associated with production conditions in the wage goods sector.

When Mill, then, explicitly moves into considering the classical dynamics in Book IV, his method remains one of considering all possible cases. Moreover, methodologically the analysis proceeds in terms of tendencies and counter-tendencies. This is particularly true in the chapter on the tendency of the rate of profit under conditions of land scarcity to fall until the economy reaches the stationary state. Having presented the standard Ricardian analysis of the tendency, Mill asks:

> What, then, are these circumstances, which, in the existing state of things, maintain a tolerably equal struggle against the downward tendency of profits, and prevent the great annual savings which take place in this country from depressing the rate of profit much nearer to the lowest point to which it is always tending, and which, left to itself, it would so promptly attain?
>
> (733)

He goes on to discuss four such counter-tendencies: the loss of capital in the commercial crisis, technological improvements, foreign trade, and the outflow of capital to the colonies and other countries.

However, for our purposes there are two points here. First, it is clear that Mill understood that empirically the profit rate was not falling, and that this did not constitute a refutation of the theory. Second, we see a clear application of certain methodological positions Mill established in his earlier writings. The first point is directly relevant to the view that Mill is in some sense trying to rescue Ricardo from the historical fact that his predictions were not materializing. As Hollander states it:

> This charge turns on a failure to recognize that Ricardo like Smith before him did not design his economic models with an eye to specific historical prediction; and that Mill formally adopted this 'classical' position in his own writings on method. Nothing in British economic experience (particularly the movements of wage and profit rates) reflected adversely on Ricardian doctrine. ... In particular, Ricardianism provided general tools of analysis, including a fundamentally important theorem of distribution, which proved indispensable to Mill in his social preoccupations quite independently of the actual path of agricultural productivity and real wage rates.
>
> (EJSM: 945)

Our brief encounter with Mill's handling of the fundamental theorem and the falling rate of profit indicate that Hollander's conclusion here is essentially correct.

It is, however, a mistake to assume that Mill's method empties the framework of empirical content, or renders it unscientific because it becomes irrefutable. Contrary to some critics of *EDR* (O'Brien 1981: 358–9), a general framework is not empty theorizing. Indeed, as Mill clearly recognized, the fundamental theorem was falsifiable, and he was concerned that contemporary data seemed to refute it. Thus, the combination of high profit rates and high wages in the United States worried Mill, but the constancy of the British profit rate did not.

That Mill would treat theoretical political economy as providing a general framework of analysis, not a set of historical predictions, reflects a central tenet of his methodological writings: "In social phenomena the Composition of Causes is the universal law" (Mill 1988: 65). Without entering deeply into Mill's philosophy of social science, suffice it to say that this composition and plurality of causes in social science was the basis of his view of political economy as a deductive science set within a general social science: the science of ethology, the formation of national character. Any partial science, such as political economy, would focus deductively on the plurality of causes within its domain – hence Mill's approach to dynamics in terms of tendencies and counter-tendencies, each deduced within the confines of appropriate *ceteris paribus* assumptions.

The general science of ethology Mill viewed as empirical in nature, and it would situate political economy within its appropriate cultural and behavioral domain. In particular, behaviorally political economy concerned itself with those aspects of human nature which were associated with the drive to create and acquire material wealth (Mill 1974: 140). As Hollander concludes, "far from being represented as of 'universal' relevance, the axiomatic foundation of political economy [wealth maximization] was said to be pertinent only to well-defined environmental conditions" (EJSM: 104ff.). Culturally he confined it to the workings of the competitive capitalist system, although its method was universal. This, then, gives the *Principles* its institutional eclecticism which is its characteristic feature. By positioning political economy as a partial science of human nature and of human society, Mill believes he is able to maintain it as a deductive, Ricardian science of tendencies while rescuing it from the apologists and the sentimentalists. "His adherence to Ricardian procedure may be simply understood by the fact that it was envisaged as quite consistent with an appreciation of the 'provisional' nature of institutions and a preoccupation with social reform" (*EJSM*: 927–98).

Hollander's conclusion that Mill's view of the provisional nature of political economy is consistent with Ricardian procedure rests crucially on the notion that political economy must be understood as providing a framework of analysis, not a specific set of predictions and/or policy positions. That some of the most self-consciously Ricardian doctrines to be found in the *Principles* are explicitly presented in this way certainly adds plausibility to Hollander's position. It should be clear, for example from our review of the fundamental theorem, that Mill saw its import as a powerful tool of analysis, not as the basis for a prediction of a falling rate of profit. Mill's reformism and his historicism may be seen as part of a consistent program to rescue Ricardian political economy and place it on what he thought was a solid methodological foundation which was already implicit in the original. In this way he was able to demonstrate that Ricardian political economy was amenable to a broader, historical treatment, rendering the *Principles* a text in the Ricardian tradition.

There is much more to Mill and to *EJSM*, but, in keeping with the main themes of interpretation which Hollander's work raises, I have confined myself to Mill's treatment of the fundamental theorem and how it relates to other central issues of interpretation. *EJSM* reinforces the continuity thesis in two directions. First, our consideration of Mill's derivation of the theorem shows more clearly its roots in a general equilibrium model of relative price determination with value and distribution being interdependent phenomena. As such it is quite consistent with later neoclassical models. Second, by explicitly treating the theorem along with the classical dynamics as providing a framework of analysis, we were able to argue that the institutional and historical material of the *Principles*, far from being a departure from Ricardian political economy, was part of an overall strategy of rescuing it from apologists, second-raters, and sentimentalists.

## Conclusion

As I have indicated along the way, I think the main lines of Hollander's interpretation, at least those aspects which deal with value, distribution, and growth, hold up very well under the withering criticism to which they have been subjected. The fact that extensive reviews of these books appeared in major journals is itself testimony to their importance. In addition to the views expressed, Hollander's scholarly style also proved to be a source of discontent among his readers. Simply put, Hollander's books are not easy to read. As many reviewers have complained, they are extremely long, closely reasoned, and loaded with extensive quotations from the original sources – more so than any other secondary work.

Some reviewers have suggested, quite reasonably, that Hollander's scholarly style is rooted in his Talmudic training.[12] To me his books are stylistically similar to biblical commentaries. The entire extant text, including unpublished material, is taken extremely seriously as communicative of the thought of a single, unified mind. The result is extensive quotation followed by commentary, the use of materials from the whole extant body of primary materials, and an interpretative strategy which treats inconsistency as a last resort. A common reaction is Blaug's complaint that *EJSM* is "twice too long; there is much here that can only be explained by the author's propensity to revel in detail for its own sake and to multiply quotations from original sources beyond all the requirements of scholarship" (1986).

This is an understandable reaction from a reviewer who had to read the books straight through. As biblical-styled commentaries, however, they are not necessarily meant to be approached in that way. They should be viewed as references, each chapter of which can be consulted independently of the whole. This is not to say that there are no general themes which unite the books, far from it. But Hollander provides frequent summaries at the beginning and end of chapters, and the final chapter of each book contains a fairly extensive summary of the main points of the book.

While recognizing that Hollander's scholarly style has proven to be a stumbling block for many reviewers, I would also suggest that it is one of the main strengths of his work. As Ronald Meek said of *EAS*, "his judgements, however controversial they may at first sight appear, are always so well documented that it is very difficult to catch him out" (1974: 99). Surely no one would have taken Hollander's highly controversial view of the classical economists at all seriously if his interpretations had not been so thoroughly grounded in the primary source material.

I am reluctant to engage in predicting whether the central Hollander theses which I have reviewed in this chapter will ultimately win the day. Certainly there are and will continue to be adherents (and occasionally converts), for example, to the continuity thesis, the "new view" of Ricardo, and Malthus's reversal on agricultural protectionism. I have also alluded above to the beginning of some recognition of these views in the history of economic thought textbooks. However, given that there is no objective measure of the difference between a change of emphasis and a "drastic" change of emphasis (Blaug 1996: 4; also 291), it is entirely possible that debate will continue indefinitely.

In his summary comments on *EAS*, Meek made the following prediction: "If the remaining volumes in his planned series turn out to be of the same calibre as this, his total contribution to the history of economic thought will indeed have been a remarkable one" (1974: 100). Twenty-five years and three major installments later, we can conclude that Meek was indeed correct in his forecast. This, as yet unfinished body of work is indeed a remarkable one. Regardless of one's position in the controversies which continue to rage, there is no question that Hollander's is that rare sort of work which requires its audience to rethink long held positions and to look at old texts in new ways. It cannot help but produce a major shift in the way historians teach and write about the classical economists.

## Notes

* I wish to thank the editors of this volume for helpful comments on an earlier draft. The usual disclaimer applies to the final product.
1  Examples would include the exchanges between Hollander and D. P. O'Brien (1981, 1982), A. Roncaglia (1982), and P. Garegnani (1982). It is also worth noting that in each case the respective journals published full-scale review articles, which, given the scarcity of space in top journals, is surely indicative of the importance of EDR. Mark Blaug gives a characteristically blunt assessment of EDR by first laying out what he sees as its ten key propositions and then concludes: "I believe that every one of these ten assertions is false" (1985: 147). Lastly, I believe it is fair to suggest that EDR and its sequels were a major provocation behind Terry Peach's (1993) book-length reassessment of the Ricardian record.
2  In denying the "surplus" interpretation I do not mean to imply that Ricardo had no concept of surplus. He did have such a concept as income available for taxation and/or accumulation. Moreover, with wages above subsistence except in the stationary state, part of the surplus accrued to labor as well as land and capital.
3  Samuelson, for example, points out that the "new view" dynamics represent the general model while he presents the traditional subsistence wage model merely for "pedagogical simplicity" (1978: 426). The latter is then clearly a special case of the former.
4  If one denies outright the validity of the method of rational reconstruction there is the reverse danger of completely severing all ties between contemporary theory and its history. Since modern economics obviously came from somewhere it has legitimate antecedents, and it can be a useful aid in understanding them, even in identifying the "true" ancestors.
5  Joan Robinson once pointed out to me in personal correspondence (October 11, 1978) that Production of Commodities was the Marxian $c + v + s$ with the emphasis on $c$.
6  David Levy (1976) has formalized this in a model of rational choice where an individual must trade off per capita consumption against marriage age – that is, number of children.
7  It is a curious fact that much of the weight of evidence cited for the corn-model interpretation of Ricardo rests on things Malthus said, not Ricardo.
8  In fact, Hollander holds the view that they were not committed to the doctrine of free trade in principle, regardless of the resulting resource allocation. Their advocacy of free trade in grain in France in the eighteenth century turned on their presumption that under such a regime France would be a net exporter of food, causing resources to be redirected from trade and manufacturing to agriculture (CE: 51).
9  Some recent examples would include Eltis (1980), Costabile (1983), and Costabile and Rowthorn (1985).
10  I certainly do not want to denigrate Sraffa's own monumental contribution in the Works and Correspondence of David Ricardo. However, I think that fully sorting out the problem required a thorough investigation of the works of both Ricardo and Malthus.
11  See for example the review by P. J. Kelly who notes that

it must be said that this is a very important work for two reasons; firstly it is the definitive work on Mill's economic writings, and secondly the chapter on

"Utility and Liberty" is in my view the most important essay on Mill's reaction to Bentham and its effects on his utilitarianism and his theory of justice.

(Kelly 1987: 55–6)

12 Hollander agrees that his Talmudic training has had a significant impact in the way he approaches the original texts (Young 1998).

# Bibliography

Blaug, Mark (1985) *Economic Theory in Retrospect*, fourth edition, Cambridge: Cambridge University Press.

—— (1986) "Review of *The Economics of John Stuart Mill*," *History of Economic Thought Newsletter* 36, Spring.

—— (1996) *Economic Theory in Retrospect*, fifth edition, Cambridge: Cambridge University Press.

Bronfenbrenner, Martin (1997) "Review of *Ricardo: The New View*," *History of Political Economy* 29, 1: 159–61.

Casarosa, Carlo (1978) "A New Formulation of the Ricardian System," *Oxford Economic Papers* XXX, March: 38–63.

Costabile, Lilia (1983) "Natural Prices, Market Prices and Effective Demand in Malthus," *Australian Economic Papers* 22, June: 144–70.

Costabile, Lilia and Rowthorn, Bob (1985) "Malthus's Theory of Wages and Growth," *The Economic Journal* 95, June: 418–37.

Eltis, Walter (1980) "Malthus's Theory of Effective Demand and Growth," *Oxford Economic Papers* 32, 1: 19–56.

Garegnani, P. (1982) "On Hollander's Interpretation of Ricardo's Early Theory of Profits," *Cambridge Journal of Economics* 6, 1: 65–77.

Hicks, Sir John and Hollander, Samuel (1977) "Mr. Ricardo and the Moderns," *Quarterly Journal of Economics* XCI, August: 351–69.

Hollander, Samuel (1973) *The Economics of Adam Smith*, Toronto: University of Toronto Press.

—— (1979) *The Economics of David Ricardo*, Toronto: University of Toronto Press.

—— (1981) "Marxian Economics as 'General Equilibrium' Theory," *History of Political Economy* 13, 1.

—— (1982) "*The Economics of David Ricardo*: A Response to Professor O'Brien," *Oxford Economic Papers* 43, 1.

—— (1984) "Marx and Malthusianism: Marx's Secular Path of Wages," *American Economic Review* 74, 1.

—— (1985) *The Economics of John Stuart Mill*, Toronto: University of Toronto Press.

—— (1987) *Classical Economics*, Oxford: Basil Blackwell.

—— (1992) "Malthus's Abandonment of Agricultural Protectionism: A Discovery in the History of Economic Thought," *American Economic Review* 82, 3.

—— (1995a) *Ricardo – The New View: Collected Essays I*, London: Routledge.

—— (1995b) "More on Malthus and Agricultural Protection," *History of Political Economy* 27, 3: 531–7.

—— (1997) *The Economics of Thomas Robert Malthus*, Toronto: Toronto University Press.

—— (1998) *The Literature of Political Economy: Collected Essays II*, London: Routledge.

Hutchison, Terrence (1988) *Before Adam Smith: The Emergence of Political Economy, 1662–1776*, Oxford: Basil Blackwell.

Kelly, P. J. (1987) "The Influence of Bentham on the Thought of J.S. Mill,"*The Bentham Newsletter* 11, June: 53–7.

Knight, Frank (1935) "The Ricardian Theory of Production and Distribution," *The Canadian Journal of Economics and Political Science* 1: 3–25, 171–96.

Levy, David (1976) "Ricardo and the Iron Law: A Correction of the Record," *History of Political Economy* 8, 2: 235–52.

Malthus, T. R. (1986) *Principles of Political Economy Considered with a View to Their Application*, second edition, New York: Augustus M. Kelley.

—— (1992) *An Essay on the Principle of Population*, ed. Donald Winch, Cambridge: Cambridge University Press.

Meek, Ronald (1974) "Review of *The Economics of Adam Smith*," *Journal of Economic Literature* XII, 1: 99–100.

Mill, J. S. (1974) *Essays on some Unsettled Questions of Political Economy*, second edition, New York: Augustus M. Kelley.

—— (1987) *Principles of Political Economy With Some of Their Applications to Social Philosophy*, ed. Sir William Ashley, New York: Augustus M. Kelley.

—— (1988) *The Logic of the Moral Sciences*, La Salle, IL: Open Court.

O'Brien, D. P. (1975) *The Classical Economists*, Oxford: Oxford University Press.

—— (1981) "Ricardian Economics and the Economics of David Ricardo," *Oxford Economic Papers* 33, 3: 352–86.

Pasinetti, Luigi (1960) "A Mathematical Formulation of the Ricardian System," *The Review of Economic Studies* XXVII, 2: 78–98.

Peach, Terry (1993) *Interpreting Ricardo*, Cambridge: Cambridge University Press.

Prendergast, Renee (1986) "Malthus's Discussion of the Corn Ratio Theory of Profits," *Cambridge Journal of Economics* 10, 2: 187–9.

Pullen, John (1995) "Malthus on Agricultural Protection: An Alternative View," *History of Political Economy* 27, 3: 517–29.

Rashid, Salim (1998) *The Myth of Adam Smith*, Cheltenham: Edward Elgar.

Ricardo, David (1951) *Principles of Political Economy and Taxation, Works and Correspondence of David Ricardo*, Vol. I, ed. Piero Sraffa, Cambridge: Cambridge University Press.

Robbins, Lionel (1998) *A History of Economic Thought; The LSE Lectures*, ed. Steven G. Medema and Warren J. Samuels, Princeton, NJ: Princeton University Press.

Roncaglia, Alessandro (1982) "Hollander's Ricardo," *Journal of Post-Keynesian Economics* IV, 3: 339–59.

Samuelson, Paul (1978) "The Canonical Classical Model of Political Economy," *Journal of Economic Literature* XVI, December: 1415–34.

Schumpeter, Joseph A. (1954) *History of Economic Analysis*, Oxford: Oxford University Press.

Smith, Adam (1976) *An Inquiry into the Nature and Causes of the Wealth of Nations*, ed. Andrew S. Skinner and R. H. Campbell, Oxford: Clarendon Press.

Sraffa, Piero (1951) "Introduction," *Works and Correspondence of David Ricardo*, Vol. I, Cambridge: Cambridge University Press.

—— (1960) *Production of Commodities by Means of Commodities*, Cambridge: Cambridge University Press.

Staley, Charles E. (1989) *A History of Economic Thought: From Aristotle to Arrow*, Oxford: Basil Blackwell.

Stigler, George (1965) "Textual Exegesis as a Scientific Problem," *Economica* NS XXXII, 128: 447–50.

Walras, Leon (1977) *Elements of Pure Economics*, trans. William Jaffe, New York: Augustus M. Kelley.

Winch, Donald (1987) *Malthus*, Oxford: Oxford University Press.

Young, Jeffrey T. (1991) "Review of *Classical Economics*," *History of Political Economy* 23, 1: 167–70.

—— (1998) "Interview with Samuel Hollander," 9 July.

# 9 S. Todd Lowry and ancient Greek economic thought

## An interpretation

*Spencer J. Pack**

## Introduction

S. Todd Lowry has a vision of economics as the study of administrative or managerial efficiency. His position may be viewed as a generalization of the more orthodox view of economics as the study of market efficiency. For Lowry, human administrators may or may not use the market. Human administrators will also decide on how the markets will be organized and structured. The market for Lowry is not some naturalistic force outside of human control and management. Efficiency for Lowry means that administrators must make choices about how to achieve ends. These choices will be based upon hedonic, cost–benefit analyses, having to deal with pleasure and pain, or pleasure and non-pleasure. Western economic thought based upon this conception of economics, economics as the study of administrative or managerial efficiency, where efficiency involves the making of hard choices based upon careful hedonic calculations, has a long history. It goes back at least as far as the ancient Greeks. It is up to historians of economic thought to rediscover, explore, and develop this ancient, rich heritage. In effect, Lowry has an extensive research program which he invites the rest of the discipline of the history of economic thought to pursue.

The chapter is organized as follows. First it discusses methodological issues arising from Lowry's approach, and the nature and scope of the subject matter of economics. Then it discusses Lowry's work in resource and environmental economics. This is followed by a short discussion of Lowry's views on legal and contract theory, and a brief, general overview of his position concerning ancient Greek economic thought. The chapter then gives an account of Lowry's interpretation of the economic thought of Xenophon, Plato, the participative view in ancient Greek thought as found in such sources as the Homeric epics and the sophists (especially Protagoras), and Aristotle. The chapter concludes by suggesting avenues for future research which arise from Lowry's seminal work.

## Methodological issues

Lowry is most noted for his deep expertise in ancient Greek economic thought. He has been particularly concerned with the relationship between ancient

Greek economic thought and the modern economic thought of the past quarter millennium. Lowry has outlined and detailed his position in a series of articles published both before and after the appearance of his major work, *The Archaeology of Economic Ideas: The Classical Greek Tradition* (1987a). The *Archaeology of Economic Ideas* itself presents the most comprehensive account of Lowry's views; much of the most valuable material is discussed in the extensive footnotes. Warren Samuels, in a review in *History of Political Economy*, has characterized the book as "a brilliant exercise of the intellect by one of the finest intellects and brilliant historians of thought in the discipline" (1989: 160). For Samuels, the work "is a tour de force and is recommended to any economist seeking to appreciate the larger dimensions of the discipline and to all historians of economic thought" (ibid.).

Yet, why is the book so important and why would historians of economic thought, let alone general economists, even be interested in ancient Greek economic thought? The answer is complex.

If one takes a narrow neoclassical view of economics, and equates the study of economics with the study of competitive market prices, then one may not be too interested in ancient Greek thought, nor, indeed, find any economic thought there.[1] After all, ancient Greece does not seem to have been what one would call a market society. Many products did not exchange through the market. The prices of those goods that did exchange through the market were frequently administered by state authorities, or else they were the result of isolated bilateral bargaining. Market prices appear to have been rarely the result of many competitive market buyers and sellers. Consequently, there appears to be little or no ancient Greek economic thought concerning the workings of a more or less self-regulating competitive market price mechanism.

On the other hand, if one takes the more recent view that neoclassical economic thought is actually the theory of choice,[2] then one will be keenly interested in ancient Greek economic thought, and hence Lowry's work. As Lowry repeatedly demonstrates, the ancient Greeks were consumed with the problem of choice. How does one choose to be a good person? How does one choose to divide the produce after a successful hunt or military/pillaging expedition? What sort of familial, social, and political institutions should be adopted to facilitate the individual choice of virtue or excellence? These are the sorts of questions which deeply concerned the Greeks and which they attempted to solve. Lowry's work demonstrates that the Greek answers to these questions form the foundations of modern economic answers to similar questions concerning choice and how humans should make decisions among options.

On another hand, suppose one takes a narrow Marxist view of political economy, that political economy is the study of the production and reproduction of the capitalist mode of production. Here, again, one may not be too interested in ancient Greek thought. After all, ancient Greece does not appear to have been a capitalist society. It was to a large extent a slave-based society, or in any case its economic production was not dominated by the free wage–labor capitalist social relation.[3] Yet, if one takes a broader view of Marxian political economy as the study of the production and reproduction of the means of production and the relations of production in societies in general, then one would again be keenly interested in what the ancient Greeks thought. The Greeks had a great deal to contribute to the understanding of how societies should be organized; indeed, they largely began the Western tradition of political and social thought. Marx himself was keenly interested and influenced by ancient Greek thought (Marx, 1973; Meikle 1985; 1995).[4]

It is from the institutional point of view that the importance of the study of ancient Greek economic thought is perhaps least problematic; and this is indeed Lowry's basic approach. For Lowry, "[i]nstitutionalists seek to build a more realistic analysis of economic interactions based on empirical observation, historical or evolutionary understanding and anthropological and sociological insights" (1994b: 47). Lowry defines economics as the study of how human beings "have sought food, shelter and clothing, the essential elements of physical survival" (1987a: 2). It is the study of administrative efficiency.[5] Therefore, "economic thought must ... have a very long history" (ibid.). By this definition, the Greeks, as with all other human societies, must have had an economy. Furthermore, what they thought about their economy is absolutely crucial to understanding modern economic thought, because their thought forms the foundations of the intellectual tradition out of which modern economic thought developed. Granted, current economists may be completely ignorant about the ancient Greek roots of economics. Indeed, it is not quite correct to say that contemporary economists have forgotten these ancient roots since "you can't forget what you never knew" (Proctor 1998: Preface).[6] Yet, the great classical economists such as Smith, Bentham, and Marx who forged the modern discipline of economics certainly knew their ancient Greek thought. It is through them that the ancient Greek intellectual tradition has been transmitted into the most contemporary of economic works.[7]

## Resource and environmental economics

Lowry's institutional approach manifests itself clearly in his earlier work in resource and environmental economics. His Ph.D. dissertation "A Survey of Early Economic Thought on the Problem of Resource Analysis"[8] led not only into papers such as his "The Classical Greek Theory of Natural Resource Economics" (1965); it also led into such questions as the proper administrative management of the US South's forest, timber, and pulp and paper industries. In "The Appalachian Regional Development Act of 1965 and the Timber Development Organization Dilemma" (1966), Lowry carefully considered the many smallholdings of timber in the hands of marginal farmers or rural residents. He argued that for them, higher prices or lower transportation costs simply increased the cutting or harvesting of timber, but not the actual planting and production of timber. Lowry urged that the forest be treated as a flow resource rather than merely as a fund to be liquidated. He continued this theme in "The Future of the South's Forest Industry" (1967). There he argued in the name of administrative efficiency that forests be considered as flow resources, likened to fisheries, pasture land or water power. Lowry emphasized that the cutting of forest products is not their real production; it is only their harvesting. Indeed, when high prices cause the landowner to clear-cut the land and then put it to pasture, then the harvesting of timber will be up; but the production of wood products will actually be down.

Lowry furthered his theoretical analysis in "The Kinked Cost Curve and the Dual Resource Base under Oligopsony in the Pulp and Paper Industry" (1974c). He argued that there was an oligopsonistic structure in the raw materials market in industries with significant captive resource bases, such as the pulp and paper industry. There large firms had a choice to expand the harvest or production on their own land or to buy from outside sources. Lowry argued that a close institutional analysis of how the pulpwood buyer actually makes its decisions was needed. It could be that with a rise in the price of output, monopsonistic and oligopsonistic firms would choose not to raise input prices, and not to buy more from their outside suppliers. Instead, they would choose to harvest more from their own lands. The firms would rationally treat the two sources of supply differently. More empirical investigations were needed to ascertain how often firms really did this.

Lowry continued to evince a concern for the precise institutional specifications of the forest market in "Some Perspectives on Raw Material Costs in the Forest Industry" (1976b). He argued that it keenly matters whether a mill acquires its input from company-owned land (inside wood) or outside wood supplied by the small landowners. Furthermore, closer public and private administrative attention needs to be paid to the difference between the harvesting and the production of timber. Lowry also argued that the entire administrative efficiency of the forest industry in the United States is impaired because of "the lack of a culturally established forestry tradition in the country" (1976b: 65) which embodies a suitably long time horizon. Hence, suggests Lowry, "ethical and ideological developments" may be needed to help "induce a stable, longrun land management pattern" (1976b: 64).

Lowry continued his theme of the lack of a healthy vital forestry tradition in the United States, and the frequently deleterious effects this has had on US forests in "The Nature of Pre-Industrial Forest Planning" (1977). Lowry pointed out that in France, physiocratic doctrine led to reduced forest land. Lowry viewed US Jeffersonian agrarian thought as a US projection of the physiocratic justification for land clearing. Lowry harshly criticized "lumbermen who helped themselves to public timber in New England," who were "merely men in an institutionally fluid society in which short-run economic aggrandizement was the order of the day, and stealing newly accessible public timber was an efficient way to get rich quick" (1977: 26). Indeed, Lowry argued, "it is questionable whether the open market for timber products has ever charged any consumer the full social cost of its production" (ibid.). He further argued that there is a need for established custom, aesthetic ideal, or legal restraint to lengthen time horizons of people longer than an individualistic point of view to properly manage the nation's timber resources properly (ibid.: 28). This argument is indicative of Lowry's general attitude. He sees a need for a reform, in this case a dramatic lengthening of the time horizon for the efficient management of timber. However, he appears agnostic as to whether the reform should be achieved through changes in the law, aesthetic ideals, or customs, or some combination of the above.

Lowry sees a more clear-cut need for a legal or direct administrative approach in dealing with large shopping center malls in "The Impact of Large-scale Private Land-use Decisions: The Theory of Cut-throat Development" (1980). Lowry argues that with shopping centers, developers build a series of shopping malls. Each one is bigger than the one before, and each new shopping center completely beats out the older shopping center. Eventually, this process leaves behind a mess of old shopping centers with deteriorating parking lots, empty stores, and ruined agricultural land. In this situation, Lowry sees the need for an administrative approach in the tradition of public utility regulation to regulate the mall developers. Otherwise, there will just be megamalls with other small, older decaying malls littering the landscape.

Lowry further reflects on the need for environmental protection and conservation in "An Economist's View of Preservation" (1976a). He argues that "[t]he respect for manual arts and the appreciation of beauty in both city and country is more than just a faddish flight of elitist indulgence or a frightened conservatism clinging to the past out of fear of the future" (1976a: 28). Rather, we do need to preserve wilderness areas, rural landscapes, and urban buildings. The difficulty is how to value and appraise the need for social assets, as well as to compare between current and future values. A particularly acute problem is that many subjects have completely unique characters; once they are destroyed, these characters are lost for ever.

Generally, in dealing with environmental, political, or theoretical issues, Lowry is quite calm, measured, professorial, courteous. Once in a while he gets testy, particularly in dealing with the formalism of neoclassical economics,[9] for example:

> a slow creeping sense of depression came over me. What have we done in the development of higher education that guarantees that no one will raise the obvious questions so that we go on mechanically expounding tenuous platitudes designed to simplify reality, but that seem primarily to succeed in training students quiescently to embrace the unreal, patiently and unquestioningly assimilating narrowly conceived inverted pyramids of elaborated assumption?

> (1979b: 228)

## Legal and contract theory

A key aspect to Lowry's institutional analysis is his knowledge of legal theory. Lowry, who acquired a law degree before he switched to the field of economics,[10] has "an appreciation of legal theory or jurisprudence as the carrier of many intellectual patterns into modern thought" (1987a: xiii). This knowledge is perhaps most evident in his papers "Lord Mansfield and the Law Merchant: Law and Economics in the 18th Century" (1973) and "Bargain and Contract Theory in Law and Economics" (1976c). In his paper on Lord Mansfield, Lowry demonstrated how Mansfield brought "the usages and customs of the merchants, the so-called 'Law Merchant', into the mainstream of English common law" (1973: 606). Mansfield was the father of commercial law, bringing "under formal legal supervision and management a system that had perpetuated and maintained itself for centuries as a voluntaristic unmanaged structure of rules developed by the merchants themselves for the conduct of business" (ibid.: 609).

This law enforced contracts and contracts need to be seen as a vital instrument of economic planning. These ideas are developed in Lowry's article on bargain and contract theory (1976c).[11] There Lowry criticized Coasean theory since Coase naively assumed law-abiding citizens who will not destroy each other's property or being. Rather, according to Lowry, one needs already to have an established system of order, where there is conformity to socially accepted and legally enforceable laws. Moreover, Lowry argues, it is preferable to commence an economic analysis with an extended family to understand social and economic relations, than with the presumed rationality of isolated individuals. Bargaining for Lowry necessarily occurs in a social or institutional arena and is really part of ongoing social relations. Contracts themselves further structure unique patterns of commitment and obligation. They organize and plan future economic relations, thus promoting stability. Contracts are more than mere one-time transactions or bargains or exchanges, since they involve planning and ongoing relations.

## Ancient Greek economic thought

Turning now to Lowry's work in ancient Greek economic thought, Lowry attempts to trace economic ideas to their earliest formulation, to study them in their "infant nakedness" (1991d: 142). So, for example, in looking at the development of contract theory, he studies the ancient myth of Prometheus,[12] the benefactor of mankind who stole fire from the gods for mankind. Lowry investigates the Promethean meat division between Prometheus and Zeus from an economic and legal perspective. The essence of the deal is that one divides a pile of meat into two, and the other chooses the pile he wants. The results of the division stand, the free choice is made, a deal is a deal even if the chooser (who was Zeus himself) then feels that he chose the worse pile. The choice is binding; this is a "nascent legal precedent in the evolution of contract theory" (1991c: 55; see also 1987a: 126–31).

Lowry emphasizes that, institutionally, the Greeks lived in a risky world, a world of piracy, raiding, and much warfare. The environment could be viewed as a high-stakes game, and the Greeks developed a "success culture" (1987a:

26–9) where defeat in war meant death for the adult males and enslavement for the women and children (1991a). In this environment the Greeks stressed leadership, administrative control (1991b; 1988b), and the improvement of human qualities (1965; 1995a). Moreover, "the diffusion of the patriarchal success ethic to the head of every nuclear family unit established the male citizen as an individual decision-maker" (1987a: 29) – a person who had to make hard, difficult choices.

Among the ancient Greeks, Lowry concentrates on a few key individuals who were associated with classical Athens. Also, there is a dialectic to Lowry's approach, where there is Plato, Plato's antagonists the sophists (particularly Protagoras), and the attempted synthesis in the thought of Aristotle (1998). Yet, these were all "high-brow" theorists. There was also the more practical, man of action/experience/business approach of Xenophon. Let us turn to Lowry's interpretation of Xenophon.

## Xenophon

Xenophon (c. 428–354 BC) was a professional soldier; although an Athenian, he took up arms against Athens and for Sparta. For this, he was exiled from Athens. The decree of banishment was not lifted until near the end of his life in 365 BC. In spite of his banishment, Xenophon was keenly concerned with Athenian affairs. His article "Ways and Means" was written to advise Athens on how to raise its public revenues. Observes Lowry, "as late as the 18th century his 'Ways and Means' was studied for its practical analysis of economics and administrative problems" (1987a: 46). Lowry describes Xenophon's writings as a "vivid combination of romantic adventurism and practical common sense" (ibid.). They were vitally important in the education of the wealthier classes in Western Europe up to modern times. Xenophon emphasized the importance of the individual decision maker, "whether military commander, public administrator, or head of an extended family estate" (1987a: 47). He urged the "dedicated emulation of heroic role models as the most effective avenue to greatness" (1987a: 46). This promoted the "great man theory of history" (1987a: 51). Xenophon emphasized the importance of managing an enterprise, be it an army, the state, or a private estate. He stressed organization, efficient leadership, and the acquisition of skills and knowledge. His emphasis on improved skills to solve problems was a recognition of the importance of human capital (1987a: 50). Training, more than the initial allotment of character or productivity traits, was the key to Xenophon's administrative approach. Self-command, discipline, the giving of direction to underlings, and the view of humans as the key productive variable in management and control characterize Xenophon's writings. Lowry remarks that "Xenophon was not concerned with the market or of market processes as such" (1987a: 55). Rather he was concerned with estate and military management and leadership, with mental and physical training, with finding the best experts to assist the leaders, and with how to order and combine things correctly to get efficient results. As with the other ancient

Greeks, Xenophon tended to assume "that all potential, both material and human, was already in existence" (1987a: 66). The key was to maximize this potential by diligently "putting existing elements together in new or better ways" (1987a: 73).

Xenophon argued, as Adam Smith would several thousands of years later, that improved craftsmanship depended upon the extent of the market. With increases in the size of the market, the quality of the product would improve; moreover, gross physical productivity itself would also increase (1987a: 71–3). Xenophon gave a description of assembly-line methods of shoe production. He had a subjective measure of value suggesting "that one who is completely satisfied with very little may be richer than one who has much but is still desirous of more" (1987a: 78).

Lowry argues that when Xenophon did consider exchange, he thought more in terms of isolated exchange, rather than in terms of an established market. Hence, Xenophon was concerned with bargaining over unique goods. Yet, this bargaining over goods was just a minor part of the royal art of military leadership, or of household or estate management. Xenophon was developing a general administrative or managerial art, or form of knowledge based upon hedonism (or a hedonistic theory of choice), subjective use value, and the idea of the manager or leader "as a capital asset which can augment wealth" and promote efficiency (1987a: 274, n. 66). Xenophon also discussed cost–benefit analysis, for example in his account of Socrates' explanation of how an entertainer could maximize audience pleasure while minimizing work effort and risk (1987a: 81). Xenophon's work merits much more attention from modern historians of economic thought; it is in need of a general reevaluation from the point of view of economics as the study of administrative efficiency.

## Plato

Plato (c. 427–347 BC), although Xenophon's contemporary, was a very different type of person. Both studied under Socrates; but while Xenophon went off at a relatively young age to seek his fame and fortune pursuing a military career, Plato pursued the life of the mind. He is, of course, considered one of the great thinkers of the Western world.

Plato presented his ideal administrative state in *The Republic*. For Lowry, "[a]s in Xenophon, the administrative problem is here posed as the application of administrative expertise or organizational skills" (1987a: 85). The work is a blueprint for a perfect society, an administered utopia, and it reflects "Plato's irritation at the failure of the public assemblies and law courts to accept what he considered to be rational leadership" (1987a: 87). In *The Republic* a semi-deified lawgiver brings order to the community; the community is static, efficient, and self-sufficient. Ruled under the benign authority of an intelligent leader, there is the assumption that there is one best function for each member of the society. The rationally organized state uses experts who have true knowledge. Plato displays disdain for democratic institutions. Mere rhetoric for Plato is a process used to subvert the influence of the true expert. Hence, Lowry explains that for Plato "rhetoric or public persuasion is thus rejected as a process that in and of itself will lead to valid social consensus and proper order" (1987a: 89). Instead, rhetoric enables the ignorant or the unjust "to *appear* to know more than the real expert" (1987a: 90; emphasis in original).

The wise and the experts will be ruled by an ethical hedonism based on either happiness or internal harmony. They "will be concerned with limiting their need for material goods through temperance so as to avoid creating any imbalance in the harmony of their souls" (1987a: 92). Plato rejects "the characterization of the economic process as the impingement of unlimited wants on limited or scarce resources" (ibid.). Rather, for Plato, the use of reason in the pursuit or choice of ethical self-interest and ethical hedonism "will prevent any individual – and most particularly a ruler – from voluntarily being unjust to others because this would damage the inner harmony of his own psyche or soul" (1987a: 115). Justice, rationally chosen by rational individuals, is necessarily beneficial since it leads to inner peace.

Thus, Plato "develops a concept of an objective ethical standard for justice that can be used as a basis for criticizing any given system of laws inconsistent with 'true knowledge'" (1987a: 94). Following reason, the ruler will choose to devote "himself only to the interests of his subjects" (1987a: 95). Like Veblen's technocrat, the expert will practice his art efficiently. There will be rigorous education and training for the elite. As with captaining a large ship, political expertise is "a specialty that could be competently mastered by only a few" (1987a: 111).

Lowry finds that Plato gives "about as clear a statement of the economic genesis of a state based upon subjective mutuality as one could expect" (1987a: 104). People form a state because they need each other for the production and distribution of food, shelter, clothing, etc. Economic specialization is the basis for mutual interdependence. It is also the source of efficiency and productivity, and it leads to the reciprocal exchange of products. The state is formed due to this economic interdependence growing out of the production and distribution of goods. In Plato's ideal state, the superior intellect or lawgiver assigns roles to individuals on the basis of their natural differences in skills and capacity. Each citizen "achieves the greatest happiness by performing his most efficient role in society" (1987a: 108).

For Lowry, Plato presents an update of the patriarchal tradition. In Plato's world, while there is a vertically structured hierarchy of duty, there is no definition of individual rights (ibid.). Also, Plato is "completely lacking in any theory of a participative political or economic process for arriving at the just or orderly state" (1987a: 110). Instead, he assumes that "the knowledge which gives the expert 'true' ideas is a fixed entity so that there would be no disagreement" (1987a: 113). Thus, there is only one rationally chosen agreed-upon destination for the ship of state; and Plato "never finds it necessary to give any criteria by which the objectives of the expert can be judged" (1987a: 121).

## The Greek participative tradition

Plato is reacting to what he considers to be the excesses of Athenian democracy, under which his great teacher Socrates was put to death for allegedly subversive teachings. This Athenian democracy had developed a remarkable tradition of a participative process in reaching both private and public decisions (or choices). Lowry explores various aspects of this tradition.

One aspect was the use of Greek myths to develop processes that do not depend upon raw physical power, or might makes right. Hence, as discussed above, Lowry demonstrates how the myth of Prometheus in Hesiod's *Theogony* structured a procedure for the "quarrel-free distribution (but not exchange) of a jointly acquired good in an isolated setting" (1987a: 128). There, even though Zeus himself was unhappy with his free choice, he honored the distribution of meat. Similarly, Lowry demonstrates how Homer's *Iliad* was in part "an economic and legal confrontation between Achilles and Agamemnon over the distribution of the returns of warfare (booty)" (1987a: 131). The *Iliad* teaches that rather than kill Agamemnon, Achilles should fight with words. Their "confrontation occurs against the background of a public debate before an assembled multitude where the views of experienced elders are heard" (1987a: 136). There is a formalized structure of debate in a gathering place. The work introduces the "image of a public process for the settlement of disputes" (ibid.).

For the Greeks, words begin to take on a life of their own; justice becomes a procedure. Justice is arrived at by a process of negotiation which is carried out rhetorically and in public view. The emphasis is on effective, persuasive speech where disputants must work out their private disagreements in a public arena.

While Lowry demonstrates how the *Iliad* may be read as an essay on law and the economics of distribution, he argues that Homer's *Odyssey* "can be read as a study of the law and economics of hospitality" (1987a: 146). For Homer and the Greeks, people have a burden to offer hospitality to strangers, including beggars, and to succor and protect suppliants. In this framework, the Cyclopes, obviously, were a paradigmatic example of bad hospitality.

Lowry argues that, as reflected in Homer and other sources, the Greeks developed the crucial idea that crime is an offense against the entire community. Crime becomes a social phenomenon, and it demands correction by a social process, not by private vengeance or clan warfare. Additionally, the Greeks developed the idea of contracts being legally enforceable; contracts become voluntary distributions and/or commitments, protected by a legal framework. Thus, the concept of the polis was born, which included, among other things, both the concept of duty to one's peers as well as enforceable rights against one's peers (1987a: 156).

According to Lowry's reading, the idea of justice as a social process was further developed by the sophist Protagoras (c. 490–420 BC). For Protagoras, "man is the measure of all things" (quoted in Lowry 1987a: 162). Lowry explains that this "man-measure doctrine is the parent idea of both the labor theory of value and the notion of subjective individualism" (1987a: 159). Moreover, for Protagoras, whatever the state decides to make a law is lawful for that state. The key ingredient for Protagoras is the process. The wise leader in a democracy explains to the populace "the elements of a utilitarian calculus for use in collective decision making" (1987a: 158). This wise leader persuades but does not force the populace to accept better council. The state itself is largely held together by *aidos* or fellow feeling (similar to and anticipating Adam Smith's theory of sympathy in *The Theory of Moral Sentiments* (1987a: 215)). For Protagoras, no individual or state is necessarily wiser than any other; there is no standard for objective truth. His emphasis on the decision-making process parallels with "our modern legal concept of due process of law in that it sets up the procedure or process itself as the measure of justice" (1987a: 170). Protagoras claimed to be able to teach his listeners success and virtue in managing the affairs of both their own household and the city. For Lowry, he was, in effect, teaching economics.

## Aristotle

In Lowry's interpretation, Aristotle (384–322 BC) attempted to synthesize the emphasis by Protagoras and the sophists on process, rhetoric, and public debate, with the more elitist, static, teleological views of Plato. According to Lowry, rhetoric for Aristotle became "a form of analysis to be employed in convincing decision-makers about the utility of different choices" (1987a: 178). In practice, Aristotle would begin his treatment of a subject with a review of received opinions, since any belief accepted by common sense or wise men must be at least partly true. This corresponded "to the generative potential which Protagoras ascribed to the participative political process" (1987a: 296, n.19). Lowry finds that in the *Topics* Aristotle took account of scarcity and use value, where, according to Aristotle, "what is rare is a greater good than what is plentiful" (quoted in 1987a: 179). Aristotle used marginal analysis in the *Topics* in dealing with arguments, persuasion, and choice, and demonstrated "that a careful, systematic analysis of hedonic comparisons will convince an opponent of the superiority of one choice over another" (1987a: 177).

In the *Nicomachean Ethics* Aristotle presented a mathematical analysis of how to determine just price in a two-party exchange. In this situation, Aristotle does not seem to have been dealing with an impersonal market price. Rather, he had in mind an isolated bargaining situation where justice in exchange was framed in terms of means and proportions, quite possibly harmonic means and proportions. Thus, Lowry interprets Aristotle as using proportions and means to mathematize his discussion of justice in exchange. Furthermore, according to Lowry, Aristotle's possible use of the harmonic proportion also reflects a concern with the maintenance of Greek social structure. Aristotle was concerned with "settling disputes between individuals and in maintaining a rational balance between individuals in a community" (1987a: 211).

Of the harmonic proportion, Lowry explains: "The harmonic proportion, by assigning intermediate points in terms of opposite extremes, provides a framework for visualizing this relationship by identifying different quantifications of

reciprocal justice (or injustice) – 'more or less' – from the subjective perspectives of two different parties" (1987a: 190; see also Lowry 1969). Lowry argues
that for Aristotle

> the measurement of the benefits of trade from the subjective perspective of
> each participant in an exchange independent of the basis of value used by
> the other is most easily represented by the harmonic proportion since it
> permits measurement from two different reference points, in other words
> dual subjectivity.
>
> (1987a: 191)

Although Aristotle's math is obscure,[13] it is clear that he is dealing with a zone
of indeterminacy between two negotiating parties, and is trying to ascertain a
proper exchange ratio. This zone of indeterminacy served as the basis for
Edgeworth's "contract curve" (1987a: 191). It may also have served as a zone for
some scholastic notions of just price. For Aristotle, justice is a kind of mean, too
much or too little being unjust. There is a zone of mutual benefit which the
trading parties will receive from their exchange. Aristotle's formulation of the
gains from trade is the general case from which the theory of comparative
advantage of international trade is a particularization. Lowry argues that "a
careful retranslation and analysis of the manuscripts from which our
Aristotelian material is taken" by someone with a mathematical and/or
economics background "may very well reveal clues to a systematic quantitative
expression of mutuality" (1987a: 209). This might clarify the ambiguities in
Aristotle's mathematical analysis of just exchange between two isolated transactors.

For Lowry, Aristotle's Platonic side is evident in his *Politics*, where

> he stays within the shadow of Platonic teleology by insisting that the whole
> or ultimate end of combinations is what gives meaning and character to
> constituent elements, so that they cannot be understood except in the
> context of the general system or ideal type.
>
> (1987a: 216)

There is a tripartite structure to Aristotle's political economy. The household
provides goods of the body; these are of first and lowest order of priority. The
village provides external goods; these are of second order of priority. The polis
or city-state provides psychic goods, goods of the soul; these are the ultimate
and highest order of goods (1987a: 219). For Aristotle, there is diminishing
marginal utility to lower goods of the body and external goods, but not to
psychic goods (the goods of the soul).

Aristotle demonstrates that the exchange of commodities generates money,
and Lowry argues that Aristotle discussed four functions of money: as medium
of exchange, measure of value, store of value, and standard of deferred payments
(1987a: 226). For Aristotle, the exchange of commodities, with money as an

intermediary (C – M – C'), is legitimate and natural. This is mutual need satisfaction, the reciprocal pattern of complementary surpluses and shortages.
However, the use of money to make more money (M – C – M') or usury (M –
M' – M'') is deemed unnecessary and unnatural. This part of Aristotle's analysis
influenced Marx's work in the early parts of *Capital* (1987a: 319, n.39).[14] The use
of money to make more money encouraged people to become too acquisitive. It
was chrematistics – the unlimited desire for more money. In contradistinction,
Aristotle's natural political economy was directed "to an analysis of the management and satisfaction of the needs of the household and state and not to the
study of a market oriented toward profit maximization" (1987a: 231). For
Aristotle, there were natural limits to human desire (Lowry 1974a; Pack, 1985a).
Yet, "in chrematistics made possible by monetary exchange, there is no internal
limiting factor" (Lowry 1987a: 233). Hence arose the

> need for the regulation of retail trade necessitated by the absence of any
> natural forces adequate to protect the citizen of the Greek city-state from
> the possible predatory accumulation of coined money by the useful but
> suspect metic [resident foreign commercial] population.
>
> (Lowry 1974a: 63)

Lowry finds that in time, this perceived need for the human, administrative
regulation of commerce jarred so

> with the eighteenth-century discovery of the apparently rational resource-
> allocating capacities of the self-regulating market system and the liberating
> potential of economic expansion that the older administrative approach of
> the ancient Greek science of oikonomia, with its emphasis on stability and
> self-sufficiency, was deemed an anachronism, and no longer relevant.
>
> (1987a: 240)

Nonetheless, this ancient system of thought formed the archaeological foundations of modern economic thought (1987b; 1987c). Hence, to take just one
example, even Adam Smith's formulation of a largely self-regulating market
seems to be none other than an example of a Platonic ideal type. Smith himself
knew and was able to clearly articulate Plato's theory of eternal blueprints or
models and theory of forms and substance (Lowry 1993a). Of course, the same
can hardly be said for today's economists, or even historians of economic
thought. However, concludes Lowry, echoing Theodor Gomperz, "we shall
never be free of the ancient Greeks until we understand the origins of our intellectual past" (1987a: 251).

## Avenues for future research and conclusion

Lowry's deep, rich work suggests many avenues for future research. The
following are among the most salient:

1   Following Lowry's lead, more work could be done delineating the connec-
    tions between the ancient Greek theorists and modern economic
    thought.[15]
2   Work can and needs to be done filling in the historical blanks of the
    Western tradition of economics. Essentially, Lowry has extensively
    discussed two endpoints: the ancient Greeks and modern economics.[16]
    Much more work needs to be done tracing the tradition from the classical
    Greeks, through the Hellenistic period (Natali 1995), to the Romans, to
    the ancient and medieval Arab, Persian (Hosseini 1998), and Jewish
    scholars,[17] to the medieval/scholastic period, and beyond. In a sense, this
    necessitates rewriting and correcting Schumpeter's *History of Economic
    Analysis* from the broader more inclusive perspective of economics as the
    study of administrative or managerial efficiency. This task seems to be the
    general direction that much of Lowry's recent work is taking (e.g., 1995b,
    forthcoming).
3   Detailed studies could also be made of the significant differences and
    disjunctions between the Greeks and the moderns. For example, the
    Greeks and the moderns differ greatly on their notions of history and
    change. The Greeks tended to have a cyclical view of history; the moderns
    an evolutionary view (Hayek 1966). The Greeks tended to give teleological
    explanations of causality, much more so than the moderns (Fleetwood
    1997). And, of course, modern mainstream economics tends to celebrate
    monetary connections; not so for the Greeks.
4   When economics is viewed as the study of administrative efficiency, then
    there must have been more than one tradition in the world of economic
    thought. Any relatively complex society must have had some sort of study
    of administrative efficiency. Hence, there must be an Indian, a Chinese,[18] a
    Japanese, and other traditions of economic thought. Comparative studies
    could be broached. For example, Lowry has extensively documented the
    archaeology of the circulation concept in Western economic theory
    (1974b). To what extent did this concept appear in other traditions?
    Lowry's general framework opens up the door to the extensive explorations
    of non-Western traditions of economic thought.[19]

This chapter has argued that Lowry has a comprehensive research program
based upon his conception of economics as the study of administrative or
managerial efficiency. It discussed methodological issues arising from his institutional approach, Lowry's work in resource and environmental economics, his
approach to legal issues and contract theory, and his work on ancient Greek
economic thought. Among the ancient Greeks, this chapter emphasized Lowry's
interpretation of the economic thought of Xenophon, Plato, Protagoras, and
Aristotle. Lowry's work provides a detailed account of ancient Greek economic
thought, as well as its relationship to the modern economic theory of the past
quarter millennium. His fertile, rich scholarship suggests many new areas of
research, including (among others) further studies on the similarities and

differences between the ancient Greeks and modern economics; a complete reworking of the history of Western economic thought based upon economics understood as the study of administrative efficiency; and detailed studies of non-Western traditions of economic thought. Lowry has mapped out an erudite, ambitious research program which beckons to be studied, pursued, and developed.

## Notes

* I thank S. Todd Lowry for his extensive assistance on this project, as well as my colleague at Connecticut College, Dirk Held, Professor and Chair of Classics, for his warm help and encouragement; also Jolane Solomon, J. Alan Winter, Lester Reiss, John Coats, James MacDonald, Steven Medema, and Warren Samuels. A one-semester sabbatical, as well as the general support of my colleagues in the Economics Department at Connecticut College, also gave me a nurturing environment, and the time and intellectual space needed to undertake this study.

1  See Lowry (1979a). Finley (1970), relying upon Schumpeter (1954) and Polanyi (1968), essentially follow this approach, as does Neusner (1990), in his study of ancient Jewish Mishnaic economic thought.

2  The work of Gary Becker (among others) has been influential in furthering this view of the subject matter of economics. See, for example, Becker (1976) and Becker and Becker (1997). Economics as the study of the theory of choice is a logical development of Lionel Robbins' definition of economics as "the science which studies human behaviour as a relationship between ends and scarce means which have alternative uses" (1949: 16).

3  Although see Wood (1988) for an argument on the importance of laboring citizenry (including working peasants, craftsmen, and even casual laborers) in ancient Athens.

4  And Greek art (Marx 1973: 110–11).

5  In modern times, the work of Herbert Simon is perhaps most noted for focusing attention on administrative efficiency. See, for example, Simon (1976).

6  See Proctor's "Preface to the Second Edition" where he explains why he changed the title of his book from Education's Great Amnesia to Defining the Humanities.

7  Lowry is concerned with clearly defining intellectual traditions. This concern is perhaps most evident in his review essays of other writers. See, for example, Lowry (1992, 1993b, 1994c, 1999).

8  Ph.D., Louisiana State University, 1958. Lowry also earned an MA in natural resources and geography from Louisiana Sate University in 1956 with a thesis entitled "Henry Hardtner: Pioneer in Southern Forestry."

9  Perhaps because of his intimate knowledge of neoclassical economics, some classicists have apparently thought that Lowry himself wrote from a neoclassical perspective; see, for example, Meikle (1989).

10  LLB, University of Texas Law School, 1951.

11  See also Lowry (1994a).

12  In my opinion, this is Lowry at his creative and imaginative best. His handling of the economic implications of ancient myth should serve as a model for future work in this area, and as an example of the benefits which can be gained from searching for economic insights in such seemingly non-economic source material.

13  For early discussions of the harmonic mean, see Masi's translation of Boethian Number Theory (1983: 165–88) and D'ooge's translation of Nicomachus of Gerasa: Introduction to Arithmetic (1926, Book II: chapters XXI–XXIX).

14  See also Pack (1985b: Appendix D, "Aristotle and Marx on the Origins of Capital").

15  For a recent example, see Calkins and Werhane (1998).

16 Although, strictly speaking, it may be misleading to call the ancient Greeks an endpoint. There was no doubt important economic thought before them; perhaps most notably from the ancient Egyptian and Babylonian empires.

17 Eventually, historians of economic thought will also have to more grapple fully with the question: to what extent is it useful to think of and trace the development of one overarching tradition of Western economic thought; and when is it preferable to trace the development of various, at times competing and at other times complementary, multiple schools of Western economic thought?

18 So, for example, the *Records of the Grand Historian of China* (Watson 1961), which dates from approximately the second century BC, has chapters on "The Biographies of the Money Makers" and "The Treatise on the Balanced Standard" (managing the economy).

19 Other areas of research suggested by Lowry's work include, but are not limited to, the following:

(a) A history of home economics, or estate management and its relationship to political economy. This would no doubt demonstrate, among other things, that the use by the classical economists of the term political economy needs to be juxtaposed not only against the neoclassical use of the term economics, but also against domestic or home economics.

(b) A closer attention to and development of the history of law, and its relationship to economics.

(c) A closer analysis of when administrative efficiency is fostered by a top-down approach (what Lowry calls the administrative approach) and when it is better served by a bottom-up approach (what Lowry calls the participative process approach).

# Bibliography

Becker, Gary (1976) *The Economic Approach to Human Behavior*, Chicago: University of Chicago Press.

Becker, Gary and Becker, Guity (1997) *The Economics of Life*, New York: McGraw-Hill.

Blaug, Mark (ed.) (1991) *Aristotle (384–322 BC)*, Brookfield, VT: Edward Elgar.

Calkins, Martin J. and Werhane, Patricia H. (1998) "Adam Smith, Aristotle, and the Virtues of Commerce," *Journal of Value Inquiry* 32: 43–60.

D'ooge, Martin Luther (1926) *Nicomachus of Gerasa: Introduction to Arithmetic*, New York: Macmillan.

Finley, M. I. (1970) "Aristotle and Economic Analysis," *Past and Present* 47, May: 3–25; reprinted in Mark Blaug (ed.) (1991) *Aristotle (384–322 BC)*, Brookfield, VT: Edward Elgar, 150–72.

Flashar, Hellmut, Issing, Otmar, Lowry, S. Todd, and Schefold, Bertram (1992) "Aristoteles und seine 'Politic': vademecum zu einem klassiker des Antiken Wirtschaftsdenkens," Handlesblatt-Bibliothek *Klassiker der Nationalokonomie*, Dusseldorf: Wirtschaft und Finanzen.

Fleetwood, Steve (1997) "Aristotle in the 21st Century," *Cambridge Journal of Economics* 21: 729–44.

Hayek, F. A. von (1966) "Dr. Bernard Mandeville," *Proceedings of the British Academy* 52: 125–41; reprinted in C. Nishiyama and K. Leube (eds) (1984) *The Essence of Hayek*, Stanford, CA: Hoover Institution Press, 176–94.

Hosseini, Hamid (1998) "Seeking the Roots of Adam Smith's Division of Labor in Medieval Persia," *History of Political Economy* 30, 4: 653–81.

Lowry, S. Todd (1965) "The Classical Greek Theory of Natural Resource Economics," *Land Economics* XLI, 3: 203–8.

—— (1966) "The Appalachian Regional Development Act of 1965 and the Timber Development Organization Dilemma," *Journal of Forestry* December: 785–91.

—— (1967) "Southern Business Summary: The Future of the South's Forest Industry, Highlights and Shadows," *Atlanta Economic Review* XVII, 7: 9–12.

—— (1969) "Aristotle's Mathematical Analysis of Exchange," *History of Political Economy* I, 1: 44–66.

—— (1973) "Lord Mansfield and the Law Merchant: Law and Economics in the Eighteenth Century," *Journal of Economic Issues* VII, 4: 605–22; reprinted in *The Economy as a System of Power*, Vol. 1, New Brunswick, NJ: Transaction Books, 1979, 243–60.

—— (1974a) "Aristotle's 'Natural Limit' and the Economics of Price Regulation," *Greek, Roman, and Byzantine Studies* 15, 1: 57–63.

—— (1974b) "The Archaeology of the Circulation Concept in Economic Theory," *Journal of the History of Ideas* 35: 429–44.

—— (1974c) "The Kinked Cost Curve and the Dual Resource Base under Oligopsony in the Pulp and Paper Industry" (with John Winfrey), *Land Economics* 50: 185–92.

—— (1976a) "An Economist's View of Preservation," *Pioneer America* 8, 1: 28–35.

—— (1976b) "Some Perspectives on Raw Material Costs in the Forest Industry," *Economics of Southern Forest Resources Management*, Baton Rouge: Division of Continuing Education, Louisiana State University, 53–65.

—— (1976c) "Bargain and Contract Theory in Law and Economics," *Journal of Economic Issues* X, 1: 1–22; reprinted in *The Economy as a System of Power*, Vol. 1, New Brunswick, NJ: Transaction Books, 1979, 261–82 and *State, Society and Corporate Power*, New Brunswick, NJ: Transaction Books, 1989, 41–62.

—— (1977) "The Nature of Pre-Industrial Forest Planning," in Frank Convery and Charles W. Ralston (eds) *Forestry and Long Range Planning*, Durham, NC: School of Forestry and Environmental Studies, Duke University, 18–29.

—— (1979a) "Recent Literature on Ancient Greek Economic Thought," *Journal of Economic Literature* XVII: 65–86; reprinted in Mark Blaug (ed.) (1991) *Aristotle (384–322 BC)*, Brookfield, VT: Edward Elgar.

—— (1979b) "Notes and Communications: A Nightmare in Introductory Economics," *Journal of Economic Issues* XIII, 1: 225–8.

—— (1980) "The Impact of Large-scale Private Land-use Decisions: The Theory of Cutthroat Development," *Land: Issues and Problems*, Virginia Cooperative Extension Service, #52, April.

—— (1981) "The Roots of Hedonism: An Ancient Analysis of Quantity and Time," *History of Political Economy* 13, 4: 812–23.

—— (1985) "Review of Karl Pribram," *A History of Economic Reasoning, Research in the History of Economic Thought and Methodology* 3: 259–65.

—— (1987a) *The Archaeology of Economic Ideas: The Classical Greek Tradition*, Durham, NC: Duke University Press.

—— (ed.) (1987b) *Pre-Classical Economic Thought, from the Greeks to the Scottish Enlightenment*, Boston: Kluwer-Nijhoff.

—— (1987c) "The Greek Heritage in Economic Thought," in S. Todd Lowry (ed.) *Pre-Classical Economic Thought, from the Greeks to the Scottish Enlightenment*, Boston: Kluwer-Nijhoff, 7–30.

—— (1988a) "From Aristotle to Modigliani on Surplus and Intergenerational Transfers," *Bedrifts Okonomiens Helhet: Spenning Mellom Analyse og Humaniora*, Alma mater Forlag As, 246–53.

—— (1988b) "Insights from Ancient Views on Distribution," in Y. S. Brenner, J. P. G. Reijnders, and A. H. G. M. Spithoven (eds) *The Theory of Income and Wealth Distribution*, Brighton: Wheatsheaf Books, 226–38.

—— (ed.) (1989–1995) "The Invisible College of Ancient, Medieval and Renaissance Research in the History of Economic Ideas," with Introductory Essays and Bibliography of Participants (Newsletter).

—— (ed.) (1990) *Perspectives on the History of Economic Thought*, Vols VII and VIII, Aldershot: Edward Elgar.

—— (1991a) "Pre-classical Perceptions of Economy and Security," in C. D. Goodwin (ed.) *Economics and National Security*, Durham, NC: Duke University Press, 5–21.

—— (1991b) "Understanding Ethical Individualism and the Administrative Tradition in Pre-Eighteenth Century Political Economy," in William J. Barber (ed.) *Perspectives on the History of Economic Thought*, Vol. V, Aldershot: Edward Elgar.

—— (1991c) "Distributive Economics and the Promethean Meat Distribution: Myth, Folklore, and Legal Precedent," in Morris Silver (ed.) *Ancient Economy in Mythology: East and West*, Lanham, MD: Rowman and Littlefield, 45–55.

—— (1991d) "Are There Limits to the Past in the History of Economic Thought?" (Presidential Address, History of Economics Society), *Journal of the History of Economic Thought* 13: 134–43.

—— (1992) "MacIntyre's *Whose Justice? Which Rationality?* A Review Essay," *Research in the History of Economic Thought and Methodology* 9: 201–7.

—— (1993a) "A Note on the Idea of Models: From Plato to Adam Smith," *Brock Review* 2, 2: 201–5.

—— (1993b) "The Aristotelian Connection to the Mishnah: Review of Jacob Neusner's *The Economics of the Mishnah*," *Research in the History of Economic Thought and Methodology* 11: 205–12.

—— (1994a) "The Market as a Distributive and Allocative System: Its Legal, Ethical, and Analytical Evolution," in N. De Marchi and M. Morgan (eds.) *Higgling: Transactors and Their Markets in the History of Economics*, Durham, NC: Duke University Press, 25–46.

—— (1994b) "Institutional View of the Market," in *The Elgar Companion to Institutional and Evolutionary Economics*, Vol. II, Brookfield, VT: Edward Elgar, 47–53.

—— (1994c) "McCarthy's Marx and the Ancients: Classical Ethics, Social Justice, and Nineteenth-Century Political Economy: A Review Essay," *Research in the History of Economic Thought and Methodology* 12: 169–74.

—— (1995a) "The Ancient Greek Administrative Tradition and Human Capital," *Archives of Economic History* VI, 1: 7–18.

—— (1995b) "Social Justice and the Subsistence Economy: From Aristotle to Seventeenth Century Economics," in M. Silver and K. D. Irani (eds) *Social Justice in the Ancient World*, Westport CT: Greenwood Press, 10–24.

—— (1998) "The Economic and Jurisprudential Ideas of the Ancient Greeks: Our Heritage From Hellenic Thought," in S. Todd Lowry and Barry Gordon (eds) *Ancient and Medieval Economic Ideas and Concepts of Social Justice*, Leiden: Brill, 11–37.

—— (1999) "Review of *Economy and Nature in the Fourteenth Century: Money, Market Exchange, and the Emergence of Scientific Thought* by Joel Kaye," *Journal of the History of Economic Thought* 21: 195–8.

—— (forthcoming) "The Search for a Populist Medieval Monetary Theory."

Lowry, S. Todd and Gordon, Barry (eds) (1998) *Ancient and Medieval Economic Ideas and Concepts of Social Justice*, Leiden: Brill.

Marx, Karl (1973) *Grundrisse: Foundations of the Critique of Political Economy*, New York: Random House.

Masi, Michael (1983) *Boethian Number Theory: A Translation of the De Institutione Arithmetica*, Amsterdam: Rodopi.

Meikle, Scott (1985) *Essentialism in the Thought of Karl Marx*, La Salle, IL: Open Court.

—— (1989) "Et in Arcadia Chicago, a review article of S. T. Lowry, *The Archaeology of Economic Ideas*," *Polis* 8, 1: 25–34.

—— (1995) *Aristotle's Economic Thought*, Oxford: Clarendon Press.

Natali, Carlo (1995) "Oikonomia in Hellenistic Political Thought," in Andre Laks and Malcolm Schofield (eds) *Justice and Generosity: Studies in Hellenistic Social and Political Philosophy*, Cambridge: Cambridge University Press, 95–128.

Neusner, Jacob (1990) *The Economics of the Mishnah*, Chicago: University of Chicago Press.

Pack, Spencer J. (1985a) "Aristotle and the Problem of Insatiable Desires," *History of Political Economy* 17, 3: 391–3; reprinted in Mark Blaug (ed.) (1991) *Aristotle (384–322 BC)*, Brookfield, VT: Edward Elgar, 271–3.

—— (1985b) *Reconstructing Marxian Economics: Marx Based upon a Sraffian Commodity Theory of Value*, New York: Praeger.

Polanyi, Karl (1968) "Aristotle Discovers the Economy," in Karl Polanyi, Conrad M. Arensberg, and Harry W. Pearson (eds) *Trade and Market in the Early Empires*, Glencoe: The Free Press, 1957, 64–94; reprinted in George Dalton (ed.) (1968) *Primitive, Archaic and Modern Economies: Essays of Karl Polanyi*, New York: Anchor Books, 78–115.

Proctor, Robert (1998) *Defining the Humanities: How Rediscovering the Humanities Can Improve Our Schools*, Indianapolis: Indiana University Press.

Robbins, Lionel (1949) *An Essay on the Nature and Significance of Economic Science*, second edition, London: Macmillan.

Samuels, Warren J. (1989) "Review of S. Todd Lowry, *The Archaeology of Economic Ideas*," *History of Political Economy* 21, 1: 158–60.

Schumpeter, Joseph (1954) *History of Economic Analysis*, Oxford: Oxford University Press.

Simon, Herbert A. (1976) *Administrative Behavior: A Study of the Decision-Making Process in Administrative Organization*, third edition, New York: Macmillan.

Watson, Burton (1961) *Records of the Grand Historian of China, Translated from the Shih chi of Ssu-Ma Ch'ien*, Vol. II, New York: Columbia University Press.

Wood, Ellen Meiksins (1988) *Peasant-Citizen and Slave: The Foundations of Athenian Democracy*, London: Verso.

# 10 Ronald Meek and the rehabilitation of surplus economics

*M. C. Howard and J. E. King**

## Introduction

Ronald Lindley Meek was born in Wellington, New Zealand, in July 1917. Here he studied first law and then economics, and joined the Communist Party, under whose auspices he published a well-meaning but (for modern tastes) rather paternalistic pamphlet on *Maori Problems Today* (1943). In 1946 he moved to Cambridge, where he wrote his Ph.D. on "The Development of the Concept of Surplus in Economic Thought From Mun to Mill". Booth Piero Sraffa and Maurice Dobb[1] encouraged Meek in his work on the "surplus tradition" in the history of economics, which he saw as running parallel with – and antagonistic to – the supply and demand tradition which culminated in neoclassical theory. In 1948 Meek took up a lectureship in the Department of Political Economy at the University of Glasgow, leaving Scotland in 1963 on his appointment as Tyler Professor of Economics at the University of Leicester. He died suddenly in August 1978, at the age of 61.

Meek published prolifically, over three decades, in four distinct but closely related areas: the economic ideas of the physiocrats; the social and economic thinking of the Scottish Enlightenment; Marxian political economy and the economics of socialism; and (after the publication in 1960 of Sraffa's *Production of Commodities By Means of Commodities*) on the integration of Sraffian analysis and Marxian economic theory. The influence of Marx on Meek's own thinking was quite unmistakable, and it was not significantly weakened by his departure from the Communist Party in 1956, his brief involvement with the New Left in the late 1950s, or the social democratic views which characterized the last, politically inactive, fifteen years of his life. There was, perhaps, a shift in the orientation of his thinking after 1956, a gradual movement away from being a Marxist who made good use of the history of economic ideas, to an intellectual historian strongly influenced by Marxism. But this should not be exaggerated: Meek remained a historical materialist, and never wavered in his belief that an undogmatic Marxism offered the best approach to the history of economic thought since 1750.

## The economics of physiocracy

Two aspects of Meek's contribution to the study of the French physiocrats[2] need to be emphasized: his scholarship and his interpretation. After publishing a number of seminal articles in the 1950s, he produced several volumes of translations which made available, for the first time in English, the most important writings of the major physiocratic thinkers. The first was *The Economics of Physiocracy* (1962a), which contained, in addition to his own interpretative essays, over 200 pages of original translations from Quesnay. A decade later three further books appeared: an entire volume devoted to the work of Turgot on "progress, sociology and economics" (1973b); a selection of pieces by "Precursors of Adam Smith", which included extracts from Mirabeau, Quesnay, and Turgot (1973c); and the important edition of the *Tableau Économique*, jointly translated and edited by Meek and Marguerite Kuczynski (1972).[3] As Peter Groenewegen emphasized in his memorial tribute, before 1962 very little systematic work on physiocracy had appeared in the English language, so that Meek was responsible almost single-handedly for the rehabilitation of the school (Groenewegen 1979). Later writers, while often critical of the details of his analysis, are invariably respectful towards Meek's contribution (see e.g. Pressman 1994).

Meek's interpretation of the physiocrats, very clearly derived from Marx and the product of extensive contacts with Marxist historians in France,[4] was consistent throughout his career. It is lucidly summarized in a 1968 article, on which we draw heavily in the following paragraphs. According to Meek, the physiocrats developed their doctrines in direct response to the economic problems of their time. They employed a method of analysis that was, in all but name, historical materialism. And the substance of their theory was the unique ability of the agriculturalists to generate an economic surplus, and the necessity for appropriate policies and institutions to encourage the productive accumulation of this surplus. The physiocrats were early advocates of what, much later, would be described as the "surplus approach" to economics.

Meek regarded physiocracy as "the economic reflection of the difficulties facing French agriculture under the *ancien régime*". For Quesnay and his colleagues, "the fundamental problem set by the environment of their time was how to increase the national income of an underdeveloped country like France from a low level to a high one" (1968a: 45). The solution, they believed, was

> the widespread introduction of large-scale agriculture under the direction of capitalist entrepreneurs. Two main obstacles standing in the way of this in contemporary France were believed to be, first, the arbitrary and oppressive tax system, which fell with particular severity on the farmer, and, second, the corn laws, which prevented a *bon prix* being obtained for the farmer's product. ... The doctrine of the exclusive productivity of agriculture, and the *Tableau Économique*, were "oriented" towards these problems in much the same way as Keynes' key concepts were "oriented" towards the problem of chronic unemployment.

(47)

This, Meek concluded, was the first time that "modern" notions of economic development had come to the fore. Specifically, the physiocrats were the first to suggest that economic advancement was possible without the need (which many mercantilists had asserted) to beggar your neighbour in the process.

In methodology, the physiocrats' central innovation was "their notion that social and economic processes were law-governed in a more or less mechanistic way". This "truly revolutionary" principle, which had originated in England with John Locke and Dudley North, made it "possible for the general analytical methods developed in connection with the natural sciences to be successfully applied to the study of the economic behaviour of men in society" (48). It was no accident, Meek maintained, that the concept of the economic machine had emerged when it did. The metaphor[5] could be persuasive only with the rise of an economic order which was both highly integrated and evidently subject to impersonal and regular laws of motion; and this required the development of market exchange.

Finally, Meek identified the substance of physiocratic doctrine: the concept of a "circular flow", almost certainly suggested to them by the agrarian cycle of seed-time and harvest, and the insistence that agriculture alone was capable of producing a net product, or surplus of output over necessary inputs. "This doctrine of the exclusive 'productivity' of agriculture was indeed the lynch-pin of the Physiocratic model." It allowed them to draw "the vital distinction ... between productive and sterile occupations and was the foundation for 'their classification of basic groups according to economic function'" (51). The physiocrats argued that manufacturing was inherently incapable of yielding a surplus over necessary cost. Their vision was thus of

> a "capitalist" society in the broad sense, but a capitalist society in which the landowning classes, by accommodating themselves to the new conditions, would be able to retain their old position of prominence. Marx called their ideal society "a bourgeois reproduction of the feudal system", which expresses the point quite aptly.
>
> (56)

Indeed, Meek's entire interpretation owes a great deal to Marx's analysis in volume I of *Theories of Surplus Value* (Marx 1969: chapter II), with respect not only to the role of the economic surplus but also, and more fundamentally, to the significance of "external" or environmental influences and of ideology in the development of economic theory. This Marxian influence was apparent also in Meek's discussion of the basic defects of physiocratic thinking. The physiocrats were wrong to identify the economic surplus with the landed proprietors' rent, and consequently unable to offer an adequate account of the nature and origins of profit, since they denied the productivity of labour employed in manufacturing industry, and saw industrial profit as nothing more than a deduction from rent.

## The Scottish Enlightenment

These problems reflected the physiocrats' social vision. "It was not so much the wrong horse they backed, but rather the wrong rider" (Meed 1968a: 57). Except, perhaps, for Turgot, whom Meek increasingly came to see as a crucial link between physiocracy and the classical political economy of mid-eighteenth-century Scotland (Groenewegen 1979: 15–16). Crucially, Turgot was the first to put forward "the idea of progress which we particularly associate with the second half of the eighteenth century", to link social progress to economic development, and to emphasize "the crucial importance of the emergence in the agricultural stage of development of a *social surplus*" (Meek 1973b: 8–9). His "stadial theory of the development of early society" (5) was very similar to that of the Scottish historical school, and pointed clearly in the direction of a "materialist" theory of history, and he was much clearer on the distinction between rent and profit than Quesnay or any of the other physiocrats (20–1, 32–3).

The British contribution to Marxist thought, Meek wrote in a 1954 essay, went far beyond the well-known achievements of classical political economy, which itself "grew up in close association with a more general system of ideas about the structure and development of society which we can perhaps call Classical sociology" (1954a: 85). The core of this "Scottish Historical School" was made up of Adam Smith, Adam Ferguson, Lord Kames, John Millar, and William Robertson; Meek later added Sir James Steuart to the list (see 1967: 3–17). Under the influence of Continental thinkers, above all Montesquieu, the Scottish sociologists "tried, with some success, to bring to the study of men's relations to one another in society the same scientific attitude which had recently been so brilliantly brought to the study of men's relations to nature" (1954a: 88). History was not to be seen as the sum of the activities of "great men". Rather society developed blindly, in accordance with impersonal laws. Differences in legal codes and political institutions, the Scottish sociologists maintained, were due to differences in the "mode of subsistence". This "causal connection between property relationships and the form of government ... is constantly emphasized by all the members of the School" (87). It led them to articulate the famous "four stages" theory of social development, clearly stated by Millar and by Smith in his *Glasgow Lectures*, according to which hunting, pasturage, agriculture, and commerce followed one another in a necessary historical progression.

Meek returned to the four-stages theory in his *Social Science and the Ignoble Savage* (1976a), where he traced its evolution from early accounts of North American society through the works of Smith, Turgot, Quesnay, and their followers (for a critical assessment see Skinner 1982). The eighteenth century, Meek argued, saw the beginnings of comparative sociology, as parallels were drawn between the customs and behaviour of the "barbarians" of classical antiquity and the apparently very similar culture of the North American "savages". Knowledge of the American Indians was critical in suggesting a general materialist interpretation of social development: the "ignobility" of the "savages" could be explained by their economic circumstances, by the primitive and precarious way in which they earned their living:

> The comparative studies of primitive people ... coupled with the concept of the ignoble savage which was derived from it either directly, or indirectly by way of reaction to Rousseau, were closely associated with the emergence of the momentous idea that the *mode of subsistence* played a key role in determining the configuration and development of human societies.
>
> (1976a: 224; emphasis in original)

And this, in turn, was the foundation of the four-stages theory.

Thus Meek saw the "ignoble savage" as an important factor in the evolution of classical economics:

> There was a certain sense, of course, in which the great eighteenth-century systems of "classical" political economy in fact *arose out of* the four stages theory. In a surprising number of cases, the builders of these systems set out by elaborating some kind of scheme of socio-economic progression which started with an American-type society and ended with the "commercial" system of contemporary Europe, and then spent the rest of their lives making a sustained economic analysis of the working of this commercial system.
>
> (219; emphasis in original)

Meek stressed, once again, the way in which "the general ethos of the four stages theory" came to be incorporated in classical economics:

> In particular, the notion that *historical* processes were autonomous but law-governed led to (or was closely associated with) the notion that *economic* processes in a commercial society possessed the same characteristics.
>
> (220; emphasis in original)

The classical economists inferred from this that one could best understand the operation of the economic machine in a "commercial" society by comparison with the way in which it had worked in a previous stage. This methodological device was used not only by Smith and Ricardo. It also constituted, as we shall see in the following section, a major element in Meek's interpretation of Marx's economic method.

Meek wrote much more on Smith than on Ricardo, devoting his energies in the final years of his life to painstaking editorial work on the *Lectures on Jurisprudence* (Meek et al. 1978) and entitling the final volume of his essays *Smith, Marx and After* (1977). This led one of us to suggest that "Meek regarded Smith much more favourably, relative to Ricardo, than did either Dobb or Sraffa" (Howard 1992: 350). On reflection, we now believe that this point is difficult to sustain. Certainly Meek praised Smith for his contribution to

Scottish historical materialism and for his lucid formulation of a three-class model of capitalist society in which landlords, capitalists, and workers were explicitly distinguished for the first time in terms of their economic role and the source of their income – rent, profit, and wages respectively (Meek 1973c: vii–viii). But these are precisely the strengths that Marx had identified in Smith, and Maurice Dobb at least would have endorsed Meek's stance unreservedly (Marx 1969: chapter 3; cf. Dobb 1937: chapter 2).[6] If Meek paid less attention to Ricardo, it was because Sraffa and Dobb had got there first. In 1951 he reviewed the new edition of Ricardo's *Principles* in a Third Programme radio broadcast. Sraffa's "brilliant introduction", Meek asserted, sought to rehabilitate not only Ricardo but also the theory of value and distribution with which he was associated. If Sraffa succeeded, "it is even possible that we may eventually come to the conclusion that it was not Ricardo, but Jevons, who 'shunted the car of economic science onto a wrong line'" (1951a: 548).

## Marxism I: the Stalinist phase

This hostility to Jevons, of course, was a quintessentially Marxian position, and his appraisal was written at a time when Meek was still a loyal communist and warm admirer of Joseph Stalin. He had taken a similar line in his assessment of Keynes in the previous year. By 1950, he maintained, Keynes's ideas had come to hold more appeal for the right than for the left. "The so-called 'Keynesian Revolution'" had turned out to be "a 1688 of economic theory, rather than the 1640 which many people hoped it would be" (1950a: 34). (The "Glorious Revolution" of 1688 was an essentially conservative move initiated by the English ruling class to preserve its hegemony; the uprising of the 1640s, which culminated in the execution of the king and the proclamation of a republic, was an altogether more radical affair.) Keynes's definition of "classical economics" was profoundly misleading, Meek argued, glossing over as it did the "vital differences between Classical and post-Ricardian thought" (39). The most important of these differences concerned

> the labour theory of value, a peculiarly Classical product ... [which] is in essence simply another way of stating that the relations between men and men in the field of production ultimately determine their relations in the field of exchange.
>
> Marx inherited this attitude, made it explicit, and developed and applied it in an extraordinarily fruitful manner. But in bourgeois economic thought it virtually perished with Ricardo.
>
> (38)

Meek devoted a separate article to the decline of Ricardian economics, which he attributed very largely to revulsion at the dangerous influence of the labour theory of value on early socialist critics of British capitalism (1951a). His attack on Keynes continued by noting how, in the 1820s, and as a direct consequence of this ideological reaction:

The gradual descent towards modern neo-Classical orthodoxy began. The descent was marked in particular by the emergence of a subjective theory of value (based on an analysis of the desires of consumers) in place of the objective labour theory of Ricardo, and, eventually, by a theory of distribution which abstracted completely from the *real* distinctions between social classes, lumping them all together as the owners of certain "factors of production" which were distinguishable only by reason of the difficulty of substituting one for another.

(1950a: 38; emphasis in original)

Meek objected equally to Keynes's treatment of Say's law in classical economics. "In Ricardo's system, broadly speaking, Say's Law played a progressive role" (39) as a weapon against landlords and other "unproductive consumers". It was not fundamental to Ricardian theory, as Keynes maintained. "Certainly Marx found little difficulty in rejecting Say's Law categorically while at the same time accepting a great part of Ricardo's structure as a basis on which to build" (40). Nor was Keynes's own macroeconomic analysis an unqualified improvement on the classical theory of development: it was confined to the short run, and intended only as a supplement to neoclassical economics, not as a replacement. Meek rated Keynes very unfavourably indeed by comparison with Marx, who was both "in an important sense ... 'the last of the Classical economists'" and their most perceptive critic. Marx's "aim was to liberate Classical political economy from its bourgeois prison", by means of his "two epoch-making discoveries" – the theory of exploitation and the theory of the trade cycle (44). On the latter question, both Marx and Keynes focused on fluctuations in investment due to variations in the rate of profit. But, while Keynes concentrated exclusively on the role of effective demand, Marx added an entire layer of analysis relating to the impact of technical change and the class struggle over the rate of exploitation, factors which Keynes simply ignored. Keynes's reliance on *aggregate* demand and on the supposedly "psychological" determinants of consumption was quite alien to Marx, Meek concluded. Keynes was "an outstanding bourgeois thinker who, precisely because he was a *bourgeois* thinker, succeeded only in substituting a new collection of illusions for an older collection, which had become a little shop-soiled" (51; emphasis in original).

Not surprisingly, Meek showed none of Keynes's enthusiasm for Malthus. In 1953 he edited a volume of writings by Marx and Engels on Malthusian population theory, which contained what are probably the first extracts from Marx's *Theories of Surplus Value* to be published in English.[7] Meek's lengthy introduction revealed his unremitting hostility to the notorious parson.[8] Interestingly, Meek's fundamental objection was a methodological one which foreshadowed points that he was later to make against Marxian "tendency laws":

But our suspicions concerning the ratios must inevitably be confirmed when the theory which is based upon them is found to be capable of accommodating not only this general rule [that population constantly tends to increase up to the limit of subsistence] but all the exceptions to it as well. ... The Malthusian theory, by trying to explain everything, merely demonstrates its incapacity to explain anything. ... The original rule that population constantly tends to increase up to the limit of subsistence disappears in a mist of exceptions and qualifications.

(1954b: 26–7)

At this stage Meek's attitude to Marx was largely uncritical. "It is true", he wrote, "that Marx and Engels, when dealing with Malthus, were often rude and sometimes wrong, but few critics have come as close as they did to a real understanding of the defects of Malthus's theory" (31). They were right to insist that laws of population should be historically and socially specific, and correct in their rejection of the law of diminishing returns. Population pressure was not a natural or biological phenomenon, Meek argued, but a social problem with social solutions. Contemporary neo-Malthusians were "quite absurdly pessimistic" (47), and had utterly failed to appreciate that "the population problem of the imperialist stage of development was in its essence economic and political, and could be solved only by the abolition of imperialism" (39).

There was a distinctly Stalinist tone to this assessment, which drew unfavourable comments from at least one reviewer (Hutchison 1954: 80). Meek had already identified himself in print as a loyal supporter, not only of the USSR but also of Joseph Stalin as a major intellectual figure and a faithful interpreter of Marxian thought (1951b). In a 1953 radio broadcast just before the death of the dictator, Meek praised Stalin's article, "Economic Problems of Socialism", for providing "a much more sober and realistic blueprint than many which have been drawn up by writers in the USSR (and elsewhere) in recent years". Stalin believed it appropriate to apply the labour theory of value to the Soviet economy, and conceded that communism (and the associated withering away of commodity production and its economic laws) was not "just around the corner" (1954c: 239).[9] Meek defended Stalin in the Glasgow journal *Soviet Studies* against attacks by J. Miller and M. Miller (1950c, 1951b), and in *Oxford Economic Papers* against P. J. F. Wiles (1955b). As late as 1955, reporting on a visit to Moscow and Tbilisi as part of a Scottish cultural delegation, Meek was still praising Stalin and taking a most apologetic line on the question of academic freedom in the USSR (1955a).

The final fruit of Meek's Stalinist period appeared earlier that year, in the form of a 300-page book, *Studies in the Labour Theory of Value*, and an *Economic Journal* article on the transformation problem which was, in effect, a technical appendix to it. As he explained in the preface, the "book really owes its origin to a long correspondence on certain matters of theory which the author had in 1951 with Mrs Joan Robinson", in which he had failed to persuade her that "the labour theory was good sense and good science" (1956a: 7).[10] In essence, *Studies* is a long, scholarly application of the Marxian principles set out in Meek's 1950 appraisal of Keynes to the history of the labour theory of value, from the very beginning down to the mid 1950s. After an opening chapter on the theory before Adam Smith, Meek traced its development in Smith's thinking from the *Glasgow Lectures* to the *Wealth of Nations*, devoting a third chapter to Ricardo's theory of value. Meek's understanding of the classical labour theory of value is throughout very close to that of Marx, as interpreted by Dobb and Sraffa.

The core of the book is contained in the two long chapters on Marx's value theory. Meek begins by denying that "the labour theory of value necessarily implies a particular ethical or political viewpoint" (125), for Smith, for Ricardo, or for Marx. The theory of surplus value was not "derived" from it, Meek maintained. On the contrary:

> historically at any rate, so far from the existence of surplus value being derived from the labour theory, the labour theory was in fact evolved precisely in order to explain the manifest existence of surplus value in the real world. The emergence of a value-difference between input and output, which eventually resolved itself into rent and profit and which was not significantly attributable to any expenditure of productive effort on the part of its recipients, was regarded by the Classical economists as a simple fact. One of the main tasks which the labour theory was asked to perform was that of accounting for the origin and persistence of this surplus value and measuring its extent.
>
> (126–7)

Once again, the influence of Maurice Dobb is apparent here (cf: Dobb 1937: 22, 30–3).

Meek explains the evolution of Marx's thinking on value from the start of his intellectual career, supporting his argument by original translations from early writings which were not – in 1956 – accessible to an English readership.[11] By 1847, in *The Poverty of Philosophy*, Marx

> had by now arrived at the notion that the labour theory of value is in essence another way of stating the proposition that "the mode of exchange of products depends upon the mode of exchange of the productive forces". Once this point had been reached, the period of early development of Marx's thought comes to an end, and the period of mature development, refinement and application begins.
>
> (146)

Meek continued by outlining Marx's "logical-historical method", which he had applied to value theory by analysing the implications of the social division of labour under different types of property relations, culminating in capitalism. Marx had

concentrate[d] on distinguishing the way in which the law of value operated under capitalism from the way in which it operated under all those
earlier systems taken together in so far as they were characterised by
"simple" commodity production in which the normal exchange was one of
"value" for "value".

(155; original emphasis deleted)

In capitalism, unlike simple (or classless) commodity production, commodities
no longer exchanged at ratios equal to the relative quantities of embodied
labour contained in them. But this "did not mean that exchange ratios ceased
to be *a function* of embodied labour ratios". The law of value did operate under
capitalism, but "in a different and more complex way ... so that although ratios
were still *ultimately determined* by embodied labour ratios, the two were no
longer necessarily (or even normally) equivalent to one another" (155–6;
emphasis in original).

   After a brief discussion of the concept of value in volume I of *Capital*, Meek
outlined the refinement of the concept with reference to Marx's notion of
labour as the "substance" of value; the so-called "reduction" of skilled to
unskilled labour; and the fetishism of commodities. Next he showed how Marx
had applied his theory of value to the determination of wages and profits.
Finally Meek turned to the transformation problem, arguing that "Marx's
Volume III analysis of exchange ratios in terms of prices of production ought
properly to be regarded as a modification, rather than as a refutation, of the
Volume I analysis in terms of values" (189). He set out Marx's numerical solution and discussed its generalization by Bortkiewicz, Winternitz, and May, but
played down the significance of the whole question:

> It may well be, as Sweezy has suggested, that Marx would have dealt with
> this problem in more detail if he had lived to work over Volume III again.
> On the other hand, the relative importance of the problem in Marx's
> general theoretical scheme is hardly very great, and my own feeling is that
> he would probably have left most of the relevant passages much as they
> are.
>
> (197)

During the feverish debates of the 1970s on the transformation problem this
might have seemed an unduly complacent conclusion (see Howard and King
1992: part IV). But the Marxian economists of the "classical", Second
International period would have agreed with Meek, and we suspect – from the
perspective of 2001 – that he was right.

   Meek's uncritical account of the Marxian labour theory of value is
sustained in the two final chapters. His assessment of the critics of the theory
gives short shrift to Vilfredo Pareto, Eduard Bernstein, A. D. Lindsay,
Benedetto Croce, Oskar Lange, Rudolf Schlesinger, and Joan Robinson; oddly,
he ignores Eugen von Böhm-Bawerk, the most celebrated *Marx-Kritiker* of all.

As one hostile reviewer observed, with pardonable exaggeration, "Mr Meek never once admits that any critic has ever scored a single point against Marx on any subject whatsoever" (Hutchison 1957: 163). The book concludes with a chapter on later developments, where Meek first attacks the marginal utility theory of value and then considers the operation of the labour theory under socialism. He notes that Marx and Engels had consistently maintained the specificity of value and the "law of value" to commodity production; the concepts themselves would therefore disappear with the abolition of commodity production. Meek surveyed the recent Soviet controversies on this issue, reaffirming his support for the position taken by Stalin in *Economic Problems of Socialism*.[12] Finally, Meek makes a highly original – if largely unsuccessful – attempt to use Marx's logical–historical method as the basis for applying the labour theory of value to monopoly capitalism. He distinguishes "three more or less consecutive stages" in the development of capitalism (291). In the "transition stage", when capitalism is just beginning to emerge from simple commodity production, actual prices will generally deviate from prices of production. These deviations are very largely eliminated in the second, "competitive stage", when there are strong pressures towards the equalization of the rate of profit in all sectors. Then, in the "monopoly stage", "the relations of production once again take a hand, as they did in the earlier transitional stage, in causing prices to deviate from [competitive] supply prices" (292). But this is purely formal; Meek has very little of substance to say about the determinants of monopoly prices. Even sympathetic reviewers like Dickinson (1957: 503–4) and Tsuru (1957: 702) found his argument here rather unconvincing.

Consistent with his views on the relative unimportance of the transformation problem, Meek chose to publish his own solution as an article in the *Economic Journal* (1956b), rather than including it in his book. Marx had wrongly supposed that *two* conditions could in general be satisfied by his own algorithm: equality between the sum of values and the sum of prices, and equality between the sum of surplus values and the sum of profits. In fact, as Bortkiewicz and others had demonstrated, only one of these conditions could be met unless quite exceptional circumstances applied. Meek now suggested an alternative condition, which he believed more accurately to reflect the spirit of Marx's thinking: the ratio between total output and total wages should be the same in both value and price terms, since this was "the fundamental ratio upon which profit depended" (1956b: 98).[13] Meek used a numerical example to show that this new condition could indeed be satisfied, but only "upon the assumption that the organic composition of capital in the wage-goods industries is equal to the social average" (104). In fact this is no less restrictive than the assumption required for Marx's *two* conditions to be satisfied.[14] Although Meek reprinted the article, unamended, in his *Economics and Ideology* (1967: 143–57), he subsequently repudiated it in favour of a quite different, Sraffian approach to the transformation problem (1977: 122).

## Marxism II: the new left

By the summer of 1956 Meek, who was already involved in a very bitter internal struggle within the Communist Party of Great Britain, was becoming increasingly disillusioned with the Party. The final straw came later in the year when he found himself in Poznan with a group of Cambridge economists when the Polish workers' rising broke out.[15] Thus Meek broke with communism before the even more dramatic events in Budapest, after which thousands left the Communist Party of Great Britain in protest against the bloody Soviet suppression of the Hungarian Revolution. The immediate effect on Meek was profound. While he did not discuss the events of 1956 with his students, they "did notice a change: instead of the formal didactic style, he delivered his lectures seated, and smoked incessantly. Later we realised how distressed he must have been."[16]

The collapse of party membership was especially pronounced among the intellectuals. Freed from the stifling constraints of "democratic centralism" they began to develop their critique of Stalinism in a variety of new publications, one of which was the New Reasoner, "a quarterly journal of Socialist humanism".[17] Here, between 1957 and 1959, Meek published three pieces reassessing the respective strengths and weaknesses of Marxian and bourgeois economics. Inevitably, this involved him in the initial stages of a profound auto-critique. The first of these articles was a highly critical review of John Strachey's (1956) book Contemporary Capitalism. It revealed a Meek much more open to a Marx–Keynes synthesis than he had been in 1950. Keynes's biggest failing, Meek now argued, was his neglect of oligopoly, while Marx's predictions of stagnant real wages and increasingly severe cyclical crises "must also be regarded with suspicion" (1957a: 42). While cautioning against "throwing out the Marxist baby with the Stalinist bathwater" (47), Meek savaged Marx's theory of wages. "There is little doubt", he wrote, "that Marx would have been extremely surprised at the extent of the rise in real working-class earnings which has taken place in, say, Britain and America since his day" (49). The source of Marx's error was political, rather than narrowly economic: he had failed to anticipate the extent to which working-class pressure would be able to extract concessions from the system. It could still be argued that Marx had identified an underlying tendency for real wages to decline under capitalism. "But here an important methodological question arises. If a 'tendency' is continuously and permanently modified, so that it never gets a chance of actually displaying itself, can it really be said to exist in anything other than a metaphysical sense?" (50). This objection, which Meek had earlier raised against Malthus, was now applied to Marx himself.

On the issue of economic crises Meek was more supportive of Marx. The absence of a major depression in the previous twenty years could be explained by armaments expenditure, technical progress, the rise in real wages, and the increasing use of self-finance by oligopolists, which made aggregate investment less volatile than before:

Does the appearance of these new features, then, mean that capitalist economies are becoming more controllable than they used to be? Up to a point, and in so far as the features can be regarded as permanent, I think it does.

(54)

But there were also "political and economic disincentives" which served to discourage capitalists from accepting Keynesian counter-cyclical remedies, including the perceived threat to private enterprise that would be posed by really large public works expenditures and a radical reduction of income inequality:

> My own feeling is that unless the remedies were associated with an exten-sion of the state sector so considerable as to amount to something like a transcendence of the capitalist system, they would probably prove ineffec-tive in the face of a large fall in profit expectations. At any rate the chances of failure are sufficiently great to prevent us from talking as if we now knew for certain how to avert slumps, or as if a Keynesian "mixed economy" could be made to lead more or less automatically and painlessly to a demo-cratic socialist society.
>
> All in all, then, there seems to be a case for continuing to use a model (like that of Marx) which lays emphasis on the inherent instability of economic activity in a predominantly capitalist economy, and which sees this instability as one of the expressions of a basic contradiction between the social character of production and the private character of appropriation.
>
> (56)

Meek concluded, however, that Marx's crisis model needed further develop-ment, "in part by the absorption of some of the Keynesian tools and techniques" (57), if it were to deal effectively with the new problems posed by contemporary capitalism.[18]

What, then, of bourgeois microeconomics, which Meek had formerly denounced as ideological nonsense? His second *New Reasoner* article reviewed a book on this question by the Soviet economist I. G. Blyumin. While "a major part of bourgeois economics is concerned, although largely unconsciously, with apologetics" (1958: 58) this did not for Meek justify the blanket dismissal of Western economic theory in its entirety:

> It is true that there are certain basic bourgeois theories which are so much affected by the traditional tendency to abstract from the relations of production as to be virtually unusable by Marxists – the marginal utility theory and Marshallian theories of value, for example; the marginal productivity theory of distribution; and those theories of crisis which (like Keynes's) overemphasise psychological at the expense of sociological factors. But the concept of the margin can surely be divorced from the

marginal utility theory, and the concepts of elasticity, marginal and average cost, and the long and the short period from the Marshallian theory; and the techniques of demand analysis which these theories have inspired are surely just as useful in a socialist as they are in a capitalist society.

(60)

There was thus considerable scope, Meek maintained, in a (no doubt unconscious) echo of Joan Robinson's aphorism,[19] for economists "to apply non-Marxist analytical methods to some of the most important of the problems posed by Marx" (60). Lange and Lerner had shown, for example, that modern welfare economics could be adapted to the economics of socialism. Meek ended the article with two (implicit) items of self-criticism. Marxists should not allow their justified distaste for Malthus to degenerate into an unqualified rejection of population as an economic variable. And they should not attack the great majority of bourgeois economists as "hired prize-fighters of the bourgeoisie" because of the bad faith shown by a small minority.

Meek's third contribution to the *New Reasoner*[20] was rather more supportive of Marx, on the grounds that

the positive results of the use of bourgeois visions and methods have been so insignificant in relation to the enormous amount of energy which has gone into their production as to constitute a real challenge to those who believe that the alternative Marxist vision and method are likely to be more useful.

(1959a: 31)

Significantly, though, Meek himself never did produce the new model of contemporary capitalism incorporating monopoly, and a significant role for the state and for the organized working class, that he called for in this article (26). Instead, in two final essays in *Science and Society*, he continued his critique of Marxian macroeconomics.

The first dealt with Marx's theory of the falling rate of profit, on which Meek had already expressed strong reservations.[21] Drawing heavily on a recent article by Roman Rosdolsky (1956), Meek discussed the two principal objections to the treatment of this issue in volume III of *Capital*. Both concerned the so-called "counter-acting tendencies": under certain conditions, technical progress would increase the rate of exploitation and reduce the organic composition of capital, thereby reversing the Marxian tendency and *increasing* the rate of profit. Marx had recognized both factors, Meek conceded, but had not been able to analyse them with sufficient clarity or rigour. Meek's own procedure was to accept a continuous increase in the organic composition and, by means of a series of simple numerical examples, trace out the effect on the profit rate under different assumptions as to movements in the rate of exploitation. In almost all cases the initial effect of technical change was to increase the rate of profit. Thus, on the basis of Marx's model, "it is virtually impossible to predict how the rate of profit will in fact behave" (1960a: 50). In place of precise predictions, there was merely "a conceptual framework within which many problems relating to the behaviour of the rate of profit can be usefully considered", and a valuable reminder that "changes in the rate of profit depend not on technical factors alone, but rather on the interaction of these with sociological factors" (50).

In the second *Science and Society* article Meek returned to the "increasing misery doctrine". After repeating many of the criticisms that he had directed in 1957 to Marx's theory of wages, he now assessed their broader implications. For Marx it was the immiseration of the working class which would make it the agent of revolutionary change. Thus "the prediction of 'increasing misery' was no minor or incidental part of Marx's analysis: on the contrary, it formed an essential and extremely important constituent of his theory of the transition from capitalism to socialism" (1962b: 438). Nor was it the only one of Marx's predictions to be "falsified by the facts". On the contrary: "if we are honest, we must surely recognise that it is merely the leading species of a genus – a genus which embraces a significant proportion of Marx's most famous and most crucial 'laws of motion of capitalism'" (438). Only the law of concentration and centralization of capital had manifested itself in capitalist reality. Marx's expectations with respect to the falling rate of profit, and the increasing severity of cyclical crises, had proved to be unfounded, no less than the law of increasing misery. A major revision of Marxian theory was required, Meek concluded, or "Marxism as a scientific theory of the development of contemporary capitalism will most surely die" (440).

## Marxism III: the social democratic phase

This was the last article Meek published in a political, rather than a purely professional, journal. It was also very nearly his last work on Marxian economics for a decade. Meek's bibliography shows a slackening after 1962 in his hitherto prodigious output rate, associated with his move to Leicester in the following year as head of the economics department, and a pronounced shift in his interests away from the history of thought towards welfare economics. At Leicester, Meek set up a Public Sector Economics Research Centre and produced a series of papers on the problems of electricity pricing. For the most part these were highly technical, revealing Meek's new interest in formal welfare theory and his extensive command of the relevant French and Soviet literature. One paper did explore the philosophical implications of public sector economics, and found Meek speculating on the possible emergence of "a new science of 'economic management' or 'social engineering', replacing either wholly or in large part economics as it has traditionally been known" (1963b: 36).

Apart from a handful of book reviews and a brief comment (1968b) on a conference paper by Paul Sweezy, his only writing on Marxism between 1962 and 1972 is found in perhaps his best-known book, *Economics and Ideology and Other Essays* (1967). Characteristically, Meek put a great deal of work into this volume:

> I have tried in a number of ways to prevent the book from becoming merely another volume of "collected essays". Some of the pieces contain sections which are substantially new, and in almost all of them I have done an appreciable amount of rewriting. So far as possible, I have tried to bring the views expressed into conformity with those which I hold today. I venture to hope that the essays as they now stand will be found to tell a reasonably clear and continuous story.
>
> (1967: ix)

They included relatively uncontentious pieces on Thomas Joplin, Adam Smith, and Sir James Steuart, in addition to Meek's review of Sraffa (to which we return in the next section). Of the four papers on Marx, the 1956 article on the transformation problem was reprinted largely intact, while the amendments to the 1960 analysis of the falling rate of profit involved only a rearrangement of some of the original material. Meek made more substantial changes to his 1962 discussion of the "law of increasing misery",[22] removing the political manifesto in the introduction and significantly rewriting the conclusion, which was noticeably less optimistic than before. If a new Marxian model of the "innate tendencies" of modern capitalism were not forthcoming – and Meek's tone suggests that he thought it unlikely – then

> it is clear that Marxists will have to settle for something less than rehabilitation. Capitalism will have proved to be more resilient, and the Marxist economic analysis of it more transitory, than we might reasonably have anticipated. But the heavens will not fall, surely, if this turns out to be the case. We have learned an incredible amount from Marx, and we may still have a great deal to learn from him – particularly, as I have suggested in the last essay, in the sphere of methodology. ... In the long run – let us face it – none of us can really expect to go down in history as more than just another genius; and no one is exempt from the universal law of the mutability and eventual diffusion of systems of thought.
>
> (1967: 128)

"The last essay" to which Meek refers in this passage is a largely rewritten version of his 1959 *New Reasoner* article, with the new title "Karl Marx's Economic Method". Here Meek summarizes Marx's " 'vision' of the capitalist economic process" (95) with great lucidity: his overriding emphasis on the production relations between capitalists and workers; his "logical-historical method" of analysis; and "the important notion", which Marx had taken over from classical political economy, that if one wished to analyse capitalism in terms of relations of production the best way of doing this was to imagine capitalism suddenly impinging upon a sort of generalized pre-capitalist society in which there were as yet no separate capital-owning or land-owning classes.

(97)

All of this is to be found in *Studies in the Labour Theory of Value*. What is different, in 1967, is Meek's much more sceptical approach to the Marxian "laws of motion" and – most importantly – the new and more critical attitude that he adopts towards the labour theory of value.

Marx had gone too far in his attempt to integrate economics and sociology, Meek now suggested:

> The role of the theory of value (in the traditional sense of a theory of price determination) in the general body of economic analysis is much more modest today than it was in Marx's time, and there is no longer any very compelling reason why a theorist wishing to bring sociology or economic history into his economics should feel obliged to start by reforming the theory of value.
>
> (105)

In fact Meek went further than this: "In my more heretical moods, I sometimes wonder whether much of real importance would be lost from the Marxian system if the quantitative side were conducted in terms of something like the traditional supply and demand apparatus" (106), so long as it was clearly understood that the "Marxian sociological factors" lay behind the supply and demand schedules themselves. The continued strength of Marxian economics was methodological more than substantive in nature:

> Broadly speaking, and subject to a number of qualifications which will be made below, it can properly be said that all that really remains of Marxian economics today is the body of general methods and tools of analysis which Marx employed to analyse the facts of his time.
>
> (110)

These tools and methods had been infiltrated into bourgeois economics with great success by writers like Kalecki, Lange, Robinson, and Sraffa.

Evidently this implied a rather different view of orthodox economics from that of the Stalinist Meek, or even his New Left cousin. As the title suggests, *Economics and Ideology* has a lot to say about the question of *Wertfreiheit* in mainstream theory and the possibility of rescuing that theory from ideological contamination. Meek made some important changes to his 1950 article on the decline of Ricardian economics. Surprisingly, these had the effect of strengthening his indictment of Ricardo's critics, who were reacting against "the disharmonious and pessimistic implications" of his system that had deeply influenced the early English socialists (1967: 69):

> It is hardly too much to say that every new development in economic thought in England about this time had the objective effect of cutting the ground from under the feet of writers like Hodgskin and William Thompson. And at least in some cases there can be little doubt that the critics of Ricardo knew exactly what they were doing and why they were doing it.
>
> (70)

There is nothing this strong in the original article (cf. 1950b: 62).

Apart from abbreviations, Meek left his 1954 assessment of the Scottish contribution to Marxist sociology unchanged. A third version of the 1950 appraisal of Keynes added further major amendments to those that he had made in the 1957 New Reasoner version. They included an element of self-criticism:

> Those of us who prophesied in the years following the publication of the General Theory that the framework of orthodox economics would soon show itself sufficiently flexible to accommodate Keynes's analysis, and that talk of a "Keynesian Revolution" was therefore ill-judged, have simply been proved wrong.
>
> (192)

Meek was much more generous in his recognition of Keynes's achievement in shifting the focus away from microeconomics towards the more pressing problems of macroeconomics, and acknowledged the increasing tendency for "Keynes's essentially micro static theory" to be transformed into "a more realistic and far-reaching macro dynamic theory" (193). This, Meek suggested, came much closer to classical and Marxian development models than anyone had originally anticipated.

Meek further elaborated on the relationship between economics and ideology in the long and influential final essay, which bore that title. The first half was devoted to a critical discussion of the relevant sections of Joseph Schumpeter's History of Economic Analysis,[23] which had argued forcibly for the unbiased, strictly scientific nature of progress in mainstream theory after 1830 (Schumpeter 1954: Part I, chapter 4). Meek was still unconvinced. He continued to assert the clear scientific superiority of the classical labour theory of value over earlier analyses, and to insist on the important "ideological overtones of the marginal utility theory" (1967: 208).[24] Meek's disagreement with Schumpeter concerned the history of economic thought rather than the methodological desirability of "securing an ideology-free economics" (1967: 223), which he regarded as a very important task. But it was, he believed, more difficult than Schumpeter had supposed, and neoclassical economists had not succeeded in accomplishing it.

The second part of the essay, dealing with recent books by Joan Robinson and Oskar Lange, was new to *Economics and Ideology*. "Let us now proceed from Schumpeter", he wrote, "who sees economic analysis as more or less free from ideology, to Joan Robinson, who sees it (up to a certain point) as chock-full of it" (209). Once again Meek came to the defence of the classical theory of value against the Robinsonian onslaught:[25] "it does not help much to insist on describing the very *concept* of value as 'metaphysical'. If one insists on doing so, it is 'metaphysical' and not 'value' which becomes 'just a word'" (212; emphasis in original). He objected also to Robinson's lionization of Keynes, who, "it seems, was the first great economist who was able to inoculate himself more or less successfully against ideological infection" (213–14). A more balanced view could be found in Oskar Lange's *Political Economy* (Lange 1963), which introduced "praxiology", or "the science of programming", into Marxian economics and demonstrated that a synthesis of bourgeois and socialist theory was at last feasible, East and West. Meek concluded by rejecting Robinson's "counsel of despair" (223). Ideology *could* be banished from economics, he maintained, given "the rigorous application of the ordinary rules of scientific reasoning" (222).

## Marx after Sraffa

The initial critical response to Piero Sraffa's *Production of Commodities By Means of Commodities* (1960) was a mixture of bewilderment (Reder 1961) and confusion (Harrod 1961). Of the early reviews in English,[26] only those by Dobb (1960) and Robinson (1961) demonstrated any real understanding of the book. But it took some years before Robinson fully appreciated Sraffa's achievement,[27] while Dobb's review was – despite its title – extremely short. It is fair to say, in fact, that only Meek's assessment, published almost simultaneously in *Science and Society* and the *Scottish Journal of Political Economy* early in 1961, and reprinted largely unchanged in *Economics and Ideology*, did any real justice to Sraffa's terse masterpiece.

Meek regarded it not merely as a critique of marginalism, and as a distinctive if unorthodox economic model in its own right, but above all as "a sort of magnificent rehabilitation of the classical approach to certain crucial problems relating to value and distribution" (1961: 119). Sraffa's starting point was the basic classical problem – "what happens to prices and profits when a class of capitalists arrives on the scene to share the net product of the economy with labour?" (125). Smith, Ricardo, and Marx had all agreed that a positive rate of profit, in an economy with different proportions of means of production to labour in the various industries, would cause relative prices to deviate from relative labour values; this is the essence of Marx's "transformation problem". Sraffa expressed this problem in Ricardian rather than Marxian terms. A change in distribution – for example, an increase in the real wage and a corresponding fall in the rate of profit – would alter the relative prices of all commodities except for that of a "borderline industry" in which "the ratio of the value of the industry's net product to the value of its means of production would always remain the same whatever change took place in the wage" (129). Such a borderline industry could be constructed, Sraffa showed, from any actual economic system by taking particular fractions of all its "basic" industries. One unit of output of this composite or "standard" industry constituted what he termed the "standard commodity".[28] It had the important property that:

> The rate of profits *over the economy as a whole* is determined as soon as we know R (the ratio of net product to means of production in the "standard" industry, which is equal to the "maximum rate of profits"), and w (the proportion of the net product of the "standard industry" going to wages). Or, to put the point in another way, when the proportion of the net product of the "standard" industry going to wages is given, the average rate of profits over the economy as a whole depends upon the level of R.
>
> (132; emphasis in original)

Marx, too, had sought to identify a borderline industry, with an organic composition of capital equal to the social average, the output of which could be used as a numeraire in the solution of the transformation problem.[29] Sraffa had demonstrated the virtual impossibility of using any individual industry in this capacity, since it would be necessary not only for its own organic composition to equal the economy-wide average, but for this to be true also of the industries which supplied it with means of production, and of the industries which supplied them, and so *ad infinitum*. However, the Sraffian "standard commodity" had precisely this property. "In other words," Meek concluded,

> Sraffa is postulating precisely the same relation between the average rate of profits and the conditions of production in his "standard" industry as Marx was postulating between the average rate of profits and the conditions of production in his industry of "average organic composition of capital".
>
> (136; original emphasis deleted)

In this way Sraffa had provided an "implied rehabilitation of the classical labour theory of value in something very like the form which it assumed in the hands of Marx" (133).

The significant word here is "implied". Sraffa gave no indication of his views on the Marxian labour theory of value, either in *Production of Commodities* or elsewhere; indeed, apart from a brief reply to Harrod he published nothing between 1960 and his death in 1983. Some Sraffians, like Steedman (1977), eventually interpreted his work as a prescription for dispensing with the labour theory of value altogether. The full implications of Sraffa's book took some time to sink in, but by the beginning of the 1970s a fierce controversy was raging among radical economists in Britain, the United States, France, and Italy over the significance of the Sraffian system for the future of Marxian political economy. On one side were ranged those who argued, like Meek, that Ricardo and Marx occupied the same theoretical terrain, with Sraffa representing a major advance on both of them. A crucial (if belated) intervention on this side of the debate came from Maurice Dobb (1970), followed by the more technical analyses of Medio (1972) and Eatwell (1975), whose interpretations of the Sraffian "standard commodity" were very similar to that of Meek (1961). On the other side were the Althusserian Marxists, who claimed that Marx's economic method was utterly opposed to that of classical political economy – Marx as an "a-Ricardian", to cite the title of de Brunhoff (1973) – and that Sraffian economics was fatally undermined by its commodity fetishism and neglect of the class relations of capitalist production. A key text here was that of another Cambridge economist, Bob Rowthorn (1974). Sraffa, to repeat, kept his own counsel on all these matters.

When Meek was approached by the publishers of his *Studies*, who wanted a second edition, he did something quite uncharacteristic. Leaving the first edition totally unchanged, he instead wrote a long, incisive, and profoundly original introduction to it (1973a: i–xliv), in which he met the challenge of the "fundamentalist Marxists" head-on. Meek did what (it could be argued) Sraffa should have done, either in *Production of Commodities* or in response to the misunderstandings that the book provoked: he applied Marx's logical–historical method to Sraffa's formal models, showing how at each stage of the argument a particular set of production relations was presupposed and making explicit the socio-economic framework that had remained, for the most part, implicit in Sraffa's text (xxxii–xli). Meek's five, "Sraffa-like" models begin with an elementary simple commodity production in which there is no surplus product, and move successively through simple commodity production with a surplus; an early capitalist economy in which capitalists appropriate the entire surplus, but with competition insufficiently strong to equalize the rate of profit; a mature capitalism where Marxian prices of production prevail; and a final model in which "the workers have combined and forced the capitalists to return to them some of the surplus" (xxxviii).

This rational reconstruction of Sraffa showed very clearly that the fundamentalist Marxists were wrong:

> our Sraffa-type sequence of models does essentially the same set of jobs which the Marxian labour theory was designed to do; it starts, as Marx's system did, with a "prior concrete magnitude" which limits the levels of class incomes; it is based on the same view about the order and direction of determination of the variables as Marx's system was; it is just as well suited to the application of a "logical-historical" method of approach; and it has the great additional advantage that it contains a built-in solution of the "transformation problem". And on the qualitative side, it is at least arguable that Sraffa's procedure reflects the basic idea which Marx was trying to express in his labour theory – the idea that prices and incomes are ultimately determined by relations of production – more clearly and effectively than Marx's own procedure did.
>
> (xiii)

As Meek put it in a conference paper written in the same year and published in 1974, Marx and Sraffa bear "a strong family resemblance" (1974: 259).

These remarks were not directed at anyone in particular. Towards the end of his life Meek used to describe himself as a "Meeksist" rather than a Marxist.[30] He took no part in the heated discussions of the early 1970s in the Conference of Socialist Economists in Britain, paralleled by those in the Union for Radical Political Economics in the United States and in various Communist Party forums in Italy, from which there emerged by the middle of the decade a coherent "Sraffian" version of classical or surplus economics which its fundamentalist opponents derided as "neo-Ricardian".[31] Something of an academic loner, Meek remained aloof from these controversies, issuing forth only to defend himself (with very limited success) against the objections raised to the concept of simple commodity production by Michio Morishima and George Catephores (1975, 1976; cf. Meek 1976b).

A more serious challenge to the Marxian labour theory of value came from those who, like Ian Steedman (1977), argued that Sraffa had rendered it superfluous. Since prices of production and the rate of profit could be derived from the Sraffian production equations, plus a distributive variable (the wage or the profit rate, both determined outside the production system), where, Steedman asked, was the need to calculate values and surplus values? In a 1975 paper with the subtitle "Was Marx's Journey Really Necessary?",[32] Meek claimed to "have some sympathy for both points of view", and to be "no longer at all religious about such matters" (1977: 123–4). However, "I find myself leaning much more towards the 'neo-Ricardians' than towards their critics" (124). Marx had good reasons for starting with labour values, Meek suggested. "But certain grim realities have to be faced by Marxists" (131):

> With the specification where necessary of the appropriate institutional datum, then, and with remarkably little modification and elaboration, a sequence of Sraffian models can be made to do essentially the same job which Marx's labour theory of value was employed to do. We can start, as Marx did, with the postulation of a prior concrete magnitude which limits the levels of profit and rent. We can adopt the same kind of view about the order and direction of determination of the variables in the system as Marx did. Up to a point, the same kind of quantitative predictions about the relation between price ratios and embodied labour ratios can (if we wish) be made; and the analysis based on the models can readily be framed (again if we wish) in logical-historical terms. The same kind of scope can be left for the influence of social and institutional factors in the distribution of income; and the transformation problem (or its analogue) can be solved in passing, as it were, without any fuss whatever. In the light of all this, the fact that we do not need to tell our Sraffian equations anything at all about Marxian values seems superbly irrelevant.
>
> (133)

Game, set, and match to the "neo-Ricardians".

## Conclusion

There was much more to Ronald Meek than political economy. He had a life-long passion for the theatre, and it was this – or so his Leicester colleague Ian Bradley understood – that first led him to the Communist Party as a young man in Wellington. In later life he found time to learn the piano and to stride the hills of his adopted Scottish homeland, and even to write a guide to hill-walking in Arran (1963a). Craufurd Goodwin remembers him as "a person of great wisdom and good humour who was especially friendly and encouraging to young people (e.g. me)", and a warm supporter of the establishment – in 1969 – of *History of Political Economy*.[33] He was an impressive lecturer both in his delivery and his appearance, described by one former Glasgow student as "Roman senatorial"; he taught modern economics through the medium of its history, taking care not to allow his politics to intrude into his teaching.[34] Academically, in fact, Meek was something of a loner, with few collaborators and even fewer disciples. Although there is certainly no "Meek school" in the history of economic thought, we suspect that his influence was nevertheless considerable. He wrote with verve and clarity, if also with a certain didacticism that prevents him from being considered a really great stylist. As a scholar of unflagging energy and unfailing attention to detail, Meek rehabilitated the physiocrats almost single-handedly, and (along with Roy Pascal and Duncan Forbes) introduced the Scottish historical materialists first to economists and then to historians of social science more generally.

His role in the propagation of Marxian economics was even more substantial. As Meghnad Desai explained, soon after Meek's death,

> Ronald Meek's contribution to Marxian economics was twofold. First, along with Paul Sweezy, Paul Baran and Maurice Dobb he kept alive the study of Marxian economics in the English speaking world at a time when the environment was hostile. This he did by patient and clear exposition of what Marx had said, explanation of the economic and non-economic context of Marx's work and by teaching through written and spoken word.
> ...
> But his more important contribution in the *Studies* and the articles written separately was to advance an understanding of Marx's theory which was free of any mechanistic – vulgar Marxist or vulgar Neoclassical – rehashing of old half truths, which was critical of Marx in the creative sense of the word and which was replete with many suggestions as to how the theory should be developed, updated and revised.
>
> (Desai 1980: 11)

Rereading *Studies in the Labour Theory of Value*, Desai was struck by the originality of Meek's interpretation, developed at a time when neither the 1844 Paris Manuscripts nor the *Grundrisse* were available in English (ibid.).

Twenty years on, after the dust has settled on the sectarian controversies of the 1970s, it is clear that Meek's view of Marx has stood the test of time, and to some extent the same can be said of his work on Sraffa. It is difficult to gauge the precise influence that Meek exerted in the neo-Ricardian debates, since his undoubtedly important contributions were all made, as it were, from the outside. He took no part in the contemporary Italian discussions on the relationship between Marx and Sraffa which (perhaps coincidentally) flared up again in 1973, the year in which he published his "logical-historical" reformulation of the Sraffian system.[35] The least that can be said is that his was a major voice, calm but authoritative, on the neo-Ricardian side of an unusually noisy debate.

At the Adam Smith bicentenary celebrations in 1976, George Stigler described the author of *The Wealth of Nations* as "alive and well and living in Chicago" (Meek 1977: 3). In one of his last articles, Meek put the record straight. Marx had been right to distinguish the "esoteric" from the "exoteric" Smith, Meek maintained, so that Smith had to be seen as the source not only of modern neoclassical orthodoxy but also of materialist political economy. Thus

> Smith must be regarded as a precursor of the intellectual tradition within which Marx worked. Smith provided Marx (and of course Ricardo) with a model of the new tripartite framework of class relationships characteristic of capitalist society; he formulated a new concept of surplus in which profit was emancipated from its former dependence upon rent and ascribed to the productivity of labour in general; and he outlined a new theory of the development of society and the nature of socio-historical processes in general which, whether Marx himself was aware of it or not, set the stage for the eventual emergence of the materialist conception of history.
>
> (1977: 16)

Today, with neoliberalism in the ascendancy and Marx's version of the history of economics once again on the defensive, there is still much to learn from Ronald Meek.

## Notes

\*   We are grateful for comments from A. W. Coats, Craufurd Goodwin, Steven Medema, Dorli Meek, Henk Plasmeijer, Alessandro Roncaglia, Warren Samuels, Michael Schneider, Andrew Skinner, and Ian Steedman; the usual disclaimer applies.

1   In the preface to his *Economics of Physiocracy* Meek thanks Dobb and others, but not Sraffa (1962a: 10), and his *Smith, Marx and After* (1977) is dedicated to Dobb's memory.

2   The qualifier is not redundant, as there were also physiocrats in Italy. Meek took little interest in them, perhaps because he did not read Italian.

3   Apart from his co-editorship of works by Quesnay and Smith, this was the only occasion on which Meek shared authorship with another historian of economic thought.

4   Personal communication from H. W. Plasmeijer, 27 March 1998.

5   Meek's inaugural lecture at the University of Leicester, entitled "The Rise and Fall of the Concept of the Economic Machine", makes some perceptive – and highly prescient – comments on the use of metaphors in economic discourse (1965).

6  So, we may surmise, would Sraffa, who never wrote anything significant on Adam Smith. As Meek noted, Smith's three-class model had been anticipated, in the 1760s, by Turgot (1973b: 20–1).

7  Meek translated four extracts from *Theories of Surplus Value* (the three English volumes of which appeared only in 1969–72), together with three extracts from the Marx–Engels *Gesamtausgabe* and two previously untranslated letters (to Bebel and Danielson).

8  An expanded version of Meek's introduction was published in 1954 in the independent US Marxist quarterly, *Science and Society*; all quotations are from this source (Meek 1954b).

9  "Stalin as an Economist" originated as a paper presented to the Edinburgh Economics Society in February 1953. An abbreviated version was broadcast (and the text published in *The Listener*) in the same month. It appeared in the *Review of Economic Studies* in the following year (1954c).

10 Robinson's position was made brutally clear in her "Open Letter from a Keynesian to a Marxist" (Robinson 1953), whose strictures were directed against (the unnamed) Meek.

11 See the lengthy translated passages in (1956a: 133, 138–9, 140).

12 Even Meek's hastily appended note on the de-Stalinization process begun at the Twentieth Congress of the CPSU ends by reaffirming his belief that "Stalin's position in history, both as political leader and as Marxist theoretician, is a very great one" (1956a: 284).

13 This bears a superficial but quite misleading resemblance to the so-called "new solution" advanced in the 1980s by Duménil, Foley, and Lipietz (see Sinha 1999).

14 For which the organic composition of capital in the luxury goods industries must equal the social average (see Howard and King 1985: 134–40).

15 Personal communication from.Mrs Dorli Meek, 15 December 1997.

16 Personal communication from L. A.W. Skinner, 28 November 1997

17 Meek was on the editorial board of the *New Reasoner* and also, briefly, its successor, *New Left Review* (Chun 1993: chapter I).

18 For the views of other leading Marxian economists see the collection *Has Capitalism Changed?* (Tsuru 1961), and the discussion of this book in Howard and King (1992: chapter 4).

19 "If there is any hope of progress in economics at all, it must be in using academic methods to solve the problems posed by Marx" (Robinson 1942: 95). Meek invoked this aphorism in *Studies* (1956a: 238).

20 In January 1960 the *New Reasoner* merged with *Universities and Left Review* to form *New Left Review*, which continues to be published. Details of the coup which removed Meek and his allies (E. P. Thompson, John Saville, and others) from the board of *New Left Review* are given by Chun (1993: chapter III) and Kenny (1995: chapter 1). Meek published only one article in the *Review*, an extended book review in which he urged the New Left to take "a much more positive and uninhibited attitude towards the economic achievements of the socialist world" than it had to date (1960b: 67).

21 See his review of Joseph Gillman's *The Falling Rate of Profit* (Meek 1959b; Gillman 1957).

22 Compare (1967: 113–14) with (1962b: 423); and (1967: 127–8) with (1962b: 439–40).

23 This is an amended version of an article published in the *Scottish Journal of Political Economy* (1957b), with some of the more polemical references to Schumpeter's misunderstandings of Marx toned down (compare 1957b: 12–17 with 1967: 207–9) or deleted (notes 6 and 8 on pp. 3 and 5 of 1957b).

24 A significant shift towards Schumpeter's position can, however, be detected in Meek's (1972) paper on marginalism and Marxism.

25  The references are to her *Economic Philosophy* (Robinson 1962: chapters 2–3).
26  Both qualifications are necessary, in view of the perceptive reviews by Harcourt and Massaro (1964), which was a substantially delayed reaction, and Napoleoni (1961), which – in addition to its rather Delphic tone – became available in English only in 1992.
27  See, for example, her subsequent re-review (Robinson 1965), duly acknowledged by Meek (1967: 161, n.1), and Luigi Pasinetti's verdict that she *never* really understood what Sraffa had done (Pasinetti 1998: 381).
28  For the definitive account of these and all other questions relating to Sraffian economics, see Kurz and Salvadori (1995).
29  In Marx's case it was Department III, producing luxuries; in Meek's 1956 solution, it was the wage goods industries of Department II.
30  Personal communications from A. W. Coats and M. P. Schneider.
31  There is as yet no satisfactory history of these (often very bitter) controversies; something of the flavour can be inferred from Steedman *et al.* (1981).
32  This was an allusion to wartime propaganda aimed at discouraging inessential use of public transport by means of posters asking "Is Your Journey Really Necessary?"
33  Personal communication from C. D. Goodwin, 16 April 1997.
34  Personal communication from A. W. Skinner, 28 November 1997.
35  Personal communication from A. Roncaglia, 25 May 1997.

# Bibliography

There is an almost complete bibliography of Meek's writings in Bradley and Howard (1982: xi–xiv), but some articles in political journals are not included there. The list included under his name below contains only those works cited in the text.

Bradley, I. and Howard, M. C. (eds) (1982) *Classical and Marxian Political Economy: Essays in Honour of Ronald L. Meek*, London: Macmillan.
Brunhoff, S. de (1973) "Marx as an a-Ricardian: Value, Money and Price at the Beginning of 'Capital'", *Economy and Society* 2, 4: 421–30.
Chun, L. (1993) *The British New Left*, Edinburgh: Edinburgh University Press.
Desai, M. (1980) "Ronald Meek's Contribution to Marxian Economics", *History of Economic Thought Newsletter* 24, Spring: 11–17.
Dickinson, H. D. (1957) "Review of Meek (1956a)", *Economic Journal* 67, 267: 499–504.
Dobb, M. H. (1937) *Political Economy and Capitalism*, London: Routledge & Kegan Paul.
—— (1960) "An Epoch-making Book", *Labour Monthly* October: 487–91.
—— (1970) "The Sraffa System and the Critique of the Neo-classical Theory of Distribution", *De Economist* 118, 4: 347–62.
—— (1973) *Theories of Value and Distribution Since Adam Smith*, Cambridge: Cambridge University Press.
Eatwell, J. (1975) "Mr. Sraffa's Standard Commodity and the Rate of Exploitation", *Quarterly Journal of Economics* 89, 4: 543–55.
Gillman, J. M. (1957) *The Falling Rate of Profit*, London: Dobson.
Groenewegen, P. D. (1979) "Ronald Meek and Physiocracy: An Appreciation", *History of Economic Thought Newsletter* 23, Autumn: 12–20.
Harcourt, G. C. and Massaro, V. G. (1964) "Mr. Sraffa's Production of Commodities", *Economic Record* 40, 91: 442–54.
Harrod, R. F. (1961) "Review of Sraffa (1960)", *Economic Journal* 71, 284: 783–7.

Howard, M. C. (1992) "Ronald L. Meek (1917–1978)", in P. Arestis and M. Sawyer (eds) A Biographical Dictionary of Dissenting Economists, Aldershot: Edward Elgar, 347–52.

Howard, M. C. and King, J. E. (1985) The Political Economy of Marx, second edition, Harlow: Longman.

—— (1992) A History of Marxian Economics, Volume II: 1929–1990, London: Macmillan and Princeton, NJ: Princeton University Press.

Hutchison, T. W. (1954) "Review of Meek (1953)", Economica NS 21, 81: 79–80.

—— (1957) "Review of Meek (1956a)", Economica NS 24, 94: 163–4.

Kenny, M. (1995) The First New Left, London: Lawrence and Wishart.

Kurz, H. D. and Salvadori, N. (1995) Theory of Production: A Long-period Analysis, Cambridge: Cambridge University Press.

Lange, O. (1963) Political Economy, Oxford: Pergamon and Warsaw: Polish Scientific Publishers.

Marx, K. (1969) Theories of Surplus Value, Volume I, London: Lawrence and Wishart.

Medio, A. (1972) "Profits and Surplus-Value: Appearance and Reality in Capitalist Production", in E. K. Hunt and J. G. Schwartz (eds) A Critique of Economic Theory, Harmondsworth: Penguin, 312–46.

Meek, Ronald L. (1943) Maori Problems Today, Wellington: Progressive Publishing.

—— (1950a) "The Place of Keynes in the History of Economic Thought", Modern Quarterly 6, Winter: 34–51.

—— (1950b) "The Decline of Ricardian Economics in England", Economica NS 17, 1: 43–62.

—— (1950c) "Preface to Bettelheim: On the Problem of Choice between Alternative Investment Projects", Soviet Studies 2, 1: 22–6.

—— (1951a) "The Rehabilitation of Ricardo", Listener 4, October: 547–8.

—— (1951b) "Some Notes on an Interpretation of Stalin's Contribution to the Linguistics Controversy", Soviet Studies 3, 2: 174–84.

—— (1953) Marx and Engels on Malthus: Selections from the Writings of Marx and Engels Dealing with the Theories of Thomas Robert Malthus, London: Lawrence and Wishart; reprinted as Marx and Engels on the Population Bomb, Berkeley, CA: Ramparts, 1971.

—— (1954a) "The Scottish Contribution to Marxist Sociology", in J. Saville (ed.) Democracy and the Labour Movement, London: Lawrence and Wishart, 61–89.

—— (1954b) "Malthus Yesterday and Today", Science and Society 18, 1: 21–51.

—— (1954c) "Stalin as an Economist", Review of Economic Studies 21, 3: 232–9.

—— (1955a) "Some Conversations with Soviet Economists", Soviet Studies 6, 3: 238–46.

—— (1955b) "Some Thoughts on Marxism, Scarcity and Gosplan", Oxford Economic Papers 7, 3: 281–99.

—— (1956a) Studies in the Labour Theory of Value, London: Lawrence and Wishart. Second edition, 1973.

—— (1956b) "Some notes on the 'transformation problem'", Economic Journal 67, 261: 94–107.

—— (1957a) "Economics for the Age of Oligopoly – 1: Mr Strachey's Economics", New Reasoner 8: 41–57.

—— (1957b) "Is Economics Biased? A Heretical View of a Leading Thesis in Schumpeter's History", Scottish Journal of Political Economy 4, 1: 1–17.

—— (1958) "Economics for the Age of Oligopoly – 2: Professor Blyumin's Economics", New Reasoner 9: 50–67.

—— (1959a) "Economics for the Age of Oligopoly – 3: Karl Marx's Economics", *New Reasoner* 10: 14–31.

—— (1959b) "Review of Gillman (1957)", *Economic Journal* 69, 273: 132–4.

—— (1960a) "The Falling Rate of Profit", *Science and Society* 24, 1: 38–52.

—— (1960b) "Rates of Growth", *New Left Review* 6, November–December: 63–8.

—— (1961) "Mr. Sraffa's Rehabilitation of Classical Economics", *Scottish Journal of Political Economy* 8, 2: 119–36; reprinted in *Science and Society* 25, 2: 139–56, 1961.

—— (1962a) *The Economics of Physiocracy*, London: Allen and Unwin.

—— (1962b) "Marx's 'doctrine of increasing misery'", *Science and Society* 26, 4: 422–41.

—— (1963a) *Hill-Walking in Arran*, Isle of Arran: Arran Tourist Association. Second edition, 1972.

—— (1963b) "The Allocation of Expenditure in the Electricity Supply Industry: Some Methodological Problems", *Scottish Journal of Political Economy* 10, 1: 36–60.

—— (1965) *The Rise and Fall of the Concept of the Economic Machine*, Leicester: Leicester University Press.

—— (1967) *Economics and Ideology and Other Essays: Studies in the Development of Economic Thought*, London: Chapman and Hall.

—— (1968a) "Ideas, Events and Environment: The Case of the French Physiocrats", in R. V. Eagly (ed.) *Events, Ideology and Economic Theory*, Detroit: Wayne State University Press, 44–64.

—— (1968b) "Discussion", in R. V. Eagly (ed.) *Events, Ideology and Economic Theory*, Detroit: Wayne State University Press, 120–3.

—— (1972) "Marginalism and Marxism", *History of Political Economy* 4, 2: 499–511.

—— (1973a) "Introduction to the Second Edition", in Ronald L. Meek, *Studies in the Labour Theory of Value*, second edition, London: Lawrence and Wishart, i–xliv.

—— (1973b) *Turgot on Progress, Sociology and Economics*, Cambridge: Cambridge University Press.

—— (1973c) *Precursors of Adam Smith 1750–1775*, London: Dent.

—— (1974) "Value in the History of Economic Thought", *History of Political Economy* 6, 3: 246–60.

—— (1976a) *Social Science and the Ignoble Savage*, Cambridge: Cambridge University Press.

—— (1976b) "Is there an 'historical transformation problem' ?: A Comment", *Economic Journal* 86, 2: 342–76.

—— (1977) *Smith, Marx and After: Ten Essays in the Development of Economic Thought*, London: Chapman and Hall.

Meek, Ronald L. and Kuczynski, M. (1972) *Quesnay's Tableau Economique*, London: Macmillan for the Royal Economic Society.

Meek, Ronald L., Raphael, D. D., and Stein, P. G. (eds) (1978) *Adam Smith, Lectures on Jurisprudence*, Oxford: Clarendon Press.

Morishima, M. and Catephores, G. (1975) "Is there an 'historical transformation problem'?" *Economic Journal* 85, 2: 309–28.

—— (1976) "The 'historical transformation problem': a reply", *Économic Journal* 86, 2: 348–52.

Napoleoni, C. (1961) "Sulla teoria della produzione come processo circolare", *Giornale Degli Economisti* 20: 101–17. English translation, "An Essay on the Theory of Production as a Circular Process", in L. L. Pasinetti (ed.) *Italian Economic Papers, Volume 1*, Bologna: Il Mulino and Oxford: Oxford University Press, 1992, 251–64.

Pasinetti, L. L. (1998) "Piero Sraffa: An Italian Economist at Cambridge", in L. L. Pasinetti (ed.) *Italian Economic Papers, Volume III*, Bologna: Il Mulino and Oxford: Oxford University Press, 365–83.

Pressman, S. (1994) *Quesnay's Tableau Économique: A Critique and Reassessment*, New York: Augustus M. Kelley.

Reder, M. W. (1961) "Review of Sraffa (1960)", *American Economic Review* 51, 4: 688–95.

Robinson, J. (1942) *An Essay on Marxian Economics*, London: Macmillan.

—— (1953) "An Open Letter from a Keynesian to a Marxist", in J. Robinson, *On Rereading Marx*, Cambridge: Students' Bookshop, 19–23.

—— (1961) "Prelude to a Critique of Economic Theory", *Oxford Economic Papers* NS 13, 1: 53–8.

—— (1962) *Economic Philosophy*, London: Watts.

—— (1965) "Piero Sraffa and the Rate of Exploitation", *New Left Review* 31, May–June: 28–34.

Rosdolsky, R. (1956) "Zur neueren Kritik des Marxschen Gesetzes der fallenden Profitrate", *Kyklos* 9, 2: 208–26.

Rowthorn, R. (1974) "Neo-classicism, Neo-Ricardianism and Marxism", *New Left Review* 86, July–August: 63–87.

Schumpeter, J. A. (1954) *A History of Economic Analysis*, London: Allen and Unwin.

Sinha, A. (1999) "Transformation Problem", in P. O'Hara (ed.) *Encyclopaedia of Political Economy*, London: Routledge, 1169–73.

Skinner, A. S. (1982) "A Scottish Contribution to Marxist Sociology?", in I. Bradley and M. C. Howard (eds) *Classical and Marxian Political Economy: Essays in Honour of Ronald L. Meek*, London: Macmillan, 79–114.

Sraffa, P. (1960) *Production of Commodities By Means of Commodities*, Cambridge: Cambridge University Press.

Steedman, I. (1977) *Marx After Sraffa*, London: New Left Books.

Steedman, I. *et al.* (1981) *The Value Controversy*, London: Verso.

Strachey, J. (1956) *Contemporary Capitalism*, London: Gollancz.

Tsuru, S. (1957) "Review of Meek (1956a)", *American Economic Review* 47, 5: 701–2.

—— (ed.) (1961) *Has Capitalism Changed?*, Tokyo: Iwanami Shoten.

# 11 Philip Mirowski as a historian of economic thought

## S. Abu Turab Rizvi

> The smallest subdivisions of science taken separately are dealt with purely in relation to themselves – the general, great sciences, on the contrary, regarded as a whole, call up the question – certainly a very non-objective one – "Wherefore? To what end?" It is this utilitarian consideration which causes them to be dealt with less impersonally when taken as a whole than when considered in their various parts.
>
> (Nietzsche, *Human, All-Too-Human*, sect. 6)

People write the history of economics for a variety of reasons. Philip Mirowski reveals some of his own motivations in his "Confessions of an Aging *Enfant Terrible*":

> Thus, when I read a particular economist's advocacy of regarding children as consumer goods, or another insists that Third World countries should be dumping grounds for toxic industrial wastes since life is cheap there, or a third proclaims that no sound economist would oppose NAFTA, or a fourth asserts confidently that some price completely reflects all relevant underlying fundamentals in the market, or a fifth pronounces imperiously that no credible theorist would recommend anything but a Nash equilibrium as the very essence of rationality in a solution concept, I do not view this as an occasion to dispute the validity of the assumptions of their "models"; rather, for me, it is a clarion call to excavate the archeology of knowledge that allows such classes of statements to pass muster, as a prelude to understanding what moral presuppositions I must evidently hold dear, given that I find them deeply disturbing.
>
> (Mirowski 1998a: 216)

This passage reveals a number of characteristics of Mirowski's writing: the long sentences with a pile of clauses, forcing you to tarry and absorb the message; the message itself delivered straight on, inviting controversy, certainly challenging and pulling no punches; the mixture of practical economics and high theory; the impatience with small questions and approaches, always looking for the big picture; the discomfiting reference (for most economists) to Continental philosophy; and the palpable and very personal opposition to mainstream economics. But most of all, it reveals Mirowski's concern with why certain claims gain currency in particular intellectual milieus. It is the examination of this issue that stands out in his contributions to the history of economics.

Philip Mirowski's methods of inquiry and influential theses have had an enormous impact on the history of economic thought, precisely because his work is about why "classes of statements" pass muster. To write about this issue of legitimacy and appeal, Mirowski has had to consider illegitimacy, and has had to take into account areas of thinking beyond economics. This has, in turn, caused his work to be influential and controversial at the same time. Some important Mirowskian concerns discussed in this chapter, with these issues in mind, are the genesis of neoclassical economics, the methodology of economics, the place of the history of thought in the economics profession, the relation between the natural and the social, mathematical expression in economics, and cyborg science.

## Education and early projects

Philip Mirowski graduated from Michigan State University in 1973 with a degree in economics. He had moved to economics from anthropology, in which he found a lack of attention to theoretical foundations of the subject. His only undergraduate course in the history of economics was with Warren Samuels. He pursued graduate study at the University of Michigan, earning a Ph.D. in economics in 1979. His experience of graduate school was disappointing, and he recalls poor teaching and his own lack of interest in much of what he was taught. His first academic appointment was at Santa Clara University, where he began teaching history of economic thought (Heinonen 1993: 508). Mirowski's early publications were in economic history (with history of thought thrown in) on topics ranging from business cycles to eighteenth-century stock markets in England (e.g., Mirowski 1985).

Other than Warren Samuels, Mirowski's early influences included the economic historian Gavin Wright – who joined him in reading books such as Feyerabend's *Against Method* – and Larry Sklar, the philosopher of science. Mirowski attributes a great deal to his intensive interaction with fellow members – mostly students – of the Union for Radical Political Economics (Heinonen 1993: 508–9).

Two related features of this early history stand out. First, Mirowski developed some lifelong interests: in history of economic thought, methodology, and the philosophy of science. Second, like many economics graduate students with unorthodox tendencies (who have the "moral suppositions" quoted earlier), he gravitated towards those fields that have been traditionally most congenial to this outlook. These include economic history which, before the introduction of cliometrics and formal modeling into it, was a refuge for those who wished to address the economic reality in a relatively direct manner, without much help from orthodox economic analysis;[1] history of economic thought, which permitted consideration of alternatives now forgotten in the march to the current state of the art; and methodology and philosophy, since these too permitted looks into the periphery, beyond the blinkered focus of the majority of economists, and provided legitimacy for questioning the foundations of the field.

## Histories of economics

And question the foundations of the field he certainly did. Mirowski is best known as the author of More Heat Than Light. In this work, he made a series of claims, most famous among which is the view that "the progenitors of neoclassical economic theory boldly copied the reigning physical theories in the 1870s ... they copied their models term for term and symbol for symbol, and said so" (Mirowski 1989a: 3). Naturally, then, his work has been controversial. Many historians of thought and economists generally have found it hard to know what to make of him. Where was he "coming from?" Where did he fit? In order to answer these questions, let us consider the more usual approaches to the history of economics, so that Mirowski's can be seen in relief.

For some time, it seemed that histories of economic thought fell into several categories. Of course, some histories spanned more than one category. First there were those historians who did careful work with the primary texts, paraphrasing and clarifying major themes and figures, constructing chronologies of ideas, illuminating primacy issues, publishing and annotating manuscripts, and the like. This was history of economics pretty much for its own sake. The watchwords here are painstaking, careful, and rather dry. Given the paucity of new texts, and the esoteric nature of the work, this was not to be a flourishing breed within the economics profession. Here, one is reminded of Mirowski's disparaging remark about the "antiquarian pursuits" of historians of economics (1989a: 202). Others, those in the next two categories, seemed rather more motivated by particular economic doctrines. Thus the elder statesmen and others of the neoclassical persuasion would seek precursors of their current ideas in previous writings. This accounts for much work on utility, marginalism, demand, and so on. Mirowski certainly disparaged the Whiggish "business of searching for precursors of neoclassical economics theory [which] does seem to be one of the few precarious niches that most historians of economic thought have carved out for themselves in the modern economic profession" (1989a: 202). For neoclassical economists, the history was in a sense optional. It contributed little to contemporary economics other than providing a pedigree and some legitimacy. The real economics was done elsewhere. Here, too, one can see that historians of thought would not be a growing school. A third approach belonged to those who did not appreciate such appropriation of their favored historical figures. They sought to revive the true message of a particular economist, and adapt it to the modern context. They opposed the mainstream contemporary theory and sought an alternative foundation in earlier writing. Hence the interest in history of thought for Marxists, post-Keynesians, neo-

Ricardians, and Austrians who want to clarify what Marx, Keynes, Ricardo, or Hayek really meant in contrast to what these figures mean to those with a neoclassical mindset. But though these historians championed an alternative to the orthodoxy, they were not a thriving camp, either.

Mirowski has little praise for most historians of thought, citing the field as a moribund specialty (1992a, 1994f). He pulls no punches as he talks of its "catastrophic failure," inability to provide reflexive distance and perspective, its obsolescence, repetition, incapacity to surprise and entertain, and its irrelevance (1998: 13–14). We shall have occasion to return to his views on the profession shortly. For now, what is important is that while Mirowski shares something with many of the historians in the three categories, that is not the whole picture. That he shares something with those in the first and third categories is clear. He has worked in the first mold and is certainly responsive to issues surrounding the historian's craft. He has edited some of Edgeworth's papers (Mirowski 1994c) and five volumes of Thornton's collected economic writings (Mirowski 1999). Nearly all of his writings show familiarity with more well known as well as obscure texts and the relevant archival record. He has sniffed manuscript dust with the best of them. Moreover, he can be seen as being united with the third group in his opposition to the mainstream. Yet he has not been a champion of particular figures in the way of the third group. While he certainly shows a great deal of respect for economists such as Veblen and Georgescu-Roegen (and dedicated *More Heat Than Light* to the latter), his own positive contributions to economics (Mirowski 1991a; Mirowski and Somefun 1998) are not based on reconstructions of these figures. Since his view of economics as being analogous to contemporaraneous physical theories does not exclude Ricardo or Marx, say, the current champions of these figures have themselves disputed Mirowski's claims. Overall, it is difficult to place Mirowski in one of the three categories. But if Mirowski is not "just" doing history, finding precursors, or rehabilitating a historical figure, what is he doing?

My suggestion is that he represents a way of writing history of economics that is more aware of contemporary intellectual trends than any of the categories of historian I described. While Mirowski is certainly not the only one to do so, he has responded to (though he has certainly not always agreed with) the intellectual currents of the past three decades. I refer to upheavals in the philosophy and anthropology of science, the rise of science studies, feminist thought, postmodernism, structuralism, constructivism, hermeneutics, relativism, and so forth – that is, some of the trends that more conservative historians such as Blaug have caricatured as mere "anti-modernism, anti-foundationalism, post-structuralism, hermeneutical deconstructivism, discourse analysis, radical relativism, end-of-philosophy critique" (Blaug 1994: 130). One example of Mirowski's broadening of what constitutes legitimate history of economics can be seen when he writes that

> some of the most profound and imaginative work in the history of economics is done by historians such as Lorraine Daston, Ted Porter, and

Tim Alborn, and that the history of economics must shake off its Smith/Ricardo/Marx/Keynes complex and its Whiggish bias and evince a truly interdisciplinary imagination if it is to survive.

(Mirowski 1992a: 221)

In this quotation, he finds a great deal of value in the work of (general and science) historians rather than in the typical occupations of historians of economic thought. The expansion of the disciplinary landscape makes Mirowski's work challenging for  traditionally trained historians of economics, but also makes it more contemporary. This background also helps to explain Mirowski's reluctance to stay safely within the boundaries of typical economic discourse. Economics is "de-centered" by being seen as part of general intellectual trends; similarly, its history has also to be part of general intellectual history. We will return to this theme.

## More Heat Than Light

In *More Heat Than Light*, Mirowski proposes a new and universal approach to the history of economics. He asks us to think about the importance of ideas about the natural world in our approach to social phenomena such as the economy. What allows economic theories to have acceptability is that they resonate well with the physics or other natural science of their time. Specifically they resonate well with contemporary conceptions of the interrelations among the triad of body, motion, and value. Mirowski advances the thesis that the metaphors of body (anthropometrics), motion (physics), and value (economics) are interconnected (1989a: 99–138). In a slow-moving but relatively stable sense, an idea in one of these areas serves to underpin those in the others. This is how the theories get their validity. So the focus on labor as a determinant and measure of value that we find in Quesnay, Smith, Ricardo, and Marx – in classical political economy generally – reflects the physics of conserved substances derived from Leibnizian and Cartesian rational mechanics (1989a: 139–92). The classics had a substance theory of value, the substance being labor – hence body. It was augmented in production, diminished in consumption, and preserved in circulation (1989a: 143) – hence motion. Body and motion as seen through contemporary physical theories provide the resonant metaphors by which the value theory gains its power.

When the underlying physics changed, the reasonableness of classical political economy became suspect. This occurred in the mid nineteenth century with the rise of what Mirowski calls proto-energetics (1989a: chapter 2). Indeed, Mirowski begins the book by explaining the concept of energy – which by "the 1870s ... became coextensive with the entire range of physics" – its conservation, its mathematical representation as field theory, dynamics, determinism, entropy, thermodynamics, relativity, and quantum mechanics (Mirowski 1989a: 11–98). With proto-energetics, energy was conceived with the help of field formalisms, and not as a conserved substance. Value was no longer associated with body substances such as labor but with mental phenomena (utility and later preference). Neoclassical economics was based on a different physics from classical theory, but the categories of body, motion, and value were still pertinent and provide the continuity against which a change in theory can be seen (1989a: 195–7). Here we get the Mirowskian claim, cited earlier, that "the progenitors of neoclassical economic theory boldly copied the reigning physical theories in the 1870s ... they copied their models term for term and symbol for symbol, and said so" (Mirowski 1989a: 3). The marginalists substituted utility for energy and so made economics from the available physics of the mid nineteenth century.

By itself, this foray into physics represented a challenge to historians of economics, who were comfortable with a fairly self-considering history of economic ideas and, so far as other disciplines were concerned, might dip into political philosophy. But this isolationist view ignores the reality that earlier times did not have the disciplinary distinctions we now possess, and Mirowski was convincing with textual evidence that the marginalists were copying field formalisms.

Problematically, the neoclassical theory of the twentieth century retained the mid-nineteenth-century physics in order to hold on to its unifying principle of utility (or preference) maximization subject to constraint. The is the same principle we see in Samuelson's *Foundations of Economic Analysis* (1947) and every other neoclassical treatise to this day. The underlying physics, however, changed into its more modern forms. What problem does this cause other than modeling the enterprise on an outdated physics (Leonard 1993: 250)? This important question is discussed in the next section.

Mirowski's approach in *More Heat Than Light* permitted him to reevaluate the status of figures in the history of economics. He was intent on overlooking the "orthodox hagiographies" of the precursor type and to situate writers such as Canard, Bentham, and Cournot according to the body–motion–value paradigm. Against this new background, the various figures recede and others advance: "the rejected and despised Canard grows in esteem, whereas Bentham is marginalized and discounted, and in the case of Cournot, the explicitly nonneoclassical themes loom larger" (1989a: 203). Such shifts in valuation, too, presented a challenge to conventional historians. Mirowski has continued in this vein with new evaluations of Edgeworth, Marshall, Henry Ludwell Moore, and Von Neumann and Morgenstern (Mirowski 1994b, 1990a, 1990b, 1992c). Some of these pieces, those that revalued figures downward, were so shocking that the celebrants of the figures involved took clear umbrage. Thus Denis O'Brien, reviewing the book in which Mirowski's chapter on Marshall appeared, called Mirowski's work "an extraordinary tirade," was baffled by the nineteenth-century physics, and chose to "pass by without comment" (cited in De Marchi 1993: 3).

On the other hand, many historians of economics found Mirowski's book revolutionary and bracing and it has had significant influence on the history of economics. E. Roy Weintraub (1993) calls it an important, unsettling, and epochal book for historians of economics. More than anything else, he sees its historiographic stance as being subversive: the view of the history of economics interconnected with texts from physics, psychology, philosophy, and other disciplines; the use of a variety of texts, from treatises to letters to popular accounts; the situating of economics in a history of ideas; the interest in what makes an economic account convincing beyond its internalist successes. Weintraub's contribution appears in a volume edited by Neil De Marchi (the special issue of *History of Political Economy* for 1993). Fifteen other contributions in the volume follow up on matters raised by Mirowski, apply his ideas, or dispute them. The topics range from Mirowski's use of metaphor, mathematical formalism, the physics–economics thesis and historiography. The entire volume marks the importance of Mirowski's work for historians of thought. As De Marchi writes, "If the measures are the number of interesting questions formulated and provocative propositions adumbrated, or the freshness of the approach devised, he has to be taken very seriously" (1993: 3). Similarly, an even larger number of essays in *Natural Images in Economic Thought* (Mirowski 1994b) analyze the Mirowskian theme of the relation between the natural and the social in economics. In both of these contributions it is clear that Mirowski's work has influenced not only historians of economics but also historians of science. This raises the issue of the relation of the two fields, a topic that Mirowski has addressed.

### Two answers to "so what?"

What follows from Mirowski's book? Was this a harmless story of origin, or did it have "insistent implications" for further development of the theory? What problem does this borrowing of physical formalisms cause? These lead to the "so what?" question. To this there are at least two sorts of answers. The first is broader and is represented really by most of Mirowski's work since *More Heat Than Light*. It is to consider the various possible relations between the natural and the social and to see what alternatives there are to the sort of correspondence he identified there. For example, his inaugural lecture at Notre Dame and the contributions of others to the conference on that occasion (Mirowski 1994b) are in this spirit. Here, Mirowski notes that:

> In appropriating the formalisms of mid-nineteenth-century energy physics and adapting them to the language of utility and prices, the progenitors and their epigones adopted a certain worldview, one that had to stress the extreme near identity of physics and economics. Veering so close to becoming subsumed in pure identity could be attractive only to a personality who was convinced of a far-reaching unity of science, one necessarily founded on the bedrock of a natural law external to all human endeavor.
>
> (1994c: 10–11)

Thus this is just one possible position to take concerning the relation between the natural and the social. From the point of view of current intellectual developments, there are many other positions available to economists (and social scientists generally) or to historians of economics. At this point, Mirowski outlines a very useful taxonomy of relations between the natural and the social, and this shows what is more broadly possible (the names are representative holders of the various positions):

1. The Natural and the Social are identical in
   a. Every respect (extreme reductionism)
   b. Laws (Churchland)
   c. Epistemic methods (Glymour, Cartwright)
   d. Metaphorical structure (Schumpeter)

2. The Natural and the Social are disjunct but individually lawlike due to
   a. Epistemic status (Windelband, Rickert, Weber, Kuhn)
   b. Ontological status rooted in psychology (Dilthey, Taylor)
   c  Purposes (Habermas, Dreyfus)

3. The Natural is objectively stable, whereas the social is patterned on it but is not stable, implying
   a. A sociology of collective knowledge (Durkheim, Mannheim)
   b. Sociology as epistemology (Douglas, Bloor, Shapin)

4. The Natural and the Social are both unstable and hence jointly constructed as mutually supportive
   a. Out of interests (Latour, Haraway, actant-network theory)
   b. Out of practices (modern pragmatists, Hacking, Rouse)
   c. Out of will (Nietzche, Foucault)

(Taken from Mirowski 1994e: 11, Table 1.1; see also the slightly different list in Mirowski 1993: 319)

In doing this, Mirowski gives historians of economics and economists a view of the possibilities. This sort of taxonomy is important to make sense of where different authors are "coming from." It also raises the stakes for those who would do history of thought. There is a great deal to know beyond economics and a little methodology. In addition, it is important to note that not only are there philosophers and historians in this taxonomy, but also there are those who write or wrote social science. Thus for economists, it is vital to see not only where the history, methodology, or appraisal of economics belongs in this classification, but also where economics belongs. To find most of economics in a very narrow ambit, whereas social theory is so much broader, ought to be eye opening. Thus those economists who would approach the subject in a different manner can benefit by contemplating the various ways of conceiving these relations and possibly following other approaches.

In his own more recent work, Mirowski has found the alternative approaches to the natural and social to be liberating. He writes:

> With the banishment of all residual traces of historical representation from the faculties of most departments of economics, I doubt there remain any reasonable grounds to think the situation can be reversed from within. Therefore, I will suggest that the next best hope for the reorientation of the history of economics comes from without – namely, a coalition of writers from the social studies of science (Pickering 1995; Heims 1991), anthropologists and philosophers of science (Latour 1993), and modern third-generation feminist thought (Fox Keller 1995; Haraway 1991), all of whom have recently recast the entire question of the post-World War II relationship of the natural and the social sciences. While they have not *specifically* addressed the situation of modern economics, their observations concerning biology, computer science, operations research, and other collateral disciplines can be readily extended to economics, with potentially far-reaching consequences.
>
> (Mirowski 1998: 14)

In this article and in a forthcoming book (called *Machine Dreams: Economics becomes a Cyborg Science*) Mirowski seeks to fill in the importance of these "cyborg sciences" for economics. In earlier work, Mirowski noticed an interesting disjuncture between types of recent economics. On the one hand, we have what might be called the main style of economics. It is largely axiomatic and formal, atemporal, and mechanical, and inclined to assert an Archimedean perspective. Examples would be general equilibrium theory, IS–LM-type macroeconomics, and associated econometrics. In contrast to this classical view, we have a more romantic one (Mirowski 1996: 15). Its methods are more inclined to holism, its approach to time more evolutionary, its claims more guarded. It sees diversity as a plus and not a problem, experimentation as a virtue and a necessity, computational and the numerical methods as valuable when compared to the analytical and the exact; and it takes a perspectival approach as a given. Mirowski's example of such an approach was the Santa Fe Institute's complexity theory. He now sees what he previously called the romantic impulse as a "cyborg" science, reflecting the importance in the post-WWII period of human–machine interactions in scientific and other research, for example operations research, artificial intelligence, information theory, and cybernetics. From complexity theory, Mirowski's scope expands to include evolutionary and computational themes more generally. He covers prominent contemporary trends such as game theory and bounded rationality.

In general, Mirowski has championed the application of the historical apparatus to contemporary and recent economics and he is joined in this by a number of historians of economics. This was the theme of the special issue of the *History of Political Economy* (1998) edited by John B. Davis in which

Mirowski's cyborg essay appeared. Historians such as Esther-Mirjam Sent and Robert Leonard and others have made such explorations their chosen subject matter. Similarly, the interest evinced by historians of economics in the history of game theory or econometrics follows a similar impulse. Mirowski (1989b, 1991b, 1992c, 1995) has contributed to these areas as well.

Connected to the relation between the natural and the social is the issue of mathematical and verbal expression in economics (Mirowski 1991a). One of the larger issues that Mirowski has dealt with is the manner of expression chosen by economists (verbal, mathematical, etc.). An idea of his approach to economic rhetoric can be gained from his article on McCloskey's *Rhetoric of Economics* (1985). McCloskey claimed that rhetoric provided a way to understand argument and debate among economists – debate that was supposed to be occurring according to "scientific method." Mirowski makes a more enveloping claim. He says that to understand the role of rhetoric in economics, you have to understand how economics has evolved to champion a scientific, objective, and mathematical style that considers words fuzzy and imprecise. It is true that economics, like any social science, employs metaphors. But to the extent that rhetoric and mathematics – to use shorthand – could be seen to be opposed, and economists had chosen the latter, the former was not a viable option. Looked at this way, simply turning to rhetoric for understanding, as McCloskey suggests, would "sound dissonant and appear self-contradictory" especially since McCloskey champions important aspects of the neoclassical program (Mirowski 1988: 120). Metaphor as seen by McCloskey, then, is a slippery slope and if economists step onto it, much of their received wisdom recedes and then vanishes into the background. Mirowski then proceeds to explore neoclassical economics with the analogy between energy and utility along the lines we have discussed. Contrary to McCloskey, Mirowski sees important differences between poetic and scientific metaphors. In the case of the energy = utility metaphor, he argues that the proponents of the theory never saw it for what it was, with awkward consequences. Metaphors have consequences that are not just aesthetic.

This brings us to the second answer to the "so what?" question: why does *More Heat Than Light* matter for contemporary historiography and economics? It seems that there was originally some confusion on this narrower and more technical issue, but that has now been resolved. I refer to Mirowski's claim about integrability and conservative vector fields in neoclassical economics. The issue is what problems for the theory does the copying of proto-energetics cause? And the answer is of clear importance to contemporary economics. Studying this in detail demonstrates the importance of Mirowski's work for historians of economics and for understanding economic theory. Some of this matter has been discussed by Wade Hands (1993), whom Mirowski has called an ideal reader of his work. Hands is also a co-author of his (Mirowski and Hands 1998) and the two authors plan a book called *Agreement on Demand*, which will explore the history of demand theory.

In *More Heat Than Light*, Mirowski claimed that the copying of proto-energetics by the marginalists led to an important obfuscation in economic theory. He argued that conditions sufficient for the integrability of demand are also sufficient to guarantee that prices form a conservative vector field. For example, he wrote that the "key to understanding neoclassical economics is to realize that prices constitute a conservative vector field" (Mirowski 1989a: 223). If this claim is accepted (and Mirowski wrote that it is accepted as a matter of course in neoclassical theory) then he further argued that it led to unreasonable and embarrassing implications, such as "the sum of expenditure and utility is conserved" (Mirowski 1989a: 233; also 371, cited by Hands 1993: 120). Because of these implications, Mirowski held that these matters involving integrability were left obscure by the neoclassical economists.

Yet Hands shows with a three-good example that Mirowski's original premise is not generally true: it does not follow from the standard Slutsky conditions or an equivalent condition for the integrability of demand that prices will form a conservative vector field (Hands 1993: 121). Rather, Mirowski's claim is true only for the special cases showing symmetry of the Jacobian or Walrasian demands, cases that involve, relatedly, zero income effects, homothetic preferences, and compensated demand. At this point, Hands notes an irony by contrasting the Chicago tradition of using compensated demand as opposed to the general equilibrium tradition that Mirowski criticizes. If only the Chicago approach had been followed, stability and uniqueness could have been demonstrated (Hands 1993: 125).

While Mirowski's initial claim is not in general true, he was able to revise it by appealing to results on the arbitrariness of aggregate excess demands that had been proved in the 1970s. In his response to the participants of the conference at which Hands's contribution was delivered, Mirowski refers at several points to these results (1993: 312–13, 333–5). These arbitrariness results are very important for judging the status of neoclassical microeconomics (Rizvi 1994). Because of this arbitrariness, uniqueness, stability, comparative statics, econometric identification, and microfoundations of macroeconomics cannot be typically established in general equilibrium theory. In other words, general equilibrium theory – the fullest culmination of neoclassical economics – has reached a dead-end since it cannot progress beyond demonstrating the existence of equilibrium. Since the conditions under which the arbitrariness does not hold are vacuous or very special, Mirowski's appeal to the Sonnenschein–Mantel–Debreu results is the correct way to locate the crucial weakness of neoclassical price theory. The irony here (stated somewhat differently from Hands) is that Mirowski's original claim (of prices forming a conservative vector field) would suffice to establish uniqueness and stability and would have caused general equilibrium theory to be a comparative success. The reason why Mirowski's original claim did not hold is precisely why the general equilibrium program has failed to make headway. Moreover, some of the areas in which Mirowski has written after More Heat Than Light, such as chaos, complexity, and non-linear dynamics (Mirowski 1996; 1998; and the forthcoming cyborg science book), all depend for their interest on "open" rather than "closed" (i.e., conservative) systems (Prigogine and Stengers 1984).

This second answer to the "so what?" question (namely, why does the physics–economics analogy matter for understanding contemporary economics?) can now be stated with some specificity. It was not possible for economists to copy every bit of proto-energetics and maintain complete symmetry between economics and physics because this would lead to accepting absurd conditions such as gross substitutability, zero-income effects, identical and homothetic preferences, compensated demands, and the like. Yet without these, the general equilibrium program was stalled and could not address key desiderata such as uniqueness, stability, comparative statics, microfoundations of macroeconomics, or econometric identification. The theory could have some results (beyond existence) at the sacrifice of great realism or some realism without many results to speak of, but not both. Thus there is a great deal of importance for contemporary economics in following through on the choices the marginalists made, and which Mirowski has so ably illuminated in his work.

Thus the significance of Mirowski's work is quite apparent. Not only is his work important for appraising the core of neoclassical economics, but also it challenges historians of economics with a broader suggestion. His writing can certainly be seen as history of economics but it has also moved vigorously beyond the confines of the field conventionally defined. Much of his recent and projected work (such as *Machine Dreams*), especially, is intellectual and cultural history that has a broader audience and ambition. This trajectory – with its expansive interest in the theoretical elaboration of the relation between the natural and the social, and in the acceptability of that theory – thus moves beyond the conventional ambit of the field. It represents, therefore, a criticism of a narrower history of economics and provides a boundary-defying response to that criticism.

## Notes

1 Mirowski himself has asserted the "fact that Fogel and his cliometrics movement were the vanguard of the penetration of neoclassical economics into a stronghold of institutionalists, historicists, and other disgruntled types united by their distaste for the atemporal character of neoclassical economic theory" (1988: 123).

## Bibliography

Blaug, Mark (1994) "Why I am not a Constructivist: Confessions of an Unrepentant Popperian," in Roger Backhouse (ed.) *New Directions in Economic Methodology*, New York: Routledge.

De Marchi, Neil (1993) "Introduction," in Neil De Marchi (ed.) *Nonnatural Social Science: Reflections on the Project of More Heat Than Light*, Durham, NC: Duke University Press.

Hands, D. Wade (1993) "More Light on Integrability, Symmetry, and Utility as Potential Energy in Mirowski's Critical History," in Neil De Marchi (ed.) *Nonnatural Social*

Science: Reflections on the Project of More Heat Than Light, Durham, NC: Duke University Press.

Harraway, Donna (1991) Simians, Cyborgs, and Women: The Reinvention of Nature, New York: Routledge.

Heims, Steve J. (1991) The Cybernetics Group, Cambridge, MA: MIT Press.

Heinonen, Visa (1993) "Conversation with Philip Mirowski: Economics as the Physics of Society," Review of Political Economy 5: 508–31.

Keller, Evelyn Fox (1995) Refiguring Life, New York: Columbia University Press.

Latour, Bruno (1993) We Have Never Been Modern, Cambridge, MA: Harvard University Press.

Leonard, Robert J. (1993) "Chalk and Cheese: Mirowski Meets Douglas and Bloor," History of Political Economy 25 (Suppl.): 249–70.

McCloskey, Donald N. (1985) The Rhetoric of Economics, Madison: University of Wisconsin Press.

Mirowski, Philip (1985) The Birth of the Business Cycle, New York: Garland.

—— (1987) "Shall I Compare Thee to a Minkowski-Ricardo-Leontief-Metzler Matrix of the Mosak-Hicks Type? Rhetoric, Mathematics and the Nature of Neoclassical Theory," Economics and Philosophy 3: 67–96.

—— (1988) Against Mechanism: Protecting Economics from Science, Totowa, NJ: Rowman and Littlefield.

—— (1989a) More Heat Than Light: Economics as Social Physics: Physics as Nature's Economics, New York: Cambridge University Press.

—— (1989b) "The Probabilistic Counter-Revolution, or How Stochastic Concepts Came to Neoclassical Economic Theory," Oxford Economic Papers 41: 217–35.

—— (1990a) "Problems in the Paternity of Econometrics: Henry Ludwell Moore," History of Political Economy 22: 587–609.

—— (1990b) "Smooth Operator: How Marshall's Demand and Supply Curves Made Neoclassicism Safe for Public Consumption but Unfit for Science," in Rita Tulberg (ed.) Alfred Marshall in Retrospect, Brookfield, VT: Edward Elgar.

—— (1991a) "Postmodernism and the Social Theory of Value," Journal of Post Keynesian Economics 13: 565–82.

—— (1991b) "When Games Grow Deadly Serious: The Military Influence on the Evolution of Game Theory," History of Political Economy 23: 227–55.

—— (1991c) "The When, the How and the Why of Mathematical Expression in the History of Economic Analysis," Journal of Economic Perspectives 5: 145–57.

—— (1992a) "Comments on Margaret Schabas' 'Breaking Away'," History of Political Economy 24: 221–3.

—— (1992b) "Three Vignettes on the State of Economic Rhetoric," in Post-Popperian Methodology of Economics: Recovering Practice, Dordrecht: Kluwer.

—— (1992c) "What Were von Neumann and Morgenstern Trying to Accomplish?" History of Political Economy 24: 113–47.

—— (1993) "The Goalkeeper's Anxiety at the Penalty Kick," in Neil De Marchi (ed.) Nonnatural Social Science: Reflections on the Project of More Heat Than Light, Durham, NC: Duke University Press.

—— (1994a) "Confessions of an Aging Enfant Terrible," American Economist 38: 28–35.

—— (1994b) "Doing What Comes Naturally: Four Metanarratives on What Metaphors Are For," in Philip Mirowski (ed.) Natural Images in Economic Thought: Markets Read in Tooth and Claw, New York: Cambridge University Press.

—— (1994c) *Edgeworth on Chance, Economic Hazard, and Statistics*, Lanham, MD: Rowman and Littlefield.

—— (1994d) "Marshalling the Unruly Atoms: Understanding Edgeworth's Career," in Philip Mirowski (ed.) *Edgeworth on Chance, Economic Hazard, and Statistics*, Lanham, MD: Rowman and Littlefield.

—— (ed.) (1994e) *Natural Images in Economic Thought: Markets Read in Tooth and Claw*, New York: Cambridge University Press.

—— (1994f) "What Are the Questions?" in Roger Backhouse (ed.) *New Directions in Economic Methodology*, New York: Routledge.

—— (1995) "Three Ways to Think about Testing in Econometrics," *Journal of Econometrics* 67: 25–46.

—— (1996) "Do You Know the Way to Santa Fe? Or, Political Economy Gets More Complex," in Steven Pressman (ed.) *Interactions in Political Economy: Malvern After Ten Years*, New York: Routledge.

—— (1998a) "Confessions of an Aging Enfant Terrible," in Michael Szenberg (ed.) *Passion and Craft*, Ann Arbor: University of Michigan Press.

—— (1998b) "Machine Dreams: Economic Agents as Cyborgs," *History of Political Economy* 29: 13–40.

—— (1999) *The Collected Economic Works of William Thomas Thornton*, 5 vols, London: Chatto and Pickering.

Mirowski, Philip and Hands, Wade (1998) "A Paradox of Budgets: The Postwar Stabilization of American Neoclassical Demand Theory," *History of Political Economy* 30: 260–92.

Mirowski, Philip and Somefun, Koye (1998) "Markets as Evolving Computational Entities," *Journal of Evolutionary Economics* 8: 329–56.

Pickering, Andrew (1995) *The Mangle of Practice: Time, Agency and Science*, Chicago: University of Chicago Press.

Prigogine, Ilya and Stengers, Isabelle (1984) *Order Out of Chaos: Man's New Dialogue With Nature*, New York: Bantam Books.

Rizvi, S. Abu Turab (1994) "The Microfoundations Project in General Equilibrium Theory," *Cambridge Journal of Economics* 18: 357–77.

Samuelson, Paul A. (1947) *Foundations of Economic Analysis*, Cambridge, MA: Harvard University Press.

Weintraub, E. Roy (1993) "After Mirowski, What?" in Neil De Marchi (ed.) *Nonnatural Social Science: Reflections on the Project of More Heat Than Light*, Durham, NC: Duke University Press.

# 12 Donald E. Moggridge as an historian of economic thought

## John B. Davis*

### Introduction: the editor as historian of economic thought

The history of economic thought is produced through a variety of activities on the part of many individuals. Most historians of economic thought would agree that one consequence of this is that there are multiple viable accounts of most if not all of the theories, doctrines, and conceptual developments in that history. There may be a tendency for opinion on some subjects to settle over time, but most historians of thought would probably still say that the field has a pluralistic character, and that this guarantees that the history of economic thought as a whole will always be in a state of evolution. This image of the history of thought as evolving and multi-perspectival, however, is contrary to how many non-historians understand the field. Non-historians tend to think of history of all kinds in terms of "facts," and this obscures the complexity involved in thinking about a history of ideas in particular. Thus non-historians are apt to believe that when it comes to what Adam Smith said that there must be a "truth" to the matter. Historians, in contrast, know from experience that they operate with both interpretive strategies and strategies of argument, and that these invariably mediate "truth." History of economic thought methodology, as a subfield of economic methodology, investigates the significance and character of these interpretive strategies and strategies of argument. Interpretive strategies may be said to concern the assumptions and presuppositions that historians bring to the subjects they investigate. Joseph Schumpeter in a classic statement saw interpretive strategies at work when analytic efforts are built upon a pre-analytic vision:

> The first task is to verbalize the vision or to conceptualize it in such a way that its elements take their places, with names attached to them that facilitate recognition and manipulation, in a more or less orderly schema or picture. But in doing so ... we assemble further facts in addition to those perceived already, and learn to distrust others that figured in the original vision ... [while] the very work of constructing the schema or picture will add further relations and concepts to, and in general also eliminate others from, the original stock.
>
> (1954: 42)

In contrast, argument strategies concern the specific ways in which historians seek to organize and communicate their understanding of what they investigate. Sheila Dow explains this in terms of the mode of thought the historian employs:

> By mode of thought is meant the way in which arguments (or theories) are constructed and presented, how we attempt to convince others of the validity or truth of our arguments. It is as much concerned with the rhetoric used as means of communication as with the logical structure of the argument.
>
> (1996: 10)

Nonetheless, non-historians are still likely to suppose that, if not "truth," at least "what Adam Smith said" constrains the work of historians. Historians' work, it might thus be argued, results in secondary literatures rather than primary ones, and historians' strategies of interpretation and argument presuppose a resource base of primary materials and literatures upon which historians operate. What *is* the role of primary literatures in the history of economic thought, then? Might they indeed constitute a source of gravitation continually acting against the multi-perspectival, evolving character of the history of economic thought? Or might primary literatures themselves contribute to the evolution and the multi-dimensionality of that history by creating unsturdy platforms that facilitate historians' interpretive strategies and argument strategies?

In discussing Donald E. Moggridge's achievements as an historian of economic thought, specifically as the editor and biographer of J. M. Keynes, I want to suggest that an important and sometimes overlooked source of complexity and change in the history of economic thought derives from historians' production of *primary* as opposed to secondary literatures. On the surface it may seem contradictory to say that historians of economics produce primary literatures, since the history of thought is typically seen to have as its object a set of primary literatures together with their supporting histories. How could historians produce the object of their studies when those studies seem to presuppose an object of study? The untangling of this conundrum begins with recognizing that historians never begin with uninterpreted, *tabula rasae* primary literatures upon which they then bring their interpretive strategies and arguments to bear. Though the original authors of texts are indeed their primary producers, individuals other than these authors mediate secondary literature producers' access to original texts in a variety of ways. Consider the case of David Ricardo, and ask yourself what the primary text is that we label *The Principles of Political Economy and Taxation*. Ricardo himself published three editions of the book which differ in important respects. Are there then three *Principles* or one? If, as most say, the answer is "one," then by extension might it not be argued that "the text" of this three-separate-things-in-one somehow also includes other separate things, namely other works Ricardo wrote "directly" related to production of "the" *Principles*, say, correspondence written between (and perhaps before and after) the three editions, on the ground that these other writings were so much a part of the development of the *Principles* as to arguably be a part of a "single" *Principles*? If this argument appears odd, the alternative view, that each edition of the *Principles* is fully a separate *Principles*, seems not only odd, but on the surface likely to be rejected by most of us. Carrying the original proposal remorselessly ahead, then, might one also go on to ask whether it is necessary to include some of the correspondence and writings of Thomas Malthus in Ricardo's "single" *Principles*? Malthus, one could argue, was part of an exchange that ultimately produced (albeit through Ricardo's writing) what emerged as "the" *Principles*. Then, to talk about "the" *Principles* we would talk not only about its being constituted out of separate documents, but also, after a fashion, about its being the product of separate people.

Arguments of this sort may appear strained and tendentious, but they point to real dilemmas regarding the identification and constitution of primary texts. More to the point in this chapter, issues involved in determining what constitutes the *Principles* reflect just the sort of issues faced by Ricardo's various editors when they had to decide how Ricardo's "collected works" would be defined, what would be contained in them, and what "background information" such as biography and correspondence needed to be included.[1] There is no need, however, to pursue this issue further, since it seems fair to say that Ricardo's principal editor, Piero Sraffa, was, if not a *primary producer of Ricardo's texts*, at least a *producer of Ricardo's primary texts*. Sraffa obviously did not play the same role as Ricardo (and Malthus?) in creating those texts, but he was nonetheless involved in their production. Moreover, Sraffa's work as an editor is certainly different from what is traditionally understood to be involved in making contributions to a secondary literature on Ricardo. As historians of economic thought, editors thus seem to occupy a peculiar half light between being economist producers of primary literatures and historian of economics producers of secondary literatures, sharing with the former the task of constructing the materials which subsequent historians will investigate, and sharing with the latter the necessity of applying interpretive strategies and arguments to construct "original" materials.

Donald Moggridge, of course, stands out as one of the most accomplished of such individuals in recent experience. His modern peers include Sraffa, William Jaffé (Leon Walras), and R. D. Collison Black (W. S. Jevons). Note the scope and breadth of his responsibility with respect to Keynes. Of the thirty volumes of Keynes's *Collected Writings*, twenty-four were Moggridge's responsibility, including *A Revision of the Treaty*, *A Tract on Monetary Reform*, *A Treatise on Money*, *The General Theory*, *A Treatise on Probability*, *Essays in Persuasion*, *Essays in Biography*, three volumes on the preparation, defence, and development of *The General Theory*, three volumes on depression and interwar economic crisis, six volumes on World War II and the postwar international economic order, and the Bibliography and Index. Additionally, note that (as I will discuss more fully below) Moggridge's chief contribution in producing *The Collected Writings* involved not republishing previously published volumes, less than a third of the total, but in selecting, assembling, and organizing the large volume of material that constituted the far less easily defined two thirds of *The Collected Writings*.

Moggridge's achievement as a biographer of Keynes stands on its own apart from his achievement as the editor of Keynes's writings, but seeing the biography in the light of Moggridge's status as Keynes's editor places it in an important light. If one places serious emphasis on the suggestion above that a complete edition of Ricardo's *Principles* needs to include more than simply Ricardo's own writings, then one might also say that a thirty-volume edition of Keynes's *Collected Writings* should be accompanied by an entire volume of supporting information and background that provides a framework for Keynes's own writings. I say this not to deny that the biography is an historian's contribution to the secondary literature on Keynes, nor at all to belittle Moggridge's biography of Keynes, which must be ranked together with the other major Keynes biographies, but rather to draw attention to its dual character as a biography and as an interpretive system side by side with Moggridge's production of *The Collected Writings*. Seeing *The Collected Writings* merely as a collection of documents creates the temptation to regard them as a set of uninterpreted primary materials when through their organization and selection they are in fact produced primary materials. Moggridge's biography of Keynes reflects the interpretive system he employed in producing *The Collected Writings*. This does not imply, nor would he assert, that his biography of Keynes is meant to be "definitive." But it is nonetheless the Keynes biography by the editor of *The Collected Writings*, and thus has special interest for this reason, over and above its intrinsic interest as a major biography of Keynes.

Thus Moggridge is not a typical historian of economics. Indeed neither his pathway to becoming an historian of economic thought nor his achievements as an historian of thought are characteristic of the routes and achievements of many others who have devoted themselves to the history of economic thought. In the second section below I accordingly describe Moggridge's particular pathway into the field in order to suggest his specific orientation toward it. I then turn to his two principal achievements, the Keynes edition and the Keynes biography, attempting to describe them as the outcome of his entry point into the field. In the third section the Keynes edition is discussed. In the fourth section the biography is discussed. The fifth section of the chapter makes brief concluding remarks on the subject of editors of economists' writings as historians of economics.

## Point of entry: economic history

Moggridge's first interest was economic history, rather than the history of economic thought. When he completed his undergraduate degree at the University of Toronto, and went in October 1965 to King's College at Cambridge to begin postgraduate study, he had planned to specialize in economic history. Indeed at Cambridge "[t]he only lectures available on the history of thought were Maurice Dobb's," and these, he later reported, "were so boringly presented that I did not persevere after the first" (Moggridge 1997: 32). Indeed he had left Canada thinking that his particular orientation would be North American economic history, but in light of the library resources at Cambridge soon decided instead on doing a dissertation on monetary history, specifically on the effects of Britain's return to the gold standard in 1925.[2] This led first to his The Return to Gold, 1925: The Formulation of Economic Policy and its Critics (1969) and then more extended discussion in British Monetary Policy, 1924–1931: The Norman Conquest of $4.86 (1972), both based on his Ph.D. dissertation.[3]

But this projected pathway would not be sustained. At the end of 1968 Moggridge was approached by Austin Robinson about joining Elizabeth Johnson in editing Keynes's Collected Writings.[4] Moggridge agreed, and began in October. In November his Ph.D. was submitted for examination, and, after a brief period of indecision about whether to return to Toronto, he elected to stay on in Cambridge to complete his part of the Keynes editing, projected originally by Austin Robinson as likely to require three to four years. Yet as he describes it (Moggridge 1997: 36–8), the number of volumes ultimately to appear in The Collected Writings would be revised upwards a number of times, first on account of the decision in Britain to open up public records on a thirty-year basis (until January 1968 access to British public records had been on a fifty-year wait rule), then on account of the subsequent early opening of the material for all of World War II in a single block, and finally because of the discovery at Keynes's country house at Tilton in 1976 of the "laundry basket" of material that would alone contribute two large volumes to The Collected Writings relating to Keynes's Treatise on Money and The General Theory. Thus rather than having materials up through only the late 1930s, by the late 1970s everything in Keynes's life as a public servant through to his death had become available. Moreover, the volume of new material was tremendous, and thus soon there was simply no time for Moggridge to devote himself to economic history (at least apart from how he found it through the lens of Keynes's work). He continued writing monetary history through the 1970s, but thereafter it was Keynes, Keynes, Keynes until the last volume of the thirty volumes of The Collected Writings appeared in 1989 and Maynard Keynes appeared in 1992.

I believe that most historians of thought have skipped a first step such as Moggridge's. Most historians rather seem to have simply begun their intellectual inquiries with the history of thought itself, perhaps out of a fascination with ideas about the economy. Moggridge, at least initially, wanted to know more about the ideas because they were intrinsic to the history that primarily concerned him. Clearly, however, his interest in the ideas themselves soon took over – no one could have sustained the painstaking investigations required of his work on Keynes had it been only instrumental to other concerns. But it is important to remember in thinking about Moggridge as an historian of thought and producer of primary texts that the immediacy of ideas to events has always been the context in which he has operated. Moreover, should we grant that interwar monetary history laid the basis for subsequent adoption of Keynesian national economy management methods, as well as the early postwar Bretton Woods international monetary order, then that earlier economic history continues to help explain the present. Moggridge's personal context for economic thought, then, is the implication of interwar ideas for the world and economic ideas of today.

## The constitution of *The Collected Writings*

The Keynes edition, as its title indicates, is made up by the collected rather than complete writings of Keynes. The original planning committee of Kahn, Harrod, and Robinson only aimed for completeness in the case of material published by Keynes in his lifetime.[5] But there was a vast amount of Keynes's writings still to be published, and thus once they moved beyond Keynes's previously published work, the editors faced the problem of selecting which of Keynes's unpublished writings would be published. This selection was guided by "one over-riding principle" which was potentially controversial for an individual as many-sided as Keynes: "the focus of the edition was on Keynes as a working economist and participant in public affairs" (Moggridge and Robinson 1989: xi). This meant that not to be included in *The Collected Writings* was Keynes's personal correspondence unrelated to his economic writings, including that with Lydia, his wife.[6] Also not included was considerable correspondence associated with the ordinary business of Keynes's acting as the editor of *The Economic Journal* (for thirty-three years), though examples of Keynes's writings as editor or referee were included (e.g., with Bertil Ohlin). And also excluded were Keynes's early unpublished philosophical writings.

Additionally, things were more complicated when it came to previously unpublished economics material that became available with the revisions to the Public Records Act. Three exceptions were made to the principle to forgo completeness with unpublished material in the interest of providing as complete a record on a number of subjects of special importance: (1) the entire transcript of Keynes's evidence to the Chamberlain–Bradbury Committee on the Currency and Bank of England Notes issues (1924), and the entire transcript of Keynes's evidence to the Macmillan Committee on Finance and Industry (1930); (2) the Keynes–Kingsley Martin correspondence concerning *The New Statesman* and its 1931–46 editorial policies; (3) both sides of relevant correspondence between Keynes, D. H. Robertson, Harrod, R. G. Hawtrey, Kahn, Joan Robinson, and others over the drafts and texts of *The General Theory* and to a lesser extent *A Treatise on Money*.[7] In these three cases, selectivity in topic was married to completeness regarding material. But otherwise the Keynes edition could attempt to do no more than provide glimpses into important episodes in Keynes's career, if it were not to double in length. And inevitably this required that an editorial conception of certain episodes in Keynes's career be constructed that would then be documented by the inclusion of various materials illustrative of these episodes.

Thus, as with the inclusion of samples of selected correspondence of Keynes as an editor, in connection with the (thirteen!) "activities" volumes[8] the Keynes edition also included a sample of selected unpublished letters, memoranda, and speeches "to illustrate how Keynes supplemented his published essays in persuasion with other means, often orchestrating his activities with those of others" (Moggridge and Robinson 1989: xiii). Even more difficult was the decision regarding how to treat Keynes's "activities" in government service during the two world wars. Though Keynes was quite active in both tenures in government, he wrote comparatively little that would document his work and thinking. Thus "In these circumstances, the editors used the archives and Keynes's own papers not just to supplement the public record of his activities, but also to *establish the record itself*" (ibid.; emphasis added). The materials at hand were memoranda, minutes, telegrams, records of meetings, marginalia, and associated correspondence. Where possible both sides of exchanges were included. But there were two particular complications involved in putting together this material.

First, all of Keynes's efforts were not of equal value in terms of his commitment to the thinking they presupposed: "some of Keynes's forays were ephemeral, some misconceived and only some of long-standing importance" (ibid.). How was one to select among different candidate episodes around which to establish a record? Sometimes historical events showed particular "forays" to have been worthy of special attention. Sometimes it was clear from the state of opinion at the time that Keynes had special influence. But however Keynes was to be represented in his government service, judgment would necessarily need to be exercised in constructing a record. The second complication concerned deciding how much context to create so as to exhibit the significance of Keynes's role in government service. Whereas another guiding principle for *The Collected Writings* as a whole had been to minimize commentary and supporting scholarly apparatus, here it was unavoidable that some editorial explanation accompany the selection of Keynes's contributions to government policy making. The alternative would have been essentially to omit the record of Keynes's government service activities, leaving them for some other compilation. That this was thought unacceptable no doubt was because of the often close connection between Keynes's policy recommendation and his theoretical development. The former acted as a window upon the latter. But a Keynes edition that would show Keynes's development as an economist unique in his influence on public affairs also had to show how his theoretical development occurred, or more specifically how successive drafts of *The General Theory* ultimately led to the published version.

Second, then, not only were there the drafts of *The General Theory*, but there was also the extensive discussion and commentary on these early stages of the book by others (the third exception to incomplete collection noted above), as well as commentary and response by Keynes after its appearance. As Ricardo was influenced by Malthus, so Keynes was also influenced by his interaction with others. Thus, the treatment of *The General Theory* in the Keynes edition has a period of pre-publication development (volume XIII, *The General Theory and After: Part I, Preparation*) and a period of post-publication elaboration and extension (volume XIV, *The General Theory and After: Part II, Defence and Development*),[9] both of which are meant to give as complete a picture as possible of the network in which Keynes operated as he wrote.

In all these decisions concerning what would be included in Keynes's *Collected Writings*, emphasis rested upon seeing "Keynes as a working economist and participant in public affairs" (ibid.: xiv). Outside of this frame was an earlier Keynes who wrote and published on philosophical ideas, most importantly his *A Treatise on Probability*. *Probability* was included in *The Collected Writings* because of the principle of completeness regarding including all of Keynes's writings published during his lifetime. The same applies to Keynes's later commentary on his early philosophical views in "My Early Beliefs." But excluded from *The Collected Writings* were Keynes's fellowship dissertations for King's (essentially drafts of *Probability*), a collection of early philosophical papers and fragments on various subjects mostly associated with Keynes's participation in the then-secret Cambridge Conversazione Society or Apostles, and related correspondence. Nor was there much indication elsewhere in *The Collected Writings* of the nature and extent of these materials. At the same time, *Probability* alone of all Keynes's republished books received a new introduction from the perspective of the philosopher R. B. Braithwaite. Basically, as Moggridge later elaborated (1997: 39; see also Moggridge and Robinson 1989: xiv), the original conception of *The Collected Writings* was of works in economics and policy – a conception under-laid by the assumption that these were separable from Keynes's work on other subjects. Braithwaite's introduction was intended to make *Probability* accessible to non-philosophers. That the assumption that Keynes's economics and philosophy were separable and Braithwaite's particular reading of Keynes's philosophy would later be scrutinized by scholars interested in linking Keynes's economics and philosophy more closely was simply not anticipated when the original editorial committee established initial guidelines for *The Collected Writings*.

The editing of *The Collected Writings*, then, clearly involved a number of important decisions that determined the very nature of the Keynes edition, and thus the editing of this edition was a distinct contribution to the production of Keynes's primary texts. At the same time, the selection and organization of the materials that were included also creates a distinct image of Keynes – one that may very well be the dominant image of Keynes in the foreseeable future. This image of Keynes, we will see, forms the basis of Moggridge's biography of Keynes. To be sure, the main orientation on *The Collected Writings* was taken before Moggridge came on board. But that Moggridge went to Cambridge with economic history in mind certainly made him the sort of individual that the original editorial committee believed capable of being the (co-)editor of "Keynes as a working economist and participant in public affairs" (ibid.: xiv). We might say, then, that on one level, Moggridge's hands were tied regarding what kind of Keynes edition he would help produce. But Moggridge himself saw Keynes principally as an economist and policy maker. Thus while he has since come to place additional weight on Keynes's philosophical thinking (e.g.,

Moggridge 1988), as his biography of Keynes demonstrates, this accretion to his conception of Keynes has not significantly altered his fundamental understanding of the man.

## Maynard Keynes as companion to The Collected Writings

To characterize Moggridge's biography of Keynes as a companion to *The Collected Writings* is misleading in one obvious way. A volume of more than 900 pages hardly amounts to a set of elucidations and commentary to be read side by side with the volumes of *The Collected Writings*.[10] And *Maynard Keynes, An Economist's Biography* (1992) is an altogether independent achievement as the telling of the history of an individual who, as a contributor to economics and as an economic policy maker, played a major role in transforming modern thinking about the relationship between the economy and government. In fact, Moggridge's biography of Keynes has the specific ambition of joining the history of economics and economic history to one another by demonstrating how one individual in particular made economic history by writing economics. Of course Keynes was not entirely a solitary figure in producing "his" economics. Like Ricardo in his relationship to Malthus (and others), Keynes had many collaborators with whom he interacted in various ways. Thus neither Moggridge (nor most other intellectual biographers for that matter) would say that history and ideas are essentially the product of individual genius. But by telling the history of economics and economic history in terms of the story of one man, Moggridge certainly wants to say that there are extraordinary individuals who have disproportionate influence on ideas and events. Keynes in his estimation was just such a person.

At the same time, there remains an important sense in which *Maynard Keynes* is indeed a companion to *The Collected Writings*. If one man made economic history by writing economics, then the history he made, told through his own individual history, is importantly exhibited in his writings. Though it sounds odd to say, *The Collected Writings* might rather be seen as something of an "appendix" to Moggridge's intellectual biography of Keynes. Though Keynes's ideas made history, they only did so at Keynes's instigation – especially in connection with his own tireless promotion of those ideas. Consequently, we can see the ideas that made history gathered together in *The Collected Writings*, but to see the way in which those ideas had historical significance you must turn to Keynes's making of those ideas and his own intellectual history. There his ideas appear in the historical context in which they acquired leverage, and thus have a meaning that is unavailable in their more direct examination in *The Collected Writings*. Thus though it is artificial to characterize either *Maynard Keynes* or *The Collected Writings* as companions to one another, nonetheless the philosophy of the biography and economic history that motivates Moggridge creates an especially intimate relationship between the two. To understand the modern history of the relationship between state and economy, one must both know Keynes's writings and know how he used the ideas in them to produce historical influence.

From this perspective, the relative uniqueness of *The Collected Writings* as an editing project becomes apparent. In contrast to most other collected works editions of other economists, *The Collected Writings* contains an especially large volume of a "non-standard" sort of material in the way of memoranda, addresses, editorials, notes, talks, broadcasts, notices, etc., that add to the books, articles, reviews, lectures, etc., also in *The Collected Writings*, that constitute the more usual fare for economists' collected works. Indeed, who cannot be struck by the fact that out of a total of thirty volumes, volumes XV through XXVII all fall under the general title, "Activities." This part of *The Collected Writings*, also recall, required sampling Keynes's various "forays" while in government service, and, contrary to one of the edition's guiding principles of minimizing commentary and supporting scholarly apparatus, depended upon using "Keynes's own papers not just to supplement the published record of his activities, but also to establish the record itself" (Moggridge and Robinson 1989: xiii). In part, of course, this strategy was dictated by the fact that Keynes did much while in government service but published little about it. But the strategy was also dictated by Moggridge's view of Keynes's significance, as well as by his view of the influence individuals could have on economic history. Keynes's ideas did not speak only for themselves; they also spoke through his "activities." Thus, because of who Keynes was, *The Collected Writings* had to be unlike most other collected works of economists.[11]

Having briefly toured *The Collected Writings*, then, we should not be surprised to find that we already have a good idea of what we are to find in Moggridge's *Maynard Keynes*. But let us hear from Moggridge what he meant *Maynard Keynes* to be. In particular, how did he determine what aspects of Keynes's life and varied experiences should be selected and discussed to tell the story of Keynes?

> From the start one must accept that selection is shaped by the achievements of the subject. For it is the achievements that make the subject the possible object of a biography. If he or she were simply an average economist ... he or she would, it is true, be a possible subject for some aspect of the "sociology" of the discipline for which one might want biographical information, but hardly for a biography. This exceptional achievement inevitably shapes the biography.
>
> (1992: xxii)

This is not to say, Moggridge adds, that identifying what constitutes an achievement is always easy. There are issues of both what brought important developments about and who was responsible for bringing important developments about. Some developments may have been "in the cards;" some may have been the work of many individuals in collaboration. Interestingly, then, Moggridge resolves these issues in the spirit of Keynes:

> As Keynes repeatedly emphasised, at the centre of the act of creation is an intuition or insight that allows the creator to "see through the obscurity of

the argument or of the apparently unrelated data" as a result of which "the details will quickly fall into a scheme or arrangement, between each part of which there is a real connection."

(ibid.: xxiii; the quotation from Keynes is from the King's College Keynes Papers, UA/10/1, "Science and Art," 1909: 5)

Intuition, for Keynes and Moggridge, runs ahead of formal analysis, and creates the foundation for it (much as Schumpeter understood occurred with pre-analytic vision). Consequently, whereas many social and historical factors operate on producing the achievements of a single individual, and indeed many individuals collaborate in bringing the achievements of a single individual to fruition, should those achievements have their origin in that single individual's creative intuitions, then those achievements may ultimately be traced back to that individual and also be said to be the ultimate responsibility of that individual.

Intuition and creativity certainly do enable us to pick out exceptional individuals. But there is also an entire variety of not-always-compatible ways of talking about what intuition and creativity involve. In fact, one of Keynes's other biographers, Charles Hession, sought to explain Keynes's creativity in relation to his early homosexuality (Hession 1983). Moggridge does not totally reject Hession's thesis, nor does he exclude information about Keynes's homosexual experiences from *Maynard Keynes*. But he doubts such information ultimately offers us very much help in trying to understand Keynes's creativity as it was manifest in his historical achievements.

This does not mean that such information may not be biographically important in other contexts, which may be relevant to some other aspects of a subject's activities, but if one cannot find a relevance, why select it or relate it in particular degrees of detail?

(1992: xxiv)

Here clearly, "relevance" concerns Keynes as an economist and policy maker.

Thus, as the book's subtitle, *An Economist's Biography*, indicates, Moggridge's biography is written for a particular audience. This, he allows, involves something of an irony, since those who should be most interested in an influential economist's biography, contemporary economists with policy concerns, are generally likely to be reluctant to read the book. The fact is that economists today "no longer greatly value biography," largely because they apparently believe that "the history of technical economic analysis as some sort of scientific process is the only approach to the subject" of economics (ibid.: xxv). Never mind whether the latest technical "advance" is of any interest to those who influence economic policy, much less whether it has any bearing on reality. Even historians of economics, Moggridge complains, are too often prey to exaggerating "scientific" practice, and consequently under-appreciate the role of biography in the history of economics. Like practicing economists, historians of economics seem to forget that "[t]here are 'fertile' facts and 'creative' facts," and that "[s]election and arrangement do matter – both for purposes of persuasion and enlightenment" (ibid.). Thus all those concerned with economics would do well to reflect on George Stigler's thought that it would have been good to have had Ricardo as a colleague: the point was not to have an excellent technician on staff, but to be exposed to the way Ricardo's mind worked – to see his intuition at work on problems at the interface of economics and policy.

What sort of biography, then, does a man write who believes his profession rife with positivism and lack of real-world imagination? What sort of biography does he write when he believes his subject is historically notable because of his powers to intuit the outlines of solutions to problems when others were unable to "see through the obscurity of the argument or of the apparently unrelated data" (Keynes 1909: 5)? Essentially, he writes a biography that shows his subject possessed of a relative autonomy in being able to affect the course of historical events through the exercise of a set of individual powers. I emphasize relative autonomy both because Moggridge does (in recognizing the issue of joint vs. individual influence), and because doing so helps contrast Moggridge's biography of Keynes with other biographies of Keynes. Hession's biography has already been noted. His argument is that Keynes was bisexual, and this gave him a special talent for combining opposite concepts and methods, science and art, induction and deduction. In effect, then, Keynes was a creature of his psychology. While this need not imply that his choices were somehow always determined by his nature, the selection of themes Hession utilizes creates the appearance of a man in the control of deeper forces. In the same interpretive tradition is Piero Mini's psychological biography of Keynes (Mini 1994). Mini represents Keynes as an intelligent but neurotic personality who sublimated feelings of guilt. Somewhat more broadly, "we have here the picture of what I will call existentialist man, whose extremes of sensitivity, self-consciousness and cold reason often made him into a nervous wreck" (Mini 1994: 13). Again, though Keynes's talents and influence are not denied, they nonetheless seem to spring from something other than his own choices.

Thus by the idea of a relative autonomy I mean a particular kind of self-directedness. For Hession and Mini, Keynes was driven by his passions, and this explains his creativity and imagination. In contrast, for Moggridge, Keynes's creativity sprang from a unique capacity to intellectually grasp real-world problems from a theoretical perspective. That Keynes was a passionate individual, that is, was neither the cause of nor incompatible with his ability to understand issues. Thus Moggridge's reaction to psychological accounts of Keynes in general is that he simply does not see their relevance to Keynes's influence as an individual. This – *cognitivist* – view of Keynes justifies ascribing a relative autonomy to Keynes as an historical actor, because of the implied rarity among individuals of a talent for genuine understanding, despite the pressure of passion on clear-headedness. Moggridge's view is not just an anti-reductionist one that preserves the individual from him- or herself. His view is that Keynes, like other great intellects, was in the grip of a stronger power, the power to reason freely according to the dictates of a logic accompanied by a view of the world and of evidence to which he addressed that logic. This is what, for Moggridge, ultimately explains Keynes's influence.

Consider in this light the different conception of Keynes developed by Robert Skidelsky (1983, 1992). Drawing on Alasdair Macintryre (1981), Skidelsky's understanding of Keynes derives from his view of the world into which Keynes was born. Macintrye describes a world in which moral discourse has been disabled, because shared grounds for resolving disputes between individuals, such as a Christian world-view, are no longer available. In such a world most individuals become "managers" who manipulate social relations, or become "aesthetes" who pursue private sensual enjoyment. Some individuals, however, combine both characters in a carefully partitioned life – in Keynes's case, the worlds of Bloomsbury and Whitehall. Thus Keynes pursued economic management to preserve a society that contained space for artists. Many of his friends (including his wife) were artists, but his work was finance and economic stabilization, and then only so much: "[e]conomics was a game he could play, a language he could use, a powerful tool of thought; but the sources of his understanding of economic life lay outside, or beneath, its own characteristic ways of reasoning" (Skidelsky 1992: xix). Skidelsky thus follows this thread through his two volumes of Keynes's life: "looking at his ideas and plans over his lifetime there is a remarkable consistency in his *understanding* of his age" (1992: xxi). He understood that the disappearance of Victorianism left the world a place of many moral spaces, but he believed that that multiple reality could be preserved if the system of capitalist wealth creation were itself maintained. Thus it was not social revolution that Keynes feared, since such tensions did not exist in interwar Britain, but rather the steady erosion of private worlds by persistent low levels of economic activity.

Note the contrast, then, between Skidelsky's and Moggridge's views of Keynes and his world. To overdraw the comparison a bit, whereas Skidelsky's Keynes is a product of his world (not his psychology), for Moggridge the world is more a product of Keynes. In the same tradition as Roy Harrod's early biography of Keynes – "a man of genius, of intense individuality" (1951: vi) – Moggridge emphasizes what Keynes brought about through his economics. Skidelsky sees Keynes as relatively unique in his combination of public and private life, but what ultimately interests him about Keynes is how Keynes expressed this divided English world in such remarkable fashion. No doubt Moggridge appreciates Skidelsky's historical vision. But Moggridge saw himself as having a specific responsibility, namely, to write An *Economist's Biography*, strictly speaking the biography of Keynes as an economist, but also, we may suppose, a biography written by an economist with particular concerns about the attitudes and thinking of economists generally. It is not redundant to emphasize this connection once again. The retreat of economics since Keynes into an absorption with technocratic expertise has made economics less and less important to social policy making. But Keynes's example shows how economics may intelligently be brought to bear on real-world problems. It was to show this that the original editorial committee for the Keynes edition, all economists, designed a plan to publish *The Collected Writings*. Moggridge's biography of Keynes completes that commitment.

## Concluding remarks

I began this chapter by asking whether primary literatures in economics were sources of gravitation acting against the multi-perspectival, evolving character of the history of economics, or whether primary literatures actually contributed to this evolution and the multi-dimensionality of the history of economics by creating unsturdy platforms facilitating historians' different interpretive and argument strategies. My purpose in doing so was to highlight the pivotal role of editors of primary economic literatures, especially with respect to their part in helping produce those primary literatures. Thus what conclusions do we reach having surveyed Donald Moggridge's contributions as an editor of the Keynes edition and his biography of Keynes?

Moggridge's efforts, and indeed those of Austin Robinson and the original editorial committee, have certainly worked, I have tried to argue, to place Keynes's writings in a very specific light. They might consequently be said to have reinforced the gravitational effects of Keynes's writings on multiple readings of the history of twentieth-century economics, casting Keynes's economics in a set number of roles regarding macroeconomic stabilization policy and postwar international finance. Against this, however, note that Keynesianism, taken in the broadest possible sense, seems only to have proliferated in its different meanings and interpretations, rather than narrowed as Keynes and his writings have become better known. Perhaps it is too soon to judge the effects of the Keynes edition and *Maynard Keynes* on the formation of opinion. Gravitational forces may operate with a delay once a wider interest has been created. But it may also be fair to say that the availability of Keynes, both in his writings and his biographies, has created space for a range of interpretations of Keynes and Keynesianism not possible with more limited textual and scholarly resources, and that editorial production multiplies interpretation.

Here I do not attempt to settle this issue. Indeed, whether editorial production of primary literatures (and the writing of biographies) tames multi-perspectival evolution of the history of economic thought or causes it to flourish may ultimately be an irresolvable question. But there does seem to be one thing on this subject about which we can be reasonably confident. Reproducing the works of economists and telling their lives is an act of creation instrumental to the continued writing of the history of economic thought. As such it is an intrinsic aspect of that history.

## Notes

\* I thank Jacqueline Cox, Zohreh Emami, Steve Medema, and Warren Samuels for helpful comments on an earlier version of this essay. Errors remaining are my own.
1 There are in fact letters from a variety of other individuals in Ricardo's *Works*.

2  This resulted in a change of supervisor from Joan Robinson, to whom he had originally been assigned, to Richard Kahn.
3  His dissertation title was "Some Aspects of British Monetary Policy, 1924–1931,"
   and his supervisor was Kahn.
4  The editorial committee consisted of Richard Kahn, Roy Harrod, and Austin
   Robinson.
5  For the special influence of Kahn on what was to be included in the Keynes Archive
   at King's College from which The Collected Writings would largely be drawn, see Cox
   (1995).
6  Some of this latter correspondence has been independently published in Hill and
   Keynes (1989).
7  This third exception receives additional attention below.
8  Rather than a chronological ordering of Keynes's writings as characterizes many
   collected works editions, the volumes of The Collected Writings are organized into
   four categories: published books (volumes I–X), professional writings (volumes
   XI–XIV, XXIX), "activities" (volumes XV–XXVII), and social, political, and literary
   writings (volume XXVIII).
9  In addition, there is the supplementary volume XXIX.
10 A better candidate in this regard would be Moggridge's earlier, short biography of
   Keynes (1976). For Moggridge's own views on biography, see Moggridge (1989).
11 Perhaps the most like Keynes in this respect was Ricardo, whose career in parliament
   also necessitated a broad canvas for The Works and Correspondence.

# Bibliography

Cox, Jacqueline (1995) "Keynes: An Archivist's View," in A. Cottrell and M. Lawlor
   (eds) New Perspectives on Keynes, Durham, NC: Duke University Press.
Dow, S. (1996) The Methodology of Macroeconomic Thought: A Conceptual Analysis of
   Schools of Thought in Economics, revised second edition, Cheltenham: Edward Elgar.
Harrod, R. F. (1951) The Life of John Maynard Keynes, London: Macmillan.
Hession, C. (1983) John Maynard Keynes: A Personal Biography of the Man Who Revolu-
   tionized Capitalism and the Way We Live, New York: Macmillan.
Hill, P. and Keynes, R. (1989) Lydia and Maynard: Letters between Lydia Lopokova and
   John Maynard Keynes, London: Andre Deutsch.
Keynes, J. M. (1909) "Science and Art," UA/10/1, King's College Keynes Papers, 20
   February.
—— (1971–1989) The Collected Writings of John Maynard Keynes, E. A. G. Robinson and
   D. E. Moggridge (managing eds), 30 vols, London: Macmillan.
Macintrye, A. (1981) After Virtue: A Study in Moral Theory, London: Duckworth.
Mini, Piero V. (1994) John Maynard Keynes: A Study in the Psychology of Original Work,
   New York: St Martin's Press.
Moggridge, D. E. (1969) The Return to Gold: The Formulation of Economic Policy and its
   Critics, Cambridge: Cambridge University Press.
—— (1972) British Monetary Policy, 1924–1931: The Norman Conquest of $4.86,
   Cambridge: Cambridge University Press. Reprint, Gregg Revivals, 1992.
—— (1976) Keynes, London: Macmillan.
—— (1988) "Foreword," in Anna Carabelli, On Keynes's Method, New York: St Martin's
   Press.
—— (1989) "Economists and Biographers, Presidential Address to the HES, June 1989."
   History of Economics Society Bulletin 11, 2 : 174–89
—— (1992) Maynard Keynes, An Economist's Biography, London: Routledge.

—— (1997) "Among the Most Fascinating of Scholarly Subjects: A Memoir," *Journal of the History of Economic Thought* 19, 1: 24–48.

Moggridge, D. E. and Robinson, E. A. G. (1989) "General Introduction," in *The Collected Writings of John Maynard Keynes*, vol. XXX, London: Macmillan.

Ricardo, D. (1951–1973) *The Works and Correspondence of David Ricardo*, 11 vols, ed. P. Sraffa, Cambridge: Cambridge University Press.

Schumpeter, J. (1954) *History of Economic Analysis*, New York: Oxford University Press.

Skidelsky, R. (1983) *John Maynard Keynes, Volume One: Hopes Betrayed 1883–1920*, London: Macmillan.

—— (1992) *John Maynard Keynes, Volume Two: The Economist as Saviour*, London: Macmillan.

# 13 D. P. O'Brien's contribution to the history of economic analysis

## John Creedy*

### The beginning

A newly appointed assistant lecturer in the University of Belfast in 1963, with no postgraduate training but with more than two years' experience in industry, including time with British Nylon Spinners, approached his head of department with a suggestion for a research topic.[1] The proposal concerned, naturally enough, the textile industry in Ulster, but the head of department suggested that he might instead consider a topic in the history of economic analysis, such as the work of McCulloch. Despite the scale of the undertaking, which it can be certain that neither supervisor nor Ph.D. student fully appreciated at the time, the fact that McCulloch's published output was enormous and ranged over the whole of classical economics, combined with the not insignificant difficulty that the primary material was scattered across the other side of the Irish Sea throughout England and Scotland, the investigation was duly started.

This may sound more like the start of an academic farce than a successful academic career. However, the new assistant lecturer was Denis O'Brien and the head of department was Bob Black (see Black 1998). This chapter describes in broad terms the contribution to the history of economic analysis that O'Brien has made since that auspicious interview. It is impossible to do full justice to such a vast output that ranges over a very wide area. This includes the whole of classical economics, much of neoclassical economics (in particular the theory of the firm and the work of Marshall), and more recent economics (in particular, monetary economics and the work of Robbins and Hayek), though there is also much work relating to the preclassical period (such as Petty and Bodin). The following brief discussion may, without apology, be described as a panegyric. But it is hoped that this review may stimulate some readers to return, or in some cases turn for the first time, to the contributions mentioned. It is perhaps likely, given the range and dispersion of publications, that even readers who are familiar with some of O'Brien's work do not appreciate the full extent of his contribution to the subject. A list of publications is given in the bibliography; for this reason, full details are not always given in the following discussion.

Given O'Brien's propensity to pursue several different lines of research concurrently, and given the scope involved, it is not easy to produce a simple division by subject area or theme. Similarly, there is no clear division into periods or phases. Despite the inevitable overlaps, the following discussion is divided into three broad phases. While this involves a certain arbitrary element (and is in fact not always strictly followed), these very roughly cover the period in Belfast, the period in Durham from the early 1970s up to the late 1980s, and finally the more recent work of the 1990s. Having examined these "phases", the general characteristics of O'Brien's work and of his approach to the history of economic analysis are discussed. This is followed by some concluding comments.

## The first phase

### McCulloch

While carrying the burden of an assistant lecturer,[2] the Ph.D. was completed in 1969 and turned into a published book in 1970 – to a rapturous welcome by reviewers. This book alone would have been sufficient to establish a lasting reputation. The rest of us can only look back on our early work with some embarrassment. We have to begin with a narrowly defined subject that can be handled without the feeling of "going under" that results from "jumping in at the deep end". But *J.R. McCulloch: A Study in Classical Economics* displays complete maturity in the handling of a vast and complicated subject.

McCulloch's career as an economist spanned almost fifty years, during which he published far more than any other classical economist, in addition to carrying out an enormous amount of scholarly editing.[3] McCulloch had been caricatured as a slavish follower of Ricardo, but O'Brien showed without doubt that the influence of Ricardo was largely transient. Indeed McCulloch was found strongly to have rejected many of the central propositions of Ricardo and deserves to be regarded as a leading classical economist who made numerous original contributions. For example, in value theory he rejected Ricardo's concept of the invariable measure. In monetary economics, he was one of the earliest writers to argue that a note issue should fluctuate in response to the balance of payments exactly as a metallic currency would do and (contrary to Ricardo) suggested that, in order to protect convertibility, regulations are required to avoid the over-issue of notes.[4] On the question of population, his strong anti-Malthusian position also distanced him from Ricardo. His methodological position, with his strong emphasis on empirical work, was also entirely different from that of Ricardo.

As indicated by the subtitle, the book on McCulloch really involved covering almost the whole of classical economics. O'Brien's approach to his subject is entirely consistent throughout all his published work. In particular, the emphasis is placed on the economic analysis. Not only are complex views analysed and a vast literature synthesized in a wonderfully transparent way, but the analysis is related to later work, which is thereby placed in a clearer perspective. As Winch (1971: 172) mentioned, the mass of evidence on all these issues is handled with great skill and confidence. McCulloch's position is dissected and placed in contemporary perspective. O'Brien also shows that he is equally conversant with modern thinking on the same questions, which is no mean achievement when one considers that classical debate ranged over what are now a dozen specialised fields ... a major piece of scholarship.

The essential characteristic of O'Brien's writings, so clearly displayed in this first full-length work, is that the study of the history of economic analysis and the study of economics are the same thing. It should be no surprise to learn that Viner and Robbins were both acknowledged as providing an important early stimulus. With such an approach, the history of economic analysis becomes a crucial part of a training in economics. Further discussion of his approach is provided in the penultimate section below.

In the 1970s (which more strictly belong to the second phase, but are mentioned here for obvious reasons) there was some further consolidation of this earlier research on McCulloch, resulting in 1975 in a scholarly edition, again with a lengthy introduction and extensive notes, of his treatise on taxation and the funding system.[5] O'Brien's introduction is in fact a critical examination of virtually the whole of the classical contribution to public finance. This book was the first systematic treatise in English on public finance, and reflects the strong interest in the question of the national debt following its considerable increase during the Napoleonic wars.

## Overstone

During the time spent working on McCulloch, O'Brien succeeded in finding the private papers of Lord Overstone, formerly Samuel Jones Loyd. The search for these papers was initially merely a part of the work on McCulloch, in view of the friendship between the two men.[6] Overstone combined a very low public profile – indeed a strong dislike of publicity – with enormous practical influence. Robbins (1972: 20) has described him as

> one of the greatest figures in the financial and public life of the country in the middle years of the nineteenth century ... as leader of the so-called Currency School, he was one of the chief influences leading to the great Bank Act of 1844.

Similarly, Horsefield (1972: 1098) referred to Overstone as "one of the most influential, though hitherto most enigmatic, figures of the mid-nineteenth century" and *The Economist* (1972: 45) stated that "no one had a greater influence than he on shaping the major lines of monetary and fiscal policy between the 1830s and the 1860s".

The Bank Act involved the separation of the Bank of England's function into two departments, the Banking and Issue Departments. The latter was allowed to issue £14 million pounds in notes against securities, but the remainder had to be backed by specie. This was intended to ensure that, without any role for discretion, the currency (regarded as the high-powered monetary base, on which deposits were built) and therefore the money supply would follow bullion flows directly. This, it was hoped, would ensure that the convertible currency would act just like a metallic currency, thereby also providing a counter-cyclical stimulus, as in the specie flow mechanism of Hume. This would also ensure the essential maintenance of convertibility. The critics, in the form of the Banking School, argued that over-issue was impossible, so that convertibility had an inbuilt self-protection, that the money supply was demand determined, and that the Bank would need to act as a lender of last resort (which of course it eventually became). Overstone argued that there was a trade cycle that monetary policy was powerless to avoid, but that proper control of the monetary base could help to stabilize it to a degree, whereas the Banking School's proposals would only exacerbate the cycle.

In view of Overstone's importance, it is not surprising that earlier attempts had been made to find his papers, but this objective had eluded such eminent figures as Theodore Gregory, Jacob Viner, and Lionel Robbins. It had been concluded that the papers were destroyed. It might be thought that this was a lucky find – but luck had nothing to do with it; the papers were found as a result of a characteristic aptitude for detective work.[7] Indeed, it should more properly be said that the profession is extremely lucky that they were found by O'Brien. As Robbins wrote in a letter (1971), "you have conferred on all of us a quite inestimable benefit, both in the original discovery of the papers and in the meticulous and illuminating editing thereof. Both the introduction and notes seem to me to be beyond all praise."

After working, without research assistance, at a rate which the vast majority of us could not even begin to contemplate, the three-volume edition of the correspondence of Lord Overstone appeared in 1971. These volumes were compared in scholarship and editorial standards with the famous Sraffa and Dobb edition of Ricardo's works, the preparation of which was spread over many years.[8] The Overstone volumes, with their lengthy introduction and editorial notes, stand as a remarkable single-handed achievement that is unlikely to be matched.

The introduction could indeed almost stand alone as a book-length treatment of Overstone's thought, and that of his contemporaries. Horsefield (1972: 1098) summarized this as providing "a masterly analysis of his thought – on the Poor Law, on Decimal Currency, on the role of the state, on trade policy and, above all, on monetary policy". The volumes will also be of lasting value to social scientists other than economists. As Coats (1973: 690) stressed, "political historians ... will find these volumes a rich source of information and insight into political connections and parliamentary affairs, while social historians and students of nineteenth century biography will also find much of interest".[9] The comment by Robbins (1972: 20) is also worth reproducing here:

this is a book which should be on the shelves not only of historical scholars ... but also of the members of all leading City institutions ... as a pious tribute to the memory of one of their greatest figures and ... as a picture of what the life of a great Victorian banker was really like ... honourable conscience, public spirit, prudent generosity and, beneath a reserved exterior, passionate affection for one's intimates.

Having achieved "the highest ranks of international scholarship" (Robbins 1971: 20) in such a short time, this research actually provided, rather than any kind of culmination, the basic foundation for a subsequent stream of output of outstanding quality, as well as volume.[10] The research that was built on top of this scholarly foundation was spread over a vast range; the thought, to borrow a different metaphor, of continuing to plough the same furrow has never occurred to him.

## Industrial economics

What of the initial interest in industrial economics? Even before McCulloch appeared, concurrent research produced several journal articles and a full-length book on information agreements and competition policy, published in 1969 and jointly written with Dennis Swann. There is no record of the head of department's reaction to what turned out to be his failure to divert the young assistant lecturer's attention away from such studies. But he would have been unusual if he had not occasionally worried about a "lack of focus" that in more modern times would be judged to be alarming.

As with the scholarly and historical work, this early research provided merely the starting point for subsequent publications in industrial economics, competition policy, and the theory of the firm. This work cannot be reviewed here, but it should not be regarded as entirely separate from the historical work; such distinctions are difficult to make. As Black (1998: 5) has suggested in this context, "a study of his articles on both subjects shows clearly how each complements and illuminates the other". The historical work on the theory of the firm is one obvious link, but also important is the emphasis on data collection.

## The second phase

The work described above and completed in such a short time period led to rapid promotion to a readership in Belfast and then to a chair at the University of Durham in 1972.[11] Despite carrying a burden of teaching and administration that would seem deliberately designed to put an end to any further research, and which would terrify anyone working in a university in the United States (or indeed most universities in Britain), O'Brien built on the foundation of scholarship established while in Belfast in order to produce a steady flow of new work.

As always, over the same period during which this historical work was carried out, a steady stream of research in industrial economics produced several full-length books (two published in 1974 and one in 1979) in addition to numerous papers in the area.

## The Classical Economists

The year 1975 saw the publication of a treatise on classical economics that immediately became the single most valuable book on the subject. In reviewing *The Classical Economists*, Blaug (1976: 326) suggested that, "from now on all histories of economic thought can start their story in 1870, because it is difficult to see how anyone can improve on Professor O'Brien's analysis of the century that preceded it".[12]

This book should not really be considered as a textbook, although it is obviously compulsory reading for anyone studying the history of economic analysis. In its attitude towards the reader and the extensive basic research and synthesis which so often provides such a fresh view of the subject, it perhaps compares more closely with Hutchison (1953), except that it also contains an extensive amount of rational reconstruction. As Robbins (1975) commented,

> apart from the excellence of the argument – to this reviewer he seems always to pick on the significant propositions and references – the treatment is marked, where this is possible, by a translation of the main propositions involved into the language of simple geometry.[13]

A valuable feature of *The Classical Economists* is the arrangement of the material by subject area rather than by author. It is also distinguished by the valuable material in the first three chapters, including treatments of the personnel, their backgrounds, the scientific community, their preconceptions, and the roots of classical economics.[14] The book clearly shows the extent to which it is a gross distortion to describe classical economics in terms of just two people. O'Brien (1994e: xix) later described this tendency as "the bad old habit of viewing classical economics as made up of the work of Adam Smith and David Ricardo, and simply treating every other author as a regurgitating also-ran". The theme was also continued in a lengthy and valuable paper (1988a) on "classical reassessments", examining the work and influence of Longfield, James Mill, Senior, Bailey, Torrens, and Say.

## Methodology

The same period saw substantial contributions to methodology, which continued well into the 1990s. This involved the detailed analysis of research programmes covering the whole range from classical economics to the latest journal literature. Early work in this area includes his inaugural lecture, published in 1975, and the important 1976 paper on "the longevity of Adam

Smith's vision", which was substantially extended in 1984.[15] Much of the work on methodology carried out in the 1980s took as a "case study" the development of the theory of the firm; this included a paper in 1983 and a book chapter in 1984. The major emphasis of later work (which provides a link with the earlier work on the Scottish empirical tradition) is on the role of data in economics; this includes a 1991 chapter on "theory and empirical observation" and a paper in 1992 on "economists and data". A more recent contribution, from 1998, highlights four lengthy "detours" that have been made by the profession as a result of a disregard for empirical evidence. There is clearly sufficient material for a full-length work on methodology.

A strong theme running through all the work on methodology is the need for empirical work, following the approach that O'Brien identified as the Scottish Tradition in which there is a continual process of data collection, which suggests hypotheses to be tested, requiring further data collection and the revision of hypotheses, further testing, and so on. The collection and analysis of data is of course exemplified in O'Brien's work in industrial economics as well as in the history of economic analysis, particularly in monetary economics and authorship puzzles discussed below.

## Marshall

The late 1970s also saw a significant move towards work on the neoclassical period. Of special interest is the 1982 analysis of the complete work of Marshall – only "big" central subjects seem to hold any attraction. There is clearly a link with the interest in industrial economics, shown explicitly in two papers on Marshall published in 1990. Given such a strong knowledge of classical economics, the chapter in the *Principles* centenary volume, sponsored by the Royal Economic Society, on "Marshall in relation to classical economics" is of special value. This is a particularly awkward issue in view of Marshall's changing and often misleading statements about the classical economists. A valuable introduction was written for the 1994 reprinting of *The Economics of Industry*, and mention should also be made of the detailed and extensive 1997 review article on "Marshall and his correspondence". There is in fact material for a full-length study of Marshall's economics.

## Authorship puzzles

The 1979 book on industrial economics involved extensive use of non-parametric statistical methods. This same interest in non-parametric methods that informed the industrial economics was directed to statistical work on authorship puzzles in the history of economic thought, the first of its kind, leading to a book published in 1982. It is likely that the seeds of this book were also sown during the early work on McCulloch, in view of the latter's bibliographical interests and extensive work on identifying the anonymous authors of works that he was reprinting.

The approach, which is particularly useful where small samples are involved, investigates the position in sentences of high-frequency words in order to identify habits of style exhibited by the authors in question. Examples include the first word in sentences, and collocations such as the relative frequency of "the" preceded by words such as "and", "which", "of", and "by", and the frequency of "be" preceded by words such as "will", "can", and "may". Such relative frequencies are used in combination with chi-squared tests of independence. Large samples of known works can be used to identify style characteristics of potential authors, which can then be compared with the disputed text. Of course, such statistical work is regarded as complementing, rather than substituting for, the more usual kind of detailed examination of textual and other evidence. Indeed, this is necessary in order to identify putative authors.

## Robbins

The second phase also involved the writing of a book on the work of Robbins, published in 1988. Written so soon after Robbins's death, and considering the vast range of the work of this "outsize personality" who was one of the dominant figures of the twentieth century in British economics, the study presented a particularly difficult challenge. However, the result provides a model for this kind of work. Baumol (1990: 82), who knew Robbins well, enthused that the book "is a tour de force" and

> a comprehensible, careful, and systematic summary of the contributions that Lionel Robbins made to economics over the course of his long and productive career. This is no easy task since his work spanned an extraordinary broad set of fields ... Professor O'Brien does not merely record Robbins' contributions; he contributes considerably to our understanding of their substance.

## The third phase

The work produced during the 1990s also defies simple categorization, and the work on methodology during this period has already been mentioned. The solid foundation in monetary economics has of course played an important part during all phases of O'Brien's research. One significant contribution, which in some respects is part of the "second phase" but is included here for reasons that should become clear, is a lengthy survey in 1984 that traces the evolution of the main current ideas in monetary economics. In other words it achieves the very difficult task, which is unfortunately rarely attempted in the history of economic analysis, of setting modern mainstream ideas and theories in historical perspective. This is particularly difficult in view of the fact that "it is probably true that monetary theory was the first branch of economics to reach sophisticated levels of analysis and that its analytical concepts have the longest history" (O'Brien, 1984a: 3).

## Joplin

The interest in monetary economics bore further fruit, indeed a veritable harvest, in 1993 in the form of a major full-length study of Joplin and classical macroeconomics. Not only did this book produce a substantial reappraisal of classical monetary thought, but it also "marked a watershed" in O'Brien's own thinking about the positions taken by the Currency and Banking Schools. In particular, Joplin's emphasis on the country bank note issue, neglected by the two major schools of thought, produced a superior analysis of monetary control and stabilization policy. This book also displays an extensive knowledge of modern macroeconomics, along with a combination of modelling and statistical skills that are rare in work on the history of economic analysis. One review simply began with the statement "make no mistake about it: this is a major book" (Skaggs 1995: 209). It is hard to exaggerate the far-reaching implications of this reappraisal.

Joplin provides an interesting contrast with Overstone. While the latter was an "insider" with considerable influence who preferred to remain in the background, Joplin was an "outsider" who, despite strenuous efforts, failed to obtain the influence and recognition that he sought and deserved. While Joplin's role as a pioneer in joint-stock banking has been acknowledged, his other highly original contributions have been entirely neglected. This included his treatment of the monetary system and the role of the (then dominant) agricultural sector within a framework that O'Brien was able to formalize in terms of a dynamic open economy neo-Keynesian model. This has a highly sophisticated treatment of the money market, involving separate money markets for financial transactions and goods and importantly the inclusion of the role of country banks, with the balance of payments affecting the Bank of England's note issue and, with a lag, that of the country banks. Joplin's treatments of a multiplier, the concept of reciprocal demand and supply, and his elucidation of the principle of "metallic fluctuation", are shown to predate those of other economists who have previously received credit.

An important feature of Joplin's analysis, explored by O'Brien, was his methodological position, involving (in contrast with his contemporaries) the clear formulation of hypotheses to be subsequently tested using data. O'Brien's analysis of data that were available to Joplin, using modern methods, along with extensive analyses of later data, showed that Joplin's treatment was indeed superior to that of the dominant Currency School. It is ironic that Joplin died in 1847 just a few months before the first financial crisis, of the kind that he predicted, took place following the 1844 Bank Charter Act.

It is entirely consistent with O'Brien's own methodological position that it was his own empirical analysis that persuaded him of the superior value of Joplin's analysis compared with that of his contemporaries. In summarizing Joplin's achievement, O'Brien (1993: 242) pointed out that "the end result raises disturbing questions not only for nineteenth-century monetary orthodoxy, but also about the ranking of what Schumpeter called 'performance' by individual nineteenth-century economists".

## More monetary economics

Further work in the area of monetary economics in the 1990s was also entirely in line with O'Brien's consistent approach to the history of economic analysis, exemplified by the study of Joplin and discussed further in the next section of this chapter. This work included, in 1995, a detailed analysis of the stability properties of several dynamic models, in a framework containing an in-built trade cycle, that were designed to examine the implications of the Currency and Banking Schools' policy prescriptions. He found that the Currency School monetary rule, according to which (following the principle of metallic fluctuation) a balance of payments deficit leads to gold outflows and thereby a reduction in the Bank of England note issue (the high-powered monetary base) and hence in the total money supply, would result in price stability. However the "passive money supply" prescription of the Banking School, whereby money supply increases endogenously (and is therefore demand determined), can at best produce a saddle point or, with the addition of a balance of payments constraint on money supply, price fluctuations with a higher amplitude.

The work in monetary economics also includes the collection of a large database and the use of extensive econometric analyses designed to test the main propositions of the adherents of the Currency and Banking Schools of thought. A paper, published in 1998, showed that the hopes of the Currency School for monetary control, through control of the Bank of England note issue, were not realized. The same applied to the Currency School's hopes for greater economic stability, by the attempt, with the Bank Charter Act of 1844, to replicate the automatic stabilization properties of a metallic currency. This work is of course in many ways directly related to the earlier work on Joplin, and indeed finds considerable support for his argument that the country bank note issue was the most important part of the money supply. Essentially, the Currency School argument ignored the implications for the money supply of the existence of joint-stock banking; such banking had in fact been pioneered by Joplin. However, econometric causality tests showed support for the important Currency School argument that the direction of causality runs from the money supply to the price level, contrary to the position of the Banking School in which money supply is demand determined.

The more recent work, stemming directly from the study of Joplin, can therefore be seen as part of a highly productive research programme involving the application of modelling and econometric methods to a central debate in monetary history. The value of this work extends well beyond the light it throws on the history of economic analysis and monetary history itself. This is because the nineteenth-century debates, involving some of the most sophisticated and complex analyses in the whole of economics, "are still the origins of almost everything useful that economists know about money" (O'Brien 1994e: xvi). This research programme clearly promises further results of great importance.

O'Brien's unrivalled knowledge of monetary economics and its literature was also used to produce masterly introductions to six volumes on the foundations of monetary economics; these introductions could form the basis of a separate treatise. Similarly, a series of introductions to volumes on business cycle history was also produced. Overstone provides a clear influence on the interest in business cycles, given his important contributions to that area. There is of course a clear interdependence between monetary economics and the analysis of business cycles. For example, the Banking and Currency Schools held very different attitudes towards monetary policy during the different phases of the business cycle. In addition, a set of introductions to eight volumes of the works of McCulloch were recently completed. These introductions extend well beyond the type of thing that most people understand by the term "introduction"; they represent the results of extensive research into the basic and secondary literature.[16]

## Hayek

As always, work on several projects proceeded concurrently, as the stream of research continued to flow with full force.[17] More recent work has included lengthy studies of the work of Hayek. This includes a broad discussion of his work, for the British Academy in 1994, a chapter on "Hayek as an intellectual historian" also in 1994, and the more recent "Hayek: economics and law". Like the study of Robbins, this work was initially stimulated by an invitation to write a critical appreciation following the death of the person concerned. On reading the first piece, Humphrey remarked, "I cannot imagine that any other study of Hayek and his work could possibly be as clear, complete, and edifying as your paper".[18] Obviously there is material here for a full-length study of Hayek.

## The nature and approach

The enormous breadth, as well as depth, of research reflects more than an amazing energy and range of abilities.[19] It reflects an explicit view that economists should not become narrow specialists. Furthermore, a concern for the relevant economic questions should motivate study in the history of economic thought; the main emphasis should be on the analytical economic content rather than the policy views which tend to be given more prominence in "relativist" approaches. Historical work requires a solid grounding in modern economic theory and statistical methods. Black's (1998: 4) comment, made in relation to methodology, applies equally to historical work.[20] He suggested that "Denis has spent more time and effort in practising his method than in preaching its virtues". Indeed, "leadership by example" provides an appropriate description of every facet of his academic career.

## Rational reconstruction

In the context of historical work, there is no doubt about the essence of O'Brien's approach. At its heart is rational reconstruction. He does not mean the kind of "model building which (to be unfair) attempts the *Wealth of Nations* in three equations, but model building which sticks as closely as possible to the original author's own model" (O'Brien 1999a: 30). What he has in mind is stated in O'Brien (1999a: 15):

> the central concern is with the internal logic of a theory. Where there are gaps in the reasoning, the historian of economic thought can legitimately seek to ask what is required to fill the gaps, and what can reasonably be assumed as implicit knowledge on the part of the historical figure being studied … an historical dimension enters directly via the plausibility of the assumptions made by the original writer. But at the heart of the argument is the theory.

It is of course acknowledged that "historical circumstances do influence both the questions addressed by economists and the assumptions they make", but after it has been developed, "a theory becomes detached from its historical origins" (1999a: 17). In pursuing this approach, O'Brien has nevertheless brought to the study a huge historical knowledge and appreciation of the wider concerns.

Despite the vast scale of his output, a consistent characteristic is the extent of "compression" involved. A vast amount of energy may be spent in exploring all avenues that could possibly be relevant, but there is no expansive display of this. No judgement is made without consideration of every possible piece of evidence or point of view, and yet the "supporting edifice" is often left in the background in order to produce a "tight" argument that maintains a clear focus on the main issue at hand. One is reminded of Phelps Brown's description of the best empirical work, that it represents only the tip of a triangle that is placed solidly on its base, in contrast with more speculative work where the triangle is inverted and supported in a precarious and unstable equilibrium by a single assumption or piece of carefully selected evidence.

*Publishing habits*

A comment on publication practices may perhaps be made here. Most of O'Brien's research has involved, as mentioned above, "big" subjects that have led to the production of books and lengthy book chapters, despite the long list of journal papers. Many academics, particularly in the current environment that attaches so much importance to journal papers, would have produced a series of smaller pieces in addition to the books. But he has never engaged in this practice.[21] For example, before the book on McCulloch was published, only two related journal papers appeared. In the case of the Overstone work, only the three volumes appeared: yet here is a mass of material that could have been used to produce a series of separate pieces. Such papers would have given the work more exposure to a wider audience. The treatise on *The Classical Economists* also contains material that could, without too much difficulty, have been used to produce journal papers as well as being included in the book. The work on authorship puzzles in economics produced just one journal article, yet the subject offers the scope to publish a series of separate papers. Only one separate piece on Joplin was published before the full-length study, and that was in the form of a book chapter. Here again, there was ample opportunity to give parts of this work more exposure in the form of journal articles, given the range covered by the book and the extent of the original research that went into each chapter.

These comments simply reinforce the point made by Black (1998: 5) that "only in one respect can Denis O'Brien's contribution ... be described as modest – in that he has always followed the advice he has recently given to others in the profession", that is, to be more humble.[22] Any suggestion to engage in such a publication strategy, or any kind of "self-promotion", would be regarded as abhorrent and considered unworthy of a reply. The philistine form of the so-called research appraisal now regularly conducted in British universities, in which "without any real public debate, scholarship has been not so much down-graded as eliminated" (O'Brien 1999a: 4) and whereby the journal article is elevated to a dominant position, is clearly deeply offensive.

## Concluding comments

Most academics are now generally expected to produce some research output and many accumulate lengthy CVs. However, the consistent high flow of output produced by O'Brien in difficult circumstances is nothing short of remarkable. The most striking characteristic of all of his work is that no one with any interest in the area of concern can afford to ignore it – it simply has to be read and considered, even by those who may ultimately disagree with some judgements. Indeed, it is explicitly recognized that the history of economic analysis is not a subject in which clear-cut answers are always available. His non-dogmatic style recognizes different points of view; the reader is treated as a mature and intelligent person and allowed to disagree or weight evidence differently.[23]

Not only is it impossible to ignore the work, but it is noticeable how often reviewers stress the point that it will not be necessary to go over the same ground again, while at the same time the work in question opens up further avenues and provides a stimulus to further research. On the McCulloch volume, Winch (1971: 172) remarked that "this is the first full-length study ... such is the thoroughness and finesse with which Dr. O'Brien has carried out his task that it can be said with some confidence that it will probably be the last". Robbins (1971: 321) stated that it will be "quite unnecessary for future scholars to tread the same path again". Coats (1971: 607) suggested that specialists "will be exploring its treasures for many a decade".[24] On the Joplin volume, Skaggs (1995: 210) suggested that "it is almost sure to spawn a rash of new studies of this period of monetary history ... no one doing work in this area will be able to ignore O'Brien's thesis".

Historians of economic thought must naturally take a long-term perspective.

There is no doubt that the profession will continue for very many years to be grateful that someone like O'Brien, with the necessary combination of skills and standards, has chosen to devote a career unselfishly and unstintingly to the production of major works of outstanding scholarship and lasting value, in which the study of economics and its history are shown to be integral.

## Notes

\*    I should like to thank Roger Backhouse, Robert Dixon, Steve Medema, and Warren Samuels for comments on earlier drafts of this chapter.
1    The position of assistant lecturer has been described by Baumol (1998: xiii) as "a rank so low that it has no U.S. equivalent".
2    This made Kingsley Amis's *Lucky Jim* more of a nightmare than a comedy, as the eponymous Jim was also an assistant lecturer. This novel clearly made an impression on O'Brien, who quoted it twice in three pages (1994e: xiv–xvi).
3    As Robbins (1971: 321) suggested,

> no other economist of his time covered so extensive a range or catered for so wide a public. It is to the analysis of this vast *oeuvre* and the establishment of its correct place in the perspective of intellectual history that Dr. O'Brien has addressed himself in the work under review; and it should be said at once that he has made an outstanding contribution to the literature of the subject.

4    This provides a clear link with Overstone, discussed below. However, Joplin has priority with regard to the principle of metallic fluctuation; see O'Brien (1993).
5    The notes, as well as clarifying and correcting sources, indicate changes made over the three editions of this treatise of over 500 pages, as well as indicating where McCulloch had "self-plagiarised" (used earlier work without explicit mention of the fact). A critical edition of McCulloch's *Discourse on the Rise, Progress and Peculiar Objects of Political Economy* was prepared for the Scottish Economic Society, but was not published.
6    McCulloch was of course also an early proponent of the view that a convertible currency should aim to replicate a metallic currency. Overstone paid for the publication of McCulloch's editions of several scarce volumes and, following McCulloch's death, purchased his library, of about 8,000 volumes, from his estate. Overstone made the purchase out of respect for McCulloch and his known desire to keep the library intact. Overstone's collection was eventually donated, in 1920, to Reading University, which has not yet produced a computerized catalogue.
7    He noticed a reference, in a footnote in Gregory (1928: 5), to a letter from Overstone to Norman, from volume vi of the *Political Economy Club Proceedings*, edited by Higgs. It turned out that Higgs had obtained two letters from Overstone to Norman, and thanked a Mr A. T. Loyd MP. The MP designation suggested that he ought to be in *Who Was Who*, where it was found that he had been Warden of Bradfield School, and his address was given as Lockinge. The strategy was adopted of writing to the headmaster of Bradfield, Chenevix-Trench, about the successor to A. T. Loyd and about Lockinge. Chenevix-Trench provided the name of the Master of Lockinge, Christopher Lewis Loyd. He in turn was willing to let O'Brien visit, and as soon as he went into the Lockinge library he spotted books which were not books. They were in fact book bindings containing the Overstone papers.
8    The comparison included the McCulloch volume. Robbins (1971: 322) argued that

this is perhaps the most important addition to the study of the central body of classical economics since the publication of Mr. Sraffa's *Works of David Ricardo*; and those of us who have had the privilege of seeing the proof sheets of the Letters of Lord Overstone ... already know that there is much more of the same quality of scholarship to come.

On this comparison, see also Fetter (1972: 394–5).

9   He added that it was "the most important single addition to the published source materials on British nineteenth century monetary history for many decades".

10  The work mentioned above is only a part of the story. An edited volume, *Lord Overstone: Tracts and Other Publications on Metallic and Paper Currency*, with an introduction surveying Overstone's monetary thought, was delivered to the publisher in 1967. An edited volume, *J. R. McCulloch: A Catalogue of Books, the Property of a Political Economist*, with an introduction discussing McCulloch's bibliographical activities, was delivered in 1968. Furthermore, an edition of G. W. *Norman's Essay on Taxation*, the manuscript of which was discovered by O'Brien, was delivered in 1970. These three volumes were commissioned by Augustus M. Kelley but have never been published.

11  Mention should also be made of work in the area of international trade, and particularly on Torrens, produced during this period. International trade has been a perennial interest and O'Brien has taught a high-level course on this subject for many years.

12  This book was later issued in paperback and translated into Italian and Spanish, yet the publishers have allowed it to go out of print.

13  This point was also made by Skinner (1976).

14  The inclusion of a chapter on public finance is not surprising, given the earlier work mentioned above in relation to McCulloch, but filled a huge gap in the literature.

15  The later version was published under the title "Theories of the history of science: a test case".

16  Another multi-volume set of works, with extensive introductions, on public finance is also in preparation.

17  There is also a 1992 chapter on Petty.

18  From a letter to O'Brien, in 1995.

19  No mention has been made of the numerous book reviews written over this period, displaying a great generosity of spirit as well as knowledge. There is some ambivalence here; they are regarded by their author (who does not bother to keep records) as entirely ephemeral and yet the most cursory examination will show how much can be learned from them, in comparison with the vast majority of reviews.

20  It is not surprising to find that, with regard to the study of philosophy, O'Brien (1999a: 22) suggested that historians of economic thought should "be prepared to take their courage in both hands and to 'get in over their heads'".

21  This is not meant to denigrate such practice (indeed, it describes the present writer's habits), but simply to point out a different attitude to publication.

22  His advice to "read more, think more and claim less" is also worth repeating.

23  The same point was made by Skinner (1976: 375) in reviewing *The Classical Economists*, who referred to this "appealing aspect of this excellent book".

24  Furthermore, "O'Brien's book is a classic example of a definitive historical study. No one will need to go beyond it except to follow a specialised interest" (Gordon 1971: 69), and "this work must be the beginning of all further studies of McCulloch and his time" (Maclennan 1971: 67).

# Bibliography

Baumol, W. J. (1990) "Review of *Lionel Robbins*", *Journal of Economic Literature* XXVIII: 82–3.

—— (1998) "Foreword to Lionel Robbins, A *History of Economic Thought: The LSE Lectures*", ed. S. G. Medema and W. J. Samuels, Princeton, NJ: Princeton University Press, xiii–xiv.

Black, R. D. C. (1998) "The Retirement of Denis O'Brien", *HET Newsletter* 60: 3–5.

Blaug, M. (1976) "Review of *The Classical Economists*", *Economica* 43: 325–6.

Coats, A. W. (1971) "Review of *McCulloch*", *Kyklos* 24: 605–6.

—— (1973) "Review of *Overstone*", *Kyklos* 26: 680–90.

Fetter, F. W. (1972) "Review of *Overstone*", *Business History Review* 46: 393–5.

Gordon, S. (1971) "Review of *McCulloch*", *Journal of Economic Literature* IX: 69.

Gregory, T. E. (1928) *An Introduction to Tooke and Newmarch's A History of Prices*, London: P. S. King.

Horsefield, J. K. (1972) "Review of *Overstone*", *Economic Journal* 82: 1098–1100.

Hutcheson, T. W. (1953) *Review of Economic Doctrines 1870–1929*, Oxford: Clarendon Press.

Maclennan, B. (1971) "Review of *McCulloch*", *Manchester School*: 66–7.

O'Brien, D. P. (1964) "Patent Protection and Competition in Polyamide and Polyester Fibre Manufacture", *Journal of Industrial Economics* XII: 224–35; trans. into Spanish 1970, Barcelona University.

—— (1965a) "McCulloch and India", *Manchester School* XXIII: 313–17.

—— (1965b) "The Transition in Torrens' Monetary Thought", *Economica* XXXII: 269–301; reprinted in M. Blaug (ed.) (1991) *Pioneers in Economics*, Vol. 17, Aldershot: Edward Elgar.

—— (1966a) "Information Agreements – A Problem in Search of a Policy" (with D. Swann), *Manchester School* XXIV: 285–306; reprinted in L. Needham (ed.) (1970) *Readings in the Economics of Industrial Organisation*, London: Holt Rhinehart.

—— (1966b) "J. R. McCulloch and the Theory of Value", *Scottish Journal of Political Economy* XIII: 332–51.

—— (1966c) "Torrens on Wages and Emigration", *Economica* XXXIII: 336–40; reprinted in M. Blaug (ed.) (1991) *Pioneers in Economics*, Vol. 17, Aldershot: Edward Elgar.

—— (1967a) "Information Agreements: A Further Contribution" (with D. Swann), *Manchester School* XXV: 285–8.

—— (1967b) "Leggi anti-monopolio e accordi d'informazionne" (with D. Swann), *Mercurio* X.

—— (1969) *Information Agreements, Competition and Efficiency* (with D. Swann), London: Macmillan.

—— (1970) *J. R. McCulloch: A Study in Classical Economics*, London: Allen and Unwin; reprinted by Gregg, London, 1993.

—— (1971) *The Correspondence of Lord Overstone*, 3 vols, London: Cambridge University Press.

—— (1974a) *Competition in British Industry* (with D. Swann, P. Maunder, and W. S. Howe), London: Allen and Unwin.

—— (1974b) *Competition in British Industry: Case Studies* (with D. Swann, P. Maunder, and W. S. Howe), London: Allen and Unwin.

—— (1974c) "The Development of Economics", *Scottish Journal of Political Economy* XXI: 187–99.

—— (1975a) J. R. McCulloch: A Treatise on the Principles and Practical Influence of Taxation and the Funding System, Edinburgh: Scottish Academic Press.

—— (1975b) The Classical Economists, Oxford: Clarendon Press. Reprinted, 1978; trans. into Italian, 1983 (Il Mulino, Bologna) and Spanish, 1988 (Allianza, Madrid).

—— (1975c) "Whither Economics", Economics XI: 75–98.

—— (1976a) "A New Humility in Economic Policy", in Catch '76, London: Institute of Economic Affairs, 95–102.

—— (1976b) "Customs Unions: Trade Creation and Trade Diversion in Historical Perspective", History of Political Economy VIII: 540–63; reprinted in M. Blaug (ed.) (1991) Pioneers in Economics, Vol. 22, Aldershot: Edward Elgar.

—— (1976c) "The Longevity of Adam Smith's Vision: Paradigms, Research Programmes and Falsifiability in the History of Economic Thought", Scottish Journal of Political Economy XXIII: 133–51. Trans. into Spanish, 1976. Reprinted in D. Mair (ed.) (1990) The Scottish Contribution to Economic Thought, Aberdeen: Aberdeen University Press.

—— (1976d) "Whither Geography: A Cautionary Tale from Economics" (with B. Floyd), Area 8: 15–23.

—— (1977a) "Comment", in T. Wilson and A. S. Skinner (eds) The Market and the State: Essays in Honour of Adam Smith, Oxford: Clarendon Press, 63–7.

—— (1977b) "Torrens, McCulloch and Disraeli", Scottish Journal of Political Economy XXIV: 1–18; reprinted in M. Blaug (ed.) (1991) Pioneers in Economics, Vol. 17, Aldershot: Edward Elgar.

—— (1978) "Mergers – Time to Turn the Tide", Lloyds Bank Review 130: 32–44. With a Reply, Lloyds Bank Review 132: 51–2, 1979.

—— (1979) Competition Policy, Profitability and Growth (with W. S. Howe, D. M. Wright, and R. J. O'Brien), London: Macmillan.

—— (1980a) "A Rejoinder" (with A. C. Darnell), History of Political Economy 12: 411–19; reprinted in M. Blaug (ed.) (1991) Pioneers in Economics, Vol. 17, Aldershot: Edward Elgar.

—— (1980b) "Torrens, McCulloch, and the 'Digression on Sismondi': Whose Digression?" History of Political Economy 12: 383–95; reprinted in M. Blaug (ed.) (1991) Pioneers in Economics, Vol. 17, Aldershot: Edward Elgar.

—— (1981a) "A. Marshall, 1842–1924", in D. P. O'Brien and J. R. Presley (eds) Pioneers of Modern Economics in Britain, London: Macmillan, 36–71.

—— (1981b) Pioneers of Modern Economics in Britain (ed. with J. R. Presley), London: Macmillan; reprinted 1983.

—— (1981c) "Ricardian Economics and the Economics of David Ricardo", Oxford Economic Papers 33: 1–35.

—— (1981d) "The Emphasis on Market Economics", in A. Seldon (ed.) The Emerging Consensus, London: Institute of Economic Affairs, 51–77.

—— (1982a) Authorship Puzzles in the History of Economics: A Statistical Approach (with A. C. Darnell), London: Macmillan.

—— (1982b) "Competition Policy: The Silent Revolution", Antitrust Bulletin XXVII, 1: 217–39.

—— (1982c) "Ricardian Economics", Oxford Economic Papers XXXIV: 247–52.

—— (1983) "Research Programmes in Competitive Structure", Journal of Economic Studies 10: 29–51.

—— (1983–85) Eight articles in the Economic Review: "Money and Inflation", 1–2: 19, 1983; "Monetary Control", 1–3: 41, 1984; "Trade Policy", 1–4: 31, 1984; "Government and the Economy", 1–5: 39, 1984; "Say's Law", 2: 27–8, 1984–5; "Technical Economics", 2: 39, 1984–5; "Quantitative Economics", 2: 21, 1984–5; "Giffen Goods", 2: 35–6, 1984–5.

—— (1984a) *Economic Analysis in Historical Perspective* (ed. with J. Creedy), London: Butterworths; reprinted by Gregg, London, 1992.

—— (1984b) "Monetary Economics", in J. Creedy and D. P. O'Brien (eds) *Economic Analysis in Historical Perspective*, London: Butterworths, 3–45; reprinted by Gregg, London, 1991.

—— (1984c) "The Evolution of the Theory of the Firm", in F. H. Stephen (ed.) *Firms, Organisation and Labour*, London: Macmillan, 25–62; reprinted in M. Casson (ed.) (1996) *The Theory of the Firm*, Aldershot: Edward Elgar.

—— (1984d) "Theories of the History of Science: A Test Case", in A. W. Coats (ed.) *Methodological Controversy in Economics*, Greenwich, CT: JAI Press, 89–124.

—— (1985a) "Classical Economics", in A. Kuper and J. Kuper (eds) *The Social Science Encyclopedia*, London: Routledge, 110–12.

—— (1985b) Fifty-two articles on famous economists for *Encyclopedia Britannica*: Steuart; Longfield; Edgeworth; Wieser; Robbins; Heckscher; Haberler; Torrens; Rae; Wicksteed; Fetter; Lindahl; Viner; Williams, J. H.; Simon; Fullarton; Lauderdale; Barone; Cantillon; Clark, J. M.; Ely; Gini; Hawtrey; Kantorovich; Knight; Kuznets; Myrdal; Polanyi; Robinson, J. V.; Schultz; Sombart; Thornton; Ingram; Johnson, H. G.; Jones, R.; Tooke; Böhm-Bawerk; Chamberlin; Dupuit; Frisch; Hansen; Juglar; Keynes, J. N.; Koopmans; Meade; Ohlin; Robertson; Samuelson; Seligman; Taussig; Senior; Gresham.

—— (1985c) "Patents: An Economist's View", in J. Phillips (ed.) *Patents in Perspective*, Oxford: ESC Publishing, 32–41; reprinted by Butterworths, London, 1994, and in a sourcebook on intellectual property law ed. by P. J. Groves, Cavendish, London, 1997.

—— (1985d) "Robert Denis Collison Black and the History of Economic Thought", *History of Economic Thought Newsletter* 35: 2–4.

—— (1986) "Divestiture: The Case of AT&T", in J. Coyne and M. Wright (eds) *Divestment and Strategic Change*, Oxford: Phillip Allan, 166–201.

—— (1987) Six entries in J. Eatwell, M. Milgate, and P. Newman (eds): Chalmers; Colquhoun; McCulloch; Newmarch; Overstone; Ravenstone, *The New Palgrave*, London: Macmillan.

—— (1988a) "Classical Reassessments", in W. O. Thweatt (ed.) *Classical Political Economy*, Boston: Kluwer, 179–220.

—— (1988b) "Lionel Charles Robbins, 1898–1984", *Economic Journal* 98: 104–25.

—— (1988c) *Lionel Robbins*, London: Macmillan.

—— (1989) "Robbins as a Political Economist: A Reply", *Economic Journal* 99: 479–80.

—— (1990a) "Lionel Robbins and the Austrian Connection", *History of Political Economy* 22: 155–84.

—— (1990b) "Marshall, Monopoly and Rectangular Hyperbolas" (with J. Creedy), *Australian Economic Papers* 29: 141–53.

—— (1990c) "Marshall: The *Principles* Centenary", *Scottish Journal of Political Economy* 37: 2–4.

—— (1990d) "Marshall's Industrial Analysis", *Scottish Journal of Political Economy* 37: 61–84.

—— (1990e) "Marshall's Work in Relation to Classical Economics", in J. K. Whitaker (ed.) *Centenary Essays on Alfred Marshall*, Cambridge: Cambridge University Press, 127–63.

—— (1991a) "The Macroeconomics of Thomas Joplin", in G. K. Shaw (ed.) *Economics, Culture and Education: Essays in Honour of Mark Blaug*, Aldershot: Edward Elgar, 64–78.

—— (1991b) "Theory and Empirical Observation", in D. Greenaway, M. Bleaney, and I. Stewart (eds) *Companion to Contemporary Economic Thought*, London: Routledge, 49–67.

—— (1992a) "Competition and Credit Control", in *New Palgrave Dictionary of Money and Finance*, London: Macmillan.

—— (1992b) "Economists and Data", *British Journal of Industrial Relations* 30: 253–85.

—— (1992c) "Sir William Petty", in B. Schefold (ed.) *Sir William Petty und seine Political Arithmetic*, Dusseldorf: Verlag Wirtschaft und Finanzen, 55–75.

—— (1993) *Thomas Joplin and Classical Macroeconomics: A Reappraisal of Classical Monetary Thought*, Aldershot: Edward Elgar.

—— (1994a) *Alfred and Mary Paley Marshall: The Economics of Industry*, Bristol: Thoemmes/Routledge, v–xxxvi.

—— (1994b) *Foundations of Monetary Economics*: Vol. I *The Founders*: xi–xxii; Vol. II *The Bullionists*: vii–xxvii; Vol. III *The Anti-Bullionists*: vii–xxv; Vol. IV *The Currency School*: vii–xxxi; Vol. V *The Banking School*: vii–xxv; Vol. VI *Monetary Nonconformists*: vii–xxix, London: Pickering and Chatto.

—— (1994c) "Friedrich August von Hayek 1899–1992", *Proceedings of The British Academy* 84: 347–66.

—— (1994d) "Hayek as an Intellectual Historian", in J. Birner and R. van Zijp (eds) *Hayek, Co-ordination and Evolution: His Legacy in Philosophy, Politics and the History of Ideas*, London: Routledge, 343–74.

—— (1994e) *Methodology, Money and the Firm: The Collected Essays of D. P. O'Brien*, 2 vols, Aldershot: Edward Elgar.

—— (1995a) *Collected Works of J. R. McCulloch*: Vol. I *Essay on the Question of Reducing the Interest of the National Debt*: ix–xxxv; Vol. II *The Principles of Political Economy*: v–xxxvi; Vol. III *A Discourse on Political Economy; Historical Sketch of the Bank of England; A New Bank in India; A Treatise on the Rate of Wages*: v–xlix; Vol. IV *A Treatise on the Principles and Practical Influence of Taxation*: v–xxxi; Vol. V *Treatises and Essays on Money, Exchange, Interest, the Letting of Land, Absenteeism, The History of Commerce, Manufactures, etc.*: v–xlvii; Vol. VI *A Catalogue of Books, the Property of a Political Economist*: v–xvi; Vol. VII *Syllabus of a Course of Lectures on Political Economy; Articles from the Encyclopaedia Britannica; Consequences of the Proposed Repeal of the Corn Laws; Observations on the Duty on Sea-Borne Coal*: vii–xlvii; Vol. VIII *Articles in the Edinburgh Review*: vii–lxxiii and pp. 409–41 (McCulloch bibliography), London: Routledge/Thoemmes.

—— (1995b) *J. R. McCulloch: Select Collections of Tracts on Commerce, Money, Paper Currency and Banking, the National Debt and the Sinking Fund, and Miscellaneous Economical Subjects*, 6 vols; Vol. 1, London: Pickering and Chatto, ix–xxxviii.

—— (1995c) "Long Run Equilibrium and Cyclical Disturbances: The Currency and Banking Controversy over Monetary Control", in Mark Blaug, Walter Eltis, D. P. O'Brien, Don Patinkin, Robert Skidelsky, and Geoffrey Wood, *The Quantity Theory of Money from Locke to Keynes and Friedman*, Aldershot: Edward Elgar, 50–79.

—— (1996) "Bagehots 'Lombard Street' und die viktorianische Banking – Theorie", in B. Schefold (ed.) *Walter Bagehots "Lombard Street"*, German trans. by Udo Raab, Düsseldorf: Verlag Wirtschaft und Finanzen, 133–60.

—— (1997a) "Cantillon, Richard", in D. Glasner (ed.) *Business Cycles and Depressions*, New York: Garland, 79–80.

—— (1997b) *Foundations of Business Cycle Theory*: Vol. 1: ix–xxiv; Vol. 2: ix–xxi; Vol. 3: xi–xxvii. Aldershot: Edward Elgar.

—— (1997c) "Hayek: Economics and Law", in P. Newman (ed.) *The New Palgrave Dictionary of Economics and the Law*, London: Macmillan, 217–28.

—— (1997d) "J. R. McCulloch", in H. Kurz and N. Salvadori (eds) *The Elgar Companion to Classical Economics*, Vol. II, Cheltenham: Edward Elgar, 112–16.

—— (1997e) *Jean Bodin: Response to the Paradoxes of Malestroit*, trans. by H. Tudor and R. W. Dyson, Bristol: Thoemmes, 10–38.

—— (1997f) "Joplin, Thomas", in D. Glasner (ed.) *Business Cycles and Depressions*, New York: Garland, 344–5.

—— (1997g) "Lalor, John", in D. Glasner (ed.) *Business Cycles and Depressions*, New York: Garland, 374–5.

—— (1997h) "Marshall and his Correspondence", *Economic Journal* 107: 1859–85.

—— (1998a) "Edwin Cannan", in H. Kurz and N. Salvadori (eds) *The Elgar Companion to Classical Economics*, Vol. I, Cheltenham: Edward Elgar, 65–9.

—— (1998b) "Four Detours", *Journal of Economic Methodology* 5: 23–41.

—— (1998c) "Information and Investment in a Wider Context", in N. J. Foss and B. J. Loasby (eds) *Economic Organisation, Capabilities and Co-ordination: Essays in Honour of G. B. Richardson*, London: Routledge, 104–20.

—— (1998d) "Lionel Robbins", in J. Davis, D. W. Hands, and U. Mäki (eds) *The Handbook of Economic Methodology*, Cheltenham: Edward Elgar, 424–6.

—— (1998e) "Monetary Base Control and the Bank Charter Act of 1844", *History of Political Economy* 29: 593–633.

—— (1999a) *A History of Taxation*, 8 vols, London: Pickering and Chatto.

—— (1999b) "Edwin Cannan: Economic Theory and the History of Economic Thought", *Research in the History of Economic Thought and Methodology* 17, 1–21.

—— (2000a) "Bodin's Analysis of Inflation", *History of Political Economy* 32, 2: 267–92.

—— (2000b) "History of Economic Thought as an Intellectual Discipline", in A. E. Murphy and R. Prendergast (eds) *Contributions to the History of Economic Thought*, London: Routledge, 31–54.

Robbins, L. C. (1971) "Review of *McCulloch*", *Economica* 38: 321–2.

—— (1972) "Review of *Overstone*", *Financial Times* 6 January: 20.

—— (1975) "Review of *The Classical Economists*", *Times Literary Supplement* 1 August.

Skaggs, N. T. (1995) "Review of *Joplin*", *History of Political Economy* 27: 209–10.

Skinner, A. S. (1976) "Review of *The Classical Economists*", *Economic Journal* 86: 373–5.

*The Economist* (1972) "Review of *Overstone*", 8 January: 45–6.

Winch, D. (1971) "Review of *McCulloch*", *Economic Journal* 81: 172–4.

# 14 Joan Robinson's economics

## Using the history of economic thought as a discovery tool

*Ingrid Rima*

For economists, as for others whose research agendas reflect the history of their subjects, disciplinary memory exists on two levels: there is, first, the body of knowledge scholars acquire from their intellectual forbears in the process of their professionalization and, second, the body of new knowledge which a scholar leaves to the generation that follows. Joan Robinson's life work offers an extraordinary opportunity to examine the role and construction of disciplinary memory on both levels. While Robinson is not remembered as an historian of economic thought, the doctrines that comprise the history of thought, in particular *classical* economic thought, are an important building block for her own contribution to economics, especially to the subspecialty that has become known as post-Keynesian economics.

Robinson's own disciplinary memory is in the tradition of Marshall and Pigou, as well as the classical and pre-classical thinkers who preceded them. This sets her apart from most modern economists who, lamentably, consider the history of their discipline as an intellectual furrow unworthy of their talents. Along with J. M. Keynes, she was also part of a generation that thought of values and value judgments as an integral part of economics as a moral science (Robinson 1962a: 24–5). Robinson's personal perspective was deeply influenced by the ideal of "doing good," bearing witness to the example of her great-grand-father, F. D. Maurice, who renounced his military career to work on behalf of Christian socialism. Values and value judgments dictate both a thinker's vision of the world and the way in which he or she conceptualizes reality. They are the source and inspiration for the kinds of economic questions that will be asked, the ways in which answers will be sought, as well as the kinds of answers or conclusions that are arrived at.

In the early days of her professional life Robinson was part of the tradition she later came to challenge. *The Economics of Imperfect Competition* (1933) is quintessentially Cantabridgian (Asimakopulos 1989). Despite her confession that it was inspired by Piero Sraffa's 1926 article on increasing returns (Robinson 1978: ix), *Imperfect Competition* is an outgrowth and refinement of the economics of Marshall and Pigou, in particular, Pigou's "multiple monopoly" (which concentrated chiefly on duopoly) to explore the middle ground between monopoly and competition (Pigou 1912: 192–4; 1920: 267–9). Sraffa's focus was on the inappropriateness of a partial equilibrium construct whenever the assumption of independent supply and demand curves cannot be sustained, which is the general case. Among the two alternative approaches envisioned by Sraffa, Robinson chose to "abandon the path of free competition and turn in the opposite direction, namely toward monopoly" (Sraffa 1926: 187). The economic tools she pioneered – marginal revenue and discontinuous demand curves, and the concept of monopsony and monopsonistic exploitation – remain among the fundamental tools of modern price theory to this day.

Nevertheless, she came to regard *Imperfect Competition* as a "wrong turning" because the book represents a continuation of Marshall's partial equilibrium analysis.[1] This is a shortcoming which she recognized in "Imperfect Competition Revisited" (1953), in which she wrote "In my opinion, the greatest weakness of *The Economics of Imperfect Competition* is one which it shares with the class of economic theory to which it belongs – the failure to deal with time." Even more to the point, in the preface to the second edition in 1969 she substantially disassociated herself with that work describing it as a "fudge" and a "wrong turning" in not "abandoning static analysis and trying to come to terms with Marshall's theory of development."

Robinson was probably unaware at the time that at least two of the numerous book reviews and one of the articles she undertook during 1933, the same year in which *Imperfect Competition* was published, were pointing toward new intellectual directions that would later mature into her departure from the neoclassical tradition. One among these was her review of A. da Empoli's *Theory of Equilibrium* in which she notes that "the development of the pure theory of value is in a curious state of confusion." A second new direction was embedded in her review of a new edition of Philip Wicksteed's classic book *The Coordination of the Laws of Distribution* (1894) in which she argued that the marginal productivity theory of factor rewards could hold only if competition is perfect and returns to scale are constant.[2] The third new direction was contained in her *Economic Journal* essay "The Theory of Money and the Analysis of Output" which argued that Keynes's *Treatise on Money*, which was predicated on the quantity theory of money, obscured the revolutionary theory of the determination of output that ultimately became *The General Theory of Employment, Interest and Money*. In retrospect these 1933 anticipations of the directions her future work would take, especially coming substantially on the heels of her thoroughly neoclassical *Imperfect Competition*, are truly remarkable. Yet, in spite of a voluminous number of additional articles and reviews during the 1930s, Robinson's only substantive work during that period was the distillation of Keynes's *General Theory* as her *Introduction to the Theory of Employment* (1937c). Thus, the intellectual road ahead was a very long one in the sense that the three new departures noted above were still far from fruition.

In the following decades Robinson concerned herself more specifically with the history of economic doctrines as a basis for new insight into the functioning of the capitalistic system. While this direction is foreshadowed in *Re-Reading Marx* (1935)** it does not become apparent until *An Essay on Marxism*

*Economics* (1942), which was intended to show that the roots of classical, Marxian and Keynesian schools are to be found in the economics of Ricardo. Her study of the history of economic thought is continued in *Economic Philosophy* (1962a) in which she explores the role and nature of the preconceptions and metaphysical propositions that are embedded in the thinking of classical (including Marx) and neoclassical economists. Taken together their works became part of the foundation for the body of knowledge which is Robinson's legacy to the present generation. Her chief contributions are the development of a model of economic growth in *The Accumulation of Capital* (1956) and the revival of classical distribution theory, in particular Ricardo's, which she severs from its free trade policy implications.

On a more popular level, as is appropriate for a scholar who always sought to reinterpret sophisticated ideas for lay readers, she also undertook to co-author a textbook. Together with John Eatwell, then a former student and junior colleague, now president of Cambridge University's Queen's College, *An Introduction to Modern Economics* (1973c) is a "told to the children" presentation of post-Keynesian economic principles. What is novel about this introductory text is that its Book I is a survey of economic doctrines from the eighteenth century to the present day. Her intent was to use the analytical points which can be extracted from the history of economic thought to understand how they can be used to explain the operation of modern-day capitalist economies. The history of economic thought not only is thus an integral part of Mrs Robinson's personal disciplinary memory, it also played a huge role in giving direction to the way in which she studied, taught, refined, and extended economics as a discipline. She thus also entertained the hope that "some parts of it [the text] may be of wider interest" (1973a: xvi).

This chapter lends itself to being presented under four sections: the first examines her "economic philosophy" which provides the basis for her quest to revive economics as a moral science; the second identifies the concepts or building blocks she specifically derived from classical (including Karl Marx), neoclassical, and other thinkers, including Thorstein Veblen. These lead to the third section which argues that her study of classical distribution theory, in particular Ricardo's, is the source of her own most important contribution to disciplinary memory; specifically it develops a post-Keynesian theory of income distribution which she represented as the "other half" of the Keynesian revolution (Rima 1991). Finally, the brief fourth section reflects on Robinson's personal anguish that Keynes's theoretical revolution had not, after all, succeeded in bringing back the "moral problem" laissez-faire theory had abolished, and thus made little progress in the direction of establishing economics as a moral science. Yet, despite her despairing evaluation of the state of economics in the last decade of her life, by teaching her students and many of her contemporaries the necessity for couching their inquiries about the economic system in terms of an historical process, Robinson has advanced the possibilities for human progress. Once the neoclassical equilibrium perspective is discarded, it becomes possible to refocus attention on classical growth theory and going beyond it to explore the potential for increasing (rather than decreasing) returns which necessarily underlie greater equity in the distribution of income.

# I

Robinson's life work is only incidentally that of an historian of economic thought. She is first and foremost an economic theorist who is also a social philosopher who looked to the history of her subject to identify "what are the questions?" Much of her approach to economics is traceable to her economic philosophy. *Economic Philosophy* is the title of her slender 1962 volume which, writ large undertakes to identify and explain the preconceptions she believes underlie organized thought in the social sciences and, more particularly, in economics as a discipline intended to explain market behavior and outcomes under capitalism.

How, she asks, can we distinguish ideology from "science?" An ideology is a belief or point of view for which rational explanation is impossible and which is incapable of being tested or proven wrong. Ideologies and beliefs are therefore outside the realm of science (in the sense of being falsifiable by empirical evidence). Yet, a distinguishing aspect of Robinson's work is her recognition that beliefs, or what she conceives to be "metaphysical" concepts, are essential to the investigation of social and psychological problems, for they are the foundation for the questions to which answers are sought. Unlike the vast majority who undertake the study of economic questions, Robinson came to understand fairly early in her career that "it is no good trying to pretend that we can think or speak about human questions without ethical values coming in" (1962a: 14). Along with Professor Myrdal she recognized that our "value loaded [concepts] ... cannot be defined except in terms of political valuation" (ibid.). Robinson appreciated the relevance of what is today referred to as "political correctness" in a sense that relates to the political and ideological culture that is implicit in society. It is the absence of values in the natural sciences which makes propositions that can be tested (i.e., refuted) possible, while the propositions of economics and the social sciences generally cannot. Robinson singles out *value* and *utility* as having had a particularly long history in economics as concepts for which there is no basis in fact.

## Value

The concepts of value in use and value in exchange were introduced by Adam Smith at the end of Chapter 4, Book I, of *The Wealth of Nations*, and are generally accepted as giving direction not only to his own work but to classical economics generally. His argument in Chapter 6 begins with the observation that, in that early and rude state of society before the accumulation of capital and private ownership of land, the relative values of beaver and deer were based on the respective amounts of labor time required to produce them. Accordingly, in that early pre-capitalistic state the whole value of the product belonged to the laborers who produced them.

Reflecting on this familiar passage, Robinson argues that there is neither an historical nor a factual basis for Smith's example. His reliance on them is linked with his pro-capitalist ideology and was essentially a reflection of Smith's own views about the necessity to distinguish between income from work and income from property. He had no reason to distinguish between value in use and value in exchange, in Robinson's view, except in relation to the production of wealth and the increase in productivity that follows the division of labor. The distinction is a prelude to his *real* interest, which is the accumulation of capital as a basis for profit, as is examined in Book II.[3] This observation foreshadows what were to become persistent themes of Robinson's work: that is, the nature of investments made in the light of uncertain expectations about a long future, and the need to distinguish between production and exchange and between income from work and income from property.[4]

While she regards Smith's methodology as "cumbersome" for identifying income distribution as the "real" issue of concern, Robinson credits Ricardo with correctly perceiving that Smith's concern about the accumulation of capital in Book II was a prelude to "determin[ing] the laws that regulate the distribution [of the produce of the earth] among the classes of society as the principal problem in Political Economy" (1962a: 31). According to Robinson's interpretation, Ricardo's labor theory of value reflects "a metaphysical notion [which] inspired original thought, though in itself it was quite devoid of operational meaning" (1942, 1966a: xi). Like Smith before him, Ricardo's chief analytical concern was to examine how changes in the distributive shares are related to alterations in exchange values. Disputing Smith's description of "the early and rude state of society" as an era that preceded the accumulation of capital, Ricardo maintains that a worker always required tools to abridge his labor. He conceived of different commodities as being produced in his own day with different quantities of past and present labor (i.e., different proportions of fixed and variable capital) so that changes in wages (i.e., in the value of labor) bring about changes in the distributive shares.

The concept of value took on an essentially different role in Marx's work than in Smith's and Ricardo's. *An Essay on Marxian Economics*, which appeared first in 1942 and was revised in 1966, reexamines Marx's argument in *Capital* to reassess whether the metaphysical concept of *value* is essential to his theory of labor exploitation. Robinson concludes that Marx adopted Smith's *pro*-capitalist metaphysical concept of value to support his own *anti*-capitalist view that land and capital produce *no value*, and only labor is productive. Paraphrasing Marx, she argues that owning neither capital nor property is a productive activity; thus, the margin which Marshall calls profit/interest is to Marx essentially the value of unpaid labor. The surplus created by labor is represented by Marx as $s$, while $v$ is the variable component of capital that comprises worker subsistence requirements. Thus $s/v$ represents the rate of exploitation of labor as part of the capitalist process.

Robinson rejects Marshall's explanation that capitalists deserve profit as a reward because they perform the service of "waiting" while the full value of labor's product matures. On the other hand she also rejects Marx's argument that $s/v$ properly represents the rate of labor's exploitation under capitalism as neglecting the necessity, as part of the process of production, to include a component for the depreciation of capital as part of the cost of a commodity to society.

If private property were abolished and production socialized, the prices of all commodities would correspond to their costs to society; that is, they would be proportional to labor costs plus the loss of the productive value of capital through use. A system of socialized production would provide each worker with a share in the total product that corresponds to his contribution, and also include an interest charge on all the capital used in production. Thus Marx's exploitation formula $s/v$ omitted society's need to establish prices for its output that maintain (and add to) constant capital. In rejecting the formula $s/(c + v)$ as representing the rate of exploitation Marx "keep(s) insistently before the mind of the reader a picture of the capitalist process as a system of piracy" (1966a: 22). Had Marx examined the nature of pricing as it would exist under a hypothetical case of "socialist enterprises required to earn a rate of interest on all capital allotted to them ... the last link to the theory of *value* is broken" (1966a: 28). His reliance on the metaphysical concept of value to support an analytical argument for which it was unnecessary is readily exposed by recognizing that the use of capital involves a cost regardless of ownership. For Robinson this conclusion no doubt confirmed her oft-made point that we study economics in order not to be "fooled" by the emotionally persuasive arguments of other economists.

## Utility

The notion of *utility* is, perhaps, the most central concept of the stream of economic thought that stems from thinkers who concerned themselves with the market aspects of human behaviors. From Robinson's perspective, the concept of utility is no less metaphysical than is the notion of value. Taken to mean *Desire* or *Want* there is no magnitude to measure the outcomes of these behaviors. Only when the value of money can be assumed equal to everyone (which is never the case) can measurability be inferred in the sense that it can be claimed that a commodity's utility is reflected in its purchase price. For neoclassicists it follows that everyone

> must be free to spend his income as he likes, and he will gain the greatest benefit when he equalizes the marginal utility of a shilling spent on each unit of good. ... [Analogously] the pursuit of profit, under conditions of perfect competition leads producers to equate marginal costs to prices and the maximum possible satisfaction is drawn from available resources.
>
> (Robinson 1962a: 53)

Production is determined by decisions to buy and sell as expressed in the concept of "consumer sovereignty;" that is, production is a passive response to marketplace choices, for they are the prime movers of economic activity. Thus, says Robinson, the notion of utility has become a vehicle to support laissez-faire. Its link to the distinction Smith made between value in use and value in exchange to address the distribution problem inherent in his theory of prices has been forgotten. The paradox that originated in Smith's diamond–water example remained unsolved. Unable to develop a general theory of prices (including both commodities and factors), Ricardo needed to fall back on a "labor embodied" view while also retaining Adam Smith's thesis that national prosperity is rooted in the self-serving behavior of "everyman."

The mid-nineteenth-century popularization of the metaphysical utility concept facilitated the neoclassicist shift to a theory of relative commodity prices based on subjective feelings of utility rather than objective labor. By relying on utility as the well-spring of economic activity, neoclassicists (and more particularly Austrian thinkers such as Böhm-Bawerk and von Mises) caused the issues of class conflict to at least move into the background, along with the concern about accumulation and growth that characterized classical political economy. There is another aspect to this point of view which was of concern to Robinson. Specifically, if market activity is initiated by exchange, and exchange involves property (including labor), then work is itself part of an exchange; Robinson's distinction between income and income from work thus dissolves. Accordingly, the role of utility in neoclassical theory emerged for Robinson as "an ideology to end ideologies, for it has abolished the moral problem" (1962a: 53). Its whole point has become the justification of laissez-faire, along with the "unconscious preoccupation ... to raise profits to the same level of moral respectability as wages" (ibid.: 58). These ideas without a doubt reflect Marx's influence on her economic theory; this is evident from a passage in which Robinson (1979: 5) refers to Nicholai Bukharin's (1979: 54–6) emphasis on the importance of production and accumulation as distinct from the "point of view of consumption" that characterizes the Austrian school.

As is well known, Schumpeter interpreted the role of the marginal increment (whether utility or productivity) to be essentially the same in "the hard core of Marshall's theory" as Walras's (1954: 837). However, Robinson maintained there is an important distinction to be made between them. Specifically, to Walras, Jevons, and the Austrians, the economic problem is essentially a matter of achieving an optimum allocation of resources for the given supply of productive factors.[5] For Marshall, however, the factors do not exist (except for land) in fixed quantity. They thus have a supply price in the sense that "there is a necessary rate of return that must be projected as being earnable" to remunerate prospective suppliers (i.e., capitalists) for the effort of waiting. The problem inherent in the assumption of a fixed supply as it relates to the quantity of capital is that without a methodology for establishing the rate of interest on the funds that finance capital or a rate of profit on capital assets brought into existence by past investment, the quantity of capital cannot be specified.

Robinson's argument, derived as it is from the criticism of the metaphysical nature of utility, thus appears to be a prelude to her later research program in *The Accumulation of Capital* (1956), in which she intended to refocus attention on the phenomena of accumulation and growth that characterized classical political economy. While Marshall allows the possibility that businessmen may lack confidence about the future profitability of investment, this bow to realism does not, says Robinson, disturb the neoclassical picture of a market economy operating smoothly to achieve an optimum allocation of its resources. Neoclassicists focused their chief attentions on the achievement of equilibrium in a stationary state.[6] This perspective led inevitably to the free trade doctrine as an extension of the principle of utility to the world as a whole and, along with it, the proposition that free trade is good for all countries. The chief difficulty, as Robinson was quick to point out, is that the advantage claimed for protection is an illusion, for it cannot alleviate the problem of unemployment.

## Full employment as ideology

A related Robinsonian argument is that the concept of "Full Employment" is the "great ideology bearing concept in the *General Theory*" (1962a: 89). Keynes's intimation that full employment can be meaningfully expressed in terms of the relationship between the marginal disutility of labor and the average wage rate is "irremediably metaphysical" (1962a: 92). A more appropriate interpretation would be to think in terms of a level of employment at which prices will be stable, if necessary with the help of proper policy, to keep prices and employment at this appropriate level. But neoclassical theory is so isolated from practical questions that it circumvents the very purpose of setting up hypotheses that can be tested. Neoclassical hypotheses are predicated at the outset on the premise that predicted outcomes will be attained as long as all involved have perfect foresight. There is, therefore, no point in testing.

Robinson's negative appraisal of the practical aspects of neoclassical theory was particularly clear in her criticism of the so-called "Treasury View" and, because "the total fund of savings is given," the Lloyd George proposal to solve the problem of unemployment by mounting a program of public works was certain to be self-defeating. Robinson points out that Marx was cognizant of the inherent weakness of the proposition that what is saved is invariably spent, even before Keynes's theory of aggregate effective demand vitiated this neoclassical view (1967: 43). Robinson interprets Marx's intention to have been to work out a theory in which the consumption of workers is limited by their lack of consuming power, while that of capitalists is limited by their instinct to accumulate rather than to spend. The implication is that the lack of balance in the capitalistic system is attributable to distribution of income between wages and surplus. Thus, to Robinson, the great flaw in Marx's unfinished work was his failure to address the link between the rate of profit and the inducement to invest (1962a: 50).

She considered Keynes's theory of investment as being closer to the mark than Marx's theory of capital accumulation. Keynes has it that the rate of investment depends on expectations of the profitability of future investment and the rate of interest which needs to be paid on borrowed funds. The volume of investment is not necessarily equal to the volume of savings, though savings will become adjusted to investment through the mechanism of a change in the level of income. It follows for Robinson that Keynes's analysis exposed once and for all that the degree of income inequality that characterizes the capitalistic system is tolerated only because of the conventional premise that saving is the necessary prerequisite for investment, and it is difficult to justify on any other ground. Thus, Keynes's analysis is seen as reflecting Marx's essential understanding of the capitalist process.

It is also her belief that Marx's concept of the industrial reserve army is brought into clearer perspective when Keynes's theory is extended to the long period. As the productivity of labor increases, the volume of employment which corresponds to a given level of output declines. Accordingly, the technology underlying production has a major role in determining the level of employment. Even conservative opinion now recognizes that there is no mechanism inherent in the capitalistic system that can be relied on to assure the full employment of labor resources (1962a: 94–5). The Keynesian revolution has destroyed the "old soporific doctrine" of laissez-faire as a basis for policy, but the thinness of its metaphysics leaves us "in the uncomfortable situation of having to think for ourselves" (1962a: 98). It may thus be asked, what had Robinson learned from the history of economic thought that became tools of discovery to undertake a reconstruction of economic theory?

## II

From the first, Robinson was only peripherally interested in providing useful knowledge for practical people. Her concern was to present "a box of tools [which] make only an indirect contribution to our knowledge of the actual world" (Robinson 1933: 1). "It is natural enough for the practical man to complain that he asks for bread and the economist gives him a stone. ... Yet, the economist has the responsibility to ask questions that can be answered" (ibid.). Thus, Robinson made it clear from the beginning of her career that her interest lay in helping to fill "the economist's box of tools."

### Tools to address time and uncertainty

As section I has intimated, Robinson's study of the history of economics made her cognizant that many of the discipline's propositions owe their existence and durability to the broad acceptance of metaphysical and ideological concepts that are largely without relevance to economics. None among these was more repugnant to her than the concept of equilibrium and the related notion of "logical" time. Her study of classical growth theory led her to distinguish between time as a metaphor based on space as opposed to a process moving through time. The concept of historical time remains among her most perceptive discoveries. Criticizing the notion of equilibrium she notes: "In space bodies moving from A to B may pass bodies moving from B to A, but in time the straightest possible route of one way traffic is always in force" (1959: 130). Unlike movements across space, movements in time are "irreversible." It is, for example, impossible to move forward and backward on the same supply curve. Because cost conditions become totally altered, the supply curve can, in principle, only be drawn as an historical curve so that it cannot be used to determine an equilibrium between supply and demand relations. Even more to the point, the distance and space from A to B is precisely the same as that from B to A. No such symmetry exists between movements in time, "the distance from today until yesterday is infinite as the poets have often remarked" (ibid.). Robinson was among the earliest critics of the neoclassical use of "logical" as opposed to historical time.[7] It was a perspective which led her into heated exchanges with the synthesizing efforts of neoclassical microeconomists, among them Robert Lucas (1972, 1980), who undertook to create a new orthodoxy by integrating their analysis with Keynes's macroeconomics.[8]

In a later paper, *History versus Equilibrium* (1974), the phenomenon of time is addressed in a somewhat different context: that is, in terms of the concept of stability as a mechanical balance between demand and supply. What she is calling for is the need to distinguish between the *existence* of a position of equilibrium and the *process* of getting into equilibrium. The very concept of equilibrium is incompatible with history.[9] It is a metaphor based on movements in space being applied to processes taking place in time. The dimension of space makes it possible to go to and fro and make appropriate alterations, but in the context of time, the past is irrevocable, and the future is not only unknown but unknowable; that is, the laws of probability do not lend themselves to informing us about future possibilities which, as George Shackle was to put it, can only be imagined (Shackle 1954; 1972).[10]

Thus Robinson's rejection of the Marshallian equilibrium tradition was accompanied by a research program intended to develop an analysis appropriate to examining a dynamic economic system. As she expressed this research objective in *The Rate of Interest and Other Essays* (1952: Preface): "The characteristic of a dynamic analysis in the sense which is intended here is that it cannot explain how an economy behaves in given conditions without reference to past history."

Her appreciation of the methodological problem inherent in addressing the phenomenon of time in economics is nowhere explained more clearly or carefully than in *Essays in the Theory of Economic Growth* (1962b). Specifically she notes:

A model applicable to actual history has to be capable of getting out of equilibrium ... indeed it must normally not be in it. ... The initial position (in historical time) contains the state of expectations of the characters concerned (whether based on past experience or traditional beliefs) as well as physical data. The system may be going to work itself out so as to fulfill them, or as to disappoint them.

(1962b: 24–5)

"In short, as soon as uncertainty and expectations are admitted, equilibrium drops out of the argument and history takes its place" (1979c: 80).

## Tools to measure capital and explain accumulation

It was while she was still working on the shortcomings of Marshall's notion of equilibrium and its implications for irreversibilities in time that Robinson turned her attention to the theme of accumulation and the meaning and measurement of capital in the production function (1953). The prolonged and, in the view of most, largely irrelevant controversy appears to have been initiated by Robinson's argument that the notion of capital is unable to shed light on the question of what determines the distribution of income between work and property (Harcourt 1990). Marx and the classical economists were unable to address this problem successfully, yet Robinson considered that Marx's *Capital* provides the insight that it is the rate of accumulation that undergirds the empirically observable allocation of income between classes.

After many years of controversy about the meaning and measurement of capital, Robinson was ultimately persuaded that Veblen was right in thinking that the essence of capital is the community's accumulated knowledge of the practical arts used in earning the community's livelihood; that is, capital is an intangible that is embodied in the instruments of production (Veblen 1942a; 1942b). In society's early stages, virtually everyone can master the level of knowledge inherent in the simple instruments of production in use (e.g., bows and arrows). In modern times, however, the level of knowledge becomes advanced, and is embodied in complex and expensive instruments of production. Under capitalism their ownership conveys the exclusive legal right to the product of society's common heritage; as Veblen put it, "the profitable engrossing of the community's industrial efficiency" (Veblen 1942a: 352). For Robinson, the state of imperfect competition is the counterpart of Veblen's "advanced society" in the sense that, under capitalism, capital constitutes an institutional monopoly (Gram and Walsh 1983: 530). Building on this insight, it became Robinson's central objective to extend and generalize Keynes's method to Marshall's long period in order to show the way to "the second half" of Keynes's revolution.

## Tools to analyze investment and the price level

Robinson's study of the history of economic thought provided the insight that it is necessary to establish a link between investment and the exploitation of profit opportunities rather than saving; it is also necessary to discard the quantity theory of money. These were to become major stepping stones toward extending Keynes's theory of effective demand. Robinson's recognition that the concept of abstinence as the prerequisite for investment is inherently false was largely the outcome of her rereading of Marx. It was he who led her to recognize that investment is driven by the expectation of profits and not savings, and that saving and investment are, as Keynes made it a point to argue, the result of decisions taken independently of one another so that the two sides of the process of accumulation are not linked together in a way which necessarily keeps them in harmony. "On the contrary, the very notion of private enterprise causes them to have a chronic tendency to get out of gear" (Robinson 1952, reprinted 1979c: 62–3).

Armed with this new understanding of the nature of investment, Robinson also became cognizant that finance must be available before investment can begin and that, given the stability of consumption expenditures, investment is the key determinant of the level of economic activity. Investment is the driving force in establishing the level of economic activity. A further insight of hers relates to the role of money as an asset, and that real and monetary forces interact.[11] Accordingly, the quantity of money needs to be discarded as an analytical tool for explaining the price level. It is only the enormous ideological attraction of the quantity theory which, in Robinson's view, gave it credibility for more than five decades after its logical content had been exploded.

The price level in an industrial economy "is an historical accident" (1971: 90). The primary influence on it at any moment of time is the level of wage rates which are the result of movements that have taken place in the past. This insight goes beyond Keynes's recognition that unemployment cannot be remedied by cutting wages, because this tactic would cause both prices and aggregate demand to fall. Rather it goes to the heart of the reasons why the quantity theory of money is an unacceptable explanation of the price level. Industrial prices are determined by marking up prime costs with an allowance for overhead expenses. The role of the markup is to establish that in a modern industrial economy the general level of prices depends chiefly on the level of money wage rates and worker productivity. The extent of the markup is, as Robinson learned from Michael Kalecki, dependent on the "degree of monopoly." Given an empirically established constancy of the markup over unit labor costs, the implication is that for the economy to experience a steady price level increases in wage rates must correspond to productivity increases. Robinson's study of the history of inflation theory taught her that the new "dilemma of modern capitalism ... is that no policy has been found to solve the *financial* phenomenon of rising prices without making [worse] the *real* problem of unemployment" (Robinson 1980a: 201–2). Maintaining employment without inflation requires that "market demand must be expanded as fast as potential output" (*ibid.*: 232–3). As a consequence of failing to achieve this goal, industrial nations are "gradually drifting into the situation of an underdeveloped economy" in failing to offer jobs to all available workers, "not through a temporary fall in demand ... [but because of] class war; workers must struggle to keep their share in the product of industry and corporations must struggle to prevent them from increasing it" (Robinson 1976: 5–6). Robinson's ultimate concern is thus with what she termed "the second half" of the Keynesian revolution.

## III

As has already been suggested, it is unlikely Robinson had foresight that the eventual direction of her work to reconstruct neoclassical theory would be to tackle the unresolved problem of classical distribution theory. Not until the collection of essays published under the title *After Keynes* (1973b) did she observe that *implicit* in Keynes's first revolution is a second "other half" of the Keynesian revolution whose chief objective

> is to establish that in an industrial economy the level of prices is governed by the level of money wages. This [objective] was a greater shock ... even than the concept of effective demand governed by volatile expectations ... the profession still resists taking it in.
>
> (Robinson 1973b: 104–5)

The most basic requirement is that economists change their perception of the functioning of the labor market.

It is reasonable to seek the intellectual lineage of Robinson's theory of distribution as the "other half" of Keynes's revolution in her earliest major work, *The Economics of Imperfect Competition* (1933). This is to some extent appropriate, for her application of the marginal conditions to the theory factor markets was to challenge the marginal productivity theory of wages. Specifically, in this book she set forth the case of the monopsonistic employer who is able to engage in the exploitation of his workers because he employs a smaller number than his competitive counterpart while paying them a wage that is less than the value of their marginal products (1933: chapter 26). Exploitation in the labor market occurs in a situation in which the "wage is less than the marginal physical product ... valued at the price at which it is being sold" (1933: 283). Her analysis of the implications of the breakdown of competition on the buyers' side of the market, and the possibility for correction by unions when that market is dominated by a monopsonistic employer, stands as an important insight into the process of wage setting. It has a rightful place in contemporary labor market approaches (Rima 1996: chapter 11), even though it did not lead her toward a reformulation of her theory of income distribution. The road toward this accomplishment was a long time in coming, even after her insightful critiques of marginal productivity theory.

Robinson's non-traditional view of the role of labor markets is closely associated with her study of the history of the quantity theory, particularly as it related to Germany's hyperinflation in 1921 (Rima 1991: 197). Whereas writers of the period were attributing German inflation to "a combination of deficits and increases in the quantity and velocity of money," Robinson argued that an increase in the quantity of money is not the cause of inflation. The key circumstance that Robinson identified as underlying the German inflation was trade union demands for higher wage rates in the face of low rates of unemployment in Germany in the early postwar period. In other words, inflation is not simply a monetary phenomenon, but also a political phenomenon.

The insight that changes in price, especially in an upward direction, carry political implications is one Robinson first drew from Marx, and later Kalecki, with whom she was brought into close intellectual association when he was briefly part of the Cambridge scene between 1936 and 1940 during her efforts to break out of the "Marshallian incubus" (Eshag 1977: 8–9). It was through him that she became increasingly appreciative of Marx's view that conflict over income shares is a characteristic feature of capitalist economies. Even more, her studies of Marx led her to realize that the Keynesian revolution leads back to the concept of surplus, which she regarded as "the core concept of classicism" (Gram and Walsh 1983). The most fundamental change in perception that is required is that the wage rate is the economy's "key" price, not just one price among many, and it is *wages* rather than profit which are the residual category of income (Robinson 1973b: 100).

This is an interpretation which led her to postulate that wage rates are a matter of historical accident and their movement is bound up with the effort of groups of workers to maintain their relative positions. Her perception of the functioning of labor markets is that their outcomes reflect the existence of conflict between workers and other receivers of income:

> Workers, managers and research teams bring about technical progress and accumulation, and the capital falls into the lap of shareholders who are not making the smallest contribution to the process which brings it into being. Income from property is not the reward for waiting; it is the reward of employing a good stockbroker.
>
> (1973b: 66)

The most likely way in which the wage bill will shrink relative to output is through inflation. However, as the period following World War II made quite clear, there is a maximum profit rate that workers are willing to tolerate. A significant part of postwar productivity gains accrued to workers in the form of higher money wages, thereby minimizing the erosion of their real wages, even though government intervention in the form of monetary stringency between the 1960s and 1980s in the United States, Britain, and Canada undertook to contain inflation, albeit at the expense of employment, which Robinson clearly recognized as exacerbating the conflict over shares.

Robinson lived long enough to interpret what she termed "Neo-mercantilism" as an extension of the conflict over income shares into the arena of international affairs as the newly developing nations of Africa and Asia vied to earn surpluses by pursuing export-led growth (1937a, 1966b). She recognized ever so clearly that the problem of lack of effective demand reemerges when

> the market does not grow fast enough to make room for all, [so that] each government feels it is a worthy and commendable aim to increase its own share in world activity for the benefit of its own people ... the new mercantilists believe it is not necessarily foolish to prefer to acquire sterile money rather than useful goods or profitable assets.
>
> (1973a: 4–5)

Thus, Robinson is led to distinguish between capital in the sense of stocks of equipment and capital in the sense of "command over finance." She had also become appreciative of the potential inherent in Nicholas Kaldor's rediscovery of Allyn Young's concept of increasing returns and its relevance, not only as an analytical tool, but also as an operational basis for economic growth (1979a). An expansion of industries engaged in producing capital goods, along with a relative shrinkage in the production of the consumer goods sector, is a possible source of changing factor shares because it would involve a change in sectoral employment proportions, and would be accompanied by a concurrent change in the relative wage share.[12] Its outcome is likely to be inconsistent with the constancy of the wage and capital shares which is the "stylized fact" upon which Cambridge growth theory is predicated, and could clearly cause major social, economic, and political upheaval. The question whether capital accumulation might be subject to secular shifts and the way in which the latter would relate to sectoral changes in the economies of the world, whether developed or developing, is one Robinson did not address. These changes were underway in the last decade or so of her life and, as has already been suggested, she perceived that a new phase in the historical development of capitalism was already underway.

## IV

As Robinson reflected in the closing chapter of her *Economic Philosophy* (1962a), capitalism's new phase is one in which nations have become nationalistic to a degree which "makes solidarity of the human race all the more difficult to achieve. ... The great central doctrine of the neoclassical school, the case for Free Trade *pretends* that no *nation* can ever benefit itself by protection." They offer the free trade doctrine as universally beneficent. Yet its proponents "do not argue that it is the duty of richer nations to increase the sum of *utility* in the world by subsidizing imports from the poor ones." They are guilty of "combin[ing] the doctrines of universal benevolence with the same patriotism that inspired the horsemen of Ghengis Khan" (1962a: 127). In this respect they are less honest than "the hard headed classicists [who] were in favor of Free Trade because it was good for Great Britain, not because it was good for the world" (ibid.: 124–5).

Many of Robinson's intellectual forbearers, in particular Mill and Marshall, were as repelled as she by the deleterious implications of unbridled profit-driven behavior. What Robinson read between their lines was that the capitalistic system offered the best among alternative forms of economic organization. As Marshall put it, unfortunately "no socialistic scheme yet advanced seems to make adequate provision for the maintenance of high enterprise" (Marshall 1919: 111). This Marshallian pronouncement was an ongoing source of dismay to her. She thus finds particular reason to complement James Meade for recognizing that the merits of the free market cannot be attained without the radical measure of achieving a reasonably equitable distribution of income and property (1973a: 129). On the other hand, she is profoundly distressed that his case for "equity and efficiency" is not extended beyond Great Britain, illustrating once again that a "genuinely universalist point of view is very rare." This being the case, if "economic doctrines [do] have an influence on the choice of objectives for national policy, on the whole it is obscurantist rather than helpful" (ibid.: 130). Economists have been the first to fall into the fallacy of thinking that a high level of national income and consumption expenditures is indicative of a high standard of life when, in fact, statistics on the production of output and the sale of goods do not equate either with "the satisfaction of natural wants" or "given the bias of private enterprise in favor of quick profits [that] ... investment policy [will be] socially advantageous" (ibid.).

In the last decade of her life Robinson despaired of social outcomes that are grossly at odds with the ultimate values she envisioned all nations might achieve if "their great productive powers are used to abolish poverty and create conditions in which we would prefer to devote our further energies to non-economic purposes" (1979a: 115–34; 1980a: 97; 1982a, 1982b). Her aspirations for humankind reflect "The ethical system implanted in [her] by her upbringing ... and handed to her by intellectual mentors and forbears" (1962a: 12). These were further nurtured by the Cambridge tradition in which she took her first professional steps. That was a period during which she had little doubt something could be done about the economic and human costs of the Depression. Indeed, she became an enthusiastic proponent, interpreter, and proselytizer, not only for Keynes's revolutionary economic principles, but also for Keynes's belief that capitalism could "be reformed."

This early part of her work had no direct connection with the history of economic thought. That came only later, for she was confident that Keynes had "brought back the moral problem that *laissez-faire* theory had abolished" (1962a: 48). Her rereading of Marx was sparked by her uncompromising disgust with the labor theory of value. She also thought him quite wrong in accepting orthodox teaching about the tendency for the rate of profits to fall. Thus her *Essay on Marx* was both a critique of Marx and orthodox economists. In the early 1940s Robinson was predominantly Keynesian, and it was as a Keynesian (and not as an historian of economic thought) that she became impressed by Marx's emphasis on the importance of effective demand.

As is clear in her collected papers, it was only after working her way through the problems of "accumulation" in the 1950s that her interest in Marx matured to the point that she came to see Marx as a major classical economist who, building on Ricardo, was able to ask the questions that Robinson felt economics ought to be asking in order to achieve a more moral society. It is important to bear in mind that Robinson's "vision" of a moral society is one she brought with her into economics. One's value system is a very personal characteristic that is assuredly not biologically transmitted. In Robinson's case it was not learned at Cambridge, either from her teachers or from her teachers' teachers. Thus, when she turned her attentions more specifically to the history of economic thought it was not to learn about values, but to study alternative ways to define and conceptualize problems. She learned that in contrast to the Pigou–Marshall equilibrium models on which she cut her teeth (and on which she relied in her *The Economics of Imperfect Competition*), classical thinkers couched their thinking in terms of an historical process changing over the secular long run during which economies evolve. Like Smith, they perceived that "the early rude state of society" had been replaced over time by sedentary agriculture and, in turn, by a handicraft economy which evolved into the factory system that is now becoming substantially superseded by oligopoly (monopoly) capitalism. What comes next?

To this the study of the history of thought provides no answers. It tells us only that economies evolve over time; that is, there are "stages in social history," as Adam Smith recognized in his *Lectures on Jurisprudence* (1776) which speculated about the origin of the economic surplus and its role in the relationship between "the higher and lower orders" of the economic hierarchy. His focus in the *Lectures* was on the social aspects of economic behavior and the institutions within which the economic process was carried out during the stages of economic development that preceded the nascent industrial economy of his own day.

Smith's *Lectures* are less familiar to present-day economists (and never referred to by Robinson) than either *The Wealth of Nations* or *The Theory of Moral Sentiments* from which Robinson learned Smith's perception that "When Nature formed mankind for society, she endowed him with some feeling of sympathy with his fellows. Evolution produces a conscience ... but it will not answer the greatest of all moral questions, who is my neighbour?" Her great lament became that "Humanity must take over from Nature, but it does not show any signs of doing so at the moment" (1962a: 127). Yet, Smith himself was fully cognizant of the imperfection inherent in the Man–Nature relationship. The theme of class conflict is a recurring one in *The Wealth of Nations*, although it is overshadowed in our collective disciplinary memory by the equally powerful theme that natural liberty promotes harmonious outcomes (Rima 1998). Unlike his contemporary David Hume, Smith did not believe that the introduction of order and good government would invariably operate to remove enmity between the classes (Smith 1776: 385).

What Smith did believe was that his vision of an optimal self-regulating system is subject to the caveat that it is necessary to correct failings which "might be subversive of the great purpose which it [i.e., economic system] means to promote" (ibid.: 550–1). Smith was protesting against mercantilism for bringing about a premature shift of resources from agriculture to manufacturing; two centuries later Robinson was protesting against the ideology of free trade as a vehicle which developed nations were using to prevent, or at least impede, the shift of the "plantation economies" of the underdeveloped countries toward manufacturing. As Robinson clearly recognized from her study of history, including the history of economic thought, and from her observations of the world in which she lived, mercantilism and its polar opposite, free trade, are a matter of politics. Why then was Robinson so pessimistic at the end of her lifetime that the members of her profession would be either unable or unwilling to address what she conceived to be the really relevant questions of the new world order?

The history of economic thought, especially as it relates to the study of classical economics, implicitly provided her with a "stages of history" perspective of an economic system that changes over time. Although cognizant of capitalism's potential for generating class conflict, Smith's perspective emphasized the positive role of growth. Later classicists, Ricardo, Mill, and McCulloch, compromised Smith's optimism by seriously considering the possibility of a stationary state. But that vision was eventually discarded. Not even Keynes's "under-employment" theory revived the classical stationary state. It had long since been replaced by the Marshall–Pigou equilibrium perspective. This is precisely the methodological perspective to which Robinson objected, thereby, perhaps, establishing herself as the first among post-Keynesians. In her 1977 "What are the Questions?" she particularly criticized the distinction mainstream economics makes between micro- and macroeconomics, maintaining that one cannot exist without the other. The fragmentation, she maintained, reflects once again the dominant ideology implicit in Say's law: that markets clear.

Despite Robinson's fear that the equilibrium methodology of economics would for ever be the source of its undoing, that is not necessarily the case. While her last important paper, originally called "Spring Cleaning" (1985), and published posthumously, urged economists to begin anew, she continued to work at providing a firm footing for post-Keynesian economics in the United States, Britain, Canada, and Australia. The internationalization of economics has since carried her message to many scholars in the generation that followed hers (specifically my own). While post-Keynesian economics is in no sense a single paradigm, more than a few younger economists (though unfortunately too few Americans) proceed from the "stages of social history" perspective that is rooted in classical economics. Like Robinson, they also appreciate that economic growth is the prerequisite to an improved distribution of income within nations as well as among nations. While growth is the product of profit expectations (that is, of greed), it is equally the case that if the utility of additional increments of income diminishes, economic growth also offers the greatest possibility for improving the human capacity for sympathy. This insight is an integral part of the disciplinary memory Robinson has bequeathed us. It is an understanding which has begun to resonate beyond the Robinson scholars to other non-neoclassical thinkers. Perhaps there is less need for pessimism than Robinson thought.

## Notes

1 *Imperfect Competition* also substantially ignores the empirical issues broached by (John) Clapham's "Empty Boxes" (1922) and, in retrospect, falls short of Edward Chamberlin's (1933), because the latter examines the components of strategic pricing behavior in his alternative approach to explain pricing when sellers differentiate their products.

2 Robinson refined and extended the argument in "Euler's Theorem and the Problem of Distribution," written in 1934.

3 It has recently been argued in this connection that a "stages of social history" approach to examining Smith's *Wealth of Nations* makes it clear that it is income distribution and growth and not the theory of exchange value which is of particular concern to him. See Rima (1998).

4 In a memorial review of Robinson's work, Harvey Gram and Vivian Walsh (1983) refer to the distinction she made relating from work and from property as fundamental to all of her thinking and the questions she raised about distribution and accumulation.

5 Robinson notes that Walras's modern followers (Debreu among them) have given up believing *tâtonnement* is possible, and contented themselves with identifying the conditions necessary to ensure that at least one position of equilibrium exists. See Debreu (1953: end footnote).

6 Myer Burstein, in a particularly insightful essay, suggested that Robinson was quite incorrect in identifying Marshall and Pigou as being among her enemies. Rather, he suggests, it is the "new classicals" who deserve her ire (1991: 50).

7 This is not intended to undervalue the important insights into the necessity for addressing the phenomenon of time that is inherent in Gunnar Myrdal's *ex post* concept in *Monetary Equilibrium* (1939: 122).

8 Robinson wrote disparagingly about the misguided "bastard Keynesians" who tried to integrate a market clearing mechanism into Keynesian economics via J. R. Hicks's IS–LM apparatus (1937).

9 James Tobin makes a similar point when he notes that the requirement for continuous market clearing implies an intense commitment to equilibrium against history (Tobin 1980: 21–2).

10 It is precisely Robinson's point which encouraged a later subset of post-Keynesians to focus much of their attention (in particular Davidson, Minsky, Moore, and Kregel) on the role of money as an asset and on the interaction between real and monetary factors.

11 Robinson's work is thus a critical foundation to the work of the late Hyman Minsky, especially in such works as *John Maynard Keynes* (1975), *Can "It" Happen Again?* (1972), and *Stabilizing an Unstable Economy* (1986). The writings of Paul Davidson, in particular *Money and the Real World* (1973), reflect the Robinsonian influence.

12 This Robinsonian insight has been further explored in Rima (1999).

## Bibliography

Asimakopulos, A. (1989) "Joan Robinson and Economic Theory," *Banca Nazionale del Lavoro Quarterly Review* December: 381–409.

Bukharin, N. ([1920] 1979) "The Economics of the Transition Period," in *The Politics and Economics of the Transition Period*, ed. K. J. Tarbuck, London: Routledge & Kegan Paul.

Burstein, M. (1991) "History versus Equilibrium: Joan Robinson and Time in Economics," in Ingrid Rima (ed.) *The Joan Robinson Legacy*, Armonk, NY: M. E. Sharpe.

Chamberlin, E. (1933) *Theory of Monopolistic Competition*, Cambridge, MA: Harvard University Press.

Clapham, J. (1922) "Of Empty Economic Boxes," *Economic Journal* 32: 305–14.

Debreu, G. (1953) "A Social Equilibrium Existence Theorem," *Cowles Commission Papers* NS, No. 46: end footnote.

Eshag, E. (ed.) (1977) "Michal Kalecki Memorial Lectures," *Oxford Bulletin of Economics and Statistics*, Special Issue, Oxford: Basil Blackwell.

Gram, H. (1991) "Value and Capital, Robinson Style," in Ingrid H. Rima (ed.) *The Joan Robinson Legacy*, Armonk, NY: M. E. Sharpe.

Gram, H. and Walsh, V. (1983) "Joan Robinson's Economics in Retrospect," *Journal of Economic Literature* 21: 518–50.

Harcourt, G. C. (1990) "On the Contributions of Joan Robinson and Piero Sraffa to Economic Theory," in C. Sardoni (ed.) *On Political Economics and Modern Political Economy; Selected Essays of G. C. Harcourt*, London and New York: Routledge.

Hicks, J. R. (1937) "Mr. Keynes and the Classics," *Econometrica* 5: 147–59.

—— (1974) *The Crisis in Keynesian Economics*, Oxford: Basil Blackwell.

Kaldor, N. (1959) "Economic Growth and the Problem of Inflation, Part II," *Economica* 26 November: 287–98.

Marshall, A. (1919) *Industry and Trade*, London: Macmillan.

Myrdal, G. (1939) *Monetary Equilibrium*, London: Hodge.

Pigou, A. C. (1912) *Wealth and Welfare*, London: Macmillan.

—— (1920) *The Economics of Welfare*, London: Macmillan.

Rima, I. H. (1991) "Robinson and the Other Half of the Keynesian Revolution," in Ingrid Rima (ed.) *The Joan Robinson Legacy*, Armonk, NY: M. E. Sharpe.

—— (1996) *Labor Markets in a Global Economy*, Armonk, NY: M. E. Sharpe.

—— (1998) "Class Conflict and Adam Smith's 'Stages of Social History'," *Journal of the History of Economic Thought* 20, 1: 103–13.

—— (2000) "Sectoral Changes in Employment: An Eclectic Perspective on Good Jobs and Poor Jobs," *Review of Political Economy* 12, 2.

Robinson, Joan (1933) *The Economics of Imperfect Competition*, London: Macmillan (second edition, 1969).

—— (1936) "Euler's Theorem and the Problem of Distribution," *Economic Journal* 44, September: 398–414; reprinted in Joan Robinson, *Collected Economic Papers*, Vol. 1, Oxford: Blackwell, 1951.

—— (1937a) "Beggar My Neighbour Remedies for Unemployment;" reprinted in Joan Robinson, *Collected Economic Papers*, Vol. 4, Oxford: Blackwell, 1973.

—— (1937b) *Introduction to the Theory of Employment*, London: Macmillan (second edition, 1969).

—— (1938) "Review of C. Bresciani Turroni, *The Economics of Inflation*," *Economic Journal* 48, September: 507–13; reprinted in Joan Robinson, *Collected Economic Papers*, Vol. 1, Oxford: Blackwell, 1951.

—— (1941) "Marx on Unemployment," *Economic Journal* 51, June: 234–48.

—— (1951) "The Rate of Interest," *Econometrica* 19, April: 92–111.

—— (1952) *The Rate of Interest and Other Essays*, London: Macmillan.

—— (1953) "Imperfect Competition Revisited," *Economic Journal* 64, September: 579–93; reprinted in Joan Robinson, *Collected Economic Papers*, Vol. 2, Oxford: Blackwell, 1960.

—— (1956) *The Accumulation of Capital*, London: Macmillan (second edition, 1965; third edition, 1964).

—— (1959) "Some Problems of Definition and Measurement of Capital," *Oxford Economic Papers* 11, June: 157–66; reprinted in Joan Robinson, *Collected Economic Papers*, Vol. 2, Oxford: Blackwell, 1960.

—— (1962a) *Economic Philosophy*, London: Watts; reprinted by Pelican Books, Harmondsworth, 1964.

—— (1962b) *Essays in the Theory of Economic Growth*, London: Macmillan.

—— (1966a) *An Essay on Marx in Economics*, second edition, London: Macmillan (first edition, 1942).

—— (1966b) *The New Mercantilism*, Cambridge: Cambridge University Press; reprinted in Joan Robinson, *Collected Economic Papers*, Vol. 4, Oxford: Blackwell, 1973.

—— (1966c) "Kalecki and Keynes," in *Problems of Economic Dynamics and Planning: Essays in Honor of Michael Kalecki*, Oxford: Pergamon.

—— (1967) "Social Affluence," in C. H. Feinstein (ed.) *Socialism, Capitalism and Economic Growth: Essays in Honor of Maurice Dobb*, Cambridge: Cambridge University Press.

—— (1970) "Quantity Theories Old and New," *Journal of Money Credit and Banking* 2, November: 504–13.

—— (1971a) *Economic Heresies*, London: Basic Books.

—— (1971b) "Capital Theory Up-to-date: The End of Controversy," *Economic Journal* 81, September: 597–602; reprinted in Joan Robinson, *Collected Economic Papers*, Vol. 4, Oxford: Blackwell, 1973.

—— (1972) "The Second Crisis in Economic Theory," *American Economic Review* 62, May: 1–9; reprinted in Joan Robinson, *Collected Economic Papers*, Vol. 4, Oxford: Blackwell, 1973.

—— (1973a) "The Need for a Reconsideration of the Theory of International Trade," in M. B. Connoly and A. K. Swoboda (eds) *International Trade and Money*, London: Allen and Unwin; reprinted in Joan Robinson, *Collected Economic Papers*, Vol. 4, Oxford: Blackwell, 1973.

—— (ed.) (1973b) *After Keynes*, Papers presented to Section F (Economics) at the 1972 Annual Meeting of the British Association for the Advancement of Science, London: Basil Blackwell.

—— (1973c) (with John Eatwell) *An Introduction to Modern Economics*, London: McGraw-Hill (second edition 1974).

—— (1974) "History versus Equilibrium", *Thames Papers in Political Economy*; reprinted in *Collected Economic Papers*, Vol. 5, 1979, Oxford: Blackwell, 1979.

—— (1977a) "Michal Kalecki on the Economics of Capitalism," *Oxford Bulletin of Economics and Statistics* 39, February: 7–17; reprinted in Joan Robinson, *Collected Economic Papers*, Vol. 5, Oxford: Blackwell, 1979.

—— (1977b) "What are the Questions?" *Journal of Economic Literature* 15, 4: 1318–39.

—— (1979a) *The Generalization of the General Theory and Other Essays*, London: Macmillan.

—— (1979b) Foreword to K. Kuhne, *Economics and Marxism*, London: Macmillan, vii–xv.

—— (1979c) "History versus Equilibrium," reprinted in *Collected Economic Papers*, Vol. 5, Oxford: Blackwell, 1979.

—— (1980) "Time in Economic Theory," *Kyklos* 33, 2: 219–29; reprinted in Joan Robinson, *Collected Economic Papers*, Vol. 5, Oxford: Blackwell, 1979.

—— (1982a) "The Current State of Economics," *Contributions to Political Economy* (i), March: 47–9.

—— (1982b) "Shedding Darkness," (a review of A. Leijonhufvud, *Information and Coordination: Essays in Macroeconomic Theory*), in *Cambridge Journal of Economics* 6, September: 295–6.

—— (1985) "Spring Cleaning," in G. R. Feiwell (ed.) *Issues in Contemporary Microeconomics and Welfare*, London: Macmillan (published posthumously).

Schumpeter, J. (1954) *A History of Economic Analysis*, New York: Oxford University Press.

Shackle, G. L. (1954) *Uncertainty in Economics*, Cambridge: Cambridge University Press.

—— (1972) *Epistemics and Economics*, Cambridge: Cambridge University Press.

Smith, Adam ([1776] 1937) *The Wealth of Nations*, Modern Library Edition, ed. Edwin Canaan.

—— ([1776] 1978) *Lectures on Jurisprudence*, ed. R. L. Meek, P. G. Stein, and D. D. Raphael.

Sraffa, Piero (1926) "The Laws of Return Under Competitive Conditions," *Economic Journal* 36, December: 535–50.

Tobin, J. (1980) *Asset Accumulation and Economic Activity*, Chicago: University of Chicago Press and Oxford: Basil Blackwell, 21–2.

Veblen, T. (1942a) "Professor Clark's Economics," in *The Place of Science in Modern Civilization and Other Essays*, New York: Viking Press, 186–230.

—— (1942b) "On the Nature of Capital I and II," in *The Place of Science in Modern Civilization and Other Essays*, New York: Viking Press, 324–80.

Weintraub, S. (1959a) *A General Theory of the Price Level*, Philadelphia: Chilton.

—— (1959b) *Classical Keynesianism, Monetary Theory and the Price Level*, Philadelphia: Chilton.

Young, Allyn (1928) "Increasing Returns and Economic Progress," *Economic Journal* 38: 527–42.

# 15 Henry William Spiegel

## Historian of economic thought

*Steven G. Medema and Warren J. Samuels**

At the beginning of his essay on Jacob Viner as intellectual historian, the first essay in the collection to which this collection is a sequel, Donald Winch wrote that

> Jacob Viner belonged to a generation of economists for whom the history of economic thought was neither a subspecialism within economics nor a hobby reserved for off-duty moments and the retirement years. A broad, though not necessarily profound, knowledge of those writings of past economists which had, for one reason or another, acquired classic status was a normal part of the early educational pattern; and this knowledge could keep its value later as a means of situating modern debates. No special virtue or vice was attached to this: it was more a matter of the rela-tionship between the size of the accumulated stock of accepted knowledge and the rate at which additions were being made to it than a sign of special learning or undue conservatism.
>
> (Winch 1983: 1)

This description and these sentiments apply to Henry William Spiegel (October 13, 1911–July 24, 1995) and his work as an economist and historian of economic thought. Spiegel was widely read and deeply educated. He considered training in the history of economic thought to be an important part of both liberal education and the professional training and work of an economist. He went to unusual efforts to both extend and promote the learning of historical knowledge of economic ideas. He was, alas, truly of an earlier generation in his scholarship.

Spiegel was a perceptive and judicious scholar. He was also a self-effacing and diffident man. He was not a joiner of organizations, or, if a member, not an active one; he worked largely independently, for example attending only one annual meeting of the History of Economics Society. But for all his diffidence, he did not shrink from undertaking ambitious and powerful projects in the history of economic thought, several of which were pioneering. Spiegel wrote a number of articles on the history of economic thought, though not as many as he might, and should, have. His major contributions were books: *The*

Development of Economic Thought (1952) brought together both previously published and newly commissioned materials on economists summarizing and, especially, interpreting the work of other economists. The Rise of American Economic Thought (1960) collected, introduced, and interpreted the work of some two-dozen early American economists and several important episodes prior to 1886. The Growth of Economic Thought (1971, third edition 1991) became the leading undergraduate textbook in the field, achieving something of a magisterial reputation. And so on. Through these works Henry Spiegel became, with Joseph Dorfman, one of the leading historians of American economic thought, and of general economic thought as well.

In this essay we examine the life and work of Henry Spiegel. The first section presents a biographical sketch of the man. The second treats his work as an historian of economic thought. The third considers some historiographical issues raised by his work.

## Biographical sketch

Henry W. Spiegel was born in Berlin, Germany, on October 13, 1911. His father died when Henry was 9 and his mother when he was 16. He studied classics at the Friederich-Wilhelms Gymnasium of Berlin, graduating in 1930. He studied law at the Universities of Heidelberg, Cologne, and Berlin – transferring from one university to another, as was then customary among Continental students – receiving the Doctor of Laws degree (JUD) from the University of Berlin in the momentous year, 1933. At Berlin, Spiegel was a student of Arthur Nussbaum, the founder of Rechtstatsachenforschung (a school of legal thought inquiring into the active versus inactive status of statutory law in the practice of law), a specialist in the legal aspects of money, and subsequently for many years at the Law School of Columbia University.

Spiegel's training at Berlin had been the standard one for lawyers. His eventual goal was a judicial career. Although he passed the first state examination he did not receive the usual appointment, because of the Nazis. He eventually went, in 1936, to Cornell University on a fellowship to study under George F. Warren. After one semester at Cornell, having decided that agricultural economics approached from the farm management point of view was not his interest, Spiegel transferred to the University of Wisconsin, then the center of work in institutional economics under students of the recently retired John R. Commons, many of whom were prominent in the field of labor economics. Although Commons no longer taught on a regular basis, Spiegel got to know him well. At Wisconsin Spiegel established lifelong friendships with the economist Walter Morton and the later political scientist William Ebenstein, then a fellow student. Among his other fellow students at Wisconsin were Walter Heller and Joseph Pechman, who became distinguished specialists in public finance, as was their professor, Harold Groves. Another fellow student was the development specialist, Everett Hagen. Spiegel received his Ph.D. in economics there in 1939, working under George S. Wehrwein.

As a youth Spiegel had supplemented his income through journalism. He published, inter alia, two long leaders in the Neue Zuericher, Zeitung (July 8, and August 21 and 22, 1936), the first on war economics and the second on the debate about nationalization of the munitions industry.

While at Wisconsin Spiegel regularly visited the University of Chicago and Jacob Viner and Frank Knight. Viner introduced Spiegel to the work of Pierre Nicole, the Jansenist priest who had argued that charity and self-love may be equally conducive to the welfare of society. Spiegel was the first to introduce Nicole into the English economic literature (in the first edition of The Growth of Economic Thought, 1971).

While at the University of Berlin, Spiegel's doctoral dissertation, prepared under Nussbaum, was published as Der Pachtvertrag der Kleingartenvereine (1933) (Lease Contracts of Small Gardeners' Associations). During the period 1937–39 he published eight articles mainly in law journals. These were principally in German publications but one was in the American Journal of International Law (1938) and was subsequently republished in 1969 in a collection of leading articles from that journal. His Wisconsin doctoral dissertation was published as Land Tenure Policies at Home and Abroad (1941).

Spiegel's first academic appointment, in 1939, was at Duquesne University as assistant professor of economics. There he declined an invitation, offered on the basis of his doctorate in law, to become dean of the law school; one wonders what mark he might have left on legal scholarship and education had he chosen that career. He left Duquesne in 1942 for service in the United States Army, serving first in the quartermaster corps, then in intelligence, and finally in the Office of Strategic Services (the famous OSS), along with numerous other economists, some already well known and others later to become distinguished, including Edward Mason, Moses Abromovitz, Charles Kindleberger, Charles Hitch, W. W. Rostow, E. M. Hoover, Lloyd Metzler, Albert Hirschman, Paul Baran, and others. During this period Spiegel developed friendships with Fritz Machlup and P. T. Ellsworth as well as the great jurist and legal philosopher, Hans Kelsen. After a brief tour of duty with the Department of State, in 1945 Spiegel went on a Guggenheim Fellowship to study the Brazilian economy. He returned to teaching in 1946 as associate professor at Catholic University, where he had been a part-time lecturer since 1943. He became full professor in 1950 and retired in 1977, having directed some twenty doctoral dissertations. Spiegel was a visiting professor at several universities, including Wisconsin, Johns Hopkins, Michigan State, Virginia, Washington, Maryland, California at Berkeley and Santa Barbara, and the Industrial College of the Armed Forces.

Spiegel became a naturalized American citizen on March 10, 1943 in Circuit Court in Hagerstown, MD, changing his first name from Hans (the name under which his earlier writings had been published) to Henry. He married Cecile Wassermann in 1947; they raised two sons brought to the marriage by their mother, their father having been murdered by the Nazis during the war.

Spiegel was involved intermittently in public service while at Catholic University. He served on the staff of the President's Material Policy

Commission, whose report was published in 1952. In the same year he served as consultant to the Public Advisory Board for Mutual Security, and in 1962 served as consultant to the chairman of the Committee on Public Works of the US House of Representatives. In 1958 he served on a research project concerned with the value of forest roads in Idaho, financed by the US Bureau of Public Roads.

Spiegel published pioneering works in several fields, notably *The Economics of Total War* (1942) and *The Brazilian Economy: Chronic Inflation and Sporadic Industrialization* (1949a). In 1949 he published *Current Economic Problems* (1949b) with a second edition appearing in 1955 and a third in 1961. In 1951 he published *Introduction to Economics*.

Spiegel's study of the Brazilian economy is worth noting in passing. It identified a strong tendency for "permanent inflation" as an accompaniment of development and industrialization in less developed countries. It also emphasized the sporadic nature of industrialization under conditions of both international and domestic inequality, precluding the development of a strong domestic consumption sector. Among the interrelated variables stressed by him were non-democratic and autocratic regimes, the lack of advancement in the health and education of the masses as a precondition of productivity, and the distributions of income and wealth. The volume is noteworthy for its emphasis on the political economy of development rather than the narrow, technical conditions of growth; its focus on the problem of saving and investment in a country in which most people live in poverty and the rich are not interested in industrialization; and its attempt to use limitedly available national income and other statistics.

Spiegel's principal reputation as a magisterial scholar rests, however, on his work as an historian of economic thought.

## Spiegel's work as historian of economic thought

*The Development of Economic Thought*, published in 1952, presented a unique collection of essays by great economists on the work of other great economists (a Japanese translation was published in 1955). Spiegel later revealed that it had been inspired by Edmund Wilson's *Shock of Recognition* (1943). Many entries comprised reprints of earlier writings; others were newly commissioned original assessments. The collection is of particular interest for hermeneutical purposes: The individual essays represent evaluations of individual authors from the particular perspective of other authors.

The coverage is from Aristotle on Plato to Paul A. Samuelson on John Maynard Keynes and Colin Clark on Arthur Cecil Pigou. The year 1952 was probably too early for him to have included essays on John R. Hicks and Samuelson; after all, not until 1954, and even then only with great prescience, did we read language in Joseph Schumpeter's *History of Economic Analysis* indicating that economists were then in the age of Hicks and Samuelson; at any rate, and surely wisely, they were not included (though an essay by Gottfried

Haberler on Schumpeter himself was). The entries are divided into six groups: The Dawn of Economic Science (Plato through the Physiocrats), The Classical School (Smith through Say), Socialists and Reformers (Sismondi through the Webbs), Historical and Institutional Approaches (Roscher through Mitchell), The Rise of Marginalism (von Thünen through J. B. Clark), and The Growth of Modern Economics (Edgeworth through Pigou).

Spiegel thus carried the history of economic thought up to the then near-present, although restricting his analysis to those scholars who, with the exception of Pigou, were already deceased. He did not believe that the study of the history of economic thought should cease with the previous generation. That is, of course, a matter of judgment – one with which Joseph Dorfman, for one, disagreed.

The design strategy for the volume is stated in the Preface (Spiegel 1952: ix–x). It is a story of great men discussing other great men, "who are here acting out the story of which they themselves are the heroes, telling us what they think about each other." The collection is intentionally "international in scope and representative of a multiplicity of points of view." It displays the market-place of great ideas: "The very profusion of ideas, it is hoped, will prove a challenge to the critical mind, and a wholesome antidote against any narrow dogmatism of the Keynesian or other variety." Spiegel also notes that the intended focus is both on individuals and not schools of thought, and "literary" rather than mathematical (though Frisch on Wicksell is intentionally given as an example of such work).

The Rise of American Economic Thought (1960) brought together, introduced, and interpreted the work of some two-dozen early American economists and several important episodes prior to 1886. The episodes were Puritan Economic Thought and the founding of the American Economic Association in 1885, the former comprising the beginning and the latter the end of the story told in the book. Among the individuals included were Franklin, Hamilton, Jefferson, Raymond, Cardozo, Tucker, and Mathew and Henry C. Carey, as well as Amasa and Francis A. Walker, George J. B. Clark, and Simon Newcomb. This book, together with other writings, helped make Spiegel one of the leading scholars on the development of economic thought in the United States; it helped make the history of American economic thought coherent.

The rationale for the volume is chiefly to overcome scarcity: most of the contents were not readily available to teachers of the subject.[1] The book is enriched by a ten-page bibliography divided into the following sections: American Thought, General Works on American Economics, Special Phases of Economics, The Seventeenth Century, sections on the individual authors, The Founding of the American Economic Association, and Later Developments. The mind of the reader is truly stretched.

The Growth of Economic Thought (1971; Spanish translation, 1973; 3rd edition, 1991), in contrast, is a conventional textbook, not a collection. It quickly became a, if not the, leading undergraduate textbook in the field, the standard of comparison. This great work combines the two leading approaches to disciplinary history in economics. On the one hand, Spiegel emphasized the link between economics and the humanities, relating the evolution of the field to general culture and to philosophical and other intellectual developments, all requiring a relatively broad conception of the scope and origins of economics. On the other, he attended to the details of the internal development of economic theory and technique. In both respects he avoided caricatures by relating the substance and development of economic ideas in their enormous complexity with more detail and more accuracy than is typical in such texts.

The coverage of the book is substantial – indeed, encyclopedic – comparable only in its range to Schumpeter (1954) among works of the last half-century. While lacking the minute detail of coverage evidenced in Schumpeter, it nonetheless has all of the basic elements necessary to present a well-rounded and balanced picture of the history of economic thought. The book begins with topics in biblical and ancient Greek economic thought and ends with a discussion of the development of modern general equilibrium theory and econometrics – carrying on the notion of bringing the history of economic thought up to the present that he had established in *The Development of Economic Thought*. The substantive strengths of the book reside in its elaborate attention to the development of economics between mercantilism and classical economics; its careful articulation of the liberalist origins and assumptions of orthodox economic theory; its elaborate discussion of both the Hegelian and Baconian variants of historicism; its attention to the Cambridge (England) school as such, rather than only to the contributions of Alfred Marshall; its treatment of American economic thought; and, *inter alia*, its magnificent bibliographical review. The third edition of 1991 updated its bibliographical coverage and examined the diversity and new alignments of contemporary economic thought.

Depending upon one's perspective and motives, the broad sweep of the work may be a refreshing contrast to the too-often typical view that economic thought began more or less around the time of Adam Smith and that a survey of the history of economic thought involves drawing a line from Smith to the present and rarely swerving from it. This is not to denigrate the usefulness and import of the canon; indeed, one may consider a shortcoming of *The Growth of Economic Thought* to be that it does not devote sufficient depth of attention to certain of the most important canonical works (in contrast with, for example, Blaug's *Economic Theory in Retrospect* (1996)). Putting to the side the nuances of meaning associated with the terms "thought," "analysis," and "theory," Spiegel's book is clearly, as its title suggests, a history of economic *thought* rather than of economic analysis or economic theory. Reviewers were uniformly impressed with its author's erudition, judgment, and catholicity of viewpoint. The book cemented Spiegel's place as a foremost historian of economic thought.

Only a few alterations were made in the 1983 and 1991 revisions. The first was an updating of the annotated bibliography, which ran to 130 pages of relatively small type in the first edition and expanded to 160 pages by the 1991 edition. One can make the argument that these bibliographical notes –

invaluable both for the scholar who wishes to track down all manner of sources or the student who wishes to write a term paper – can justly be considered one of the book's most valuable resources. The second alteration, made in the 1983 edition, was the inclusion of a new chapter entitled "An Expanded Profession in Search of New Frontiers," a chapter discussing the character and state of the economics profession over the period since the first edition was published and presenting Spiegel's commentary on recent trends within economic thought. The final alteration, made in the 1991 edition, was the inclusion of a new introductory chapter that discusses various historiographical issues in economics – touching on, for example, the progressivity of economic thought and the attendant potential burden of anachronistically employing ideas from one epoch in later periods to which they are not well suited, the historical contingency of ideas, the archaeology of knowledge, the role of rhetoric in economic analysis and argumentation, the forces of ideology, and the role of nationality. In doing so, Spiegel gives the reader a stronger sense not only for the perspective in which he frames his discussion, but for the diversity of historiographic perspectives from which one can examine the history of economic thought.

Some thirty or so years after Spiegel published The Development of Economic Thought, Warren Samuels approached him about updating the period of coverage in a sequel. Henry readily agreed. The concept was the same in one key respect: established economists writing on the work of other leading economists. One concept, however, was different: the economists who would be their subjects were for the most part alive. Although exceptionally well established, they often were still actively working. This became in part an exercise in contemporary history of economic thought; but perhaps more so an exercise in contemporary summarization, systematization, interpretation, and critique – substantially more contemporary than The Development of Economic Thought had been.[2] Indeed, they called the resulting two-volume collection Contemporary Economists in Perspective (1984). Neither co-editor had serious reservations about the project, though they did discuss the limitations.

Fortunately they were able to reprint the essays on the Nobelists from the Scandinavian (formerly Swedish) Journal of Economics. The others were commissioned. All but one prospective author produced the agreed-upon essay; alas, the essay on Robert M. Solow was not forthcoming, becoming a serious omission. A number of these other scholars have since become Nobelists (though it was not the editors' intention to predict winners).

Together Samuels and Spiegel chose the names of subjects and authors for commission. The general structure of the collection Samuels remembers as being largely Spiegel's idea. Part I covered Varieties of Mainstream Economics, with five subsections: Generalists; Specialists; Keynesians, Fiscalists, and Post-Keynesians; Anti-Keynesians and Monetarists; and Econometric and Quantitative Techniques. Part II was entitled Eddies in the Mainstream. Part III encompassed Varieties of Heterodox Economics, with two subsections: Marxism the Cambridge Controversy, and The Further Development of Institutional Economics (partly misprinted as Industrial Economics). The subjects who were the eddies in the mainstream, by the way, were Jacob Marschak, Kenneth Boulding, Herbert Simon, George Katona, François Perroux, James Buchanan, and George Shackle.

Samuels and his research assistant, Michael Plummer, proofread the pages, a point mentioned merely to say that it was only at that time, and not when Samuels had initially read the manuscripts, that he recognized how truly widespread was a continuing theme or subtext the presence of which he should have both anticipated and observed earlier but did not. This was the ubiquitous explicit attention given by macroeconomists to the problem of uncertainty and the diverse ways in which the subjects had dealt with it. And of course, the story of economists' handling of uncertainty did not end then.

Throughout his career Spiegel published numerous articles in economics journals on a variety of history-of-thought subjects, plus many book reviews and encyclopedia entries. His articles include work on the theory and history of the concept of the entrepreneur; economic growth and development; Adam Smith; and the business and government course in the economics curriculum.

Some of the work embodied in Spiegel's periodical articles call for extended comment. Similar to *The Development of Economic Thought*, a few of the articles were stimulated by ideas outside of the realm of economics, having emerged in philosophy of science or historical studies. They demonstrate an intellectual grasp that both went beyond economics proper and deepened his understanding of economic ideas. Spiegel's article on the history of the equilibrium concept elaborates suggestions found in Alexandre Koyre's *Metaphysics and Measurement* (1968). His article on Smith's *Heavenly City* was inspired by Carl Becker's *Heavenly City of the Eighteenth-Century Philosophers* (1932). The former article reviews the entire history of economic thought and divides its leading figures into Platonists and Aristotelians. The main branch of the Platonist tradition considers the economic universe as mathematically ordered, while the Aristotelians are inclined to practice a look-and-see approach. Side by side with the main branch of the Platonist tradition and at times intermingled with it, there is visualized by Spiegel a second branch of Platonism, one that is hermetic, mystical, or magical. These distinctions shed new light on the contributions of a number of authors, for example Petty and Boisguilbert, to name but two.

Adam Smith is generally considered to have been an illustrious figure of the Enlightenment or Age of Reason. In the second article here reviewed, Spiegel examines some thought structures of *The Wealth of Nations* that reflect spiritual and intellectual influences stemming from configurations of the mind that antedate the Enlightenment or run counter to its central tendency, the enthronement of reason that interprets the world without recourse to the supernatural. The four themes selected for discussion are Smith's view of human nature, the role of secular eschatologies in his thought, the magic of numbers, and the providential function of the market. Spiegel concludes that, while Smith did not fall under the spell of the magic of numbers, the discussion of the three other themes indicates Smith's use of pre-Enlightenment patterns of thought. Amidst the profusion of articles about Smith that were published on the occasion of the bicentennial of his great work, this article stands out in breaking a new path toward the interpretation of *The Wealth of Nations* in an approach that has an affinity also with the work of Isaiah Berlin on pre- and anti-Enlightenment forces. Spiegel's work helps place Smith's analyses in perspective and it also explains how they were grounded in several modes of thought, namely supernaturalism, naturalism, rationalism, empiricism, historicism, and so on.

In his last articles, "Ethnicity and Economics" and "Refugee Economists and the Mathematization of Economics" (Spiegel 1994, 1997), Spiegel branches out into sociology of knowledge and develops a law to the effect that as far as economics is concerned, multi-ethnicity is positively related to a higher level of abstraction in economic discourse. This general proposition, one of the few applicable to the history of economics, is illustrated with the help of several test cases arranged in ascending order of abstractness: the national appeal of the historical school, mercantilist militancy, the cosmopolitan appeal of the physiocrats, Carl Menger's pure economics, and the mathematization of economics amidst the multi-ethnic world of the twentieth century, especially that created in the United States by Austrian and other refugee economists in the 1930s. While it is often argued that multi-ethnicity makes for multicultural diversity, rivalry, or cultural domination, Spiegel maintains that with respect to economics the experience has been different.

Spiegel published in 1955 a pamphlet, reproducing for the first time, Du Pont's diagram of 1774, which, apart from Daniel Bernoulli's famous analysis of utility published in 1738, was possibly the earliest use of geometry in economics. Spiegel's contributions to *The New Palgrave: A Dictionary of Economics* – numbering twenty-one in all – were among the most numerous by a single author. These essays are illustrative of Spiegel's great breadth of expertise, as they range over Xenophon, the scholastics, Thomas Wilson, Benjamin Franklin, Alexander Hamilton, Matthew Carey, Thomas Pownall, Constantino Bresciani-Turroni, François Perroux, Arthur Burns, and numerous other figures both major and minor (Eatwell *et al.* 1987; for a complete listing, see Vol. 4: 961).[3] He also served on the editorial boards of several professional journals and was a member of several professional organizations.

## Some historiographical issues

Warren Samuels, among many other historians of economic thought, has used *The Growth of Economic Thought* as an undergraduate textbook, and for many years.[4] Samuels has used it along with the textbooks of either Ray Canterbery or E. K. Hunt. The students have been told that the Spiegel text is a straightforward account, attempting to tell the history of economic thought as it developed, without an interpretive or ideological agenda; whereas the second text, Canterbery or Hunt, presents an account that is intentionally and explicitly critical of the way in which economic thought has developed. The students have also been told that they should attempt similarly to identify the approach taken in the lectures, along one and/or another line.

But what does it mean to say that *The Growth of Economic Thought* tells the history of economic thought as it developed, without an interpretive or ideological agenda? For Samuels's students are also told that the history of economic thought is socially constructed; that much work in the field is presentist and Whiggish, the former taking as an interpretive basis what economics is today, and the latter interpreting the past as the right or wrong route to the essentially correct present; that the history of economic thought can be interpreted differently from different perspectives; that any history is inexorably selective and interpretive; and so on. Is *The Growth of Economic Thought* an ideological and interpretive book? The answer is complex and subtle but, on balance, no.

The subject matter reflects choices of inclusion/exclusion and emphasis reflective of what economics has become, and not of what it might have, but did not, become. The meaning and importance accorded particular figures is inescapably interpretive. For example, in contrast to many accounts (including Samuels's own lectures), the student reading Spiegel's account of Alfred Marshall will find him to be less epochly important. That said, it remains the case, we believe, that Spiegel's account is very little driven by ideology and selective interpretation. He attempts to present the ideas of individual writers as he thinks these authors held them, and, while by no means devoid of personal and disciplinary influence, not how others have interpreted them. More importantly, he has no agenda – no intention to promote neoclassical, institutionalist, Austrian, Keynesian, or any other school of thought, which differentiates his book from most others. Still, that he has a humanistic and philosophical approach to the subject is unquestionably an interpretive matter. Most importantly, however, Spiegel attempts to equip the reader with, as he put it in *The Development of Economic Thought*, a "critical mind, and a wholesome antidote against any narrow dogmatism" (Spiegel 1952: ix). Which is to say that for Spiegel, however much interpretation and ideology may be – yes, is – inevitable, his work as an historian of economic thought was itself the antidote to narrow and dogmatic presentism and Whiggism.

The answer, therefore, is that the question of Spiegel's ideological and interpretive position is not simply answered. In several respects his book is non-ideological and non-interpretive; in others, not so. Still, its reputation as a relatively straightforward account seems warranted. More than that, the book displays both the multiplicity of economic points of view and their deepest philosophical foundations in such a way as to enable the reader to hold ideological and interpretive beliefs at arm's length, not necessarily to reject them but to see them both for what they are and in the larger context in which they have meaning.

Moving on to another matter, it is clear that *The Growth of Economic Thought* (and most of his other writings in the field) takes a cultural and humanist, even philosophical, approach to the history of economic thought (though, as already noted, it also centers on the development of the core body of conventional, and heterodox, economic theory). Spiegel's approach was that of an intellectual historian; his was not a retrospective of economic theory alone and in a vacuum. As Ingrid Rima pointed out at the 1997 History of Economics Society conference in a session memorializing Spiegel, for him the history of economic thought was a subset of, in Michel Foucault's term, the archaeology of human knowledge.[5]

In the preface to the first edition of *The Growth of Economic Thought*, Spiegel sets out the broad-based nature of his approach to the subject, noting that:

> It has been my aim to strengthen the link between economics and the humanities and to relate the history of economic thought to the intellectual tendencies of the various periods. This meant that a cultural approach was chosen rather than a technical one that would convert earlier ideas into mathematical models. The inclusion of biographical detail again underlines the humanistic orientation of the work and enhances the human-interest appeal. If attention is paid to the spirit of an age and to the personal history of a writer, new insights are opened up that disclose why economic thought took a certain turn at a given time.
>
> (1971: vii)

While this might incline the reader to infer that Spiegel is walking down the road of relativism (externalism) here, such is not the case. It is, rather, an instance – and an early one at that – of a view of the history of economic thought as intellectual history, where ideas (but not necessarily the evaluation of their efficacy or correctness) are a function of the general intellectual milieu within which they arise. Even so, Spiegel does not neglect to attempt to discuss how ideas across time hang together, or what their relationship might be to more modern forms of economic analysis. His treatment attempts to address and bring out the answer to the question "How did a writer or his school propose to cope with the fundamental economic problem of scarcity?" (1971: vii) over the course of economic thought. As such, the book demonstrates both an organizing principle for the modern student of economics and an exposure to the relationship between economic ideas and the context within which they were developed.

Remarking on the distinction between Spiegel's text and others written in the field (including her own) during the past forty years, Ingrid Rima says that:

> The essential difference between the older history of economic thought and the newer history of economic analysis lies in the objective of giving the student proficiency in understanding the nature of the economist's "box of tools" and the way in which improvements in technique, new information, and changes in institutions over historical time have reshaped the problems of particular eras. There is no room in this approach for concern about historical antecedents for their own sake; on the other hand, the final product emerges as a historically conscious presentation of the essentials of modern economics.
>
> (Rima, in Moss 1998: 353)

Rima suggests that given the course that economics has taken over the past several decades, the modern textbook approach "seems a more meaningful approach to teaching the history of economics than teaching intellectual history to a generation of students who have little or no knowledge of the history of Western Civilization" (ibid.: 354–5).

But this approach for Spiegel was not merely a matter of exploring philosophical topics because they were relevant. For Spiegel, the history of economic thought was more complex than presentist and Whiggish accounts reveal. In particular, he appreciated that economic theory and analysis could be conducted in ways quite different from the sense most economists think to be "theoretical" and "analytical" today. The history of economic thought is, in part, precisely an account of these other forms of doing economic theory and analysis. Specifically, Spiegel was aware that while economic theory, as most economists know it, is the product of market-driven economies, economies are more than markets, and pure markets (however useful may be the concept) do not exist; actual, institutionally, and culturally driven markets exist. Harald Hagemann (in Moss 1998: 348) attributes this attitude to Spiegel's early education, noting that

> Spiegel's training in Germany was that of a lawyer. He was not an economist and certainly not a mathematical economist. But training in the law makes a person more open to institutional and historical [phenomena] than does training in mathematical factors.

For Spiegel, the history of economic thought was not merely a way of remembering past schools of thought and past thinkers; it was a way of indicating that these past authors had something to say of importance. The issue is not whether, relative to modern hegemonic theory, they were right or wrong. The issue is that they had something to say which modern hegemonic theory tends to both ignore and obfuscate. In this respect, in particular, Spiegel's work was an antidote to narrow and dogmatic presentism and Whiggism.

## Spiegel as referee

Spiegel's profound interest in the secondary literature in the field is well established through the extensive annotated bibliographies that accompanied his *Rise of American Economic Thought* and *Growth of Economic Thought*. He also played a not insignificant role in the resurgence of scholarship in the history of economic thought in the 1970s and 1980s through his work as a referee for *History of Political Economy* – at that time the only journal published in English that was devoted to the history of economic thought.[6] Spiegel refereed nearly sixty papers for *HOPE* between 1971 and 1985, and an average of more than five per year during the 1970s – a relatively high percentage of the total submissions, given the flow of manuscripts to *HOPE* at that time. His recommendations were fairly evenly distributed between acceptance and rejection. The papers that he was asked to review run the gamut of the field, no doubt derivative of the generalist strength evidenced in his published works. His reports are very brief and to the point – only a few run beyond a one-page letter, and many are as short as a couple of paragraphs. Yet one would be greatly mistaken to infer from this that Spiegel devoted little effort to this process; his reports are direct and straight to the heart of the matter of why the paper in question was or was not suitable for publication in HOPE, and in a way that indicated deep acquaintance with the paper's contents.

The question that seems to have guided Spiegel in his evaluation of the papers – a theme that recurs throughout his reports – is: "Will this paper hold the reader's interest?" He seems to have taken it for granted that the readership would be broadly interested in good work, just as he himself was, for he was very quick to note when a subject was novel or under-analyzed in the literature and the usefulness of bringing this to the attention of the journal's readers. His reports also evidence his broad acquaintance with the primary and secondary literatures, from the prominent to the highly obscure. Yet, he was charitable in acknowledging when he was out of his element and in suggesting the names of additional reviewers (sometimes from other disciplines) whom he felt might be able to provide a different and better perspective than that reflected in his own comments – particularly when his review was negative.

His ideas of what would or would not interest the reader – in a sense, his standards for good work – are much in evidence. He had little tolerance for the simple *presentation* of ideas without accompanying *analysis* of them. In one instance, he lauds a paper because "It does not merely report but investigates some sort of hypothesis" (letter of November 21, 1973). In another case, he said: "I can discern no theme, no organization of the material, no attempt at disciplined thinking. What I find is only vapid rhetoric" (letter of October 19, 1982) – one of his few truly harsh assessments, for his tone in these reports was almost always highly civil. He was the enemy of sloppy writing, poor documentation, and hagiography. Despite the brevity of his reports, he tended to be a stickler for word usage. In one case, he objected to the use of the word "saeculo," pointing out that "This is the dative case of the word saeculum. I am unable to see why the dative case would be appropriate here" (letter of June 18, 1975). Regarding hagiography, remarking on a paper dealing with a tremendously obscure subject which the author (but not the referee) obviously thought was of enormous import, Spiegel offered that "the presentation is much too uncritical and reads like an advertisement of a patent medicine" (letter of January 27, 1984).

His reactions also evidence a desire to see the sort of "big picture" – that is, the history of economic thought as intellectual history – perspective reflected in his own work. In one instance, he suggested the publication of a paper authored by a French scholar in the early 1970s because "It will give our readers a taste of the French approach to the history of economics, which has much of the charm of literary criticism" (letter of November 21, 1973). On the other side of the coin, he criticizes another paper because:

It is a somewhat austere piece, exclusively about [—]'s *thought*, with little background information about the man himself, his role in the [—] movement, the ideas which influenced him and which he influenced, and the socio-economic forces which may have conditioned his thought.

(Letter of May 7, 1973; emphasis in original)

And he had little sympathy for the sort of Whiggishness that harshly condemned the work of earlier thinkers based upon modern standards. Reacting to a paper that demonstrated and criticized the incompleteness of and contradictions within [—]'s value theory and argued that it was simply a by-product of his policy concerns, Spiegel pointed out that: "There are only a few ideas in the history of economics that emerged immediately in the form of a comprehensive and consistent theory. Often they first emerge as fragments, replete with contradictions, and loaded with policy implications" (letter of April 10, 1983). It was Spiegel's view that this type of reasoning was OK, and needs to be understood as such. Considering ideas in context allows one to get some insight into how they emerged and why they might have taken the form that they did – that there is more to doing the history of economic thought than analyzing and evaluating in terms of "A was wrong and B was right." It is not that such judgments did not matter for Spiegel; it is just that this is only one part, and perhaps even a relatively small one, of the story to be told by intellectual history.

## Conclusion

We have attempted in this essay to present a portrait of Henry Spiegel's work in the history of economic thought and, in doing so, to illustrate how, for Spiegel, examining the history of economic thought was, first and foremost, an exercise in intellectual history. Motivated by this perspective, Spiegel's work evidences the diversity that characterizes the history of economics rather than reconstructing the field along a straight line that ends in the present. He was thus at the vanguard of the movement over the last few decades away from a Whiggish approach and toward a more sensitive, scholarly treatment that provides new and richer insights into the history of the field by bringing in (in his case) cultural and philosophical factors that bore heavily on the development of ideas.

## Notes

*   The authors are, respectively, Professor of Economics at the University of Colorado at Denver and Professor Emeritus of Economics at Michigan State University. We would like to thank Craufurd Goodwin, Harald Hagemann, Cecile Spiegel, and Robert Byrd and the staff of the Rare Book, Manuscript, and Special Collections Library at Duke University for their assistance in the preparation of this essay.
1   Even today, some forty years later, the history of American economic thought (especially that prior to the twentieth century) remains an under-examined subject.

2   Since then Samuels (at times with Medema) has undertaken two and perhaps three strands of sequels. One of them is represented by New Horizons in Economic Thought (1992) and American Economists of the Late Twentieth Century (1996), which bring the task of examining contemporary economists, however incompletely, increasingly into the present. The two volumes are celebrations of diversity in economics. A possible third is in the earliest planning stage.
    The second is represented by volume 1 of Research in the History of Economic Thought and Methodology, entitled "The Craft of the Historian of Economic Thought," and by the sequel of which this essay is a part. In both, accomplished historians of economic thought summarize, interpret, and critique the work of other leading historians of economic thought.
    The third is the collection which Medema and Samuels have published, The Foundations of Research in Economics: How Do Economists Do Economics? (1996). This collection does not have the economists-on-other-economists characteristic but it does have both contemporariness, self-reflection, and celebration of diversity.
    All these projects we consider to be contributions to understanding how contemporary work participates in the working out of the development of economics as an intellectual discipline and to enabling economists to be more alert to what they are doing.
    We mention these projects because, in a very profound sense, they are the intellectual grandchildren of Spiegel's The Development of Economic Thought – grandchildren not quite in the image of the grandfather but close enough for family resemblance to be both obvious and worthy of note and acclaim for the patriarch. In these ventures our mentor has been Henry Spiegel. We are in his debt – and undoubtedly biased on that account at least.

3   Spiegel's essays on "National System" and "Scholastic Economic Thought" were also among the 100 essays from the Palgrave selected for reprinting in The New Palgrave: The World of Economics (1991).

4   Samuels has also assigned the chapters on the German and English historical schools in his graduate course, as well as recommending the book to any graduate student who might want a comprehensive account going beyond the assigned readings.

5   See Moss (1998) for the text of these remarks.

6   The material discussed in this section was gleaned from the History of Political Economy archive, which is housed in the Rare Book, Manuscript, and Special Collections Library at Duke University. We have removed those features from the quoted excerpts that might identify the author of the piece. Permission to quote from these materials is gratefully acknowledged.

## Bibliography

Becker, Carl (1932) Heavenly City of the Eighteenth-Century Philosophers, New Haven, CT: Yale University Press.

Blaug, Mark (1996) Economic Theory in Retrospect, fifth edition, Cambridge: Cambridge University Press.

Eatwell, John, Milgate, Murray, and Newman, Peter (eds) (1987) The New Palgrave: A Dictionary of Economics, 4 vols, New York: Stockton Press and London: Macmillan.

—— (eds) (1991) The New Palgrave: The World of Economics, New York and London: W.W. Norton.

Koyre, Alexandre (1968) Metaphysics and Measurement, Cambridge, MA: Harvard University Press.

Medema, Steven G. and Samuels, Warren J. (eds) (1996) Foundations of Research in Economics: How Do Economists Do Economics?, Aldershot: Edward Elgar.

S. G. Medema and W. J. Samuels on H. W. Spiegel   301

Moss, Laurence S. (ed.) (1998) "Dr. Henry William Spiegel (1911–1995): Émigré Economist, Historian of Economics, Creative Scholar, and Companion," *American Journal of Economics and Sociology* 57, July: 345–61.

Samuels, Warren J. (ed.) (1992) *New Horizons in Economic Thought*, Aldershot: Edward Elgar.

—— (ed.) (1996) *American Economists of the Late Twentieth Century*, Aldershot: Edward Elgar.

Schumpeter, Joseph A. (1954) *History of Economic Analysis*, Oxford: Oxford University Press.

Spiegel, Henry W. (1933) *Der Pachtvertrag der Kleingartenvereine*, Tubingen: J.C.B. Mohr.

—— (1938) "Origin and Development of Denial of Justice," *American Journal of International Law* 32, January: 63–81; reprinted in American Society of International Law, *International Law in the Twentieth Century*, 1969.

—— (1941) *Land Tenure Policies at Home and Abroad*, Chapel Hill, NC: University of North Carolina Press.

—— (1942) *The Economics of Total War*, New York: D. Appleton-Century.

—— (1949a) *The Brazilian Economy: Chronic Inflation and Sporadic Industrialization*, Philadelphia: Blakiston.

—— (1949b) *Current Economic Problems*, third edition, Philadelphia: Blakiston.

—— (1951) *Introduction to Economics*, New York: Blakiston.

—— (1952) *The Development of Economic Thought*, New York: Wiley.

—— (1955) *Pierre Samuel Du Pont de Nemours On Economic Curves*, Baltimore, MD: Johns Hopkins University Press.

—— (1960) *The Rise of American Economic Thought*, Philadelphia: Chilton.

—— (1971) *The Growth of Economic Thought*, Englewood Cliffs, NJ: Prentice Hall; third edition, Durham, NC: Duke University Press, 1991.

—— (1975) "A Note on the Equilibrium Concept in the History of Economics," *Economie Appliquée* 28: 609–18.

—— (1976) "Adam Smith's Heavenly City," *History of Political Economy* 8, Winter: 478–93.

—— (1992) "Economics," in *Jewish-American History and Culture: An Encyclopedia*, New York and London: Garland, 145–50.

—— (1994) "Ethnicity and Economics," *International Social Science Review* 69, 1 & 2: 3–12.

—— (1997) "Refugee Economists and the Mathematization of Economics," in Harald Hagemann (ed.) *Zur deutschsprachigen wirtschaftswissenschaftlichen Emigration nach 1933*, Marburg: Metropolis-Verlag, 343–52.

Spiegel, Henry W. and Samuels, Warren J. (eds) (1984) *Contemporary Economists in Perspective*, 2 vols, Greenwich, CT: JAI Press.

Wilson, Edmund (1943) *Shock of Recognition*, Garden City, NY: Doubleday, Doran.

Winch, Donald (1983) "Jacob Viner as Intellectual Historian," *Research in the History of Economic Thought and Methodology* 1: 1–17.

# 16 Werner Stark and the sociology of knowledge approach to the history of economics

*Charles M. A. Clark*

## Introduction

The reason we study the ideas of "dead economists," besides aesthetics or pure intellectual curiosity, is the potential that such an inquiry will offer insights into how we can better understand our own economic reality. These insights are many and manifold, from a clearer understanding of the actual economic content of economic theories (before it gets permanently lost in mathematical formalism), to an explanation of why some topics are developed and overdeveloped (the search for the existence, uniqueness, and stability of general equilibrium comes immediately to mind) while others remain underdeveloped or ignored (the problem of unemployment before Keynes). However, the most important lesson that the history of economics teaches us is that we need to take a critical view of accepted economic doctrines, for they will inevitably become obsolete.[1] This is especially the case with any economic doctrines that purport to depict universal "Truths." Moreover, this is even t he case for economic theories which, in their time and place, are substantially correct and accurate depictions of their contemporary economic reality. This reality of the "relativity of economic doctrines" is one of the great contributions Werner Stark made to the history of economics. More so than all other historians of economic thought, past and present, Stark stressed that economic ideas must be, in fact can only be, understood in their historical and social and intellectual context, that economic theories, like economic phenomena, are historical and social artifacts and thus must be placed in their historical and social context to be meaningful. Furthermore, the dynamic of economic evolution is one of the main factors that causes economic theory to evolve and change.

This chapter will introduce Stark's approach to understanding the development of economic ideas. First we will give a brief biography of Stark. This will be followed by an overview of his work on the sociology of knowledge and social theory. Third, we will consider Stark's writings on the history of economic thought as a discipline, especially his manuscript *History and Historians of Political Economy*. Lastly, we will see how Stark's approach to the history of economics formed the foundation for, and naturally led to, a critique of neoclassical economic theory (the reigning orthodoxy of his day).

## Werner Stark, 1909–85[2]

Like many important contributors to the sociology of knowledge (Veblen being the classic example) Werner Stark was an outsider in the various societies in which he lived. Born to a Jewish family in Germany (Marienbad, Bohemia) in 1909 he spent most of his professional life in England and the United States. Upon retirement, he settled in Salzburg, Austria (for the music), where he died in 1985. Stark studied the social sciences at the University of Hamburg, earning his Dr.rer.pol. in 1934. He also attended the London School of Economics (1930–1), the University of Geneva (1933), and the University of Prague, where he received a Dr.jur. in 1936.

With the demise of democracy in Germany in 1934, Stark moved to Prague. Eventually he was appointed to the Prague School of Political Science, teaching there until the German invasion of 1939. Stark was invited to join the faculty at the New School for Social Research and was set on going until the State Department of the United States of America determined that it had let in enough Jews and denied him a visa. He went instead to Cambridge, England. Stark lived in Cambridge from 1939 to 1944 and it is from this period that most of Stark's work in the history of economic thought was carried out. Stark was a guest lecturer at the University of Cambridge, and was hired by the Royal Economic Society to edit Jeremy Bentham's economic writings (Stark 1952–4), the latter on a recommendation from John Maynard Keynes.

Stark later recalled how he became acquainted with Keynes (Engel 1975: 5):

> In order to prove as quickly as possible that I had a contribution to make to the culture into the midst of which my fate had propelled me, I decided to produce next an article rather than a book, and I chose as my topic "Jeremy Bentham as an Economist." I had always been interested in the history of economic thought for its own sake, and I had wondered for a long time why the great utilitarian philosopher, who was close to such outstanding economists as David Ricardo and John Stuart Mill and no mean economist himself had never been made the subject of a monograph. I submitted my paper to the prestigious Economic Journal, and it was immediately accepted. I was invited to visit the editor, J. M. Keynes, presently to become Lord Keynes, and was kindly and cordially received. Indeed, I gained in this great thinker a true friend.

If only all academic entrées into the history of economics went so well! While at Cambridge, Stark was supported by a grant from the Society for the Protection of Science and Learning (an organization dedicated to supporting refugée scholars). The Society looked at its grants as short-term relief and placed pressure on Stark to seek employment as a German or History teacher in a secondary school. Toward this end he had no luck. When the Society threatened to cut off the subsidy, Keynes intervened, offering to fund half of the grant himself (which he eventually did, unbeknownst to Stark, until Stark was drafted into the army in

1945). Keynes argued to the Society that Stark's research was more valuable to society than any contribution he might make as a school teacher.

After the war, Stark held positions at the Universities of Edinburgh and Manchester. In the early 1960s he came to Fordham University in New York to join the Department of Sociology, where he remained until his retirement in 1975. Stark's major contributions in sociology include: *The Sociology of Knowledge* (1958c), the five-volume *Sociology of Religion* (1966–72), and his six-volume *magnum opus*, *The Social Bond* (1976–87).

## Sociology of knowledge as an approach to the history of economics

If one were to sum up Stark's contribution to the study of the history of economics it would be his highlighting the importance of historical and social context in the evolution of economic ideas – the application of the "sociology of knowledge" to the historiography of economics. It is an interesting paradox that Stark's work in the history of economics, particularly his *The Ideal Foundations of Economic Thought* (1943a) and his work on *History and Historians of Political Economy*, published posthumously in 1994 but written in the 1939–44 period (which produced the short book *The History of Economics in Relation to Social Development* (1944)) led him to broader issues that make up the sociology of knowledge. Ironically, economic theory was at the same time starting to completely eliminate historical and social context as important factors for explaining economic activity (axiomatic general equilibrium theory and mathematical formalism), a move that eventually creeps into the field of the history of economics.[3] The sociology of knowledge is so fundamental to understanding Stark's approach to the history of economics that we will consider it first, keeping in mind that it represents his most mature and developed analysis of these issues, and that when he was writing on the history of economics he only had a hint of the important issues raised by emphasizing the social and historical context of the creation and development of social ideas. No doubt, had Stark completed his research in the sociology of knowledge before his forays into the history of economics, his analysis would have had the balance many have noted as lacking in his *History of Economics in Relation to Social Development* (1944).[4]

"The sociology of knowledge," according to Werner Stark, "is concerned with determining whether man's participation in social life has any influence on his knowledge, thought, and culture and, if it does, what sort of influence it is" (Stark 1967: 475). There are both micro and macro aspects of the sociology of knowledge. An example of "micro" sociology of knowledge would be the influence that social institutions particularly associated with "knowledge" creation, such as universities, academic journals, government funding agencies, and professional academic associations like the American Economic Association, have on theory development, acceptance, and perpetuation. Directing research is a discretionary act, with the choices being not only what gets and does not get investigated, but also what are the criteria for acceptance and rejection of new "knowledge." Much of this work, since the 1970s, has been labeled the "sociology of science."

The choices that these institutions make reflect their values, as well as, to a lesser extent, the values of society, or to paraphrase John Stuart Mill, the values of "those who dispose of its active force."[5] The discretionary use of power is often apparent at this level, as the political significance of "knowledge" cannot be understated (even as the ability to control it is overstated). When we switch to the macro sociology of knowledge, the influence of values and power becomes much more subtle and difficult to detect, though no less real. The social influences that the macro sociology of knowledge investigates stem more from the wider influences the theorist's world-view (*Weltanschauung*) or "vision" has on theoretical inquiry. These macro influences are often in the form of philosophical preconceptions widely accepted, but often unnoticed, by theorists. They influence the direction of theory development by directing the questions to be asked, the parameters and criteria for acceptable answers (Veblen's "final term"), and most importantly, they provide the framework with which to categorize the multitude of chaotic observations into a coherent whole. It is from these values and vision that a theorist derives the fundamental concepts upon which social theory is then constructed: the definition of what is society; human nature, and the standard of good and bad, right and wrong.

Just about the same time Stark was intensively researching the history of economics in Cambridge, Joseph Schumpeter was starting his *magnum opus*, the *History of Economic Analysis* (1954). Few works in this field have had such an impact. With regard to the understanding of the role of historical and social context on the history of economics, Schumpeter's impact was mostly negative. Schumpeter addresses these issues in the short and unfinished section of Part I, chapter four, where he starts what appears at first to be a promising discussion on the role of a theorist's "vision." Yet, the insights developed here are not carried forward into the rest of the volume. Schumpeter, in all fairness, tips his hand before the chapter begins by stating: "Economic analysis has not been shaped at any time by the philosophical opinions that economists happened to have, though it has frequently been visited by their political attitudes" (Schumpeter 1954: 31). He then notes the importance of "vision:" "analytical effort is of necessity preceded by a preanalytical cognitive act that supplies the raw material for the analytical effort. ... [T]his preanalytic cognitive act will be called Vision" (Schumpeter 1954: 41). Schumpeter notes:

> Analytic effort starts when we have conceived our vision of the set of phenomena that caught our interest, no matter whether this set lies in virgin soil or in land that had been cultivated before. ... Analytic work begins with material provided by our vision of things, and this vision is ideological almost by definition. It embodies the picture of things as we see them, and wherever there is any possible motive for wishing to see them in

a given rather than another light, the way in which we see things can hardly be distinguished from the way in which we wish to see them.

(ibid.: 42)

Yet the issue is raised only to be dropped. Economic analysis is what Schumpeter says he is interested in, not economic thought. The tools are independent of the motives of the tool maker. Schumpeter does raise the issue of ideology, but his understanding of ideology seems to be limited to the Mannheimian and Marxist approaches to the subject. From these perspectives the sociology of knowledge is seen as a tool for separating out the "ideological" from the "scientific," which often means to label your opponent's ideas as ideological and your own as scientific.

As a starting point to a theoretical understanding of the development of economics, Schumpeter's "vision" analysis is a non-starter, as Schumpeter no doubt meant it to be. Far superior is Thorstein Veblen's earlier analysis of the role of preconceptions in the development of economic analysis contained in his three-part essay "The Preconceptions of Economic Science" (1899–1900). Veblen achieves what Schumpeter states cannot be achieved: he demonstrates how the philosophical preconceptions of economists have influenced their theories:[6] "As would necessarily be the case, the point of view of economists has always been in large part the point of view of the enlightened common sense of their time. The spiritual attitude of a given generation of economists is therefore in good part a special outgrowth of the ideals and preconceptions current in the world about them" (Veblen 1990: 86). To give an example, Veblen notes that:

The failure of their critics to place themselves at the Physiocratic point of view has led to much destructive criticism of their work; whereas, when seen through Physiocratic eyes, such doctrines as those of the net product and the barrenness of the artisan class appear to be substantially true.

(ibid.: 87)

The goal of Stark's work in the sociology of knowledge is to synthesize elements of the two competing and contrary approaches that were already in existence when he entered the field: the relativist position most closely associated with Karl Mannheim and the absolutist approach best exemplified by Max Scheler. Towards the end of his career Stark summed up his efforts as such:

As I see it, the sociology of knowledge consists of two closely connected, yet clearly distinguishable efforts. There is, first of all, a desire to understand the genesis of ideas. Ideas are not the produce of isolated brains, but of socialized men, men living in the midst of societies which are not only systems of interaction but at the same time also systems of shared values and meanings. These values and meanings can throw light on the formation of distinctive world views, be they collective or be they individual.

The sociology of knowledge has to pursue the possibilities of understanding inherent in the fact that the social matrix is the medium within which thought contents spring up and unfold. But when it does its work, or rather wrestles with this first implication of its work, it will soon find itself confronted by a second task. Analysis leads to the impression that different social systems call forth different, indeed irreconcilable, systems of ideas. In Pascal's words, what is right north of the Pyrenees, is wrong to the south of them. Analysis breeds – it is at any rate apt to breed – a relativist stance. But such relativism destroys the very concept of the truth, for truth is not really truth unless it is absolute. The sociology of knowledge, basically a positive science, a method of investigation, necessarily presents a philosophical poser, the question of Pontius Pilate: what is the truth? It cannot shirk the task of finding an answer to this fateful query for the danger of mental anarchy must be held at bay. … Mannheim was right when he insisted that there is in fact a multiplicity of worldviews and that every society, indeed every class, has one of its own. But he was wrong when he refused to see these worldviews as ultimately reconcilable, as aspects of a comprehensive absolute which is not indeed given to us *in terminis*, but which we can pursue and progressively approach. "Through the relative to the absolute" – this is the formula which I propose.

Stark's approach to the sociology of knowledge was to emphasize both (1) the intellectual *milieu* in which the theorists lived and the traditions they are working in and (2) the material conditions that they theorized about. Stark referred to the first as the "Axiological Layer of the Mind" and the second as the "Objects of Knowledge" and in typically Starkian fashion argued that understanding both is necessary if one wants to develop a full understanding of the history of ideas. Stark's first book, *The Ideal Foundation of Economic Thought*, is an early examination of the former concern, while his second, *The History of Economics in Relation to Social Development*, is an attempt at the latter. Both approaches, if carried out singularly, lead to a form of relativism for which the second book has been particularly criticized.

Stark does advocate a form of relativism in accessing the history of ideas, stating that conflicting theories can often be due to conflicting realities:

An example would be that of the conflict between the medieval and modern conception of the market price. The nineteenth century economists derided the Schoolmen because they thought that the price was given before supply and demand had so much as established contact, let alone found an equilibrium; the price was "always," they said, and "necessarily," the outcome of the higgling of the market, "never" its pre-existent norm. In a way this is true, and even an absolute truth. But the medieval conception was also within its rights. For in so far as a price manages to assume the character of a piece of custom, to establish itself within the system of customary law by which a community lives, it is in fact relatively independent of supply and demand, which must then fall into line with it, rather than *vice versa*. The difference between St. Thomas and Walras was not that the one talked sense and the other nonsense, but that the one was talking of a society of the community type where norm ontologically precedes individual action, and the other of a society of the associational type where individual action precedes the norm and creates it.

(Stark 1958c: 207; see also Stark 1956)

The economy (the object of our analysis) keeps changing; thus should not economic theory continue to adapt to reflect these changes?

Stark was an avid critic of unhistorical approaches to understanding social phenomena, for social and historical context are necessary for understanding past ideas. He also charged that the trend in modern economics toward increasing formalism was in effect an attempt to eliminate historical and social context.[7] Commenting on the formalism in general equilibrium theory Stark writes:

The truth of the matter is, of course, that though a mathematical economics à la Walras tells us everything about all markets in the abstract, it tells us nothing about any market in the concrete. Locked up as it is in its tautologies, it can find no contact with the hard facts of reality, and so we have here a science without factual content – in other words, a contradiction in terms.

(Stark 1958c: 183)

Formalism, that is social theory without historical and social context, is empty and irrelevant. Furthermore it prevents us from arriving at the truth and knowledge we seek, for although Stark was a relativist in method he felt that a science of man could be eventually gained, even if it is partial and incomplete, through the understanding of mankind's many and varied historical experiences. The final goal is not the discovery of invariant natural laws of economics but of the nature of the human person.

## Fundamental forms of social thought

We have seen in the previous section that the realm of the sociology of knowledge ranges from the "Axiological Layer of the Mind" to "The Objects of Knowledge" with the "Axiological Layer of the Mind" being socially determined by the intellectual milieu and the theorist's vision or preconceptions and the "Objects of Knowledge" being, for economics, the material conditions. In this section we will be dealing with the former aspect, specifically with the vision of "what is society?"[8]

In *The Fundamental Forms of Social Thought* (1963) Stark notes that there are three basic answers to the above posed question: "what is society?": society is a unity; society is a multiplicity; and lastly, society is a process. Using this classification schema Stark is able to expose one of the key ingredients in a theorist's "vision" – how the theorists conceptualize society. Furthermore, Stark is able to also connect specific conceptions of society with what "displaced concepts" or metaphors the theorists will use as the basic building blocks of their theoretical creations. Subsequent work in the history of economic thought, especially the work of Philip Mirowski (1989), has shown how significant the use of natural metaphors and the natural sciences has been for the development, good or ill, of economic theory.[9]

Conceiving of society as a unity entails viewing it as an organic whole, "the social order is an organism" (Stark 1963: 17). Society is seen as a single entity with the individuals that comprise the society being understood in terms of their position or place in society, much like a human organ is understood in terms of its place within the human body. Organic social theorists frequently adopt biological or physiological analogies or metaphors to act as the displaced concepts upon which to develop their ideas. The most obvious example of this in the history of economics is the work of François Quesnay, especially his displacement of his model of the circulatory system onto the economy in his *Tableau Économique*.

The contrary view of society has been much more rigorously developed – society is a multiplicity, or what can be called the mechanistic view of society. Under this set of preconceptions the individual is considered "real" while society is seen as a mental fiction. Society is really just the net result of the interaction of the individuals that comprise it, with the individuals being seen here as atomistic. This view "regards the social cosmos as essentially an equilibrium system. If only the individual is real, then the coherence of society – or rather, the coherence of individuals in society – must be due to the balancing of individual forces" (ibid.: 10). The dominance of this view of society for neoclassical economic theory is more than blatantly obvious, and we will not waste any space arguing what is indisputable. All that needs to be mentioned is the adherence to methodological individualism, the refusal to take institutions seriously, and the co-opting of physics and mechanics as the source of displaced concepts as building blocks (the most important being the concept of equilibrium).

Stark notes that both of these "views of society" contain partial truths; with each missing significant aspects of social reality. The organic perspective leaves out the individual, both in terms of allowing for free will and self-determination, and in terms of the dignity of the individual as an individual. The mechanistic perspective ignores the crucial role of social institutions and the socialization process – history and culture. Stark was particularly critical of the mechanistic view of society and its expression in economic theory – the concept of equilibrium, writing (ibid.: 56–7):

> If the social order is likened to an equilibrium system, to a kind of tension between independent energies of which the balance of a pair of scales is the simplest exemplification, then it is almost certain to be interpreted in a non-historical and unhistorical spirit. An equilibrium has no history; its

laws do not change with the centuries. The formal equations in which it can be described are of timeless validity, as all purely quantitative propositions must be. Rational mechanics is a branch of mathematics and its students glory in the fact: those social theorists who wanted to model [social theory] on rational mechanics were quite unwilling to admit the reality of developmental change.[10]

Society does, at one level, resemble an organic whole, and at another a mechanism, and society will get closer to one or the other extreme in its overall character. Yet both are incomplete descriptions and by themselves must be rejected. Individuals and society are concepts that need the other to exist. Society without individuals is a nonsensical concept, yet so is the notion of the individual fully independent of society. Humans cannot and never have existed outside of human society. Robinson Crusoe is not a good example for the mechanistic theorists to use for he was fully socialized in English society before his becoming shipwrecked (note how quickly he enslaved the local population when he discovered Friday). From society we get not only our values and mores, customs, and traditions, but also our ability to speak, think abstractly, and comprehend our environment (language). Both individuals with free will and social institutions must be included in any realistic social theory. As Stark (ibid.: 12, 218) notes (in a comment which would foreshadow much of the recent critique of the influence of the natural sciences on economics):

> Physiology and physics are spurious models in the social sciences because they are concerned with a reality which man finds, not with one which he makes ... [what is needed is] [l]iberation from the erstwhile voluntary bondage to the natural sciences. Society ... is neither a creation of the laws of mechanics nor a reflection of the laws of biology: it is man's own work, sprung from his will, sustained by his will, perfectible through his will.

This leads us to the third definition of society: as a process. This conception sees society as the interaction of individuals with free will and the social institutions that socialize individuals. Both are causes and effects of the other. Individuals are shaped and molded by institutions through the socialization process while individuals shape and recreate institutions. Society is thus an evolutionary process, but without a predetermined natural end. Such a theory loses much of the certainty and precision that mechanistic and organic social theories have, yet this is a good result for this precision was not accuracy in the real sense of the word, but a false certainty, buttressing ideological structures not the real foundations of society or social understanding.

## Stark as historian of economics

John Maynard Keynes, based on his reading Stark's articles on Bentham, his manuscript that would become *History and Historians of Political Economy*, as well as their personal conversations, commented in his letters that he thought Stark was "one of the half dozen most learned people going on in his own subject" [the history of economics] (Stark 1994: xvii). Stark's work in this field covers a wide area and is fairly extensive, especially if we consider that it is mostly produced in a small portion of his academic career (most of it in a ten-year period, 1939–49). His published writings in the history of economics consist of his editing Bentham's economic writings (Stark 1952–54), two books, *The Ideal Foundations of Economic Thought* (1943a) and *The History of Economics in Relation to Social Development* (1944), and the manuscript for *History and Historians of Political Economy* (1994), as well as numerous journal articles. Taken together, the two books from 1943 to 1944 summarize Stark's approach to the history of economics. In *The Ideal Foundations of Economic Thought* Stark demonstrates the importance of the theorists' conception of the ideal order in their theoretical work, the role of the "vision," while *The History of Economics in Relation to Social Development* looks at the preeminent role of the material conditions on the development of economic theory, how a changing economy causes economic theory to change. This second book was originally the final chapter in Stark's posthumously published *History and Historians of Political Economy*, originally having the title "The Material Contents of the History of Political Economy."

The manuscript of *History and Historians of Political Economy* is of interest for many reasons, not the least of which is that it seems to be the only history of the history of economics. It is more a work on the historiography of economics, with only the last chapter being history of economics proper. It begins with a review of the major (and many minor) works on the history of economics. This review is of particular interest as it represents a past that for the most part has been lost to the field of the history of economics. Stark finds that, as a discipline, the history of economics has concentrated on three questions: what are the origins of economics as a science; did economic theory develop by stages in schools or by historical epochs; and how does one separate the valid theorists from the quacks (the valuation of economic theories)? In answering these questions there have been two approaches: historical and theoretical. Those working in the historical tradition (the leading figures of which are Roscher, Ingram, Haney, and Gonnard) have answered these three questions in a similar manner:

> The origin of political economy they are inclined to find in antiquity – in spite of the ever present knowledge of the change of economic life they rarely perceived its entire change of character; the basis for the division of development they are inclined to seek in the great periods of cultural history, not in the small alterations in abstract theory, because the science of economics means to them only a part of the field of investigation proper to economic science, they wish to comprehend and describe the whole reflection of the economic system in the human mind – for they are reluctant to divide what really belonged together. Behind all these ideas,

however, is the great creed of the spirit born of romanticism that all life, however manifold its variety in space and time may appear, must be understood as a grand and indivisible unity.

(Stark 1994: 57)

In contrast to the historical approach, the theoretical approach (whose leading proponents are Schumpeter, Dühring, Gide and Rist and Roll) dates the origins of economics in the eighteenth century with the discovery of systematic theories: Cantillon, Quesnay, and Smith. This is so because the theoretical approach views economics as a systematic science, and "cannot therefore be conceived before the appearance of a system of ideas, before the breakthrough of the idea of system" (ibid.: 111–12). The development of economic theory is divided by schools rather than epochs, for it is the theory that matters to them, not any changes in the economic reality being studied. Finally, economic theory is evaluated based on how similar it is to their ideal of "science" – the natural sciences. Stark finds great weakness in both approaches, the most important of which is their unwillingness, for whatever reason, to engage what is for him the central question in the history of ideas, the relationship between theory and reality, between that which is to be explained and the explanation. The problem is further complicated in the social sciences by the fact that both the reality and the explanations are social creations and are not the result of blind natural forces.

In the second part of *History and Historians of Political Economy* Stark looks at how historians of economics have dealt with the problem of the relationship between theory and reality. He finds that there have been essentially three approaches to this issue: the critical; the descriptive; and the explanatory. The critical approach (with Schumpeter being the outstanding representative) denies the connection between the development of theory and a changing reality.[11] It views the essential economic reality as unchanging (invariant economic laws) and thus changes in theory cannot be due to changes in the economy. Another outstanding characteristic of the critical approach is that it views the development of economics as the progressive march toward what is the accepted dogma of the historian. In this Marx and Schumpeter are equally guilty. For Marx (see *Theories of Surplus Value*) it is the progressive realization of the idea of surplus and the labor theory of value; for Schumpeter it is the concept of general equilibrium and the emulation of the natural sciences. Stark nicely summarizes this point with regards to Schumpeter (ibid.: 149):

In the final paragraph of his historical investigation Schumpeter openly asserts the essential equality of all theories heretofore propounded. "Fundamentally the Physiocrats already aimed at what we aim at today, and if we concentrate on the matter and not on the form given to it, it is often difficult to find in a vehemently worded contest a correspondingly sharp expression of the objective differences" (Schumpeter, 1914, p. 124). Certainly Quesnay wished to fathom the character of national economy in the same way as did Marshall – just as Ptolemy and Copernicus were united in the endeavor to penetrate the laws of the universe. But nature is immutable, and society is constantly changing; so a scientific history of theoretical economics can only be built on the idea of evolution, on the idea of historical relativism, which is foreign to Schumpeter's rationalist thought.

Today we would call the critical approach "rational reconstruction" or "Whig history." Within this approach, the "historian" seems to be more interested in using the history of economics as a tool for defending a particular economic outlook or for attacking a competing viewpoint.[12] The descriptive approach also eschews any attempt at addressing the issue of the relationship between theory and reality. Those working in this tradition are content at merely describing, as honestly and accurately as possible, the ideas of past economists, making little effort to evaluate the correctness of these theories, nor explain how these theories came to be. They cannot make such evaluations since they have no criteria upon which to base their judgments. Thus, unless one addresses the issue of the relationship between theory and reality one is left with the choice of either making evaluations based on conformity with accepted dogma or making no judgments at all. This is not a happy situation.

This leads us to the explanatory approach, which is based on "the conviction that ... economic ideas must be understood as the natural products of the real and ideal order of society and economy of their time" (ibid.: 137). Much like his approach to the sociology of knowledge and the definition of society, Stark believes that both (mechanistic and organic) perspectives have something to offer the historian, as they both are glimpses, however partial, of the truth. Yet a more complete understanding must include both seemingly contrary insights. History without context is like science without observation, it is meaningless. Yet Stark does not advocate a directionless relativism, for the truth is still the ultimate goal, and the ultimate evaluation of an economic theory is determined by its conformity with the actual economy it seeks to explain. The lack of conformity of neoclassical economic theory and twentieth-century capitalism is thus problematic for the historian of economics who follows Stark's method. This is certainly the case for Werner Stark as we see him move from being an historian of economic ideas to being a critic of accepted economic doctrines, specifically the notions of utility and equilibrium, to which we now turn.

## From historian to critic

Werner Stark's early work in the history of economic thought attempted to do what most economists would argue is impossible – to argue that Mun, Quesnay, and Smith could all be substantially right, that economic theorists who disagreed on major theoretical issues might, for the most part, be correct. This is possible if you allow for the fact of a changing economic reality. Stark argues that they had each grasped important aspects of the economic reality which they were investigating. Their disagreements stemmed from the fact that each had a different economic reality (material conditions). Yet the evaluation role of the historian of economics cannot be neglected, for not every economic theorist can be correct. Economists writing about the same economic reality frequently disagree. It is not enough for the historian to be aware of his own preconceptions and the distorting effects that adherence to one set of economic doctrines has on the historian's craft as historian. The historian of economics must also critically evaluate the ideas of the past. Part of this involves the inclusion of the intellectual influences on theoretical development. Thus although Marx and Jevons were working on their respective path-breaking treatises at the same time (and quite possibly in the same room of the library of the British Museum), and thus were faced with the same economic reality, much of their differences can be explained by the differing "visions" of society and the economy, not the least of which was their philosophical orientation and method of analysis. Marx and Jevons gave different answers because they asked different questions, had differing frameworks with which they organized and understood economic observations, and based their theoretical efforts on different "final terms." Yet the historian of economics should be able, at least theoretically, to answer the question as to where these two pivotal economists were correct and where they were wrong.

In two essays published in *Kyklos* in 1947 and 1950 Stark turned from being a detached observer of the history of economics to that of being a critic of the reigning economic orthodoxy of his day. This was a natural extension of his approach to the history of economics, especially the importance of context and evaluation. These essays are reflections on two of the most fundamental concepts in neoclassical economic theory: utility and equilibrium; from the evolutionary perspective of Henri Bergson. Both were to foreshadow critiques that were to be more fully developed by others.[13]

In "Diminishing Utility Reconsidered" (1947) Stark notes that the concept of utility had somehow escaped a serious philosophical analysis, with much of the justification for its use still relying on statements that it is self-evident, or as Friedrich von Wieser put it: "Every man in the street knows that whole matter of the theory of value by self-observation" (quoted in ibid.: 321). Relying on the work of Henri Bergson,[14] Stark argues that the fundamental assumption of the marginal utility theorists, that sensations (pain or pleasure) are magnitudes, is false. The idea that sensations were quantitative "was rashly assumed by the economists of the 1870s who had nothing to guide them but untutored common sense, while [the idea that sensations were qualitative] was conclusively proved by Henri Bergson in a vigorous and rigorous scientific investigation" (ibid.: 325). Using the example of a person lifting a heavy weight, Bergson demonstrates that the person (you) will

> have the impression of a sensation of effort entirely localized in your hand and running in a scale of magnitudes. In reality, what you experience in

your hand remains the same, but the sensation which was at first localized there has affected your arm and ascended to the shoulder; finally, the other arm stiffens, both legs do the same, the respiration is checked; it is the whole body which is at work ... our consciousness of an increase in muscular effort is reducible to the twofold perception of a greater number of peripheral sensations, and of a qualitative change occurring in some of them.

(ibid.: 326–7)

Stark notes:

The economist, of course, is more interested in decreasing than in increasing desires. But, *mutatis mutandis*, the case is the same. When we are hungry, our whole being cries out for food. As we proceed in the satisfaction of this urge, one muscle after another ceases to be tense, one element after another drops out of our greed, until in the end the whole body is put to rest, and the mind which had before excluded all other interests, turns to different pursuits. Pain or pleasure, increase or decrease, the change is nowhere quantitative in the strict sense of the word.

(ibid., 328)

The economists will argue that their analysis is not based on human physiology, but on consumer choices.

After calling that pleasure which I have chosen, "greatest," the utilitarian economist pronounces that I always choose the "greatest" pleasure. This statement is true, and undeniably so, but only because it is completely meaningless. It is a simple tautology. It is not a scientific discovery but a verbal definition. It does not solve the problem but covers it with a cloak of words ... while we were choosing, we were not conscious of a comparison going on within our mind between two magnitudes, but once we have chosen, we may interpret our act *as if* we had been comparing the two alternatives open to us as we may two algebraical items or two mechanical forces. The fictional character of this procedure is undeniable. ... But, as Bergson justly observes: "Mechanics necessarily deals with equations, and ... an algebraic equation always expresses something already done. Now, it is of the very essence of duration and motion, as they appear to our consciousness, to be something that is unceasingly being done, but not duration and motion themselves." Modern economics, therefore, like its parent, associationism, "thus makes the mistake of constantly replacing the concrete phenomenon which takes place in the mind by the artificial reconstruction of it given by philosophy, and of thus confusing the explanation of the fact with the fact itself."

(ibid.: 334–5)

"The barrier," Stark continues, "against which the mathematical economist is running, is as old as thought itself, and will never disappear. It is the simple fact that the qualitative manifoldness of life cannot be adequately represented by quantitative uniformity of algebraic or geometrical forms" (ibid.: 336).

In "Stable Equilibrium Re-Examined," Stark notes that the move toward mathematical formalism is easily understood, as it has the attraction of the mantel of "science." But, as Stark notes, "what is most attractive is not always what should attract us most; mathematical economics forms no exception" (Stark 1950: 219). The essential question that must be faced in a critical manner is: can economic relations and activities be adequately represented with mathematical formalism, or does the formalism adopted by mathematical economics leave out essential aspects of the economic reality theory attempts to understand? For Stark what gets lost in the mathematical formalism that has come to dominate theoretical economics is the problem of time.

> [I]n the system of mathematical economics, time is an independent variable, because, *ex hypothesi*, the future is given alongside the past, the finished product alongside the factors of production. If the stationary state is a model of economic intercourse, it is one of those models where the handle that sets the puppets in motion and starts them on their predetermined round, can be turned as quickly or as slowly as we choose, and this is the reason why it is so profoundly unrealistic.
>
> (ibid.: 224)

> It is the bane of modern economics that it fails to appreciate the essential difference between that which is inside, and that which is outside, concrete time, between the living and the dead. Part and parcel of nineteenth century monism, it is an attempt to explain economic reality according to the principles of physics. It interprets society as an epiphenomenon of nature, and conceives sociology as an exact science. But this view of its object and of itself is the consequence of an unconscious metaphysical prejudice, of an implicit acceptance of the materialistic bias. It is this fateful and unfortunate connection of economics with crude materialism which critical epistemology must expose and attack. It has the duty to insist that, as nature and society are essentially different, there can be no science common to them that would directly explain them both. ... Economics, essentially a study of living society, cannot accept the notions applicable only to dead matter without erring from the right road and ending at long last in absurdity.
>
> (ibid.: 226; 229)

Stark's critique of neoclassical economic theory came twenty years before the so-called "crisis in economics" when the relevance of the neoclassical paradigm came into question. Yet the critique of the 1970s often centered on peripheral issues (like re-switching), failing to get to the heart of the matter.[15]

All that is wrong with neoclassical economic theory stems from its adherence to an outdated, and intellectually and morally bankrupt, "vision of society" (intellectual *milieu*) and its failure to reflect adequately the existing modern capitalist economy (material conditions). It is the lesson of the history of economics that economic theory is at its best when it is driven by a conception of society which includes both human free will and the socialization function of society (society as a process), a clear and defendable vision of the "good" or "ideal" coupled with a commitment to explaining the existing economic reality in its historical and social context. This is why we still read Adam Smith, John Stuart Mill, Karl Marx, Thorstein Veblen, Alfred Marshall, and John Maynard Keynes for profit and enlightenment. Not that they have discovered the ultimate "Truths" (though this has certainly been attributed to many of them), but that they have discovered relative truths, insights into the economic and social realities of their respective epochs. If we correctly learn this lesson from the history of economics, then as a discipline it has served its purpose of better preparing economists for the task of critically understanding and explaining their own economic and social realities.

## Notes

1 Joan Robinson put it another way, stating that we study economics to avoid being deceived by economists.

2 Much of this section is taken from my introduction to *History and Historians of Political Economy* (Stark 1994).

3 This break with social and historical context by neoclassical economic theory eventually turns Stark, and many others, into a critic of neoclassical economic theory, for, according to Stark, no economic (or social) explanation can be divorced from social and historical context.

4 This point is hinted at by Mark Blaug in his *Economic Theory in Retrospect* (1962: 2, n.1).

5 This is taken from Mill's famous passage on the distribution of income (1987: 200).

6 Schumpeter's attempt to separate economic analysis from economic thought has the net effect of reducing economics to a mere box of tools. Schumpeter's goal is to rid economics of the problem of ideology, for he sees this as only creating distortions, hindering scientific objectivity. Yet, as Stark's work has shown, and Gunnar Myrdal's as well, values and value judgments are a necessary part of all theoretical activity and no theoretical activity can take place without them. For Myrdal, the best we can hope for is an open and honest accounting of a theorist's values and value judgments. Stark, however, goes further, for he argues that the ideal and the real cannot be so easily separated, that both play an active role in human activity.

7 This case is made more fully in *Economic Theory and Natural Philosophy* (Clark 1992).

8 Yet it should be noted that material conditions play a role here also, as they tend to promote conceptions of society which match the type of society. Thus associational type societies tend toward mechanistic theories while communal societies usually produce organic theories.

9 See also my *Economic Theory and Natural Philosophy* (Clark 1992), upon which much of this section is based.

10 Neoclassical economic theory, especially its notion of rational choice, in effect also excludes free will, for rational choice is predetermined and coordinated choice, a point made frequently by George Shackle.

11 Schumpeter praised economic history as one of the most important aspects of economics, yet he rejects the notion that changes in the economy play a role in changes in economic theory.

12 The research on David Ricardo is dominated by this approach, with the Sraffians rationally reconstructing Ricardo as an early Sraffian and the neoclassical economists reading Ricardo as an early marginalist.

13 It is worth noting that the ideas contained in both essays ended up playing a major role in Joan Robinson's critique of neoclassical economics, especially the problem of time. Stark and Joan Robinson became good friends while he was in Cambridge (he mentions her having read and commented on the manuscript of *The Ideal Foundations of Economic Thought*) and they continued to correspond at least until he went to Fordham University.

14 Stark calls Bergson "the greatest philosophical genius of the last hundred years" (1947: 321).

15 Joan Robinson's writings, especially with and after "History vs. Equilibrium" (Robinson 1974), did hit many of the really important issues, the role of time, and the importance of context.

# Bibliography

Backhouse, Roger E. (1992) "How Should We Approach the History of Economic Thought, Fact, Fiction or Moral Tale?" *Journal of the History of Economic Thought* 14, 1: 18–35.

Blaug, Mark (1962) *Economic Theory in Retrospect*, Homewood, IL: Irwin.

Clark, Charles M. A. (1992) *Economic Theory and Natural Philosophy*, Aldershot: Edward Elgar.

Engel, Madeline H. (ed.) (1975) *The Sociological Writings of Werner Stark: Bibliography and Selected Annotations*, privately printed.

Mill, John Stuart ([1848] 1987) *Principles of Political Economy*, Fairfield, NJ: Augustus M. Kelley.

Mirowski, Philip (1989) *More Heat than Light*, Cambridge: Cambridge University Press.

Robinson, Joan (1974) "History versus Equilibrium," *Thames Papers in Political Economy*, No. 1.

Schumpeter, Joseph (1914) *Epochen der Dogmen – und Methodengeschichte*, Tübingen: J.C.B. Mohr.

—— (1954) *History of Economic Analysis*, New York: Oxford University Press.

Stark, Werner (1941a) "A Forerunner of Marxism: François-Jean de Chastellux," *Economica* May: 203–7.

—— (1941b) "Liberty and Equality, or Jeremy Bentham as an Economist, I: Bentham's Doctrine," *Economic Journal* 51, April: 56–79.

—— (1943a) *The Ideal Foundations of Economic Thought*, London: Kegan Paul Trench, Trubner; reprinted by Augustus M. Kelly, Clifton, NJ, 1975.

—— (1943b) "Saint-Simon as a Realist," *Journal of Economic History* May: 42–55.

—— (1944) *The History of Economics in Relation to Social Development*, London: Kegan Paul Trench, Trubner.

—— (1945) "The Realism of Saint-Simon's Spiritual Program," *Journal of Economic History* May: 24–42.

—— (1946) "Jeremy Bentham as an Economist, II: Bentham's Influence," *Economic Journal* 56, December: 583–608.

—— (1947) "Diminishing Utility Reconsidered," *Kyklos* 1, Fasc. 4: 321–44.

—— (1950) "Stable Equilibrium Re-Examined," *Kyklos* 4, Fasc. 2/3: 219–32.

—— (1952–54) *Jeremy Bentham's Economic Writings*, 3 vols, ed. Werner Stark, London: George Allen & Unwin.

—— (1954) "Fünfzig Jahre britischen Wirtschaftsdenkens" (Fifty Years of British Economic Thought), *Jahrbücher für Nationalökonomie und Statistik*, Band 166: 1–19.

—— (1955) "Joseph Schumpeters Umwertung der Wertr" (Joseph Schumpeter's Transvaluation of Values), *Kyklos* 8, Fasc. 3: 225–47.

—— (1956) "The Contained Economy: An Interpretation of Medieval Economic Thought," Aquinas Paper No. 26.

—— (1958a) "Die Dogmengeschichte der Volkswirtschaftslehre im Lichte des Pragmatismus" (The History of Economic Doctrines in the Light of Pragmatism), *Kyklos* 11, Fasc. 3: 425–30.

—— (1958b) "La'Heteronomia de los Fines'en el Pensiamento Social y Economico Moderno" (The "Heteronomy of Purposes" in Modern Social and Economic Thought ), *Revista Internacional de Sociologia* Abril–Junio: 197–222; also in *Social Theory and Christian Thought*, Chapter 1, part 2: 31–62.

—— (1958c) *The Sociology of Knowledge: Toward a Deeper Understanding of the History of Ideas*, London: Routledge & Kegan Paul; reprinted by Transaction Publishers, New Brunswick, NJ, 1991.

—— (1959) "The 'Classical Situation' in Political Economy," *Kyklos* 12, Fasc. 1: 57–65.

—— (1963) *The Fundamental Forms of Social Thought*, New York: Fordham University Press.

—— (1966–72) *The Sociology of Religion*, 5 vols, New York: Fordham University Press.

—— (1967) "The Sociology of Knowledge," in Paul Edwards (ed.) *The Encyclopedia of Philosophy*, Vol. 7, New York: Macmillan and The Free Press, 475–8.

—— (1976–87) *The Social Bond*, 6 vols, New York: Fordham University Press.

—— (1994) *History and Historians of Political Economy*, ed. Charles M. A. Clark, New Brunswick, NJ: Transaction Publishers.

Veblen, Thorstein ([1899–1900] 1990) "The Preconceptions of Economic Science," in *The Place of Science in Modern Civilization*, New Brunswick, NJ: Transaction Publishers.

# 17 Roy Weintraub's contribution to the history of economics

*John Lodewijks**

An "outsider" to our craft can bring a number of alternative perspectives to the way we do the history of economic thought. This chapter examines the historiographic perspective of E. R. Weintraub and the contribution this makes to our understanding of general equilibrium and mathematical economics and our relationship with historians of science.

## Introduction

> There is not only an opportunity for mathematics and economics, but even a duty; and on mathematicians in an unusual degree lies the responsibility for the economic welfare of the world.
>
> (Griffith C. Evans 1925, cited in Weintraub 1998b: 247)

In a review of one of his critics, Roy Weintraub (1998a: 317) commented on Roger Backhouse's "long and interesting trip" from "unabashed critical rationalist, to enthusiastic Lakatosian, to worried rationalist, to critic of rhetoric, and finally to something he calls empirical philosophy of science". It is the goal of this chapter to demonstrate that Weintraub has had an even more interesting journey, one that may have significant consequences for the historian of economic thought.

Weintraub's journey is interesting for a number of reasons. First, he is one of the very few economic theorists that turned their hand to the history of the discipline while still early in their career and was not swayed by Whiggish interpretations. Second, he brings a mathematical background capable of understanding recent developments in the discipline and an openness to engage other social scientists and historians of science in a meaningful dialogue about the history of ideas. Like Philip Mirowski, he challenges the traditional canonical approach to the history of economics. Finally, he does not shy away from taking provocative positions and controversy seems to follow every path he navigates.

## Sins of the father?

Eliot Roy Weintraub grew up in a household filled with economics discourse and controversy, where the dinner guests sometimes included Roy Harrod, Joan Robinson, and Lawrence Klein. His father, Sidney Weintraub (1914–83), was the leading American exponent of the post-Keynesian approach to macroeconomics. He was a hard-hitting critic of the neoclassical synthesis and an ardent opponent of 45-degree Keynesianism. Assisted by a sizeable financial donation from John Kenneth Galbraith, Sidney Weintraub was able to establish the *Journal of Post Keynesian Economics*, which he co-edited with Paul Davidson.

Roy completed his undergraduate degree in mathematics at Swarthmore College in 1964 and then took a Masters (1967) and Ph.D. (1969) in applied mathematics at the University of Pennsylvania. As a graduate student in mathematics he became interested in shifting to some applied mathematics field. Lawrence Klein, a family friend, heard of this and outlined a problem that was to form the basis of his dissertation on "The Stability of Stochastic General Equilibrium Models". Klein supervised the thesis, and Edwin Burmeister was on the Ph.D. committee, along with two mathematicians. Weintraub later noted that Frisch's 1933 paper on "Propagation Problems and Impulse Problems in Dynamic Economics" became the genesis of his own career in economics.

The Sidney Weintraub papers[1] reveal dimensions of a tumultuous relationship between the father and his increasingly rebellious oldest son. The early correspondence shows a father continually prodding and pushing his son, attempting to further his son's career by rustling up job offers, and giving firm instructions on what his son must concentrate on. When Roy shows a penchant for mathematics he is encouraged to "use your math on real problems" and that "in 10 years, you get the formal stuff out of your system". The elder Weintraub admits that he "can't understand the stability stuff" that so interests his son and instead encourages Roy to "mathematize" his father's own work in joint-product papers.

As the son comes to embrace general equilibrium analysis, he finds allegiance with the very economists, such as Robert Clower, Frank Hahn, and Robert Solow, who had been so critical of his father. Imagine the father's reaction to the following statement made by his son: "Keynes is now, scientifically, an historical personage of great competence, but utterly irrelevant to an understanding of either the modern economy or what economists must explain." In response, Sidney Weintraub referred to "logically impeccable but realistically nonsensical articles" with respect to the general equilibrium approach. His son's retort would be to state that general equilibrium analysis has gone a long way towards relaxing earlier restrictions and that general equilibrium reasoning is central to all economic analysis which lays claim to being scientific – it is the centrepiece of the discipline of economics. Fortunately, there is a happy ending to the Mills-like relationship, with Sidney expressing great pride in receiving a copy of his son's *Microfoundations* and Roy dedicating *General Equilibrium Analysis: Studies in Appraisal* to his father's memory.

## An economic theorist turns to history

Roy Weintraub joined the Department of Economics at Duke University in 1970 and in the space of six years was promoted to full professor. This rapid advance is not surprising given the quality of the journals that Roy was able to publish in during this period – including the *Quarterly Journal of Economics*, *American Economic Review*, *Review of Economic Studies*, *International Economic Review*, and the *Journal of Economic Theory*. Many of the articles during this period related to technical aspects of stability in general equilibrium systems.

Two short books in 1974 and 1975 on *General Equilibrium Theory* and *Conflict and Cooperation in Economics* also date from this period. In the 1974 book he states that general equilibrium is at the very centre of economic theory and this mode of theorizing can also be used for macroeconomic concerns. Indeed, a general equilibrium model may be sufficiently rich and flexible to support a Keynesian macroeconomic structure, the implication being that a general equilibrium system is simply a totally disaggregated macro model (1974: 15). This interesting juxtaposition, where a particular framework is applied to a new area to reach unexpected conclusions, characterizes much of Weintraub's later work.

As befits many leading theorists, Roy revealed an early contempt for much of what passes as conventional history of economic thought and those who practise it. He was particularly surprised at the lack of interest by historians of economics in ideas outside the economics discipline, especially those coming from the mathematics community, noting that "it is a minor scandal that there is no comprehensive history of either the rise of econometrics or the mathematization of economics" (1985a: 140). This might reflect inadequacies in the training of particularly older historians of thought or a prejudice by many historians against mathematical economics. This prejudice may derive from the fact that so many historians of economics are heterodox and critical of mathematical approaches to economics. Weintraub felt that it was crucial to an understanding of how economics had been transformed in the modern period to focus upon the interconnections between mathematics and economics in the twentieth century.

It is interesting to speculate about the reasons for Roy's increasing interest in the history of economics and the development of his ideas. We have his own statement that "early in a career, concern with the worth of one's activity is not as important as getting on with the work, and so I put aside any interest I had in appraisal and criticism" and only at a later stage in his career "allowed my 'work' to be more congruent with my interests" (1991: 1–2). Perhaps tenure and a full professorial position allowed him greater creative freedom. It is also hard to believe that his close working relationships at Duke with Neil De Marchi, Craufurd Goodwin, and later Bob Coats, and the presence of the foremost journal in the field, would not have been influential. It may also be that the general equilibrium research programme he was contributing to was failing to live up to expectations. Finally, it may be that his experiences as an academic administrator, as Acting Dean of the Faculty of Arts and Sciences and Chair of the Academic Council (Duke's faculty senate), made him increasingly aware of the intellectual isolation of historians of economics and the need to establish connections with the history of science and intellectual and social history. The influence of Stanley Fish on interpretive communities is clear and Roy has commented on how Philip Mirowski's *More Heat than Light* strongly affected his thinking, saying that the "broad substance of Mirowski's argument is not only correct but also of paramount importance for understanding modern economics" (1991: 161). But we are running ahead of the story.

## On the history and methodology of general equilibrium analysis

Weintraub's first major contribution to understanding the transformation of economics from a historical to a mathematical discipline came in the 1977 *Journal of Economic Literature* with a masterful survey of modern general equilibrium analysis that was two years later expanded into a book entitled *Microfoundations: The Compatibility of Microeconomics and Macroeconomics*. What was surprising was the Lakatosian methodology employed and the historical approach to the neo-Walrasian programme from 1930 to 1960. In 1983 arguably his best paper during the 1980s was published, "On the Existence of a Competitive Equilibrium: 1930–1954". This was reprinted and interpreted at greater length in *General Equilibrium Analysis: Studies in Appraisal* (1985a) – which he later felicitously called "an extended conversation with Mark Blaug" (De Marchi 1988: 59).

In the *Microfoundations* portions of general equilibrium analysis were reconstructed as a Lakatosian research programme. This approach involved not looking at theories in isolation, but instead examining a set of theories constituting a scientific research programme. The Lakatosian framework requires one to attempt an internal "rational reconstruction" of the history of economics. Roy Weintraub attempted to do this for the history of general equilibrium analysis. In *General Equilibrium Analysis: Studies in Appraisal*, he concentrated on that part of the general equilibrium literature associated with the most formal mathematical representations – papers on the existence of a competitive equilibrium between 1930 and 1954 – and the literature was interpreted as a hardening of a Lakatosian hard core in a progressive research programme that was both theoretically and empirically progressive (1991: 2–3).

Weintraub's creative contribution lay in modifying (enriching) the Lakatosian framework by extending the notion of hardening the hard-core postulates of a scientific research programme. He argued that the sequence of papers led to hardening of the hard core of the neo-Walrasian research programme so that it was no longer problematic (1985a: 112–13). Hardening refers to the growing fixity of the meaning of the terms of the hard-core propositions and it was stated that true hardening requires mathematization of the programme. Only in this century was economics formalized well enough for that to take place. It is in that sense that neo-Walrasian economics was better developed than theory sequences in other social science disciplines, since its guiding principles have gone through the hardening process (1985a: 141). Finally, Weintraub argued that we must use criteria appropriate for gauging mathematical progress to measure the growth of knowledge associated with the hardening of the core of the neo-Walrasian programme (1985a: 117–19).

In commenting on *Studies in Appraisal*, Alexander Rosenberg (1986: 129) stated that: "I believe that this work will become a standard source both for the history of general equilibrium theory, and for the economists' justification of its status and role for their discipline." However, critics focused on the sophisticated methodological defence of general equilibrium analysis provided rather than the rich historical narrative. Controversy surrounded Weintraub's use of a Lakatosian methodology to insulate general equilibrium analysis from the "intellectually shoddy" criticisms hurled at it from diverse quarters from the likes of Janos Kornai and Nicholas Kaldor.

Yet Weintraub has been one of the very few willing to take on the critics of general equilibrium analysis at their own game – in terms of its methodological foundations and its empirical progressivity. His work can be seen as the justification for the status and role of general equilibrium analysis in economics. In a nutshell, the methodological defence of general equilibrium analysis involved placing it in the hard core of a scientific research programme which then insulates it from conventional attacks – as if it is hidden behind a methodological shield. General equilibrium analysis can be appraised, but only in a similar fashion to appraisal of mathematical theorems, in terms of its theoretical progressivity. Not surprisingly, general equilibrium work passes such an appraisal with flying colours. Weintraub regards general equilibrium as a logical starting point – the necessary conceptual framework – for any attempt at explaining how a decentralized economic system works.

This methodological defence attracted philosophers and methodologists alike – in particular, doubting responses came from Daniel Hausman, Alexander Rosenberg, and Roger Backhouse. Weintraub's controversial "The NeoWalrasian Program is Empirically Progressive" (in De Marchi 1988: 213–27) induced Arthur Diamond to undertake empirical research to discover that Debreu had a negligible impact on empirical work. Backhouse found Weintraub's attempt to show that general equilibrium lay in the core of an empirically progressive research programme "hardly convincing" (Backhouse 1997: 24).

Perhaps the negative responses from philosophers persuaded Weintraub as to the limited usefulness of specific philosophy of science models used by historians of economics. A conference volume published in 1988, *The Popperian Legacy in Economics*, edited by Neil De Marchi, covers similar territory. At the conference, Deidre McCloskey, commenting with reference to Weintraub's *Studies in Appraisal*, asked "what have we gained by forcing science into a Lakatosian mold?" and suggested that philosophical approaches had not been of much help to the historian. Weintraub has noted that his views changed considerably after listening to the discussion at the 1986 conference in Amsterdam. He acknowledged that constructing the history in terms of a

Lakatosian rational reconstruction is only one way to tell the story and it imposes a rationality on the data that can ignore the history and the actors. A rational reconstruction of a sequence of works may impose on the history a unity and coherence that really is not there.

In 1989 the American History of Economics Society held a session entitled "Should Methodology Matter to the Economist or to the Historian of Economics?" Many commentators at this gathering answered in the negative. What we have here is a critique not only of a particular approach to methodology but of the enterprise as a whole. A key article in this movement is Weintraub's (1989) "Methodology Doesn't Matter, but History of Thought Might". Weintraub now argued that it makes no sense to view the history of economic thought through methodological spectacles. Historians should lose their interest in methodology, in terms of falsificationism, and in terms of general philosophy of science appraisal methods. A number of methodologists, including Bruce Caldwell, were stung by these views and tried to restate the merits of the methodology enterprise (Caldwell 1990).

Weintraub's new view was that methodology is to economics what philosophy of science is to science. Similarly, the history of economics is to economics what history of science is to science. By methodology is meant the attempt to appraise particular theories or research programmes on the basis of general principles of what is good science with the purpose of changing and reforming economics. Weintraub denies that there are objective criteria applicable to all science, and hence the normative role for methodology rests on a profound misconception. If we cannot judge if one theory is better than another, methodology simply does not matter. This, he says, has all sorts of implications for the way we write the history of economics.

## Constructing knowledge

Roy Weintraub over the last fifteen years has been busy trying to change the way we write the history of economics. Once a critical follower of Lakatos, he then came under the spell of Stanley Fish and literary criticism. His position early in the 1990s was that:

> We must accept that history is not presented to us raw, as a neutral case or data source, upon which we may perform tests of our methodological theories of how scientific knowledge is gained. History is not "out there" waiting to answer our questions or corroborate our hypotheses. History is not found. Instead, history is written, and is itself as much a creative enterprise as is the "theory" it is often "meant" to describe.
>
> (Weintraub 1991: 4)

Imre Lakatos (and Thomas S. Kuhn) also saw science as a communal exercise. The picture of individual scientists making revolutionary discoveries in splendid isolation is myth, not reality. Scientists pursue their craft linked closely in many ways to their colleagues and peers. Progress occurs through the activities of highly integrated sub-communities of scientists.

Economics is a social activity and is carried out in interpretive communities; these communities determine the rules according to which texts are interpreted. Individuals cannot stand apart from the communities to which they belong. What one sees in a text is always a function of the interpretive model one brings to bear on it. Meaning is not objective but comes from the interpretive community. All histories are then constructed for one purpose or another. Histories constructed for a philosophical or methodological purpose are not "neutrally" found objects waiting to answer some issue.

That histories are not mere collections of facts but of necessity involve selection and interpretation comes as no surprise to the historian of economics. Weintraub's position, however, has deeper sorts of implications for the way we write the history of economics (Backhouse 1992a). Since texts are not "fixed", for they cannot be read without being interpreted, even apparently straightforward issues like attributing priority involves interpretation. Weintraub provides a case study of this with respect to the Liapunov theory. As a result we should be less concerned about who discovered it first and more with how that knowledge is agreed upon by the community. How are individuals persuaded to accept the consensus position?

Second, the issue of what constitutes a good theory is not a matter of comparing the theory with some standard of scientific goodness (derived from the philosophy of science). Appraisal comes from within the particular community, not from outside sources such as methodology. There are different communities, with different views and beliefs. Claims by outsiders criticizing the value of work conducted inside are easily dismissed, according to Weintraub.

How do we then appraise? Weintraub says it is better to see appraisal as a social process of negotiation and argument which imposes order on the knowledge creation process in relation to the standards and aims of the particular community of economists. To examine this process we have to ask questions like how was a theory developed, how was it presented, what do its terms mean, who was the audience, how did the interpretive community react to particular contributions, and how was it linked to previous papers? This is an intellectual history which seeks to reconstruct the discourse within which the particular community worked: the central problems, conventions, customs, and rules of argument.

Weintraub's position is open to attack on several fronts. Donald Walker takes a "hardheaded positivist approach" claiming that "what has happened in the past is not malleable and cannot be altered to fit our interpretations of it. The same is true of the texts we study" (in Weintraub 1991: 126, 162). The most persistent critic has been Roger Backhouse (1992a; 1992b; 1992c; 1997). Backhouse believes that much of Weintraub's approach comes out of his concern with the mathematical economics literature and would not survive immersion in the more applied and empirical areas of economics. Moreover,

Weintraub's stance is another excellent way to defend general equilibrium analysis from its critics (Warner 1991). Empirical evidence and predictive success are ruled out of court and Weintraub dispenses with notions of "truth". Complaints from those "outside" that particular community are ignored. Backhouse (1992b: 283) states that:

> Weintraub is advocating a philosophical position that is perfect for defending general equilibrium theory. Issues concerning empirical evidence and predictive success, on which general equilibrium theory is very vulnerable, are ruled out of court. By the same token, general equilibrium theory is the ideal example with which to make the case for constructivist history. When discussing general equilibrium theory, and notions like stability of equilibrium, it is very easy indeed to dispense with the notion of truth in the sense of correspondence with reality. Had Weintraub's subject been, for example, macroeconomics or labour economics, his task would have been considerably more difficult.

## History of science and the separate disciplinary status of the history of economic thought

In recent years some prominent historians of science have taken an interest in the history of economics and some historians of economic thought are absorbing the history of science literature. Philip Mirowski (in Schabas *et al.* 1992: 221) comments that:

> I do believe that some of the most profound and imaginative work in the history of economics is done by such historians as Lorraine Daston, Ted Porter, and Tim Alborn, and that the history of economics must shake off its Smith/Ricardo/Marx/Keynes complex and its Whiggish bias and evince a truly interdisciplinary imagination if it is to survive.

He goes on to say that historians of thought will have to become sensitive to modern philosophical and historiographical currents, learn some real history of science, and stop depending on Popper and Lakatos. Weintraub, in the same volume (186), states that

> there is some expression by professional historians that historians of economics would be "better" historians if they were more open to the history of science literature, but among historians of economics there seems to be less interest in addressing the larger community of historians.

In his paper in *Non-Natural Social Science* (De Marchi 1993), Weintraub questions the separate disciplinary status of the history of economic thought. The history of economics is but one part of a more comprehensive history of ideas, and we have to become more like historians in our approach and be aware of developments in related fields. Weintraub laments the intellectual isolation of historians of economics and their reluctance to address the larger community of historians. Philip Mirowski is blunter still and complains of the "catastrophic failure of historians of economics" and asks:

> How much of what has been written under the rubric of the "history of economic thought" is now obsolete? The question is posed not only because the secondary literature has become so drearily repetitive in its demonstrated inability to surprise and entertain us concerning our past but also, more distressingly, because it has proven incapable of speaking to the concerns of the tyro and the average economist.
>
> (Quoted in Davis 1998: 13–14)

Mirowski notes that only a small minority of historians have made the history of recent economics a primary subject of research, and Weintraub's *Stabilizing Dynamics* is a prime example. D. Wade Hands (in Weintraub 1997: 732–3) claims that "the most self-consciously social constructivist book in the history of economic thought is Roy Weintraub's *Stabilizing Dynamics* (1991)".

## Stabilizing Dynamics

Some historians of economics are put off by Weintraub's various reincarnations and the latest historiographic perspective. Diamond (1988: 121) talks of Weintraub's split personality with "Weintraub 1" and "Weintraub 2". Over the decade since then, various other mutations have emerged. Others see this as a flexibility of mind and a willingness to introduce fresh perspectives to our histories. Even his critics will readily admit that he has made a very valuable contribution to our craft and the fixation on methodological controversies has obscured the more fundamental challenges made to our understanding of modern economics.

Weintraub's histories of general equilibrium and economic dynamics are exceedingly valuable. In his 1991 book the focus was how a set of ideas in economics was intertwined with related work in pure and applied mathematics. The economics discipline became mathematized, with economic theory becoming mathematical theory, between the late 1930s and early 1950s. It is a story of how the rich and confusing "talk" of the 1930s evolved into technical analysis of order and coherence in a settled field. This is reflected in how the interpretative community read the word "equilibrium" over a fifteen-year period. "Equilibrium" and "dynamics" meant different things to Lionel Robbins and Ragnar Frisch and Jan Tinbergen (Weintraub 1991: 26), and the meaning of the term equilibrium evolved in a sequence of papers over 1939 and 1954. The mathematical forms of the arguments significantly altered the substance of the economic arguments. In particular, the available mathematics defined the content of economic dynamics; problems of dynamics were recast as problems of establishing whether a system was stable or unstable.

Weintraub is particularly interested in the origins of Paul Samuelson's

*Foundations of Economic Analysis* (1947). Weintraub's account differs enormously from Samuelson's own recollections about the "mythic past of the discipline" and clearly explains why Samuelson was absorbed by comparative statics and so little concerned with stability analysis (1991: 61–2). Weintraub argues "that Samuelson's mathematical dynamics reflects in large measure the beliefs and prejudices of E.B. Wilson" (1991: 58), while:

> The mathematics of dynamic systems, through Birkhoff and Picard, the applied mathematical analysis of systems from Lotka, the thermodynamics of the late nineteenth century through Gibbs via Wilson, and the confused literature on economic dynamics of the 1930s all shaped the way Samuelson constructed his arguments in the Foundations.
>
> (1991: 66)

*Stabilizing Dynamics* also makes clear how

> the way in which the mathematics that Hicks used structured his argument in certain ways and constrained him to ask certain questions and to accept certain features of the problem situation as salient, while characterizing and then rejecting others (no less significant in the economics) as uninteresting.
>
> (1991: 32)

It also notes the curious separation between Hicks and the later stability literature.

Weintraub claims that the history of modern economics must take into account the history of mathematics and how the mathematics community has influenced economics and how mathematics itself has changed. The interaction between economics and mathematics shows that the nature of mathematics has changed considerably and that the cultural context is important too. For example, Weintraub argues that English mathematics was the antithesis of what we now think of as rigorous mathematics. The English mathematics studied by Marshall and Keynes "was a mess of applied physics, thermodynamics, optics, geometry", and hence Jevons and Marshall and Edgeworth could not provide a rigorous mathematical foundation for economic theory.

The decade of the 1940s is seen as crucial in transforming economics from a historical discipline to a mathematical one:

> Economists began to use mathematical tools once those tools became widely used by those working in applied mathematics, engineering, and other applied sciences. ... Issues of control, guidance and stability became extremely important in war-related research in applied mathematics ... the period from 1946 to the early 1950s saw wider dissemination of the results ... to the mathematical economics community.
>
> (1991:93)

However, laments Weintraub, few historians of economics have taken an interest in the mathematization of economics in the postwar period. This reluctant interest may reflect the very technical context of the issues and that the history covers many disciplines and many countries (1991: 3–4).

In 1992 Weintraub edited *Toward a History of Game Theory* as part of the puzzle relating to the transformation of economics in the 1940s from a historical discipline to a mathematical one. This game theory volume challenges much of the conventional wisdom relating to the development of game-theoretic notions in economics and noted, among other things, that there was no community in which game theory could have taken root before the 1940s and thus no possibility that the theory could have been developed before that time (1992a: 8).

Particularly insightful is a 1994 article co-authored with Mirowski on how Bourbakism came to mathematical economics. This study documents how the Bourbakist school of mathematics rapidly migrated into neoclassical mathematical economics (1994: 246) and came to uphold the primacy of the pure over the applied, the rigorous over the intuitive, and strongly influenced Gerard Debreu and the Cowles Commission. This respect for mathematical formalism and scepticism of empirical work characterized the fledgling mathematical economics community.

These themes are further developed in two 1998 publications. The first is a contribution to a discussion on "Formalism in Economics" in the *Economic Journal* (Weintraub 1998c). There Weintraub distinguishes rigour from axiomatization and notes that mathematical formalism that disdains data and applied work is not necessarily mathematically rigorous on the basis of earlier interpretations of that term. The second paper is a contribution to a volume on *From Interwar Pluralism to Postwar Neoclassicism* (Weintraub 1998b). In this paper it is demonstrated that in the first decades of the twentieth century a rigorous argument was reconceptualized as a logically consistent argument instead of an argument related to an empirical foundation. This is illustrated through the intriguing contribution of Griffith C. Evans and his view that the non-quantifiable and the non-measurable, such as utility concepts, were unfit subjects for mathematical investigation.

These articles, and the statement in *Stabilizing Dynamics* (1991: 39, 115) that the stability of a competitive equilibrium programme might be considered as progressive during the 1940s and early 1950s, but degenerated after that time, indicate that the author acknowledges that not all mathematical transfers to economics have assisted the discipline.

## Attacking lost causes

The earlier *Microfoundations* book was both popular (Robert Solow used it in his graduate classes) and controversial. Stirring up a hornets' nest and offending people has never perturbed Roy, and he excels in the heated debate. Despite his affection for Paul Davidson, Roy has often slung his arrows at the post-

Keynesians. This genre includes his 1982 critique of Sheila Dow in "Substantive Mountains and Methodological Molehills" and the less than flattering appraisal ("her flawed understanding") of Joan Robinson in the 1985 *American Economic Review* (1985c: 146). Perhaps Weintraub's disagreement with Robert Heilbroner on ideology has a place here too.

Nicholas Kaldor has also received a withering assault from Weintraub for his criticisms of general equilibrium. For example, he calls Kaldor's critique of general equilibrium foolish and irrational. It is also no coincidence that when he talks about post-Keynesians he uses the following quote from C. Vann Woodward (*New York Review of Books* January 30, 1986):

> Lost causes, especially those that foster loyalties and nostalgic memories, are among the most prolific breeders of historiography. If survivors deem the cause not wholly lost and perhaps in some measure retrievable, the search of the past becomes more frantic and the books about it more numerous. Blame must be fixed, villains found, heroes celebrated, old quarrels settled, old dreams restored, and motives vindicated. Amid the ruins controversy thrives and books proliferate.
>
> (1991: 125)

Elsewhere he writes that Marxians, institutionalists, Austrians, and post-Keynesians

> are regarded by mainstream neoclassical economists at best as defenders of lost causes, at worst as "kooks," "misguided critics," "antiscientific oddballs," etc. The status of non-neoclassical economists in the departments of economics in English speaking universities is similar to that of Lamarkians in Zoology Departments, and Flat-Earthers in Geography Departments.

Similarly his September 1996 HES-LIST editorial about what is and what is not legitimate history of economics has offended people (Weintraub 1996). Weintraub's more searching demarcation has severe implications given his position as associate editor of *History of Political Economy*. One inference was that work in the Austrian, Marxian, institutionalist, or post-Keynesian tradition could not be regarded as legitimate history of thought. Weintraub is attempting to improve the standards of the history of economics presumably to increase the relevance of this work to the profession. He is critical of traditional approaches and the type of work that gets classified as history of thought. He does not regard as a legitimate contribution work by members of various marginalized groups within the economics profession who on occasion employ historical references and cite long-dead economists.

As an example, a June 1998 Weintraub review that finds Harcourt and Riach's *Second Edition of The General Theory* "uninteresting historical scholarship" has led to howls of protest. In the *Economic Record* review, Weintraub states that: "The construction of Keynes, Keynesian economics, and the Keynesian revolution are undeveloped historical topics in economics." This is an amazing claim given the deluge of material written on Keynesianism, and only made comprehensible in terms of Weintraub's strict standards for acceptable or serious scholarship in the history of economic thought. Weintraub argues that we need to address the larger community of historians and adopt their standards of scholarship.

## The obscured light

Work on the mathematization of modern economics is a valuable activity. Attempts to break down the intellectual isolation of historians of economics and to establish connections with the history of science, and recognizing that "the history of economics is but one part of a larger and more comprehensive history of ideas" (in De Marchi 1993: 301), are also laudatory. One of Weintraub's tasks as associate editor of *History of Political Economy* is to develop symposia on outreach topics and to open the perspectives of historians of economics to work in other disciplines. These initiatives may add new life and vigour to the subdiscipline. The work of Arjo Klamer and Robert Leonard, both influenced by the Duke University connection, is a case in point. Similarly, the Economists' Papers Project at Duke University with its collection of the unpublished personal and professional papers of individual economists has been uniformly praised.

Tolerance for other approaches and interests is also a valuable asset in the study of the history of economics. Not all work in the history of economics is Whiggish and there is strong resistance to a claim that denies the separate disciplinary status of the history of economic thought. Only a minority of historians of thought have moved in the direction that Weintraub (and Mirowski) advocate. Perhaps the subdiscipline will be the poorer for this reluctance or it may simply be an aversion to the "mind-numbing bouts of jargon-filled verbless sentences" (1997: 694) associated with the sociology of science.

Weintraub's work attracts controversy and dissent. He takes bold positions. He claims: that economists are not creators of theories and assemblers of facts and do not attempt to test, or falsify, theoretical accounts by confronting those theories with the data; that the "real world" and "Truth" are uninteresting concepts; that science does not uncover truth, facts are socially constructed; and that there is no basis for judging one theory better than another. These statements are bound to attract critics. These critics are not impressed when told their criticisms simply reflect how they are misinformed about the evolution of ideas in epistemology and science studies.

In some ways the reaction to Weintraub's work reflects the old distinction between positive and normative economics. When he explains how economics was transformed in the modern period this is recognized as a valuable service to the discipline. The increasing mathematization of economics, the emergence of the neoclassical synthesis, the core role of general equilibrium analysis, the intellectual monopoly of neoclassical economics, and the marginalization of alternative schools of thought, are all accepted as part of this story. Unfortunately, it is the normative view that Weintraub seems to convey that so irritates other historians. While Weintraub applauds these developments, many lament these changes in the profession.

Weintraub argues that there is no scientific economics other than neoclassical economics, that the "mathematico-scientification" of economics is precisely the story of the emergence of neoclassical economics, and that the success of neoclassical economics is precisely connected to the mathematization of the subject. Moreover, there is a fundamental connection between progress in economics and progress in mathematics (1985a: 142; 1982a). Economic analysis is a mathematical activity so that as one's mathematical understanding becomes richer so does the ability to provide explanations for economic phenomena. Furthermore, general equilibrium analysis is the only proper mode of proceeding where mutual interdependency is the order of the day.[2]

All the above statements are problematic for many economists as well as historians of thought. For example, Weintraub states that in the 1940s Patinkin successfully embedded the Keynesian model in a neoclassical optimizing framework. Is this a positive or normative statement? It depends on what is meant by "successfully", and it will not do to say that these issues are not subject to discussion. Warren Samuels complained twenty years ago about this exclusiveness and about certain positions being outside the pale of legitimate discourse: "let economics do without ex cathedra pronouncements as to what is permissible economics" (or history of economic thought!) (Samuels 1979: 1025).

This ambivalence to Weintraub's work is reflected in Robert Heilbroner and William Milberg's (1995) book, *The Crisis of Vision in Modern Economic Thought*. On the one hand they praise "his pathbreaking book, *Stabilising Dynamics*", yet the theme of their own work is that: "The mark of modern-day economics is its extraordinary indifference to ... the connection between theory and 'reality.' At its peaks, the 'high theorizing' of the present period attains a degree of unreality that can be matched only by medieval scholasticism" (Heilbroner and Milberg 1995: 3). This is not a conclusion one finds in *Stabilizing Dynamics*.

## Notes

* I would like to thank Jeff Biddle, Craufurd Goodwin, Grant Fleming, Robert Leonard, Phil Mirowski, Roy Weintraub, the editors of this volume, and participants at the July 1998 HETSA conference for helpful comments.

1 This paragraph and the next use material from the Sidney Weintraub Papers which are located in the William R. Perkins Library, Duke University, Durham, North Carolina. I am grateful to Mr Robert Byrd for allowing me access to these papers. The quotations from the first paragraph come from a letter by S. Weintraub to E. R. Weintraub, February 24, 1970, Box 2 Folder 1. The quotation in the second paragraph comes from a letter by E. R. Weintraub to J. Kregel, October 16, 1982, Box 6 Folder 2.

2 One has to be careful here as Roy has changed his mind over time and not always pushed for consistency. Through the mid 1980s he did equate general equilibrium and neoclassical economics with scientific economics. But his understanding of

science, and claims made about science, changed in the mid–late 1980s in confrontation with emerging literatures in science studies and history of science. Perhaps now Roy might say that to call some approach to economics "scientific" is to say that it employs certain rhetorical methods, certain styles of argumentation, that have historically come to be associated with a socially constructed notion called "science". It is not a compliment, it is just a label. To say that neoclassical economics is the only scientific approach to economics is to say that it is the only approach that has convincingly (in the eyes of the relevant discourse community) adopted these methods and styles, which include mathematical argumentation. To the extent that Roy is only characterizing mainstream economics while his critics (usually aligned with some heterodox tradition) think he is praising it, they are talking past each other. I am indebted to Jeff Biddle for this point.

# Bibliography

Backhouse, Roger E. (1992a) "How Should We Approach the History of Economic Thought: Fact, Fiction or Moral Tale?", *Journal of the History of Economic Thought* 14, 1: 18–35.

—— (1992b) "Reply: History's Many Dimensions", *Journal of the History of Economic Thought* 14, 2: 277–84.

—— (1992c) "The Constructivist Critique of Economic Methodology", *Methodus* 4, 1: 65–82.

—— (1997) *Truth and Progress in Economic Knowledge*, Cheltenham: Edward Elgar.

Caldwell, Bruce J. (ed.) (1984) *Appraisal and Criticism in Economics*, Winchester: Allen and Unwin (reprints the Weintraub–Dow exchange, 424–37).

—— (1990) "Does Methodology Matter? How Should it be Practiced?", *Finnish Economic Papers* 3, 1: 64–71.

Davis, John B. (ed.) (1998) *New Economics and Its History*, Durham, NC: Duke University Press.

De Marchi, Neil (ed.) (1988) *The Popperian Legacy in Economics*, Cambridge: Cambridge University Press.

—— (ed.) (1993) *Non-Natural Social Science*, Durham, NC: Duke University Press.

Diamond, Arthur M. (1988) "The Empirical Progressiveness of the General Equilibrium Research Program", *History of Political Economy* 20, 1: 119–32.

Heilbroner, Robert and Milberg, William (1995) *The Crisis of Vision in Modern Economic Thought*, Cambridge: Cambridge University Press.

Rosenberg, Alexander (1986) "Lakatosian Consolations for Economics", *Economics and Philosophy* 2: 127–39 (Reply and Rejoinder in 3: 139–44).

Salanti, Andrea (1987) "Roy Weintraub's Studies in Appraisal", History of Economics Society Annual Meeting, June, Vol. 4.

Samuels, Warren J. (1979) "Roy Weintraub's Microfoundations: The State of High Theory", *Journal of Economic Issues* 13, 4: 1019–28.

Schabas, Margaret et al. (1992) "Breaking Away: History of Economics as History of Science. Minisymposium: The History of Economics and the History of Science", *History of Political Economy* 24, 1: 185–247.

Warner, Adrian (1991) "Appraising Weintraub's Appraisal", *History of Economics Review* 16, Summer: 119–27.

Weintraub, E. Roy (1974) *General Equilibrium Theory*, London: Macmillan.

—— (1977) "General Equilibrium Theory" and "Optimization and Game Theory", in S. Weintraub (ed.) *Modern Economic Thought*, Philadelphia: University of Pennsylvania Press.

—— (1982a) *Mathematics for Economists: An Integrated Approach*, Cambridge: Cambridge University Press.

—— (1982b) "Substantive Mountains and Methodological Molehills", *Journal of Post Keynesian Economics* 5: 295–303.

—— (1983) "On the Existence of a Competitive Equilibrium: 1930–1954", *Journal of Economic Literature* 21, 1: 1–39.

—— (1985a) *General Equilibrium Analysis: Studies in Appraisal*, Cambridge: Cambridge University Press.

—— (1985b) "Appraising General Equilibrium Analysis", *Economics and Philosophy* 1, 1: 23–37.

—— (1985c) "Joan Robinson's Critique of Equilibrium: An Appraisal", *American Economic Review* May: 146–9.

—— (1989) "Methodology Doesn't Matter, but the History of Thought Might", *Scandinavian Journal of Economics*; reprinted in S. Honkapohja (ed.) (1990) *The State of Macroeconomics*, Oxford: Blackwell.

—— (1991) *Stabilizing Dynamics. Constructing Economic Knowledge*, Cambridge: Cambridge University Press.

—— (ed.) (1992a) *Toward a History of Game Theory*, Durham, NC: Duke University Press.

—— (1992b) "Roger Backhouse's Straw Herring", *Methodus* 4, 2: 53–7.

—— (1992c) "Comment: Thicker is Better", *Journal of the History of Economic Thought* 14, 2: 271–7.

—— (1996) "What Defines a Legitimate Contribution to the Subdiscipline 'The History of Economics'?", Guest Editorial, History of Economics Society, 9 September: http://www.eh.net/ehnet/HisEcSoc/Resources/Editorials (accessed September 9, 1996).

—— (ed.) (1997) "Minisymposium: STS and the History of Economics", *History of Political Economy* 29, 4: 691–760.

—— (1998a) "Review of Backhouse's *Truth and Progress* and *Explorations in Economic Methodology*", *Journal of Economic Methodology* 5, 2: 317–22.

—— (1998b) "From Rigor to Axiomatics: The Marginalization of Griffith C. Evans", in M. S. Morgan and M. Rutherford (eds) *From Interwar Pluralism to Postwar Neoclassicism*, Annual Supplement to Vol. 30 of *History of Political Economy*, Durham, NC: Duke University Press, 227–59.

—— (1998c) "Axiomatisches Mißverständnis", in S. C. Dow (ed.) "Controversy: Formalism in Economics", *Economic Journal* 108, November: 1837–47.

Weintraub, E. Roy. and Morowski, Philip (1994) "The Pure and the Applied: Bourbakism Comes to Mathematical Economics", *Science in Context* 7, 2: 245–72.

# 18 Donald Winch as intellectual historian

*Geoffrey Gilbert*

## I

It is no accident that the title given to this essay echoes that chosen by Donald Winch for his own contribution to the 1983 volume on which the present one is modeled. In writing on "Jacob Viner as Intellectual Historian," Winch was bringing to the fore one aspect of the mind and career of the man under whom he had written his own doctoral dissertation at Princeton in the late 1950s. That he chose to address his mentor's scholarly achievements "as intellectual historian" rather than as "historian of economic thought" says something about Viner, of course: according to Winch, there had come a time in Viner's career when he "moved away from doctrinal or single-discipline history of economics toward a more broadly defined kind of intellectual history" (Winch 1983b: 10). But the choice of label may also say something about Winch himself, about the kind of intellectual perspective he looks for and prizes in the scholarship of others, and aspires to in his own. Intellectual history is what Donald Winch does, and, unlike his mentor, he has been at it his entire career.[1] How and why and over what range of subject matter are questions this essay will attempt to answer.

Before taking leave of Jacob Viner, we should pause to note a few of the qualities Winch admired in his teacher, as recorded in a memorial piece for *American Scholar* in 1981. If students model themselves on their teachers, or "learn from their example" – an indulgent hypothesis most academics will readily accept – the following quotations may tell us something about both teacher and pupil. On Viner's professionalism: "He was, quite simply, the most comprehensive and meticulous of scholars; he combined encyclopedic knowledge with that rarer gift among historians, analytical acuteness, the legacy of a distinguished career as an economic theorist." On Viner's teaching style: "What we heard in his seminars was ... akin to argumentative conversation, in which Viner excelled even when he was left to play all the parts in the argument." And on Viner's scholarly credo: "He regarded the attainment of accuracy and neutrality in reporting dead men's ideas, avoiding distortion, denigration, and undue piety, as 'an arduous and difficult art, calling for unintermitting self-discipline.'"[2]

Two years later, Winch canvassed his lecture notes and memory to come up with an expanded version of the Viner credo on the proper manner of doing intellectual history. The result bears a striking (if unsurprising) resemblance to Winch's own frequently stated historiographic views, particularly his insistence on "working outward" from text to context:

> Once accurate texts had been established [according to Viner], the next task was to concentrate on the meaning of the author in his own terms rather than those of the student. The intent of the author having been evinced by placing the text within the appropriate context, it was possible to consider wider economic and social conditions, biographical evidence, traceable influences of earlier and contemporary writings. ... All of this was merely to obtain a credible interpretation of the argument of an author in a particular text, and that text alone.
>
> (Winch 1983b: 11)

## II

The subject of Winch's first book, *Classical Political Economy and Colonies* (1965), might have led him straight into the realm of "single-discipline" or "doctrinal" history, had that been his inclination (or Viner's: the book was a thoroughly revised doctoral dissertation). Most of the theoretical and policy issues on which classical economics cut its teeth – population pressure, capital accumulation, growth, trade, and the role of the state – were raised by this topic, and most of the principal figures of the classical school from Smith to Mill weighed in on it. Yet Winch rejected from the outset an approach that would have dwelt solely upon the shaping influence of the colonial debate on the body of classical doctrine; he chose to "steer clear of the history of economic analysis for its own sake in order to remain close to the issues as seen by the participants" (Winch 1965: 3). A considerable portion of the book was devoted to the ideas and influence of a man who generally rates no more than a footnote in history-of-thought textbooks: Edward Gibbon Wakefield.[3] Given the topic, of course, Winch could hardly have done otherwise. The book also paid more attention to *political* aspects of the debate over colonies, especially in later chapters, than would have been the case in a work oriented mainly to doctrinal history – and probably *less* than if Winch were writing on the same subject today. An anonymous reviewer in *The Economist* praised the work for its "judicious" and "lucid" style, adding that "one has the comfortable feeling that, after having read Winch, one will not have to read other people, except the classics themselves" (1965: 1426).

Another quality of the *Colonies* book commended by *The Economist's* reviewer was its modesty, its holding back from "massive conclusions." Modesty seems the right word, as well, to characterize Winch's decision not to attempt an assessment of the interaction between classical ideas on colonies and the direction of government policy. The impulse to establish such a connection must have been as strong as it was natural. For surely every kind of intellectual historian, aside from the most unreconstructed Marxian, believes on some level that ideas have a bearing on the way events unfold in the "real world," or, in the pithier phrase, that *ideas matter*. To believe this in the abstract, however, and to believe oneself equipped to prove it in a concrete historical context are different things entirely. With a wisdom given to few graduate students, Winch resisted the impulse, because "it seemed more important to reconstruct and interpret the internal lines of the debate than its external influence" (Winch 1965: 3).

Resisting the impulse just mentioned has become a feature of Winch-style intellectual history as it has evolved over time. Winch's obvious preference in the work he has done on eighteenth- and nineteenth-century political economy has continued to be, as it was in *Classical Political Economy and Colonies*, to "reconstruct and interpret the internal lines of the debate" rather than attempt to demonstrate policy impacts. Not that Winch has ever denied the possibility of such impacts or such demonstrations; he simply leaves these matters to others. He is careful in his own work not to overstate the power of economic ideas to influence policy in any direct, immediate way, and he can be critical of those who do not exercise the same caution. In the course of a synoptic review of the "Emergence of Economics as a Science, 1750–1870," Winch quoted a portion of the 1870 lecture by J. E. Cairnes in which the latter claimed that Britain had been the first nation "to apply with boldness our [economic] theories to practice. Our foreign trade, our colonial policy, our fiscal system, each has in turn been reconstructed from the foundation upwards under the inspiration of economic ideas." This sweeping judgment drew a categorical reproof from Winch: "The role of ideas – as opposed to interest groups and circumstance – in producing changes in policy is exaggerated" (Winch 1971: 541–2).

In a branch of his scholarship less well known to most historians of economic thought than his various studies on Smith and Malthus, namely his work on early twentieth-century economists (Keynes in particular) and their role in helping redefine the government's economic responsibilities, Winch has waded into the very issues of policy impact he tends to skirt when doing strictly intellectual history. Consider his *Economics and Policy: A Historical Study* (1969), which examines the changing scope of national economic policy in both Britain and the United States in light of the contemporary advice coming from the economics profession. It is a daunting subject, in part because "the profession" did not always speak with one voice or maintain consistency in its recommendations; Keynes himself, as we know, took a variety of wrong turns on the way to final policy positions. As Winch's narrative makes clear, there was virtually never, on either side of the Atlantic, an instance of direct and prompt translation of professional economic advice into policy action. One takes away from this study a chastened sense of the error of thinking of ideas and policy reacting on one another in simple ways. Certainly Winch's cautions about the "snares" and "difficulties" facing any inquiry into the relationship between economic thought and policy carry the conviction of one who can claim hard-won knowledge of the matter (Winch 1969: 19). He offers a special warning to economists:

> One must be aware – as Keynes was not on all occasions – of the rationalist fallacy of believing that ideas alone are powerful enough to determine the course of events. All important economic policies require political and moral choices to be made in a context that is characterized by norms, beliefs, goals, and pressures which differ from those of an academic community. Even if economic advisers were always unanimous and relevant in their diagnoses and remedies, there would still be plenty of scope for slips twixt lip and cup.
>
> (Winch 1969: 20)

For the balance of this essay, the history of ideas proper, as opposed to the complex question of the role of ideas in determining events or policy outcomes, will be our concern.[4]

## III

At a couple of points in the 1965 book on colonies – odd, incidental points easily passed over – one can catch glimpses of the mature art of intellectual history encountered in Winch's later writings. Both, as it happens, relate to Adam Smith. The first is a footnote on page 19. Having previously mentioned, in the text, three contemporaries of Smith who sympathized with the colonial cause (Richard Price, Josiah Tucker, and David Hume), Winch uses the note to list three forerunners of Smith on the idea of a legislative union between Britain and its North American colonies: Thomas Pownall, Lord Kames, and Benjamin Franklin. After providing a few references to their writings, he adds:

> Kames and Franklin corresponded on the subject of a "consolidating union" between Britain and her colonies. There are numerous inter-connections between the writers mentioned. Tucker was translated into French by Turgot who also corresponded with Price. Hume knew both Turgot and Tucker; and Kames and Tucker corresponded.
>
> (Winch 1965: 19n.)

What a web of contacts and relationships! One can almost picture Winch pulling up chairs for them all, Adam Smith included, and proceeding to initiate a roundtable exchange on the subject of a possible British–colonial commonwealth. His role as historian/host – to extend the conceit – would be to pass the port around, spur lively debate, tease out areas of agreement and disagreement, and try later to make sense of it all for an audience far removed in time, place, and historical circumstances from the original conversation. Though fanciful, this scenario captures something of the "dialogic" quality to be found in Winch's most recent book, in which key figures of the classical school are, as it were, brought into "conversation" with prominent contemporaries, both supportive and critical, in an effort to establish the full reach of their ideas.[5]

A second clue to the Winchian art of intellectual history occurs later in the book and involves an issue of historiographic principle rather than procedure. In opening a discussion of Say's law, Winch makes the point that Adam Smith cannot be interpreted as having accepted or rejected Say's law for the simple reason that the Scotsman never was pressed to consider the problem to which it was seen as a response, namely the possibility of general overproduction. Winch continues: "This has been overlooked by modern commentators; there is a tendency to transfer back to Smith a body of analysis which was developed later to deal with a problem Smith did not envisage" (Winch 1965: 84). What we have here is an early instance, in miniature, of Winch performing a crucial if negative function of intellectual history, namely to combat anachronism. As Winch has argued on many subsequent occasions, it is unacceptable for latter-day commentators to read their own biases and preconceptions into the thoughts and texts of an earlier time. And if the avoidance of anachronism – or more positively, the recovery of original intention and meaning – is held to be one of the paramount ends of intellectual history, an obvious means of achieving that end is to "listen" carefully to contemporary voices, to enter sympathetically into the conversations of the past.

*Adam Smith's Politics: An Essay in Historiographic Revision* (1978) delivers a book-length rebuke to a particularly influential species of anachronism, one which seeks to recruit Smith retroactively into schools of thought or ideological categories beyond his own time and ken. Winch insists on disassociating Smith from such labels as "liberal capitalist," "radical individualist," or advocate of laissez-faire.[6] In the appropriate eighteenth-century framework of political discourse to which Smith belongs, and which Winch credits other scholars, chiefly Duncan Forbes and J. G. A. Pocock, with having illuminated, the most appropriate shorthand term to describe Smith is "skeptical" or "scientific Whig."[7] This designation situates Smith firmly in the Scottish Enlightenment;[8] more than that, it redirects the search for the roots of Smith's politics away from John Locke's "vulgar Whiggism" and toward Smith's fellow Scotsman, David Hume, his teacher Frances Hutcheson, and the natural law theorists of the Continent, among others.

The negative purpose of the book, as indicated, is to counter teleological readings of Smith as a way station along the road from Locke to nineteenth-century liberal capitalism. The strategy Winch adopts to accomplish this aim is two-fold: first, provide Smith with a more accurate (non-Lockean) intellectual lineage; and second – this being the book's *positive* agenda – demonstrate that, contrary to what might be expected of the putative "founding father of classical political economy," Smith had a genuine political dimension to his thought, a "political vision." Moreover, it was a politics far too complex to be reducible to slogans such as "limited government" or "*laissez-faire*." No such simplistic notions would have enabled Smith to address as he did, intelligently and coherently, contemporary issues as varied as the public debt, the colonial crisis, and standing armies versus militias. (Each of these issues receives a full chapter's attention in *Adam Smith's Politics*.) Indeed, catchphrases such as "night-watchman" or "limited government" not only do violence to the depth and subtlety of Smith's politics; they fundamentally misrepresent his view of the proper scope of state action in commercial society. As Jacob Viner pointed out many decades ago, Smith saw a "wide and elastic range of activity for government" in promoting the best interests of the population at large.[9]

A leitmotif running through most of Winch's scholarly writings on Smith is the idea of political economy as a "branch of the science of a statesman or legislator." The words are from the *Wealth of Nations* itself, and what a source of perplexity to the student of the history of economics, at least on first encounter! "Science of a legislator" seems to connote something akin to political science, and one normally does not think of political economy, or economics, as merely a sub-field or "branch" of its sister discipline. But of course all of today's "social sciences" are descendants from a common ancestor, the science of man conceived in the seventeenth and eighteenth centuries and shaped, in embryo, in the moral philosophy curriculum, notably in Scotland. As early as Aristotle, politics had been considered the overarching "master-science." For Hume, the science of politics concerned itself with "men united in society and dependent on each other." The point Winch has stressed in all of this is that Smith was of an intellectual generation – the last, in fact – whose conception of politics was so encompassing that it could include political economy. Thus the *Wealth of Nations* emerged in the first place as a fuller development of the section on "police, revenue, and arms" of the lectures on jurisprudence delivered by Smith at Glasgow University in the 1750s and early 1760s. A more finished treatment of jurisprudence, one that might have offered a bridge between the *Wealth of Nations* and the *Theory of Moral Sentiments*, or between Smith's economics and his ethics, was projected by Smith early in his career but never completed or seen into print.[10]

To have argued as persuasively as he has that Adam Smith's economics was only an offshoot of his broader "science of a legislator" and, at the same time, to have focused nearly all of his Smith scholarship on the *non*-economic aspects of that science may have made Winch, from time to time, the object of quizzical side glances within the "tribe" or "guild" of economists (his terms). He has never concealed his basic disinterest in economics for its own sake, despite his undergraduate degree in economics from the London School of Economics and his Ph.D. in economics from Princeton. On the first page of *Adam Smith's Politics*, Winch forthrightly announced, "I will have little to say directly about the economists' Smith," and a dozen pages further on, having noted the inclusion of political economy within the larger Hume–Smith conception of "politics," he added: "One of the objects of this essay will be to bring to the fore and attach historical meaning to the large remainder left after political economy proper has been set on one side" (Winch 1978: 1, 13). *Set on one side?* For many readers, especially members of the "guild," setting Smith's economics on one side must appear about as reasonable as setting Rembrandt's paintings to one side in assessing his merits as an artist. What, then, are we to make of Winch's seemingly deliberate turning aside from the economics of Smith?

In the first place, Smith the economist has already been studied in minute detail by generations of doctrinal historians. Winch has shown no interest in adding another course of bricks to the already formidable edifice of Smithian economics; indeed, he harbors real misgivings about the edifice as it now stands. To a group of economists gathered in 1976 to celebrate the bicentenary of the *Wealth of Nations*, and speaking as one of the few "accredited antiquarians" in that company, Winch voiced his concern: "Economists have not always been the most reliable or consistent interpreters of their own past, and their whiggish habits have perhaps done more damage to Smith than many later figures in the pantheon" (Winch 1976: 71). In a somewhat fuller statement of his attitude toward the accounts of Smith written by economists and "those historians of economic thought who write with economists chiefly in mind," Winch has said the following:

> Even when they wish to do more than simply retrieve modern economic meanings, often by stripping away what seem to be mere period residues, they regard the *Wealth of Nations*, first and foremost, as an *economic* classic, the magnificent opening speech in a largely autonomous form of discourse that has continued to the present day.
>
> (Winch 1983a: 255)

Needless to say, these are the sorts of commentators whom Winch would fault for the reductive and one-dimensional versions of Smith that he finds untenable. They are the kind to be found "recruiting" Smith into one modern ideology or another. And they are, he notes dismissively, "unwilling or unable to shed new light on [Smith's] project taken as a whole" (Winch 1983a: 256).[11] We shall need to consider doctrinal history again, as it relates to post-Smithian political economy, in the next section.

There must be nearly as many views of the correct way to do intellectual history as there are practitioners of the discipline. Some of the approaches are listed by Winch in the introduction to his latest book: "the study of *mentalités*, the archaeology of discursive practices, *Ideologiekritik*, cultural materialism, the new historicism, and deconstructionism" (Winch 1996: 27). He subscribes to none of these, and is in fact highly dubious about applications of "theory" and "technical apparatuses" to the writing of history.[12] Acknowledging the influence of the historian Quentin Skinner on how he thinks about texts, Winch takes a position that would *appear* entirely straightforward were it not completely at odds with one of the central tenets of modern literary criticism: "I subscribe to a humanist position which believes in the existence of authors as well as texts and discursive practices – authors who were capable of forming and sometimes succeeding in carrying out their intentions when writing" (Winch 1996: 29). Knowing how controversial the issue of authorial intention has been, Winch is careful to leave no doubt on where he stands: "The essays in this book have been written on the assumption that *we can reconstruct what past speakers were trying to express* without losing our own capacity to talk about the same subjects in the process" (Winch 1996: 29; emphasis added).

The effort to see Smith, Malthus, and others as much as possible in the social, political, and intellectual contexts of their *own* time, and not through the distorting lenses of later times, has been pursued so aggressively by Winch that he has been accused of going overboard. He has called his own *Adam Smith's Politics* "rather puritanically historicist" in its deliberate neglect of what might be termed the "forward linkages" from Smith to later thinkers, and he has come to accept the duty of historians like himself to explore the various modes by which "seminal works make their way in the world and are transformed in the process" (Winch 1988: 87; also, 1996: 16–17). The charge made by others, however, is that the Winchian brand of intellectual history demands, or seems to demand, a pretense of ignorance of the future, including future terms and tools of economic analysis, when dealing in the approved, non-anachronistic manner with earlier economic thinkers. Winch disavows this "rhetorical absurdity," arguing that anachronism can be avoided in another and simpler way – by "not writing as though our chosen authors possessed foresight" (Winch 1998: 354). To write as though they *did* commits the "proleptic" (future-assuming) error, something a careful historian of ideas will seek to avoid. With regard to Adam Smith, what Winch seems to be saying is that if we insist on viewing Smith in the anticipatory mode, as a bridge to something in his future, an episode in a larger march of ideas toward a predetermined destination, we have not really seen Smith at all.

## IV

At the Glasgow celebration of the *Wealth of Nations* bicentenary mentioned above, Professor Winch tweaked his distinguished audience with this question:

> If there was a major change of emphasis and a narrowing in the scope of the science of political economy soon after Smith's death, can economists assume quite so confidently, as they appear to be doing this bicentennial year, that they are his rightful, if not sole, heirs? If, according to modern taste, Ricardo is more of an economists' economist than Smith, are today's economists the most natural celebrants of the *Wealth of Nations*?
>
> (Winch 1976: 69)

The issue of the legacy of Smith for classical political economy is one Winch has been exploring for over two decades. Because of the way he views Smith's intellectual enterprise – as a crowning though incomplete achievement of the Scottish moral philosophy tradition, of which the *Wealth of Nations* represents but a single facet – he necessarily sees a discontinuity, even a "gulf," between Smith and the various candidates who could be put forward as his possible "successors." Removed from that list for one reason or another are Say,

Sismondi, Lauderdale, John Millar, Dugald Stewart, James Mill, J. R. McCulloch, and Ricardo (Winch 1978: 184–5; 1983c: 511–20), with Malthus less easily dismissed. Among Britain's post-Smithian political economists, there simply was not, before John Stuart Mill, the same breadth of approach one finds in Smith's science of the legislator. The difference appears in several obvious ways. Smith's great work was entitled "An Inquiry," while later economic writers, striving, perhaps, to convey the sense of a more codified and bounded science, opted for "Elements" and "Principles." The two works which might have been thought most likely to transmit the Smithian tradition to a new generation of political economists, namely Ricardo's *Principles* and Malthus's *Principles*, both lacked any equivalent to Book V (detailing the duties of the government in regard to defense, justice, education, and public works) of the *Wealth of Nations*. And post-Smithian political economists came to believe it important to separate the *policy* from the theoretical aspects of their science, in a procedure that made no sense at all in terms of the science of a legislator (Winch 1983c: 511–13).

The "gulf" between Smith and his successors appears narrowest in the case of Robert Malthus, whose complicated role in the transmission and transformation of Smith's science has long engaged Winch. Despite major differences in their respective intellectual orientations, Smith and Malthus shared a common understanding of political economy as a field standing not alone, not autonomous, but subordinate to a larger science of politics and morals. This is in fact the key to Winch's scholarship on Malthus, which, like that on Smith, has been based on the "science of politics" perspective. No one has charted this territory as thoroughly as Winch, and he is still at it.[13]

The work required of an intellectual historian in retrieving the genuine Malthus from the one-dimensional representations so often encountered in the literature is, in one respect, similar to that required in the case of Adam Smith. Just as Smith was the object of recruitment into the tradition of liberal capitalism and other ideologies of a later day, Malthus, too, has been "recruited" – by the neo-Malthusian birth-control movement of the late nineteenth century, by a John Maynard Keynes eager to establish a classical lineage for his own macroeconomic ideas, and in recent decades by some environmentalists for whom "Malthusian" has been a convenient (and ominous) adjective to apply to population trends which they associate with degradation of the natural environment. But serious students of the historical Malthus have had little difficulty in peeling away these posthumously applied labels, just as they have generally been able to screen out the noisy, often deeply uninformed, vituperation directed at the "parson" in his lifetime and ever since by assorted critics. The real challenge has not been to recover a non-modernized, non-demonized Malthus; versions of that Malthus have been available from as early as Bonar (1885). Rather, it has been to give full recognition to the intertwining in Malthus's thought of the economic with the demographic, political, theological, and moral.[14]

Winch has been highly resourceful in issuing – and justifying – new labels for Malthus, to be substituted for those now seen as anachronistic, unduly narrow, or simplistic. Malthus is variously described as a "Christian moral scientist," "political moralist," "social Newtonian," "theological utilitarian," and "moderate Whig." Winch first applied the term "political moralist" to Malthus in his essay "Higher maxims: happiness versus wealth in Malthus and Ricardo" (chapter II in Winch 1983d) as a way of capturing the polemical intent of the first *Essay on Population*, with its attack on utopianism and perfectibilism and its naturalistic defense of the existing social order. By contrast with Ricardo, who tended to analyze policy issues on the basis of wealth (economic) considerations alone, Malthus was seen to employ a more complex calculus in which happiness, health, and virtue all received serious attention along with economic considerations. Winch reminded the reader that whereas Ricardo saw political economy as a science akin to mathematics, Malthus, to his friend's occasional exasperation, held that the resemblance was closer to the science of morals and politics.

And how has our understanding of Malthus the political moralist been shaped or modified by Winch's scholarship? To start on the political side, an interesting comment was made by Walter Eltis in reviewing Winch's short monograph, *Malthus* (1987), for an economics journal. "This reviewer," he confessed, "had previously seen Malthus as an obvious Tory in view of his powerful advocacy of agricultural protection, and his inspiration of the Draconian 1834 Poor Law" (Eltis 1988: 97). The confusion is entirely understandable and could easily have been shared by Malthus's contemporary readers on the basis of the journal in which his articles usually appeared – the Tory *Quarterly Review* rather than the Whig *Edinburgh Review*.[15] Winch makes clear, however, that in terms of party labels, Malthus was a Whig and a "rather old-fashioned" one, convinced of the virtues of Britain's mixed constitution, fearful of standing armies and executive tyranny. He consistently favored the Whig causes of Catholic emancipation, religious toleration, and state-supported education (Winch 1983d: 76–7). This assessment of Malthus's political stance has been elaborated in Winch's *Malthus* (1987), in the introduction to his edition of the *Essay on Population* for the *Cambridge Texts in the History of Political Thought* (1992), and in *Riches and Poverty* (1996). He argues that Malthus was, in his early years, a Foxite Whig, opposed to the war with France and to the restrictions on civil liberties which the government imposed, using the war as justification. On this issue and some others, Winch finds a surprising similarity of viewpoint between Malthus and his supposed arch-opponent, William Godwin.

The partial overlap of political–philosophical ideas between Malthus and Godwin has been attributed by Winch to the dissenting culture out of which both thinkers emerged, if that is not too strong a way of characterizing Malthus's periods of tutelage under two well-known dissenters, Gilbert Wakefield and William Frend.[16] Winch shows us how Malthus the political moralist shared with Godwin a belief in the high importance of individual reason and conscience. As he puts it: "Both men agreed that human dignity and happiness were strongly connected with the absence of relations of paternalistic dependence, and with self-exertion and the exercise of discretionary foresight in conducting personal

affairs" (Winch 1996: 256). Herein lies the key to the crucial Malthusian recommendation of the second edition of the *Essay*, namely the prudent and moral
(celibate) postponement of marriage to which the term "moral restraint" was
given.[17] The rejection of paternalism and dependency also goes a long way toward
explaining Malthus's principled stand against the Poor Law, as outlined in chapter
V of the 1798 essay. Even in his comments on the regrettable extent of inequality
in Britain and on the failure of British economic growth to benefit the poor, the
Malthus of 1798 sounded almost as Godwinian as Smithian!

In the name of intellectual–historical accuracy, Winch (1993) has disputed
several versions of Malthus that have been put forward over the past decade and
a half. He rejects Gertrude Himmelfarb's assertion, in *The Idea of Poverty*
(1984), that Malthus "de-moralized" the science of political economy as it had
been developed by Smith; likewise, he rejects the view advanced by Mitchell
Dean, in *The Constitution of Poverty* (1991), that Malthus saw the condition of
the poor only in the light of bioeconomic laws, not that of moral philosophy
(unlike Smith). On the contrary, Winch argues, Malthus analyzed and philoso-
phized within a Christian utilitarian framework, and his efforts are better
described as "re-moralizing" than "de-moralizing" political economy, at least in
terms of his intent. That the Ricardians took a different, more secular, path
which most other political economists chose to follow is indisputable but irrelevant to the question of Malthus's intellectual bearings. Winch takes issue as
well with two historians of economic analysis, Sam Hollander and Lionel
Robbins, on the salience of the theological perspective for Malthus. As Winch
sees it, Hollander commits the same error as Himmelfarb and Dean in trying to
secularize a thinker who was avowedly and fundamentally Christian. Hollander
would classify Malthus as a *secular* utilitarian for whom theology was extraneous
to analysis; Winch insists he was a *theological* utilitarian whose positions on a
variety of policy issues cannot properly be understood without taking into
account the Malthusian sense of God's plan for the world and man's place in it.

One of the advantages that must be conceded to the Winchian intellectual
history approach over the history-of-doctrine approach to an understanding of
Malthus is its greater likelihood of bringing a musty historical figure to life.
Whatever his place in the pantheon of classical economic thinkers, Malthus
clearly looms very large indeed in the wider intellectual landscape of nineteenth-century Britain. What other classical economist could inspire such
sarcastic lines of poetry as the following:

> Oh Mr. Malthus, I agree
> In everything I read with thee!
> The world's too full, there is no doubt,
> And wants a deal of thinning out ...[18]

And this is among the *milder* expressions of contempt lobbed at Malthus by his
"literary" foes! In several chapters of *Riches and Poverty*, Winch comprehensively reviews the "prolonged campaign of abuse" against Malthus by the Lake
poets and their allies. He is able to reconstruct a more substantive political

dialogue between Coleridge and Malthus than might have been expected. As in the case of Godwin, Winch finds unexpected affinities between Malthus and some of his Romantic critics, particularly in shared attitudes toward manufacturing and toward remedies for economic depression. He breaks new ground with his focus on John Rickman, a somewhat shadowy civil servant well enough versed in data relating to poverty and population to be of considerable value to the Romantic anti-Malthusians. Winch manages to be fair-minded and balanced in his assessment of a group of writers who, in their treatment of Malthus, were conspicuously neither. In this he distinguishes himself from some sympathetic accounts of Malthus in recent years that have dealt unduly stridently with his "literary" opponents.

It may be appropriate to close this essay on a note of clarification. The most recent and in some ways most ambitious book by Winch, *Riches and Poverty*, bears a carefully worded subtitle: *An Intellectual History of Political Economy in Britain, 1750–1834*. The use of the indefinite article (An *Intellectual History*) signals one of the qualities that has long marked Winch's scholarship – a willingness to entertain the possibility of other valid approaches to the same subject matter he addresses in his own particular manner. Winch has been one of the most articulate defenders of the value of the enterprise of intellectual history. His methodological views are a matter of record. But the way in which he has *practiced* intellectual history may be as instructive as any potted pronouncements. Time and again, Winch has rejected "binary choices" and "dichotomies," preferring to offer more nuanced interpretations in their place. He has been a determined foe of Whig versions of history and every kind of anachronism. He has treated all ideas seriously, if not equally, avoiding, as Viner urged, "denigration, distortion, and undue piety" (Winch 1996: 354). Through these qualities he has made himself a trustworthy guide to some of the most interesting conversations of the past.

## Notes

1  In a recent survey of Malthus scholarship from 1933 to 1998, A. M. C. Waterman suggests that Winch's latest book, *Riches and Poverty: An Intellectual History of Political Economy in Britain, 1750–1834*, demonstrates the "state of the art" of the intellectual history (IH) approach, as opposed to the history of economic analysis (HEA) approach. The latter is exemplified, according to Waterman, in Samuel Hollander's *The Economics of Thomas Robert Malthus* (1997). The two works, and presumably the corresponding historical approaches, are declared by Waterman to be "strictly incommensurable and noncompeting." (Waterman 1998).

2  Winch (1981: 522, 524). This last quote is repeated by Winch in his comment on Waterman (1998), a strong indication of the lasting impression Viner's commitment to interpretive objectivity left on him (Winch 1998: 354).

3  A notable exception to this statement is Spiegel (1991), in which several pages are devoted to Wakefield (356–60, 751–2).

4  For some later reflections on the impact of economic ideas on policy, see Winch (1990: especially 67–70); and on the complex local circumstances under which Keynesian ideas were incorporated into state policy in Britain and Sweden, see Winch (1989).

5  In this recent work, *Riches and Poverty*, Winch cites a memorable phrase of his former collaborator, John Burrow, characterizing the kind of history they write as akin to "eavesdropping on the conversations of the past." Winch clearly places a high value on the "acuteness of hearing and sensitivity to tones of voice" that trained and skillful listeners bring to their task (Winch 1996: 28).

6  Had it been more prominently in circulation in 1978, the term "libertarian" would undoubtedly have been added by Winch to the list of anachronistic labels.

7  As for the polarity between "Country" or "oppositional Whig" and "Court Whig" ideologies, as mapped by Caroline Robbins, Pocock, and others, and outlined by Winch in some detail, it does not emerge at all clearly where Smith belongs on the spectrum, perhaps because he does not fit consistently into either camp. The ambiguity on this point is highlighted in Hollander (1979).

8  Firmly but not exclusively: Winch has argued that Smith exhibited a "cosmopolitan" rather than provincially Scottish perspective on a variety of issues, that he was much attuned to Continental thought, and that he did not go out of his way to acknowledge similarity of views or interests with his fellow Scotsmen (Winch 1983a; 1996: 19).

9  "Adam Smith and Laissez Faire," *Journal of Political Economy* 35: 198–232 (1927), reprinted in Viner (1958). This is deservedly considered one of the most influential articles ever written in the history of economic thought; Winch refers to it approvingly and often in his own writings on Smith.

10 For a carefully reasoned argument on the need to keep Smith the moral philosopher in view when trying to understand Smith the proponent of political economy, see Winch (1991).

11 Toward the end of this paper, Winch acknowledges that he has ignored the economic analysis of the *Wealth of Nations* in carrying out his main task; that is, to assess the relative weights to be given to the traditions of civic moralism and natural jurisprudence in coming to an understanding of Smith's "science of a legislator" (Winch 1983a: 268).

12 He notes that his training as an economist exposed him to "explicit theorizing," but adds: "Familiarity with the habits of economists and other social scientists ... has not convinced me that I am under any obligation to ape them when writing intellectual history" (Winch 1998: 30).

13 See Winch (1998: 363) for reference to a forthcoming article on "Poverty and Pauperism: From Smith to Malthus."

14 Of Malthus the economist, we now have as compendious and authoritative an account as we are likely to get in Samuel Hollander's *The Economics of Thomas Robert Malthus* (1997). On Malthus the demographer, perhaps the most illuminating work to date has been that of E. A. Wrigley (1983, 1986). The theological side of Malthus is brought into sharp focus in Waterman (1991), who also provides a copious bibliography to related works.

15 Malthus, of course, was denied access to the pages of the *Edinburgh Review* after J. R. McCulloch became its economics reviewer in 1818. He nevertheless was on friendly terms with the founders of that journal and a number of the writers whose work appeared in it.

16 Malthus's college at Cambridge was "at the centre of both latitudinarian and republican thinking ... in the 1780s," and even after his ordination in the Church of England, Malthus, when in London, socialized in the same dissenting circles as Frend (Winch 1996: 254). There he encountered Joseph Johnson, a friend of Thomas Paine and publisher of Godwin's *Political Justice* as well as the first English translation of Condorcet. It was Johnson who published Malthus's population essay and shortly thereafter arranged for Malthus and Godwin to meet (ibid.: 255).

17 It has sometimes been argued that Malthus borrowed, even plagiarized, the idea of prudential restraint from Godwin, or, alternatively, that the introduction of "moral"

restraint in the 1803 edition of the *Essay* represented a "capitulation" to Godwin. Most scholars, however, see little merit in such contentions. Winch goes only so far as to credit Godwin with having "influenced" Malthus to give greater weight after 1798 to the idea of a prudential check (Winch 1996: 264, 276–7).

18 From Thomas Hood's "Ode to Mr. Malthus" (1839), reprinted in Gilbert (1998, II: 133–6).

## Bibliography

Anon. (1965) "A Classic View," *The Economist* 217: 1426.

Bonar, J. (1885) *Malthus and His Work*, London: Allen and Unwin.

Dean, M. (1991) *The Constitution of Poverty: Toward a Genealogy of Liberal Governance*, London and New York: Routledge.

Eltis, W. (1988) "Review of *Malthus*," *The Manchester School* 56: 96–7.

Gilbert, G. (ed.) (1998) *Malthus: Critical Responses*, 4 vols, New York: Routledge.

Himmelfarb, G. (1984) *The Idea of Poverty: England in the Early Industrial Age*, New York: Knopf.

Hollander, S. (1979) "Review of *Adam Smith's Politics: An Essay in Historiographic Revision*," *Journal of Economic Literature* 17: 543–5.

—— (1997) *The Economics of Thomas Robert Malthus*, Toronto: University of Toronto Press.

Spiegel, H. (1991) *The Growth of Economic Thought*, third edition, Durham, NC: Duke University Press.

Viner, J. (1958) *The Long View and the Short: Studies in Economic Theory and Policy*, Glencoe, IL: The Free Press.

Waterman, A. M. C. (1991) *Revolution, Economics and Religion: Christian Political Economy, 1798–1833*, Cambridge: Cambridge University Press.

—— (1998) "Reappraisal of 'Malthus, the economist,' 1933–97," *History of Political Economy* 30: 293–334.

Winch, D. (1965) *Classical Political Economy and Colonies*, Cambridge, MA: Harvard University Press.

—— (1969) *Economics and Policy: A Historical Study*, London: Hodder and Stoughton.

—— (1971) "The Emergence of Economics as a Science, 1750–1870," *The Fontana Economic History of Europe*, Vol. III, London: Collins/Fontana.

—— (1976) "Comment," in T. Wilson and A. S. Skinner (eds) *The Market and the State: Essays in Honour of Adam Smith*, Oxford: Oxford University Press.

—— (1978) *Adam Smith's Politics: An Essay in Historiographic Revision*, Cambridge and New York: Cambridge University Press.

—— (1981) "Jacob Viner," *The American Scholar* 50: 519–25.

—— (1983a) "Adam Smith's 'enduring particular result': A Political and Cosmopolitan Perspective," in I. Hont and M. Ignatieff (eds) *Wealth and Virtue: The Shaping of Political Economy in the Scottish Enlightenment*, Cambridge: Cambridge University Press.

—— (1983b) "Jacob Viner as Intellectual Historian," in W. J. Samuels (ed.) *The Craft of the Historian of Economic Thought*, Greenwich, CT: JAI Press.

—— (1983c) "Science and the Legislator: Adam Smith and After," *Economic Journal* 93: 501–20.

—— (1983d) *That Noble Science of Politics: A Study in Nineteenth-Century Intellectual History*, with S. Collini and J. Burrow, Cambridge: Cambridge University Press.

—— (1987) *Malthus*, Past Masters, Oxford: Oxford University Press.

—— (1988) "Adam Smith and the Liberal Tradition," in K. Haakonssen (ed.) *Traditions of Liberalism: Essays on John Locke, Adam Smith and John Stuart Mill*, Sydney: Centre for Independent Studies.

—— (1989) "Keynes, Keynesianism, and State Intervention," in P. Hall (ed.) *The Political Power of Economic Ideas: Keynesianism across Nations*, Princeton, NJ: Princeton University Press.

—— (1990) "Economic Knowledge and Government in Britain: Some Historical and Comparative Reflections," in M. O. Furner and B. Supple (eds) *The State and Economic Knowledge*, Cambridge: Cambridge University Press.

—— (1991) "Adam Smith: Scottish Moral Philosopher as Political Economist," *Historical Journal* 35: 91–113.

—— (1992) Edition of Malthus's *Essay on the Principle of Population* for *Cambridge Texts in the History of Political Thought*, Cambridge: Cambridge University Press.

—— (1993) "Robert Malthus: Christian Moral Scientist, Arch-Demoralizer or Implicit Secular Utilitarian?", *Utilitas* 5: 239–53.

—— (1996) *Riches and Poverty: An Intellectual History of Political Economy in Britain, 1750–1834*, Cambridge: Cambridge University Press.

—— (1998) "The Reappraisal of Malthus: A Comment," *History of Political Economy* 30: 353–63.

Wrigley, E. A. (1983) "Malthus's Model of a Pre-industrial Economy," in J. Dupaquier, A. Fauve-Chamoux, and E. Grebenik (eds) *Malthus Past and Present*, London: Academic Press.

—— (1986) "Elegance and Experience: Malthus at the Bar of History," in D. Coleman and R. Schofield (eds) *The State of Population Theory: Forward from Malthus*, Oxford: Blackwell.

# Index

absolutism 24, 34, 306
abstraction 68
Achilles/Agamemnon confrontation 175
'adding-up' theory of price 70, 72
administrative efficiency: economics and
   173, 179
aggregate demand: Keynes's reliance on
   191; Malthus's position 150–1
agriculture: Malthus's treatment of
   149–50; unique productivity of
   149–50, 187
Althusserian Marxists 205
American Economic Association:
   president 95, 114n(8)
American History of Economics Society:
   session on methodology 325
Amersterdam, University of 53, 56
analytical–narratives approach 43
appraisal: Weintraub on 326
Aristotle: Lowry on 176–8; Spiegel on 293
art markets: De Marchi on 14, 58–9;
   Grampp on 94, 109–11
Ashley, Percy 48
Athenian democracy 175
Australian National University
   (Canberra) 52–3
Austrian economists 118, 119, 270

Backhouse, Roger: on Blaug 17–39; and
   Weintraub 320, 324, 326–7
Balfour, Arthur James: on tariff reform
   47–8
Bank Charter Act (1844) 246–7, 252, 253
Banking School 247, 252, 253
Barber, William J.: bibliography 16; *British
   Economic Thought and India* (1975) 11;
   at Brookings Institution 12; *Daedalus*
   essay (1997) 6; *Designs within Disorder*
   (1996) 13; economics education 9; *The
   Economy of British Central Africa*

(1961) 10; as editor 14; on Franklin D.
   Roosevelt 13–14; *From New Era to
   New Deal* (1985) 13; at Harvard 9; on
   Herbert Hoover 13, 14; *A History of
   Economic Thought* (1967) 11; history
   education 9; at Kansas State University
   9; as liberally educated economist
   14–15; with Myrdal 11; at Oxford
   9–10; Ph.D. research 9–10; retirement
   work 14; at Wesleyan University 10–11
bargaining: Lowry's ideas on 171
Barucci, Piero 14
Baumol, W. J. 251
Belfast, University of 244, 248
Bentham, Jeremy: economic writings 303
Bergson, Henri 314
Berlin, University of 287
Bianchi, Marina 57
biography 19, 30–1, 231, 236–41, 238,
   239, 240; and science 1
Black, Robert D. C. 244; on O'Brien 248,
   256
Blaug, Mark 17–39; as absolutist 24, 34;
   *Appraising Economic Theories...* (1991,
   co-edited with De Marchi) 55–6;
   autobiography 35; bibliography 38;
   biography of Keynes 19, 30–1;
   characteristics 33; on classical
   economics 18–19, 20–1, 23–7; at
   Columbia University 18; *Economic
   Theory in Retrospect* (1962–1996) 11,
   17, 18, 19, 21–2, 24, 25–6, 26–7, 34–5,
   36, 291; education 18; historical essays
   19; on Hollander's books 26, 129, 130,
   134, 161, 162n(1); on Keynesian
   economics 30–1; at London University
   18; and Marxism 18, 35;
   methodologically directed analysis 19,
   31–3; *The Methodology of Economics*
   (1992) 19, 22–3, 32–3, 35; reference